TUNDRA's Really SUNDAY COMICS Collection

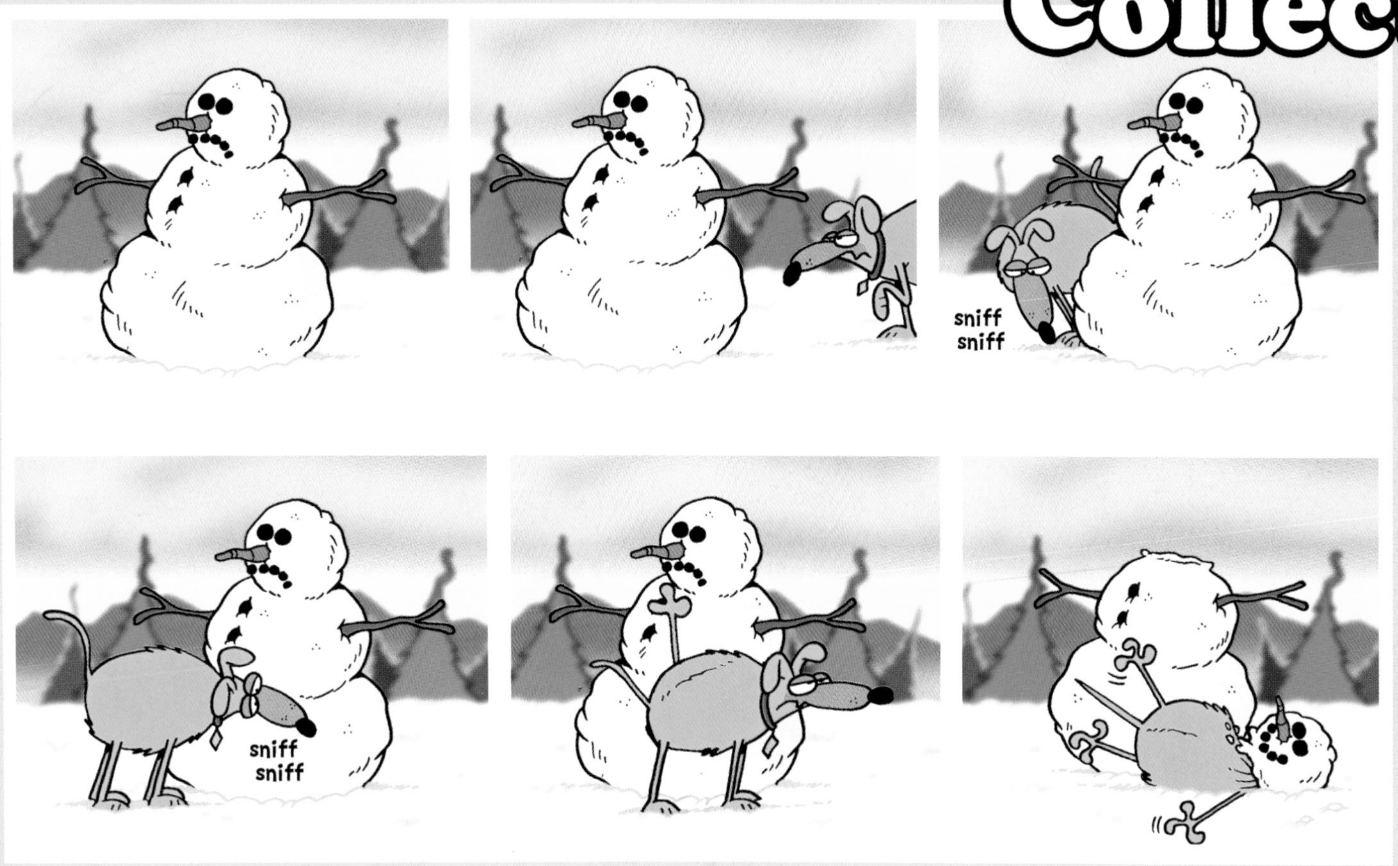
sniff
sniff
sniff
sniff

From The Files of Nature's Favorite Newspaper Comic!

TUNDRA's Really Swell Sunday Comic Collection

Colored by Karen Carpenter

Published by
TUNDRA & ASSOCIATES, INC.
PO Box 871354
Wasilla, Alaska 99687

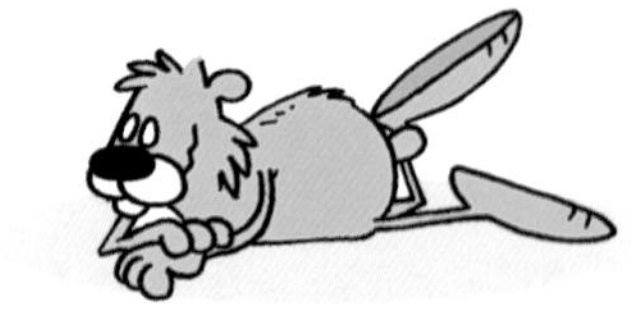

For additional copies of this or other fine TUNDRA merchandise, please visit the Official TUNDRA website at:

www.tundracomics.com

Printed in China
First Printing May 2016
ISBN: 978-1-62343-986-6

TUNDRA's *Really Swell* SUNDAY COMICS Collection

> BEFORE WE BEGIN, WE'D LIKE TO ASK THAT ALL PHONES BE SET ON SILENT AND PLEASE, NO FLASH PHOTOGRAPHY.

Bear Viewing Area

Chad Carpenter 2016

To Ma & Pa

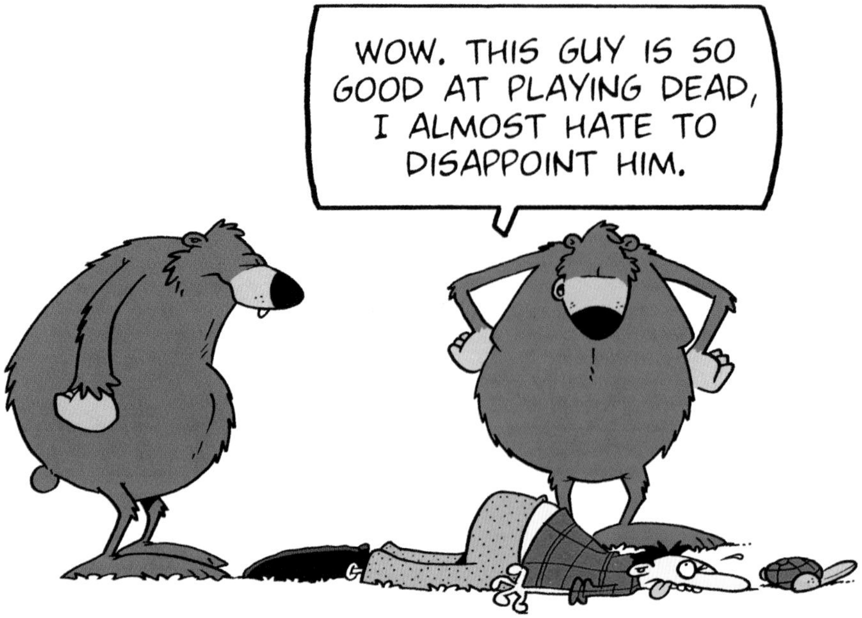
WOW. THIS GUY IS SO GOOD AT PLAYING DEAD, I ALMOST HATE TO DISAPPOINT HIM.

INTRODUCTION from Chad the Cartoonist:

Okay, you're probably thinking, "Why would a book of comics need an introduction?" I mean, it's a book full of comics – pretty self-explanatory, eh? Well, first of all, the comics don't start until the next page, and I can't stand blank pages. Ever since I was a small child, if you put an empty piece of paper in front of me, it was soon covered with scribbles, doodles and probably boogers. So, I had to fill this with something, and here it is…sans boogers.

I've always known I would eventually put together a collection of Tundra's Sunday comics but I didn't know it would take this long. Many of the strips on the following pages have never been in book form until now.

In addition to my usual single-panel comics, a good portion of the following strips feature some characters very near and dear to my heart - Dudley the bear, Sherman the squirrel and Andy the lemming, a.k.a. "The Boys." These three fellas don't show up much in my comics anymore, but at one time they made appearances on a regular basis. Many of the strips starring this trio of furry goofballs were created in collaboration with my brother, Darin. In a lot of ways, The Boys were my favorite part of drawing Tundra, but for some reason, they just slowly faded away. When folks ask me what happened to them or why I rarely draw them anymore, I don't really have a good answer. Sometimes I quip that it's due to a contract dispute with their agent or they've gone into politics, but the truth is I don't really know. What I do know is that I miss them, and that's why it's so fun for me to see them once again, leaping off the pages of this book.

Who knows? Maybe after this I'll be able to convince them to come out of retirement. Either way, I sincerely hope you enjoy their company as much as I have.

With warm wishes,

Chad Carpenter...

Chad Carpenter
Gangrene Gulch, Alaska

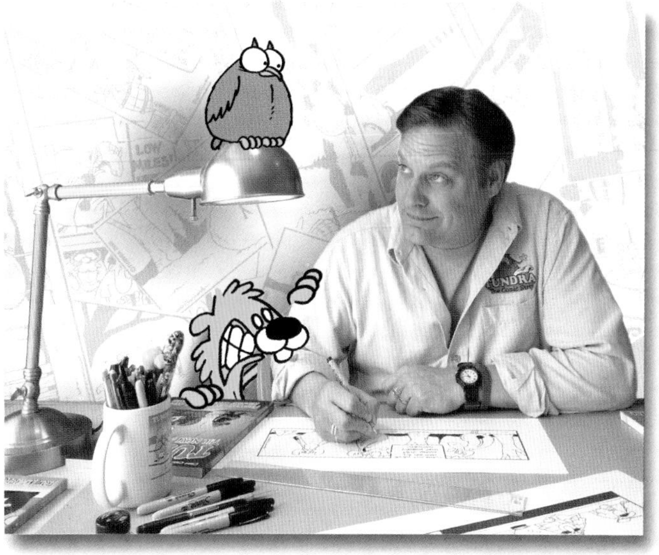
TUNDRA

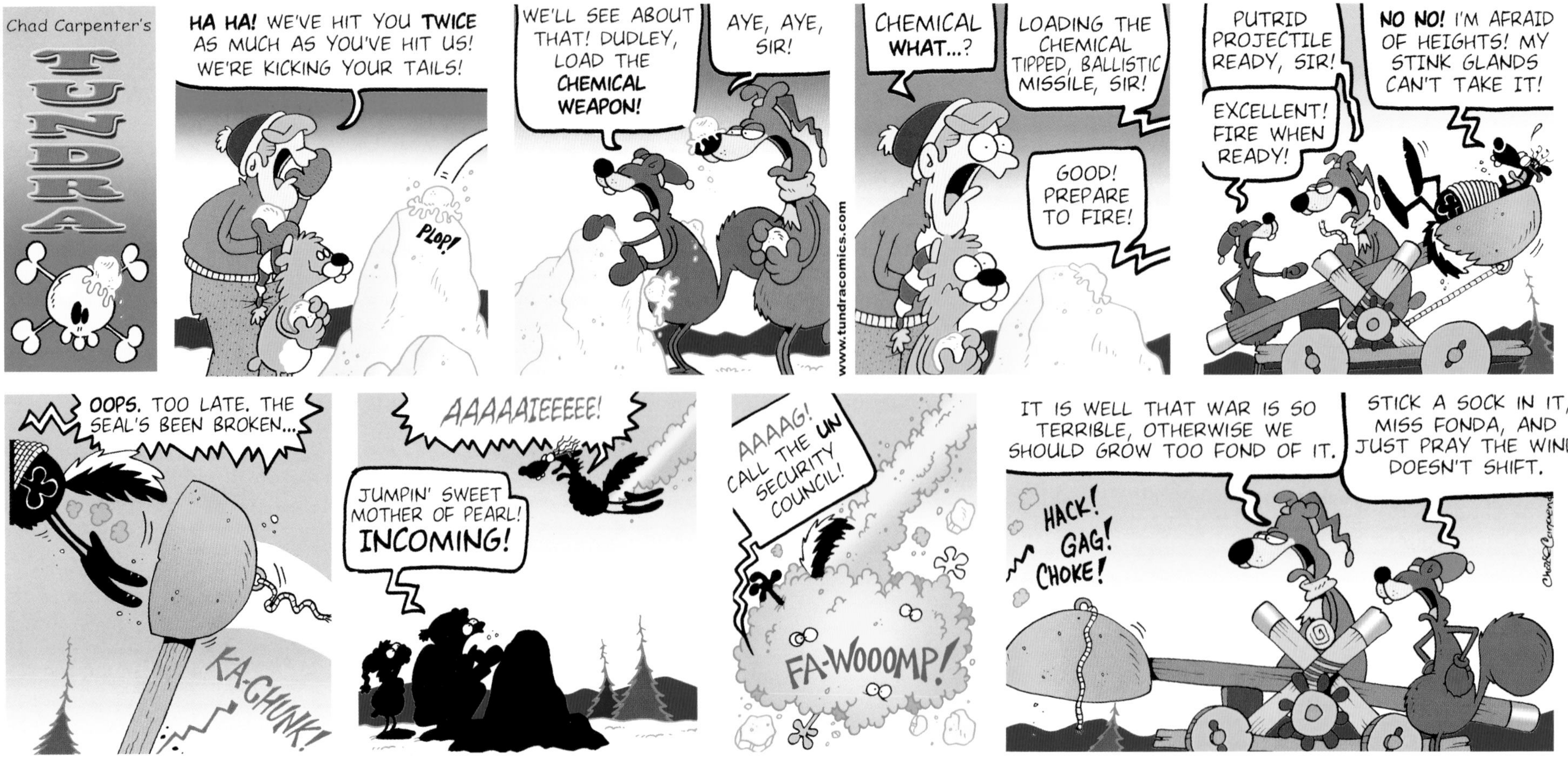
Chad Carpenter's
TUNDRA
HA HA! WE'VE HIT YOU TWICE AS MUCH AS YOU'VE HIT US! WE'RE KICKING YOUR TAILS!
PLOP!
WE'LL SEE ABOUT THAT! DUDLEY, LOAD THE CHEMICAL WEAPON!
AYE, AYE, SIR!
www.tundracomics.com
CHEMICAL WHAT...?
LOADING THE CHEMICAL TIPPED, BALLISTIC MISSILE, SIR!
GOOD! PREPARE TO FIRE!
PUTRID PROJECTILE READY, SIR!
EXCELLENT! FIRE WHEN READY!
NO NO! I'M AFRAID OF HEIGHTS! MY STINK GLANDS CAN'T TAKE IT!
OOPS. TOO LATE. THE SEAL'S BEEN BROKEN...
KA-CHUNK!
AAAAAIEEEEE!
JUMPIN' SWEET MOTHER OF PEARL! INCOMING!
AAAAG! CALL THE UN SECURITY COUNCIL!
FA-WOOOMP!
IT IS WELL THAT WAR IS SO TERRIBLE, OTHERWISE WE SHOULD GROW TOO FOND OF IT.
STICK A SOCK IN IT, MISS FONDA, AND JUST PRAY THE WIND DOESN'T SHIFT.
HACK! GAG! CHOKE!

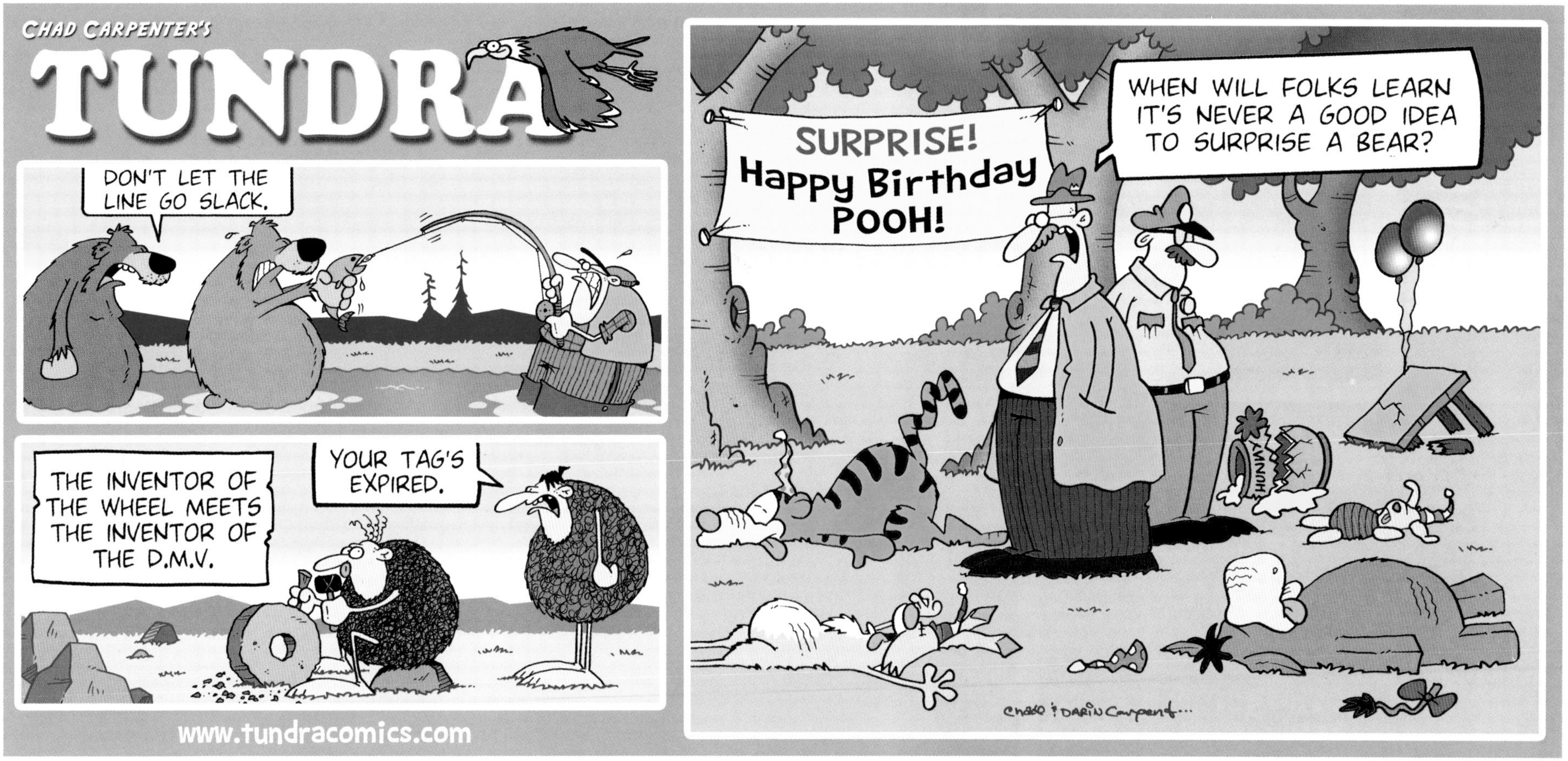
CHAD CARPENTER'S
TUNDRA
DON'T LET THE LINE GO SLACK.
THE INVENTOR OF THE WHEEL MEETS THE INVENTOR OF THE D.M.V.
YOUR TAG'S EXPIRED.
www.tundracomics.com
SURPRISE! Happy Birthday POOH!
WHEN WILL FOLKS LEARN IT'S NEVER A GOOD IDEA TO SURPRISE A BEAR?
HUNNY

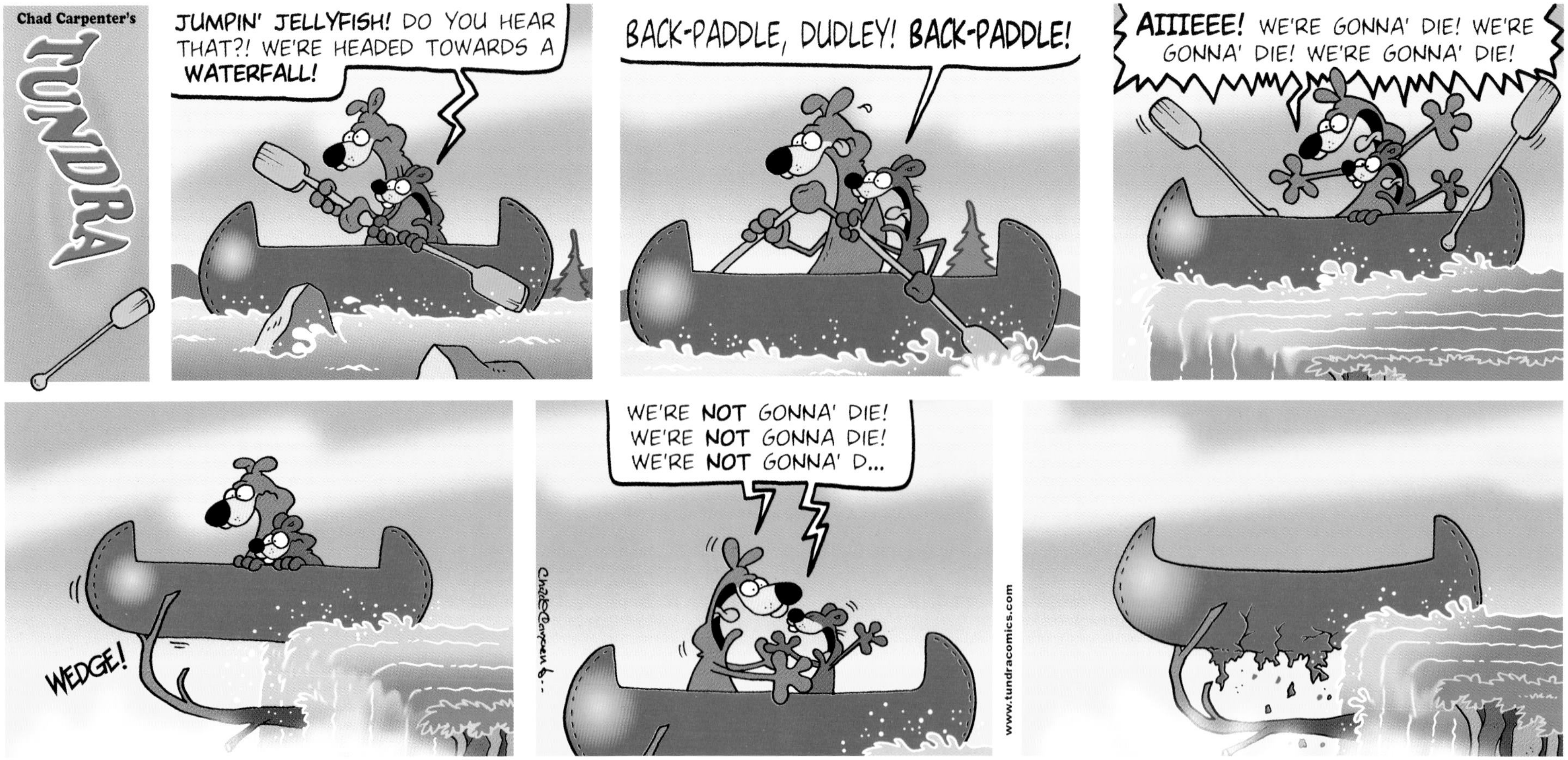
Chad Carpenter's
TUNDRA
JUMPIN' JELLYFISH! DO YOU HEAR THAT?! WE'RE HEADED TOWARDS A WATERFALL!
BACK-PADDLE, DUDLEY! BACK-PADDLE!
AIIIEEE! WE'RE GONNA' DIE! WE'RE GONNA' DIE! WE'RE GONNA' DIE!
WEDGE!
WE'RE NOT GONNA' DIE! WE'RE NOT GONNA DIE! WE'RE NOT GONNA' D...
www.tundracomics.com

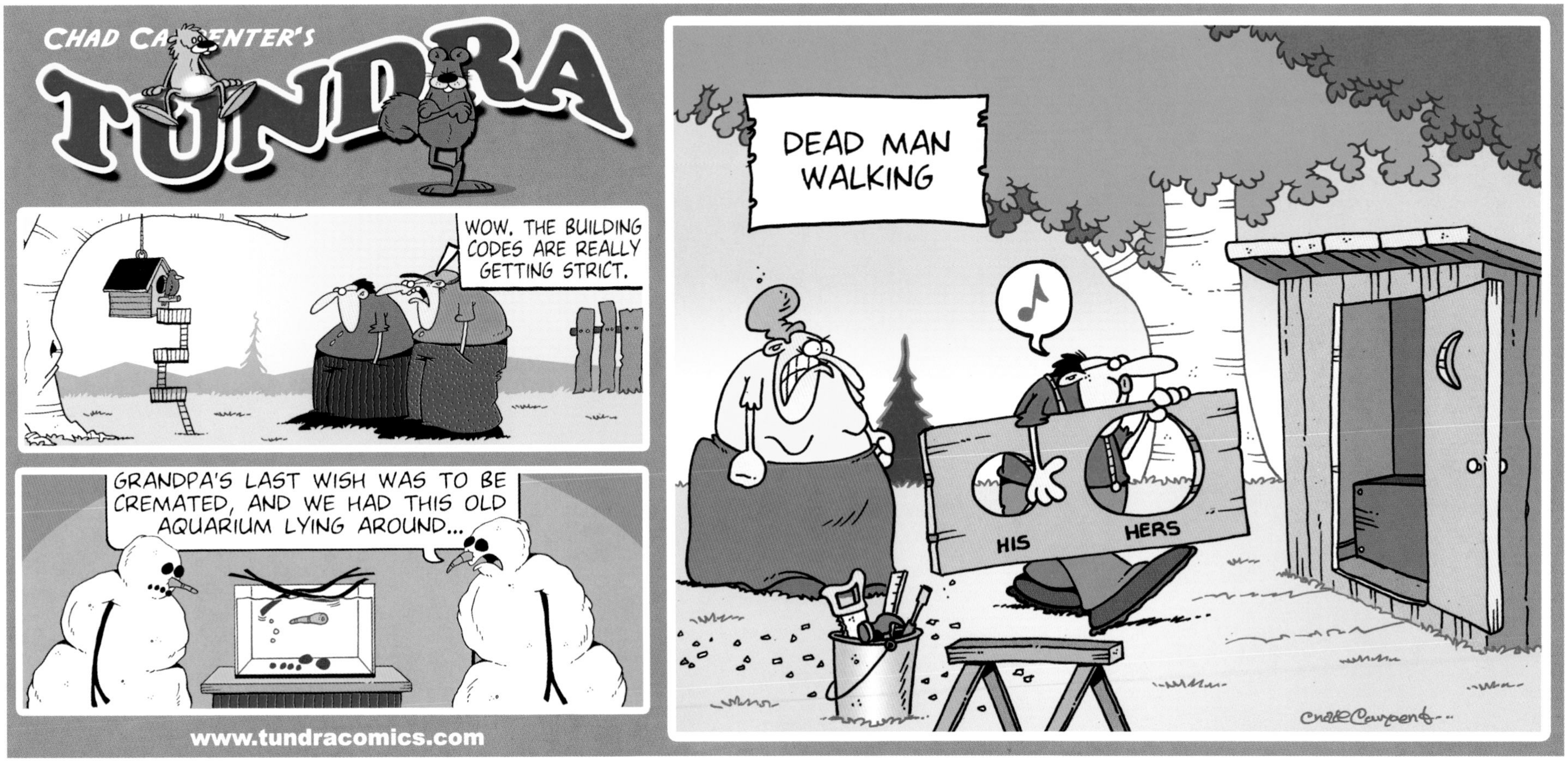
TUNDRA
WOW. THE BUILDING CODES ARE REALLY GETTING STRICT.
GRANDPA'S LAST WISH WAS TO BE CREMATED, AND WE HAD THIS OLD AQUARIUM LYING AROUND...
DEAD MAN WALKING
HIS
HERS
www.tundracomics.com

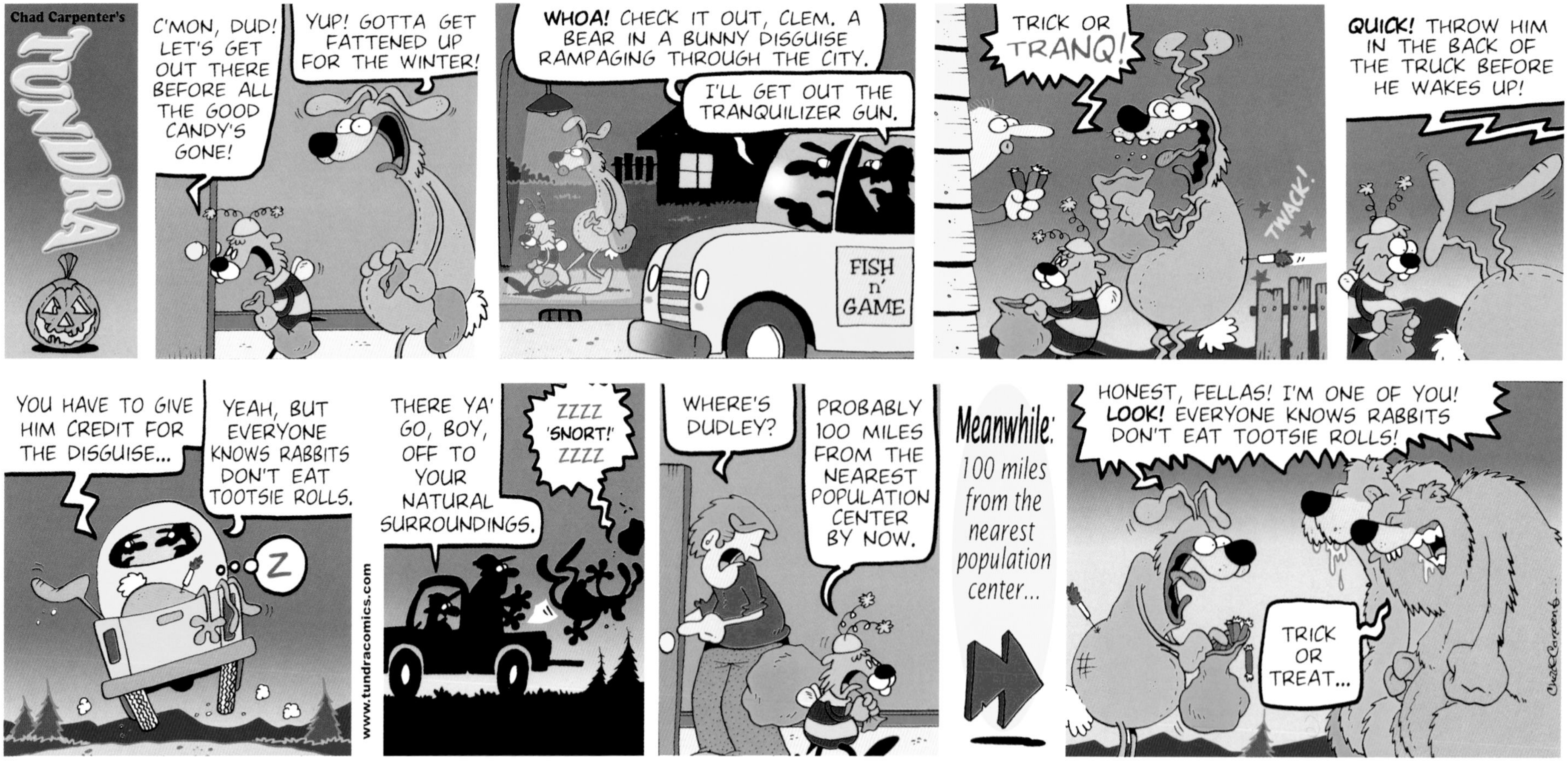
Chad Carpenter's
TUNDRA
C'MON, DUD! LET'S GET OUT THERE BEFORE ALL THE GOOD CANDY'S GONE!
YUP! GOTTA GET FATTENED UP FOR THE WINTER!
WHOA! CHECK IT OUT, CLEM. A BEAR IN A BUNNY DISGUISE RAMPAGING THROUGH THE CITY.
I'LL GET OUT THE TRANQUILIZER GUN.
FISH n' GAME
TRICK OR TRANQ!
TWACK!
QUICK! THROW HIM IN THE BACK OF THE TRUCK BEFORE HE WAKES UP!
YOU HAVE TO GIVE HIM CREDIT FOR THE DISGUISE...
YEAH, BUT EVERYONE KNOWS RABBITS DON'T EAT TOOTSIE ROLLS.
Z
www.tundracomics.com
THERE YA' GO, BOY, OFF TO YOUR NATURAL SURROUNDINGS.
ZZZZ 'SNORT!' ZZZZ
WHERE'S DUDLEY?
PROBABLY 100 MILES FROM THE NEAREST POPULATION CENTER BY NOW.
Meanwhile:
100 miles from the nearest population center...
HONEST, FELLAS! I'M ONE OF YOU! LOOK! EVERYONE KNOWS RABBITS DON'T EAT TOOTSIE ROLLS!
TRICK OR TREAT...

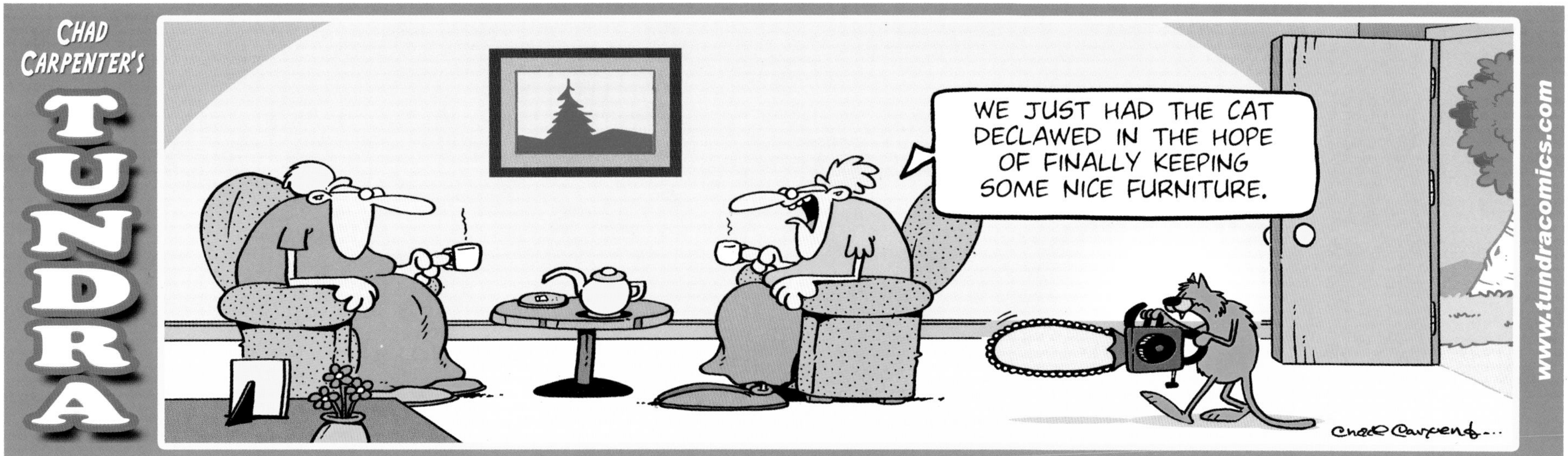
CHAD CARPENTER'S
TUNDRA
www.tundracomics.com
WE JUST HAD THE CAT DECLAWED IN THE HOPE OF FINALLY KEEPING SOME NICE FURNITURE.
Chad Carpenter...

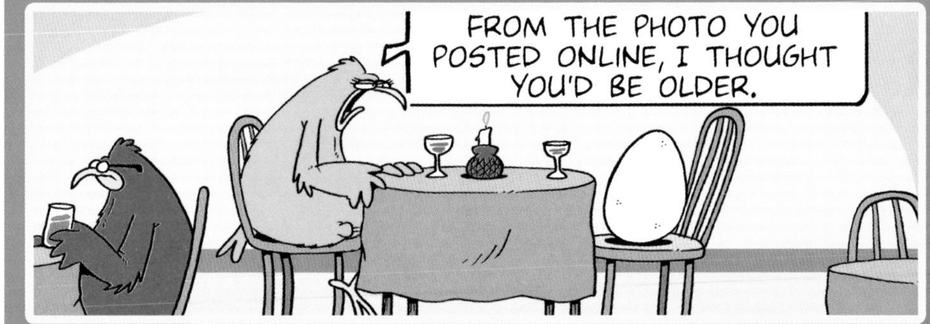
FROM THE PHOTO YOU POSTED ONLINE, I THOUGHT YOU'D BE OLDER.

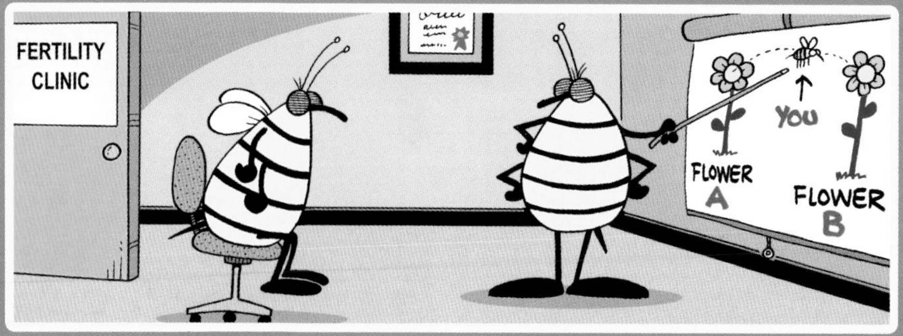
FERTILITY CLINIC
YOU
FLOWER A
FLOWER B

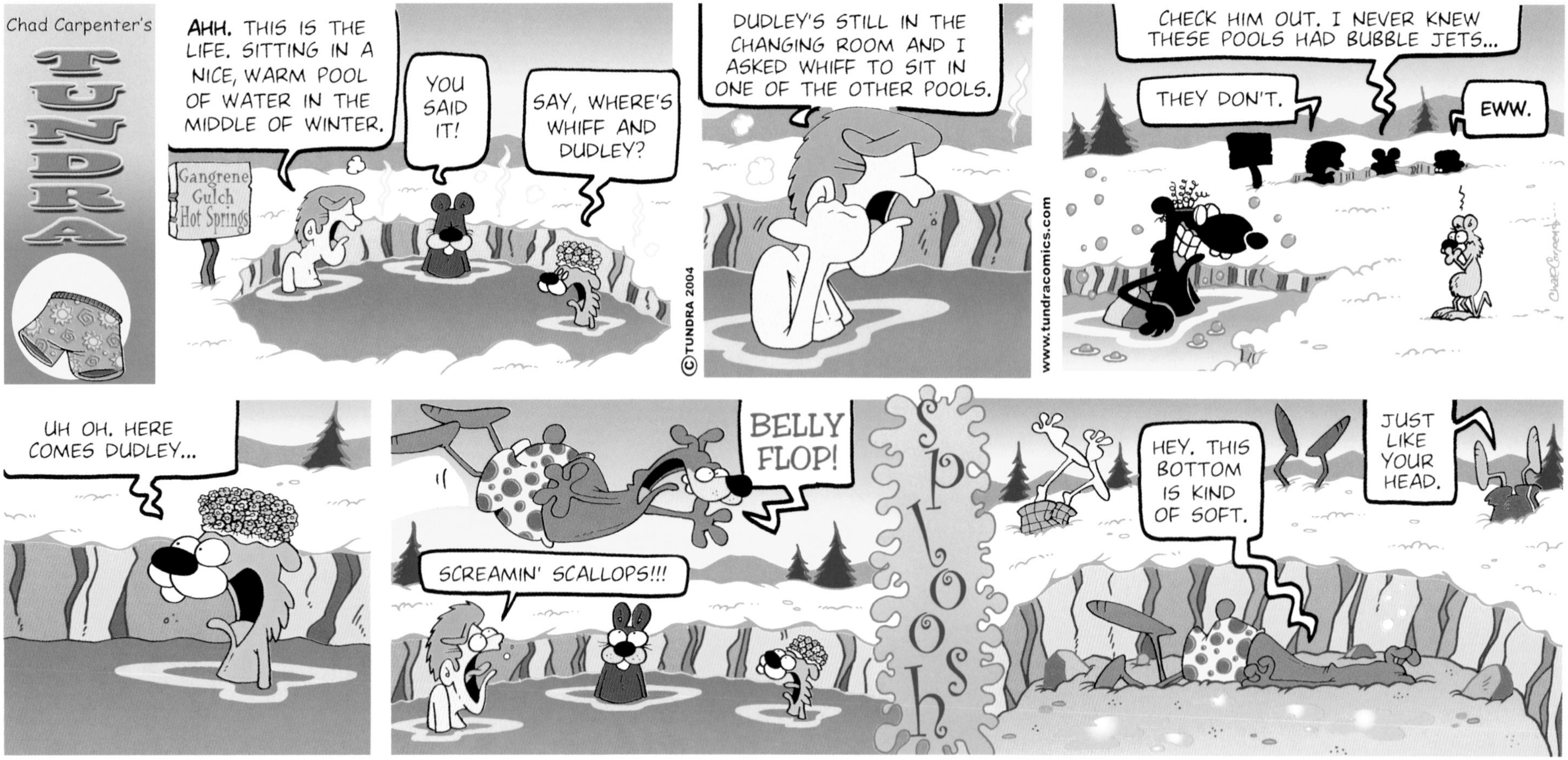
Chad Carpenter's
TUNDRA
AHH. THIS IS THE LIFE. SITTING IN A NICE, WARM POOL OF WATER IN THE MIDDLE OF WINTER.
YOU SAID IT!
SAY, WHERE'S WHIFF AND DUDLEY?
Gangrene Gulch Hot Springs
©TUNDRA 2004
DUDLEY'S STILL IN THE CHANGING ROOM AND I ASKED WHIFF TO SIT IN ONE OF THE OTHER POOLS.
www.tundracomics.com
CHECK HIM OUT. I NEVER KNEW THESE POOLS HAD BUBBLE JETS...
THEY DON'T.
EWW.
UH OH. HERE COMES DUDLEY...
BELLY FLOP!
SCREAMIN' SCALLOPS!!!
sploosh
HEY. THIS BOTTOM IS KIND OF SOFT.
JUST LIKE YOUR HEAD.

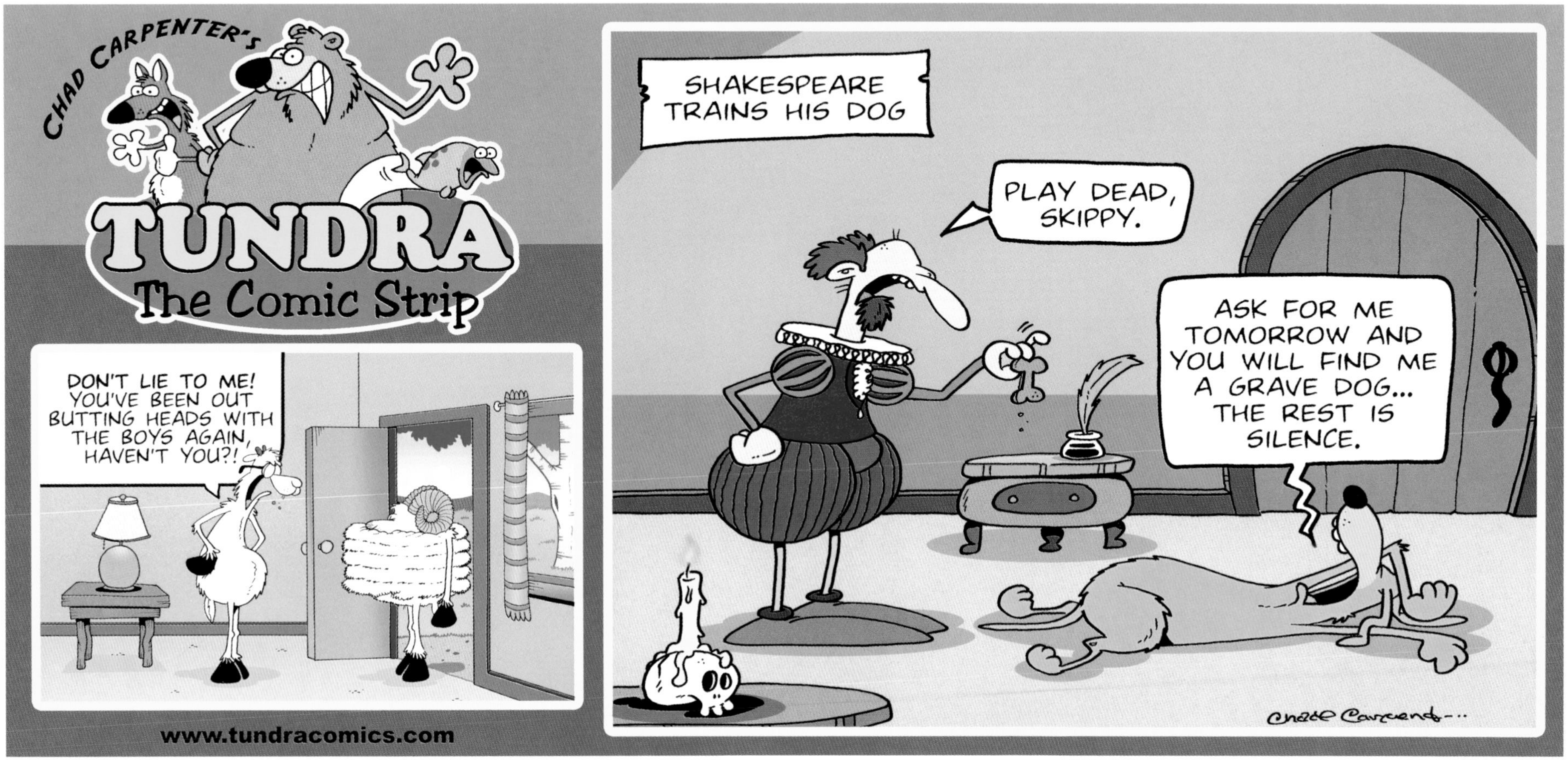
CHAD CARPENTER'S
TUNDRA
The Comic Strip
DON'T LIE TO ME! YOU'VE BEEN OUT BUTTING HEADS WITH THE BOYS AGAIN, HAVEN'T YOU?!
www.tundracomics.com
SHAKESPEARE TRAINS HIS DOG
PLAY DEAD, SKIPPY.
ASK FOR ME TOMORROW AND YOU WILL FIND ME A GRAVE DOG... THE REST IS SILENCE.

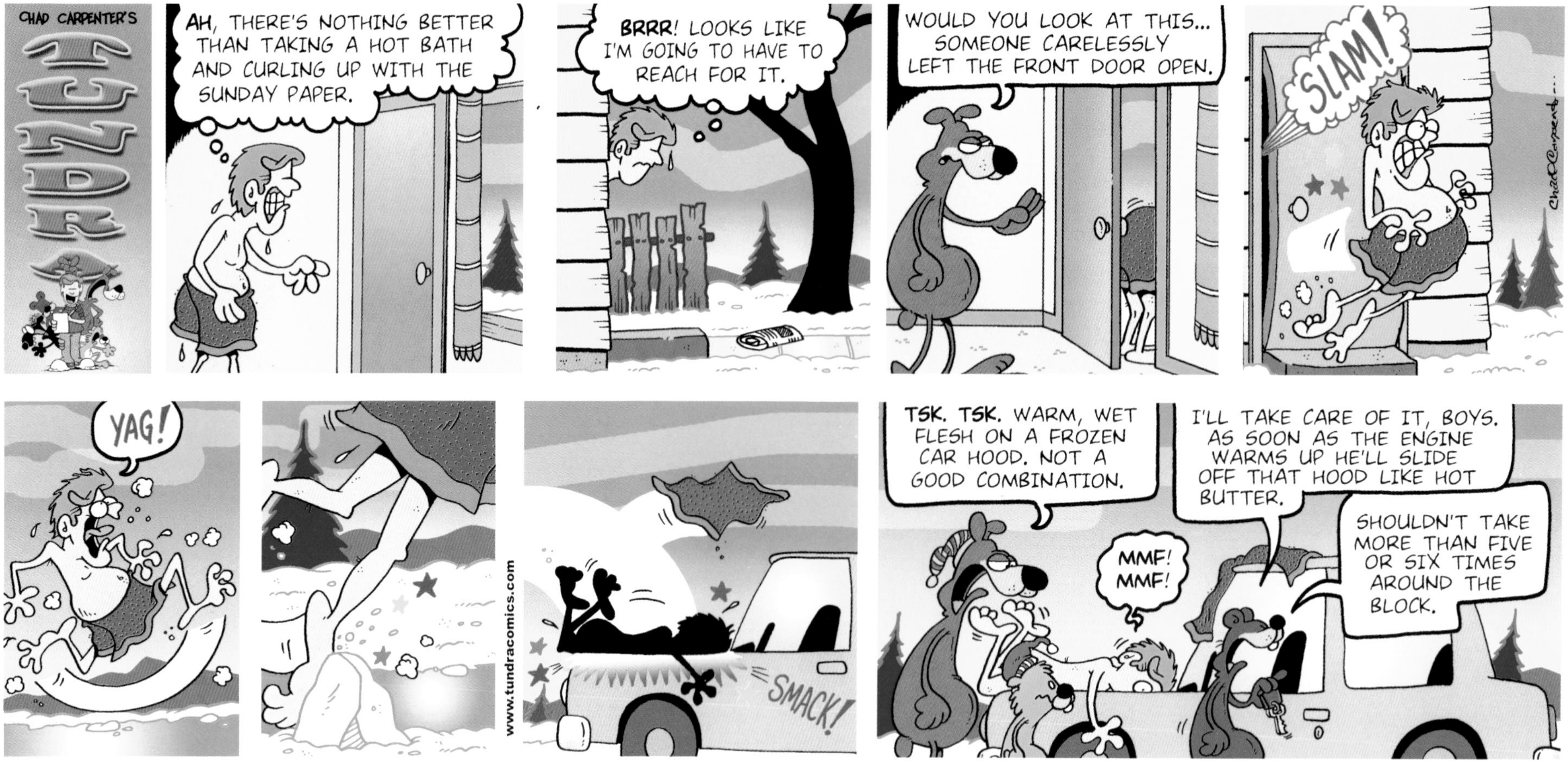
CHAD CARPENTER'S
TUNDRA
AH, THERE'S NOTHING BETTER THAN TAKING A HOT BATH AND CURLING UP WITH THE SUNDAY PAPER.
BRRR! LOOKS LIKE I'M GOING TO HAVE TO REACH FOR IT.
WOULD YOU LOOK AT THIS... SOMEONE CARELESSLY LEFT THE FRONT DOOR OPEN.
SLAM!
YAG!
www.tundracomics.com
SMACK!
TSK. TSK. WARM, WET FLESH ON A FROZEN CAR HOOD. NOT A GOOD COMBINATION.
I'LL TAKE CARE OF IT, BOYS. AS SOON AS THE ENGINE WARMS UP HE'LL SLIDE OFF THAT HOOD LIKE HOT BUTTER.
MMF! MMF!
SHOULDN'T TAKE MORE THAN FIVE OR SIX TIMES AROUND THE BLOCK.

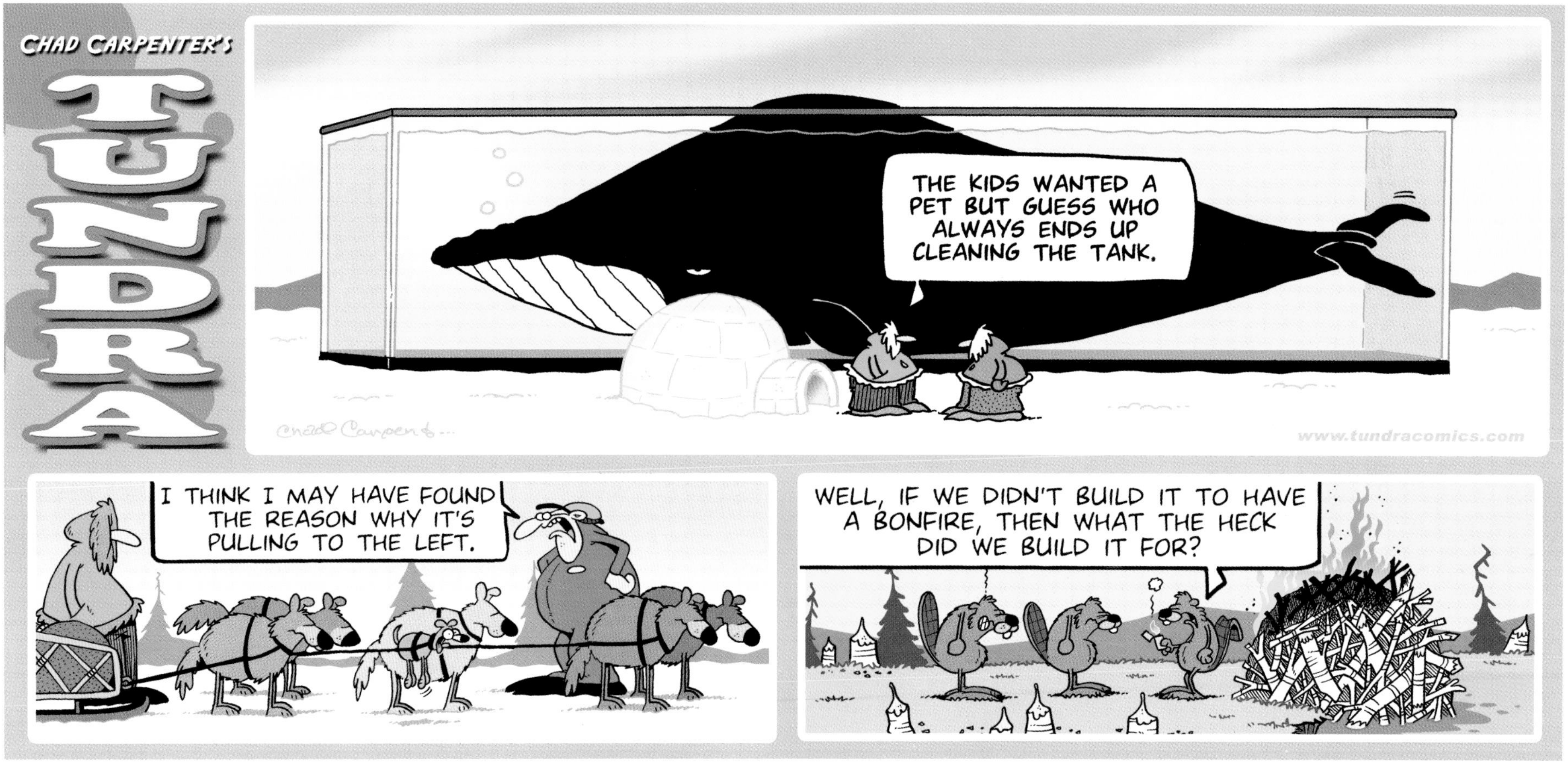
CHAD CARPENTER'S
TUNDRA
THE KIDS WANTED A PET BUT GUESS WHO ALWAYS ENDS UP CLEANING THE TANK.
www.tundracomics.com
I THINK I MAY HAVE FOUND THE REASON WHY IT'S PULLING TO THE LEFT.
WELL, IF WE DIDN'T BUILD IT TO HAVE A BONFIRE, THEN WHAT THE HECK DID WE BUILD IT FOR?

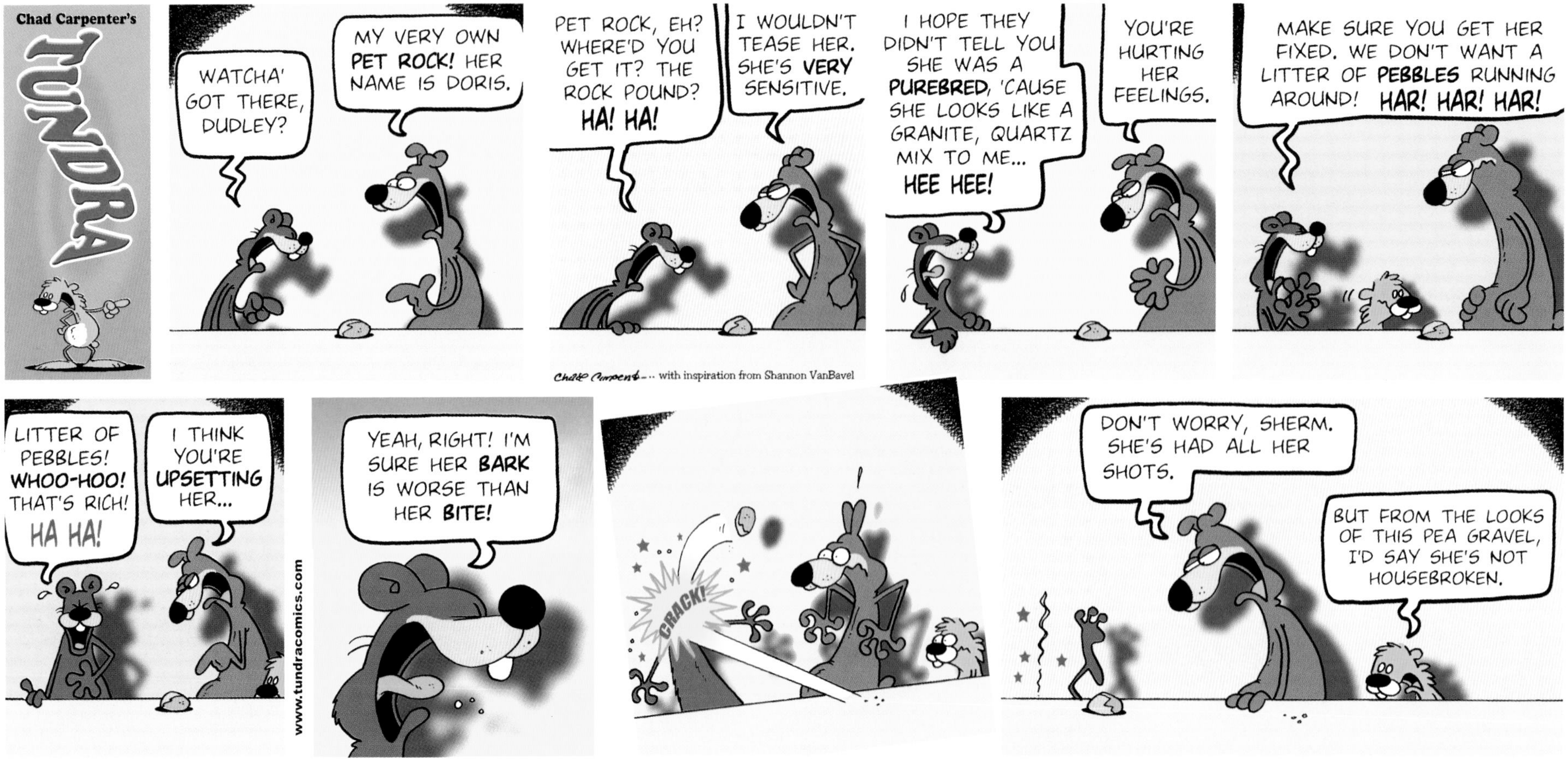
Chad Carpenter's
TUNDRA
WATCHA' GOT THERE, DUDLEY?
MY VERY OWN PET ROCK! HER NAME IS DORIS.
PET ROCK, EH? WHERE'D YOU GET IT? THE ROCK POUND? HA! HA!
I WOULDN'T TEASE HER. SHE'S VERY SENSITIVE.
I HOPE THEY DIDN'T TELL YOU SHE WAS A PUREBRED, 'CAUSE SHE LOOKS LIKE A GRANITE, QUARTZ MIX TO ME... HEE HEE!
YOU'RE HURTING HER FEELINGS.
MAKE SURE YOU GET HER FIXED. WE DON'T WANT A LITTER OF PEBBLES RUNNING AROUND! HAR! HAR! HAR!
with inspiration from Shannon VanBavel
LITTER OF PEBBLES! WHOO-HOO! THAT'S RICH! HA HA!
I THINK YOU'RE UPSETTING HER...
www.tundracomics.com
YEAH, RIGHT! I'M SURE HER BARK IS WORSE THAN HER BITE!
CRACK!
DON'T WORRY, SHERM. SHE'S HAD ALL HER SHOTS.
BUT FROM THE LOOKS OF THIS PEA GRAVEL, I'D SAY SHE'S NOT HOUSEBROKEN.

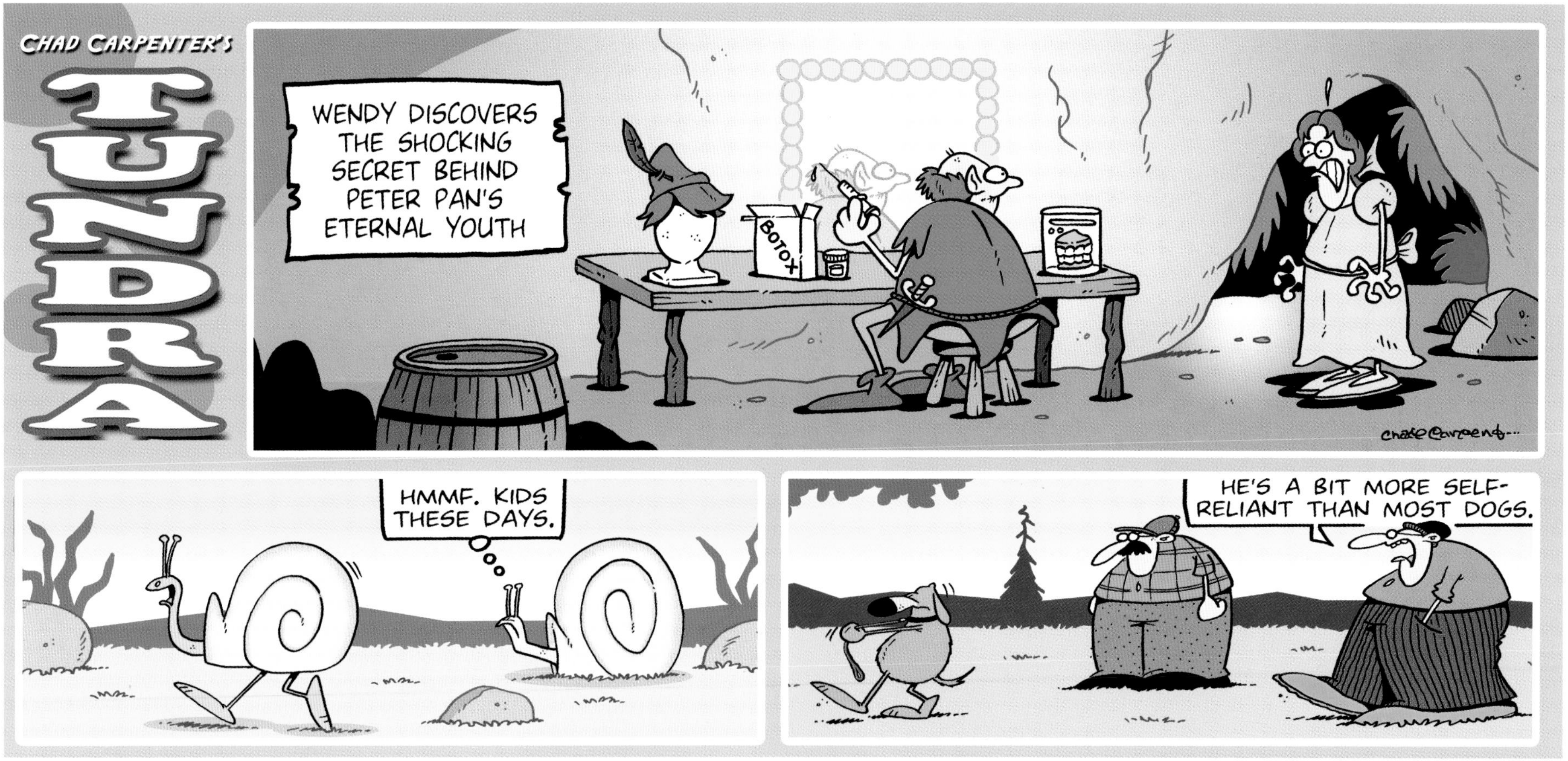
CHAD CARPENTER'S
TUNDRA
WENDY DISCOVERS THE SHOCKING SECRET BEHIND PETER PAN'S ETERNAL YOUTH
BOTOX
HMMF. KIDS THESE DAYS.
HE'S A BIT MORE SELF-RELIANT THAN MOST DOGS.

CHAD CARPENTER'S

TUNDRA

DUDLEY, THIS HAS GOT TO BE THE **LAMEST** IDEA YOU'VE EVER HAD!

ON THE CONTRARY, MY UNIMAGINATIVE FRIEND! DISGUISING MYSELF AS **GARBAGE** IS PURE GENIUS!

www.tundracomics.com

WHEN THE GARBAGE TRUCK ARRIVES, I'LL BE TRANSPORTED TO THE DUMP, AND **VOILA!** ALL-I-CAN-EAT BUFFET!

UH OH. HERE IT COMES! **QUICK!** TIE UP THE BAG!

GANGRENE GULCH Garbage Co. "You bag it, we snag it."

OOF! WHAT'S IN HERE? BOWLING BALLS?

OH, JUST SOME USELESS JUNK THAT'S BEEN LYING AROUND THE HOUSE FOR YEARS.

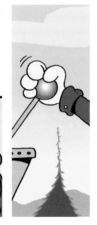

GRIND! CRUNCH! SHRED!

WHAT THE...!? AAAIEEE! THIS WASN'T IN THE BROCHURE! ...OH, THE HUMANITY!

MY MOTHER ALWAYS SAID I SHOULD HAVE THREE SQUARE MEALS A DAY...

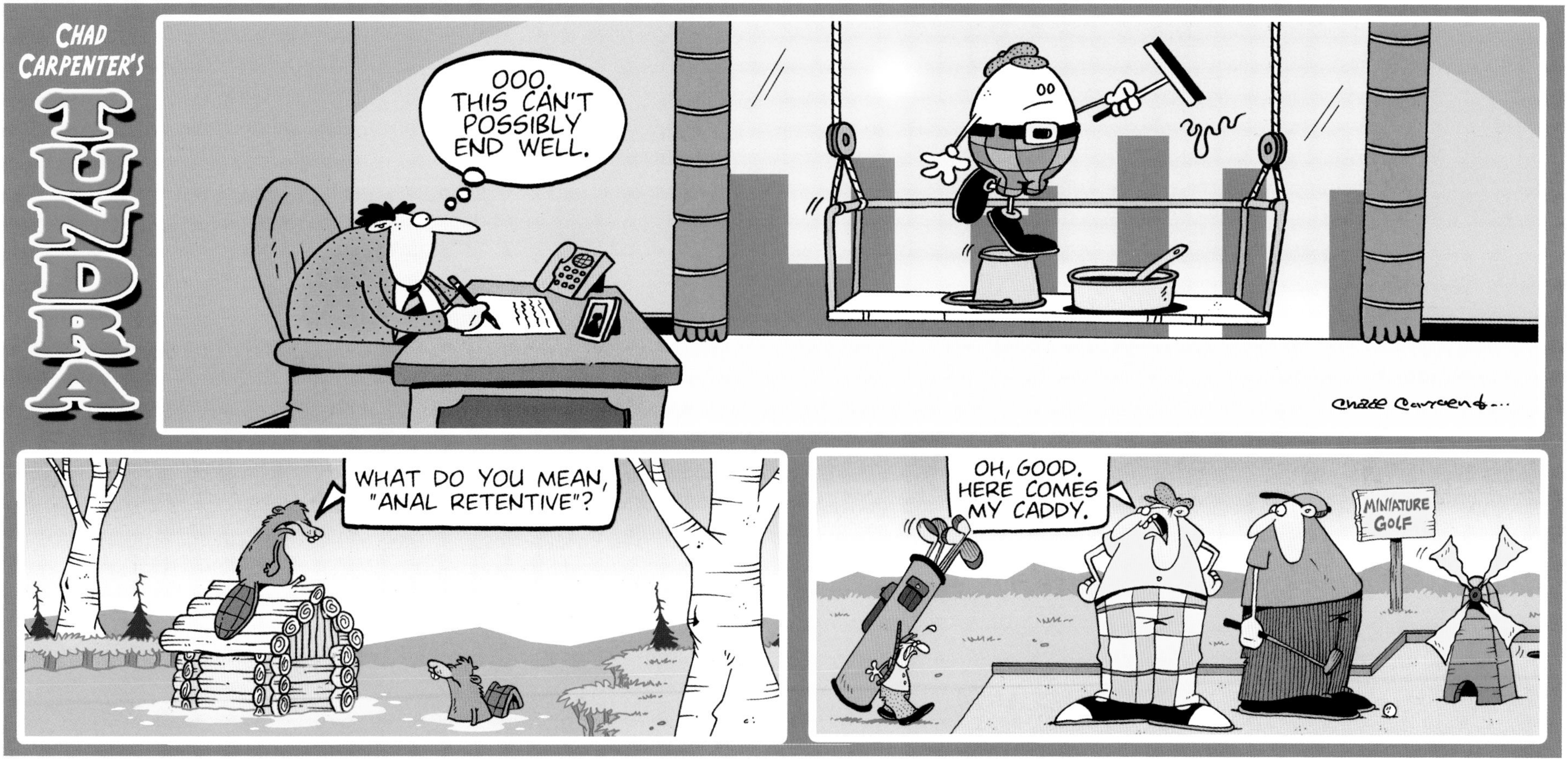
CHAD CARPENTER'S
TUNDRA
OOO. THIS CAN'T POSSIBLY END WELL.
Chad Carpenter
WHAT DO YOU MEAN, "ANAL RETENTIVE"?
OH, GOOD. HERE COMES MY CADDY.
MINIATURE GOLF

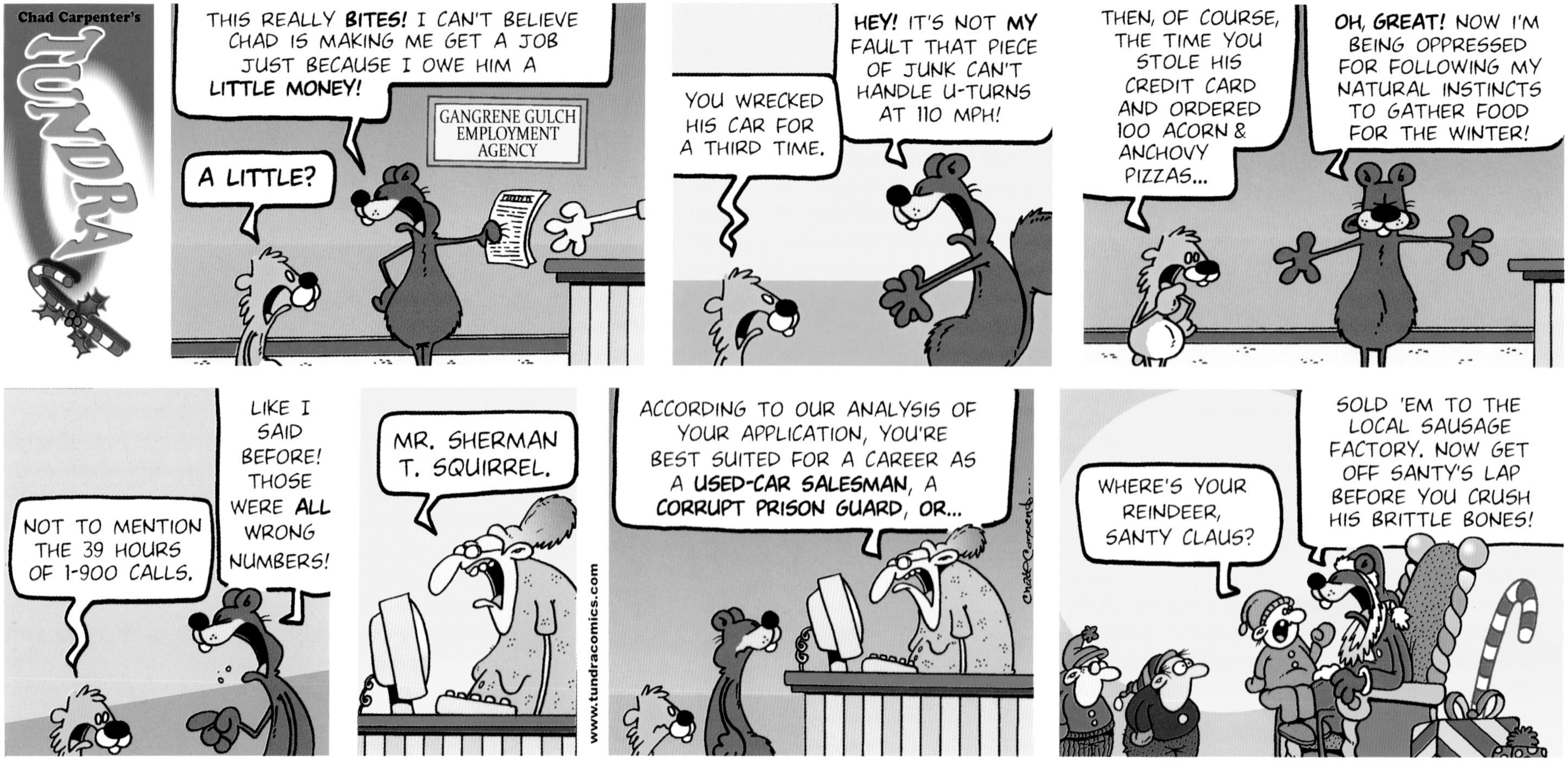
Chad Carpenter's
TUNDRA
THIS REALLY BITES! I CAN'T BELIEVE CHAD IS MAKING ME GET A JOB JUST BECAUSE I OWE HIM A LITTLE MONEY!
GANGRENE GULCH EMPLOYMENT AGENCY
A LITTLE?
YOU WRECKED HIS CAR FOR A THIRD TIME.
HEY! IT'S NOT MY FAULT THAT PIECE OF JUNK CAN'T HANDLE U-TURNS AT 110 MPH!
THEN, OF COURSE, THE TIME YOU STOLE HIS CREDIT CARD AND ORDERED 100 ACORN & ANCHOVY PIZZAS...
OH, GREAT! NOW I'M BEING OPPRESSED FOR FOLLOWING MY NATURAL INSTINCTS TO GATHER FOOD FOR THE WINTER!
NOT TO MENTION THE 39 HOURS OF 1-900 CALLS.
LIKE I SAID BEFORE! THOSE WERE ALL WRONG NUMBERS!
MR. SHERMAN T. SQUIRREL.
www.tundracomics.com
ACCORDING TO OUR ANALYSIS OF YOUR APPLICATION, YOU'RE BEST SUITED FOR A CAREER AS A USED-CAR SALESMAN, A CORRUPT PRISON GUARD, OR...
WHERE'S YOUR REINDEER, SANTY CLAUS?
SOLD 'EM TO THE LOCAL SAUSAGE FACTORY. NOW GET OFF SANTY'S LAP BEFORE YOU CRUSH HIS BRITTLE BONES!

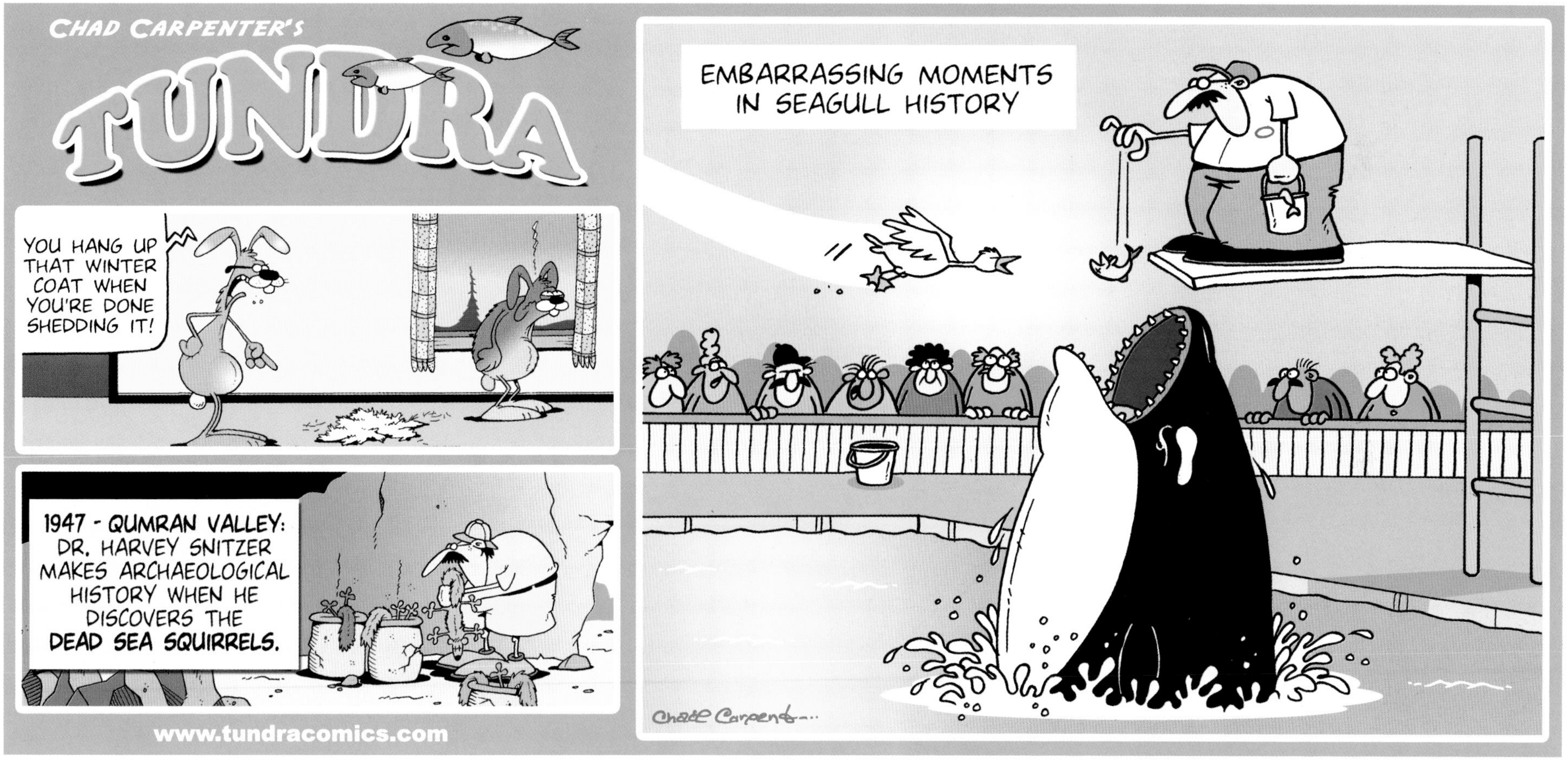
CHAD CARPENTER'S
TUNDRA
YOU HANG UP THAT WINTER COAT WHEN YOU'RE DONE SHEDDING IT!
1947 - QUMRAN VALLEY: DR. HARVEY SNITZER MAKES ARCHAEOLOGICAL HISTORY WHEN HE DISCOVERS THE DEAD SEA SQUIRRELS.
www.tundracomics.com
EMBARRASSING MOMENTS IN SEAGULL HISTORY

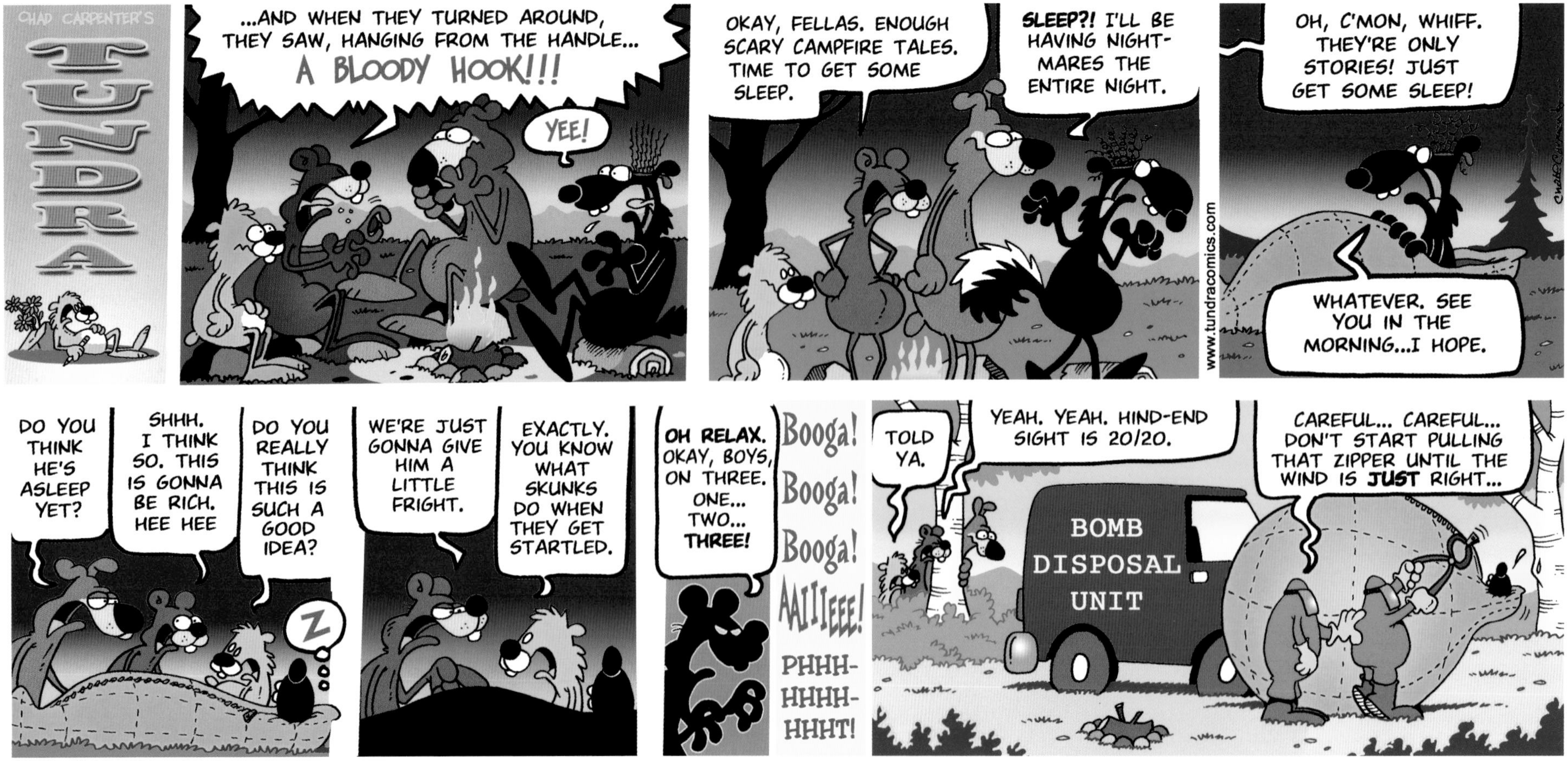
CHAD CARPENTER'S
TUNDRA
...AND WHEN THEY TURNED AROUND, THEY SAW, HANGING FROM THE HANDLE... A BLOODY HOOK!!!
YEE!
OKAY, FELLAS. ENOUGH SCARY CAMPFIRE TALES. TIME TO GET SOME SLEEP.
SLEEP?! I'LL BE HAVING NIGHT-MARES THE ENTIRE NIGHT.
www.tundracomics.com
OH, C'MON, WHIFF. THEY'RE ONLY STORIES! JUST GET SOME SLEEP!
WHATEVER. SEE YOU IN THE MORNING...I HOPE.
DO YOU THINK HE'S ASLEEP YET?
SHHH. I THINK SO. THIS IS GONNA BE RICH. HEE HEE
DO YOU REALLY THINK THIS IS SUCH A GOOD IDEA?
Z
WE'RE JUST GONNA GIVE HIM A LITTLE FRIGHT.
EXACTLY. YOU KNOW WHAT SKUNKS DO WHEN THEY GET STARTLED.
OH RELAX. OKAY, BOYS, ON THREE. ONE... TWO... THREE!
Booga! Booga! Booga! AAIIIEEE!
PHHH-HHHH-HHHT!
TOLD YA.
YEAH. YEAH. HIND-END SIGHT IS 20/20.
BOMB DISPOSAL UNIT
CAREFUL... CAREFUL... DON'T START PULLING THAT ZIPPER UNTIL THE WIND IS JUST RIGHT...

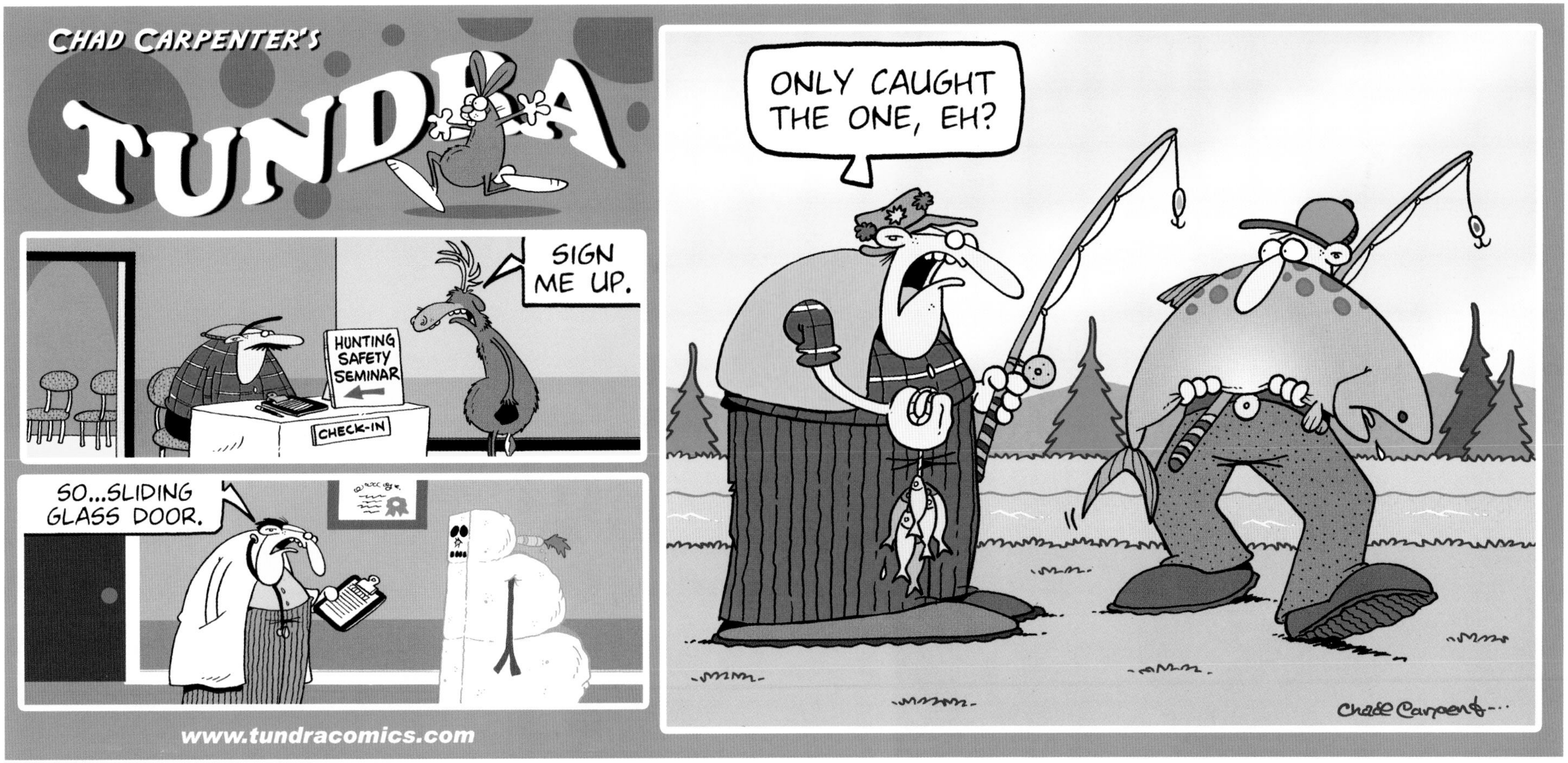
CHAD CARPENTER'S
TUNDRA
HUNTING SAFETY SEMINAR
CHECK-IN
SIGN ME UP.
SO...SLIDING GLASS DOOR.
www.tundracomics.com
ONLY CAUGHT THE ONE, EH?

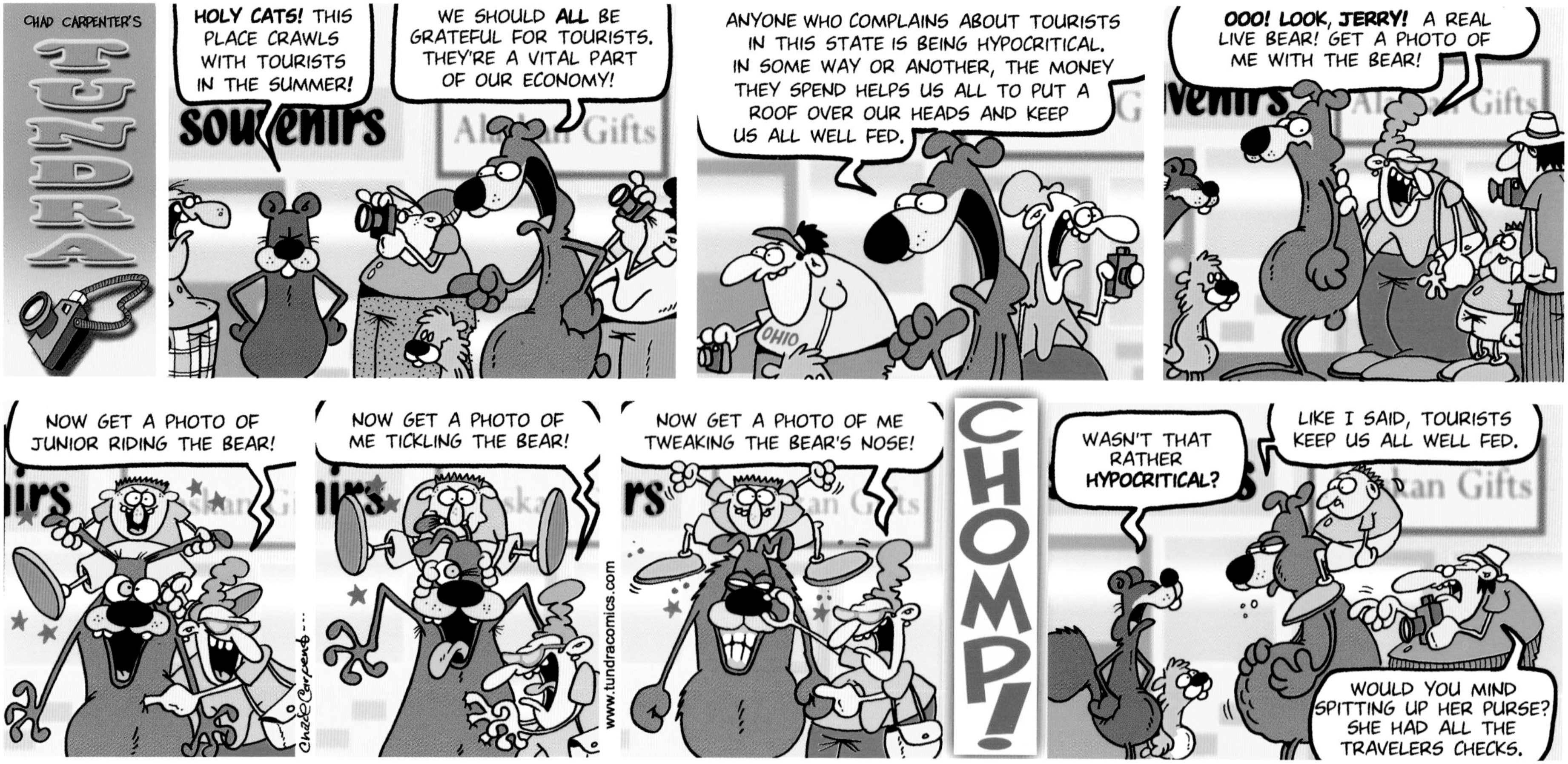
CHAD CARPENTER'S
TUNDRA
HOLY CATS! THIS PLACE CRAWLS WITH TOURISTS IN THE SUMMER!
WE SHOULD ALL BE GRATEFUL FOR TOURISTS. THEY'RE A VITAL PART OF OUR ECONOMY!
ANYONE WHO COMPLAINS ABOUT TOURISTS IN THIS STATE IS BEING HYPOCRITICAL. IN SOME WAY OR ANOTHER, THE MONEY THEY SPEND HELPS US ALL TO PUT A ROOF OVER OUR HEADS AND KEEP US ALL WELL FED.
OOO! LOOK, JERRY! A REAL LIVE BEAR! GET A PHOTO OF ME WITH THE BEAR!
NOW GET A PHOTO OF JUNIOR RIDING THE BEAR!
NOW GET A PHOTO OF ME TICKLING THE BEAR!
www.tundracomics.com
NOW GET A PHOTO OF ME TWEAKING THE BEAR'S NOSE!
CHOMP!
WASN'T THAT RATHER HYPOCRITICAL?
LIKE I SAID, TOURISTS KEEP US ALL WELL FED.
WOULD YOU MIND SPITTING UP HER PURSE? SHE HAD ALL THE TRAVELERS CHECKS.

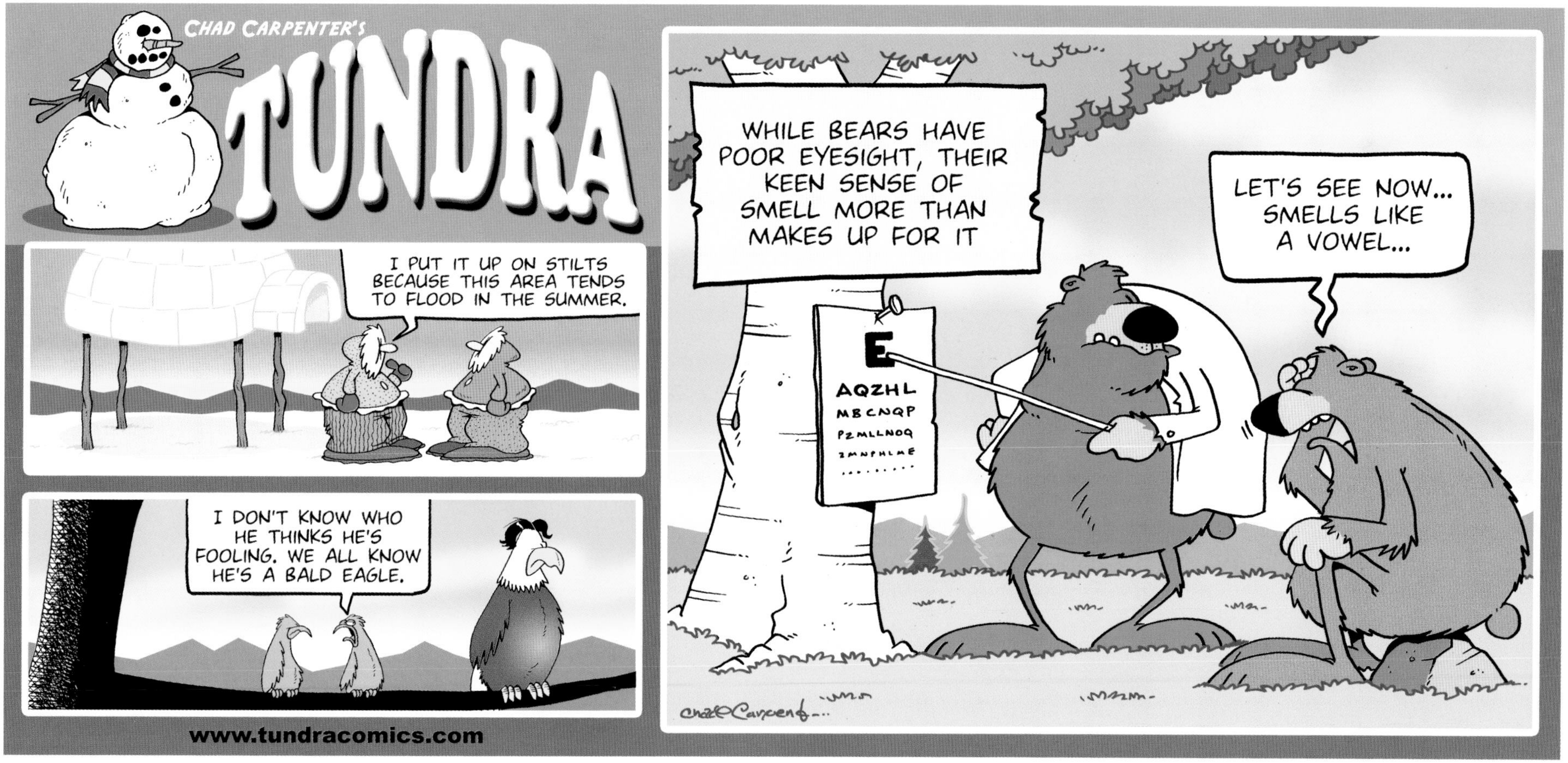
CHAD CARPENTER'S
TUNDRA
I PUT IT UP ON STILTS BECAUSE THIS AREA TENDS TO FLOOD IN THE SUMMER.
I DON'T KNOW WHO HE THINKS HE'S FOOLING. WE ALL KNOW HE'S A BALD EAGLE.
www.tundracomics.com
WHILE BEARS HAVE POOR EYESIGHT, THEIR KEEN SENSE OF SMELL MORE THAN MAKES UP FOR IT
E
AQZHL
MBCNQP
LET'S SEE NOW... SMELLS LIKE A VOWEL...

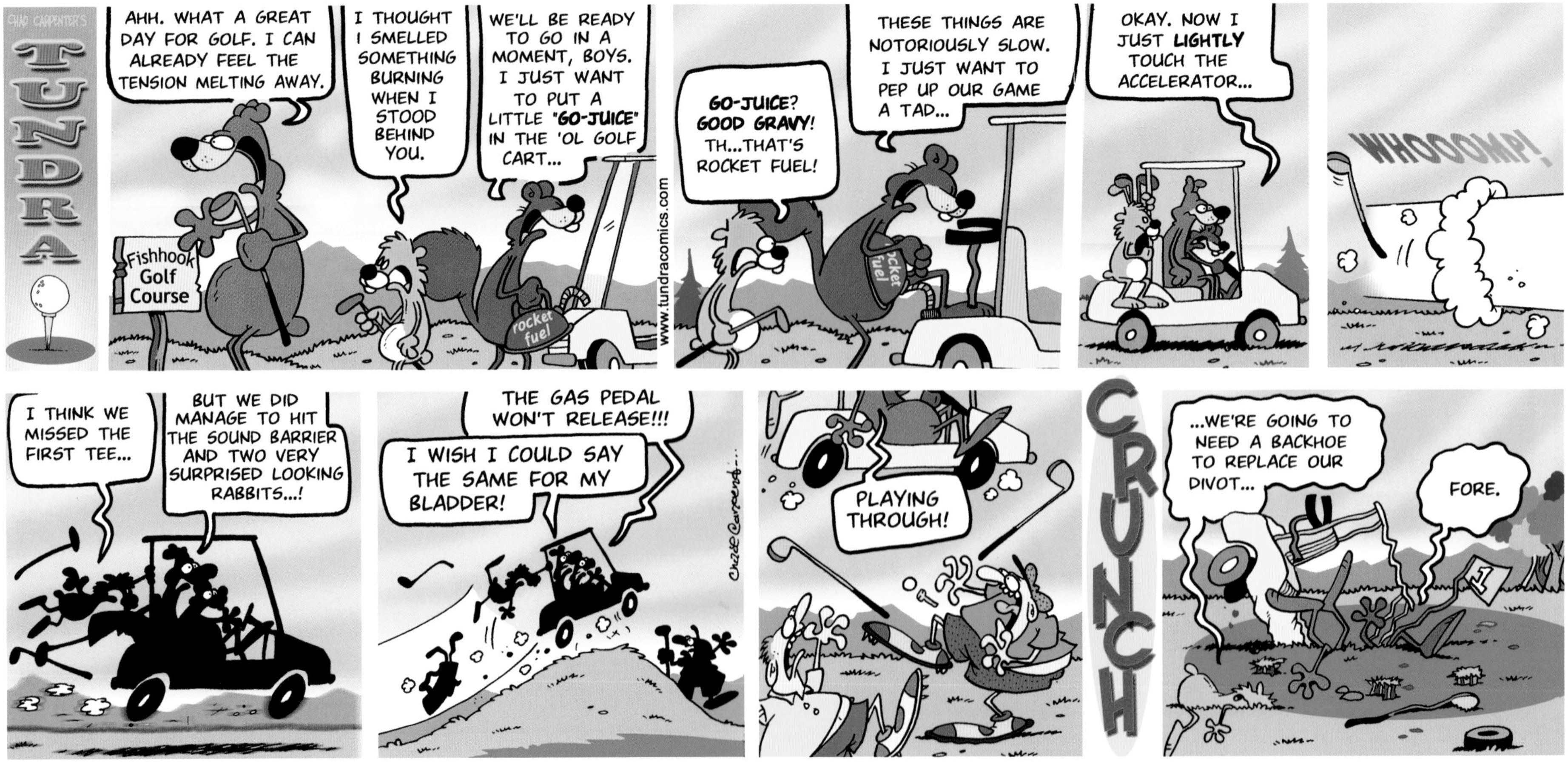
CHAD CARPENTER'S
TUNDRA
AHH. WHAT A GREAT DAY FOR GOLF. I CAN ALREADY FEEL THE TENSION MELTING AWAY.
Fishhook Golf Course
I THOUGHT I SMELLED SOMETHING BURNING WHEN I STOOD BEHIND YOU.
WE'LL BE READY TO GO IN A MOMENT, BOYS. I JUST WANT TO PUT A LITTLE "GO-JUICE" IN THE 'OL GOLF CART...
rocket fuel
www.tundracomics.com
GO-JUICE? GOOD GRAVY! TH...THAT'S ROCKET FUEL!
THESE THINGS ARE NOTORIOUSLY SLOW. I JUST WANT TO PEP UP OUR GAME A TAD...
OKAY. NOW I JUST LIGHTLY TOUCH THE ACCELERATOR...
WHOOOMP!
I THINK WE MISSED THE FIRST TEE...
BUT WE DID MANAGE TO HIT THE SOUND BARRIER AND TWO VERY SURPRISED LOOKING RABBITS...!
THE GAS PEDAL WON'T RELEASE!!!
I WISH I COULD SAY THE SAME FOR MY BLADDER!
PLAYING THROUGH!
CRUNCH
...WE'RE GOING TO NEED A BACKHOE TO REPLACE OUR DIVOT...
FORE.

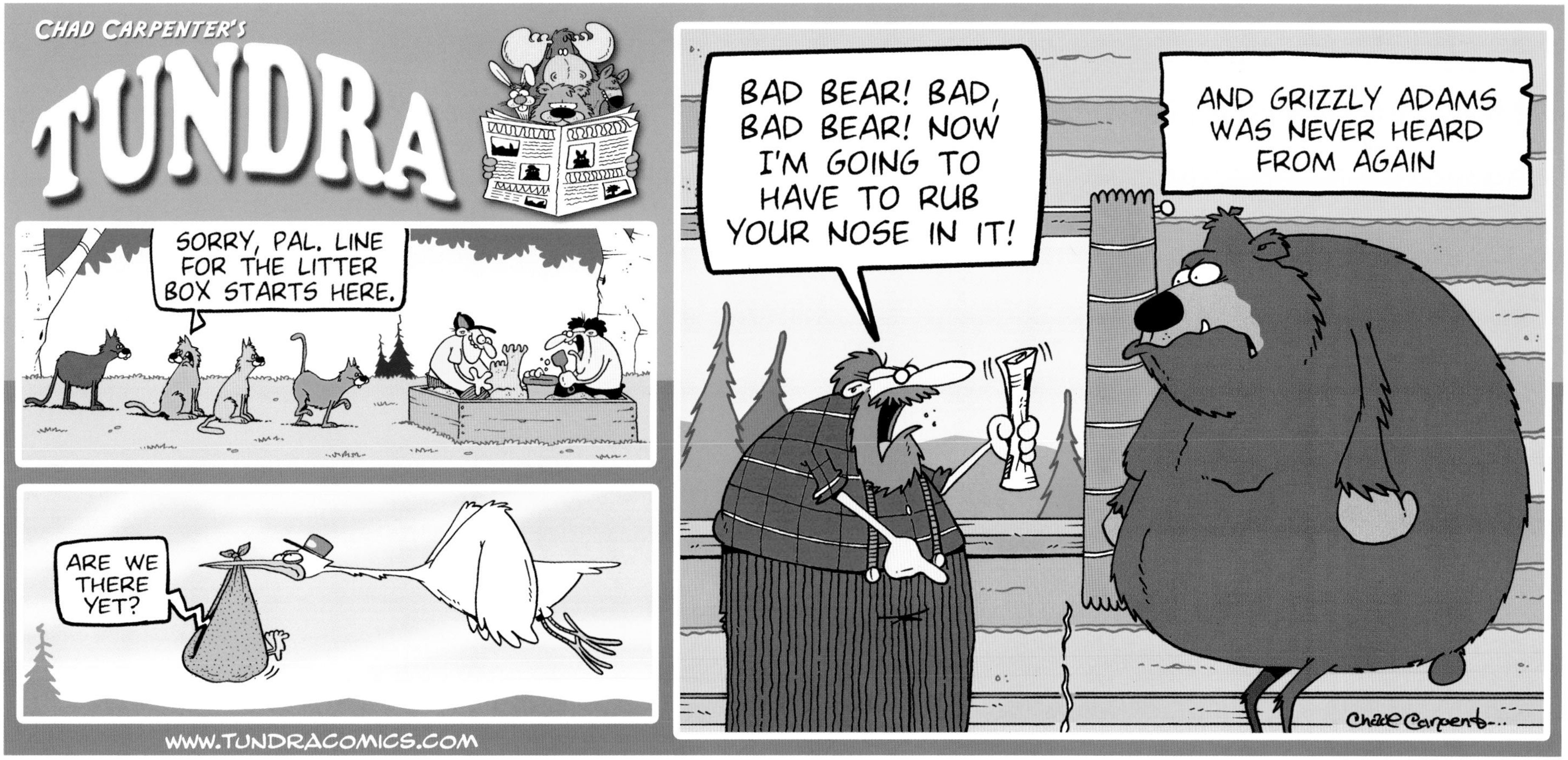
CHAD CARPENTER'S
TUNDRA
SORRY, PAL. LINE FOR THE LITTER BOX STARTS HERE.
ARE WE THERE YET?
WWW.TUNDRACOMICS.COM
BAD BEAR! BAD, BAD BEAR! NOW I'M GOING TO HAVE TO RUB YOUR NOSE IN IT!
AND GRIZZLY ADAMS WAS NEVER HEARD FROM AGAIN

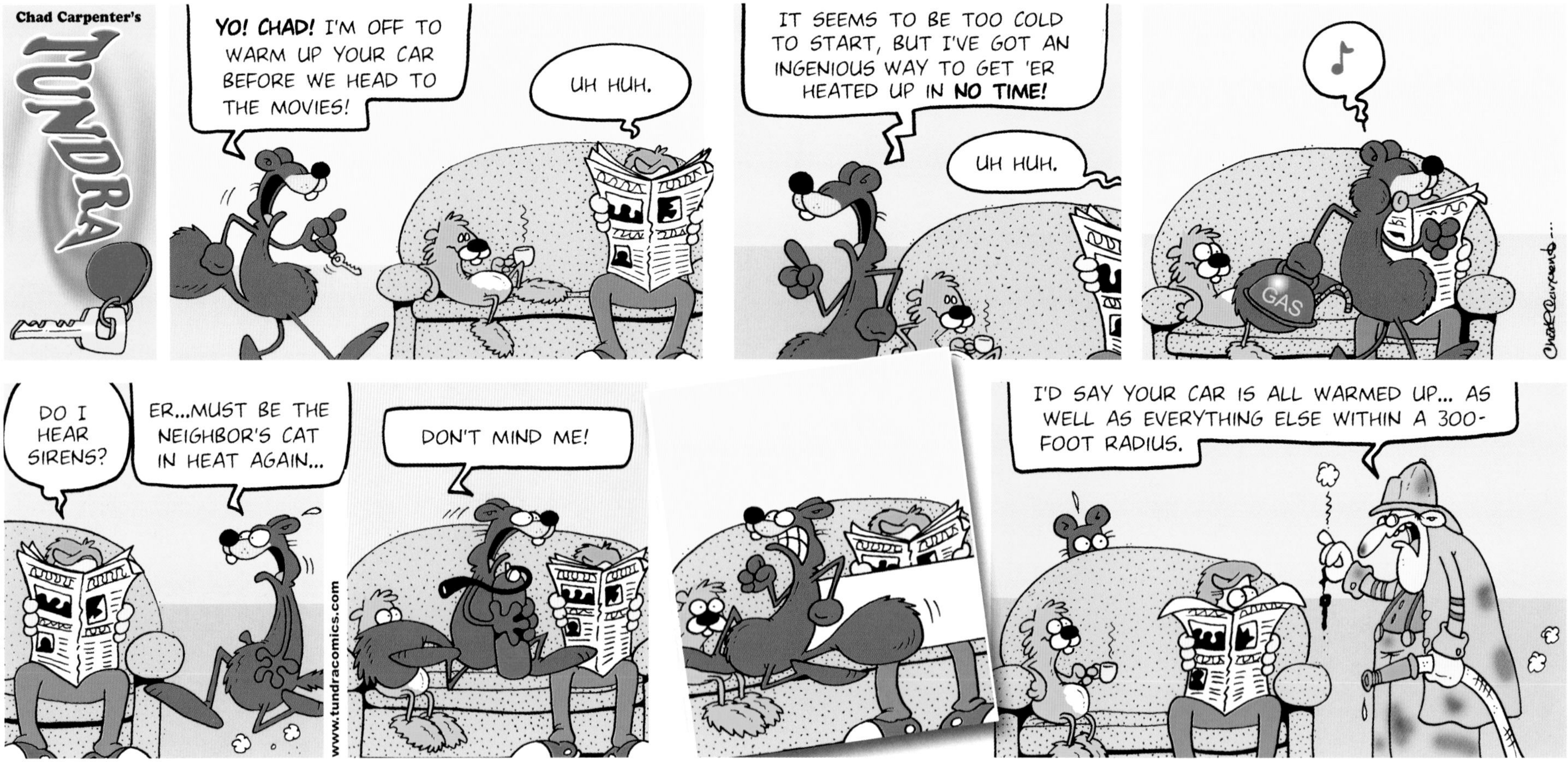
Chad Carpenter's
TUNDRA
YO! CHAD! I'M OFF TO WARM UP YOUR CAR BEFORE WE HEAD TO THE MOVIES!
UH HUH.
IT SEEMS TO BE TOO COLD TO START, BUT I'VE GOT AN INGENIOUS WAY TO GET 'ER HEATED UP IN NO TIME!
UH HUH.
GAS
DO I HEAR SIRENS?
ER...MUST BE THE NEIGHBOR'S CAT IN HEAT AGAIN...
www.tundracomics.com
DON'T MIND ME!
I'D SAY YOUR CAR IS ALL WARMED UP... AS WELL AS EVERYTHING ELSE WITHIN A 300-FOOT RADIUS.

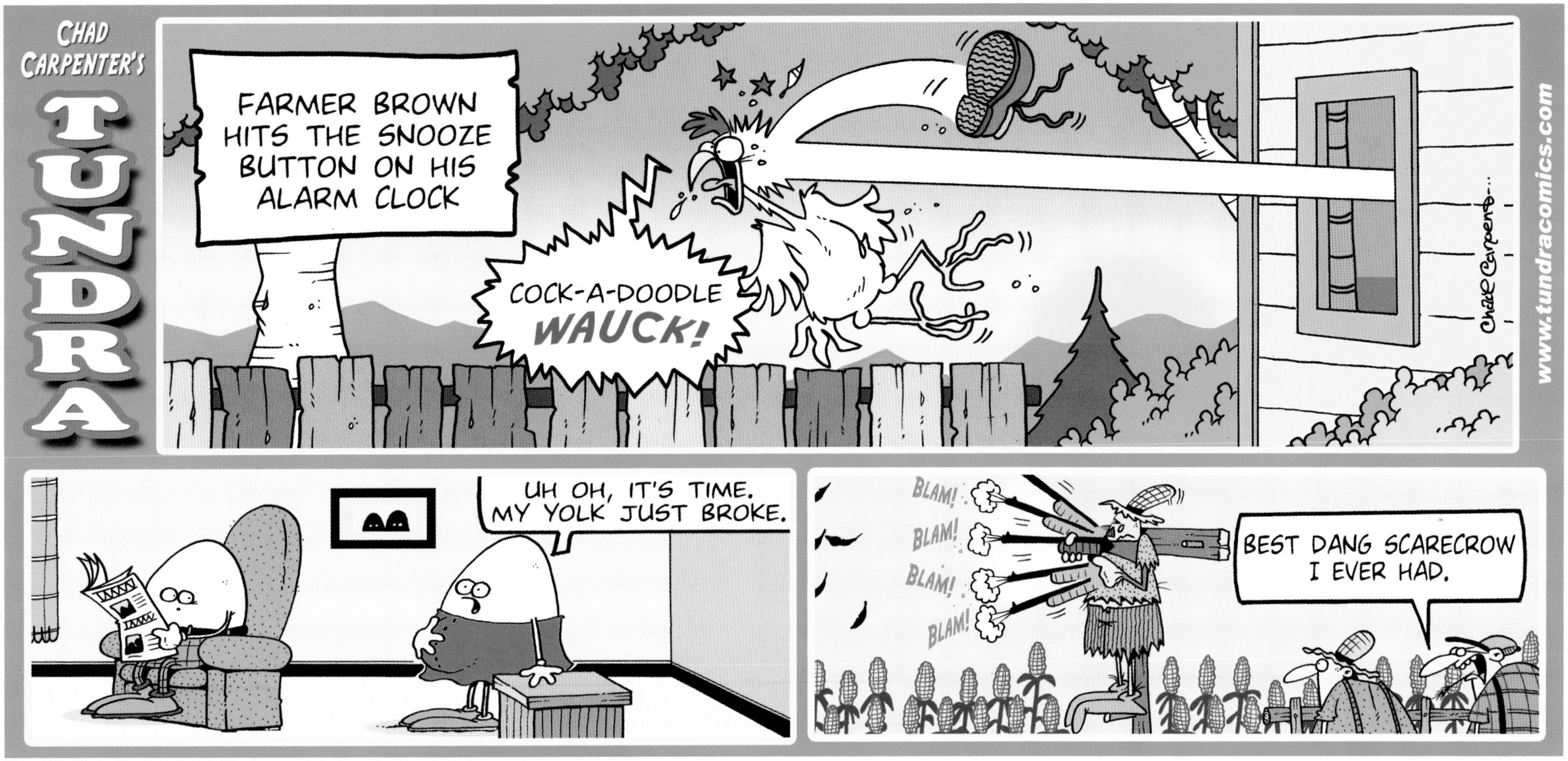
CHAD CARPENTER'S
TUNDRA
www.tundracomics.com
FARMER BROWN HITS THE SNOOZE BUTTON ON HIS ALARM CLOCK
COCK-A-DOODLE WAUCK!
UH OH, IT'S TIME. MY YOLK JUST BROKE.
BLAM!
BLAM!
BLAM!
BLAM!
BEST DANG SCARECROW I EVER HAD.

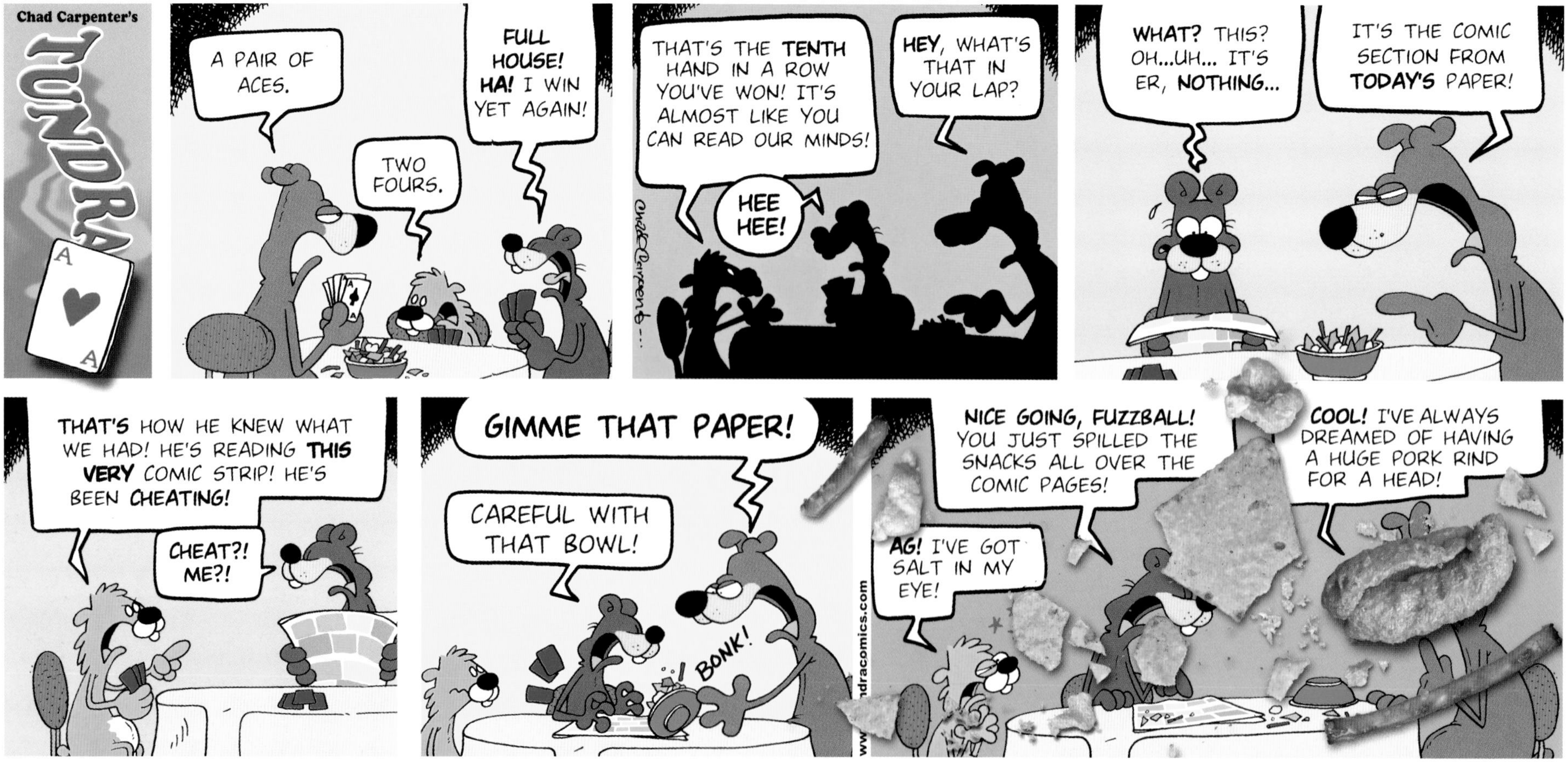
Chad Carpenter's
TUNDRA
A PAIR OF ACES.
TWO FOURS.
FULL HOUSE! HA! I WIN YET AGAIN!
THAT'S THE TENTH HAND IN A ROW YOU'VE WON! IT'S ALMOST LIKE YOU CAN READ OUR MINDS!
HEE HEE!
HEY, WHAT'S THAT IN YOUR LAP?
WHAT? THIS? OH...UH... IT'S ER, NOTHING...
IT'S THE COMIC SECTION FROM TODAY'S PAPER!
THAT'S HOW HE KNEW WHAT WE HAD! HE'S READING THIS VERY COMIC STRIP! HE'S BEEN CHEATING!
CHEAT?! ME?!
GIMME THAT PAPER!
CAREFUL WITH THAT BOWL!
BONK!
NICE GOING, FUZZBALL! YOU JUST SPILLED THE SNACKS ALL OVER THE COMIC PAGES!
COOL! I'VE ALWAYS DREAMED OF HAVING A HUGE PORK RIND FOR A HEAD!
AG! I'VE GOT SALT IN MY EYE!
www.tundracomics.com

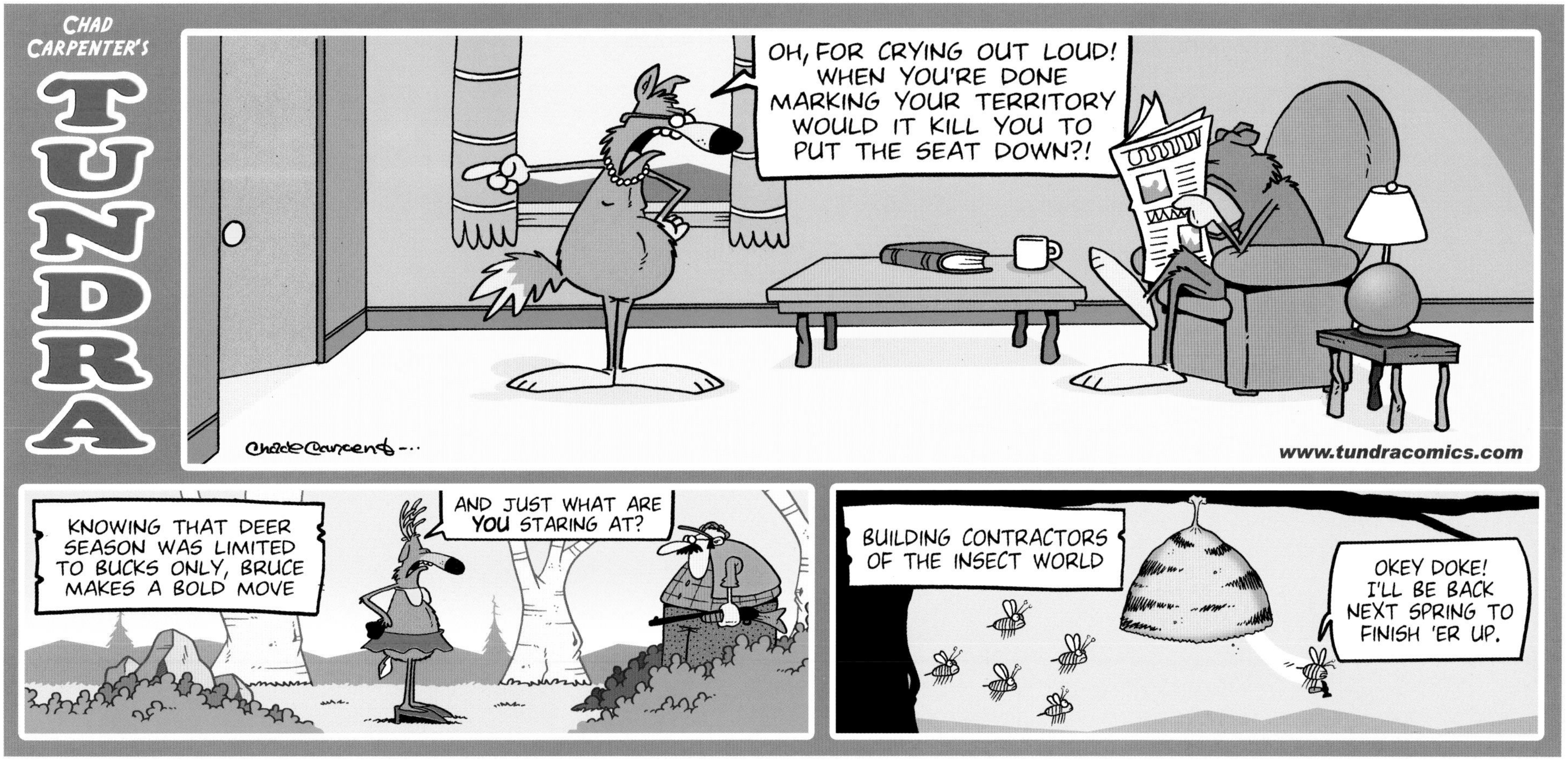
CHAD CARPENTER'S
TUNDRA
OH, FOR CRYING OUT LOUD! WHEN YOU'RE DONE MARKING YOUR TERRITORY WOULD IT KILL YOU TO PUT THE SEAT DOWN?!
www.tundracomics.com
KNOWING THAT DEER SEASON WAS LIMITED TO BUCKS ONLY, BRUCE MAKES A BOLD MOVE
AND JUST WHAT ARE **YOU** STARING AT?
BUILDING CONTRACTORS OF THE INSECT WORLD
OKEY DOKE! I'LL BE BACK NEXT SPRING TO FINISH 'ER UP.

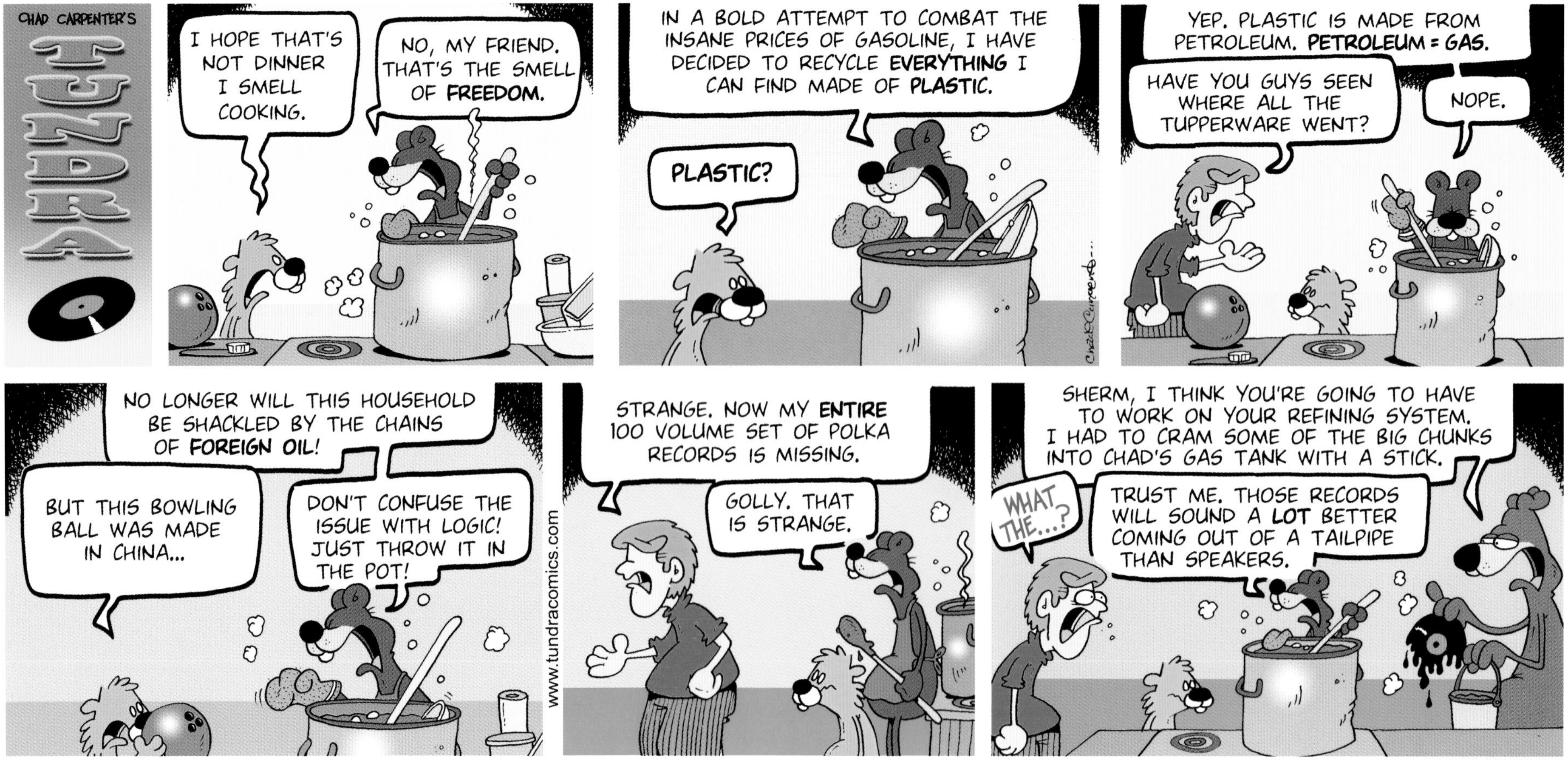
CHAD CARPENTER'S
TUNDRA
I HOPE THAT'S NOT DINNER I SMELL COOKING.
NO, MY FRIEND. THAT'S THE SMELL OF FREEDOM.
IN A BOLD ATTEMPT TO COMBAT THE INSANE PRICES OF GASOLINE, I HAVE DECIDED TO RECYCLE EVERYTHING I CAN FIND MADE OF PLASTIC.
PLASTIC?
YEP. PLASTIC IS MADE FROM PETROLEUM. PETROLEUM = GAS.
HAVE YOU GUYS SEEN WHERE ALL THE TUPPERWARE WENT?
NOPE.
NO LONGER WILL THIS HOUSEHOLD BE SHACKLED BY THE CHAINS OF FOREIGN OIL!
BUT THIS BOWLING BALL WAS MADE IN CHINA...
DON'T CONFUSE THE ISSUE WITH LOGIC! JUST THROW IT IN THE POT!
www.tundracomics.com
STRANGE. NOW MY ENTIRE 100 VOLUME SET OF POLKA RECORDS IS MISSING.
GOLLY. THAT IS STRANGE.
SHERM, I THINK YOU'RE GOING TO HAVE TO WORK ON YOUR REFINING SYSTEM. I HAD TO CRAM SOME OF THE BIG CHUNKS INTO CHAD'S GAS TANK WITH A STICK.
WHAT THE...?
TRUST ME. THOSE RECORDS WILL SOUND A LOT BETTER COMING OUT OF A TAILPIPE THAN SPEAKERS.

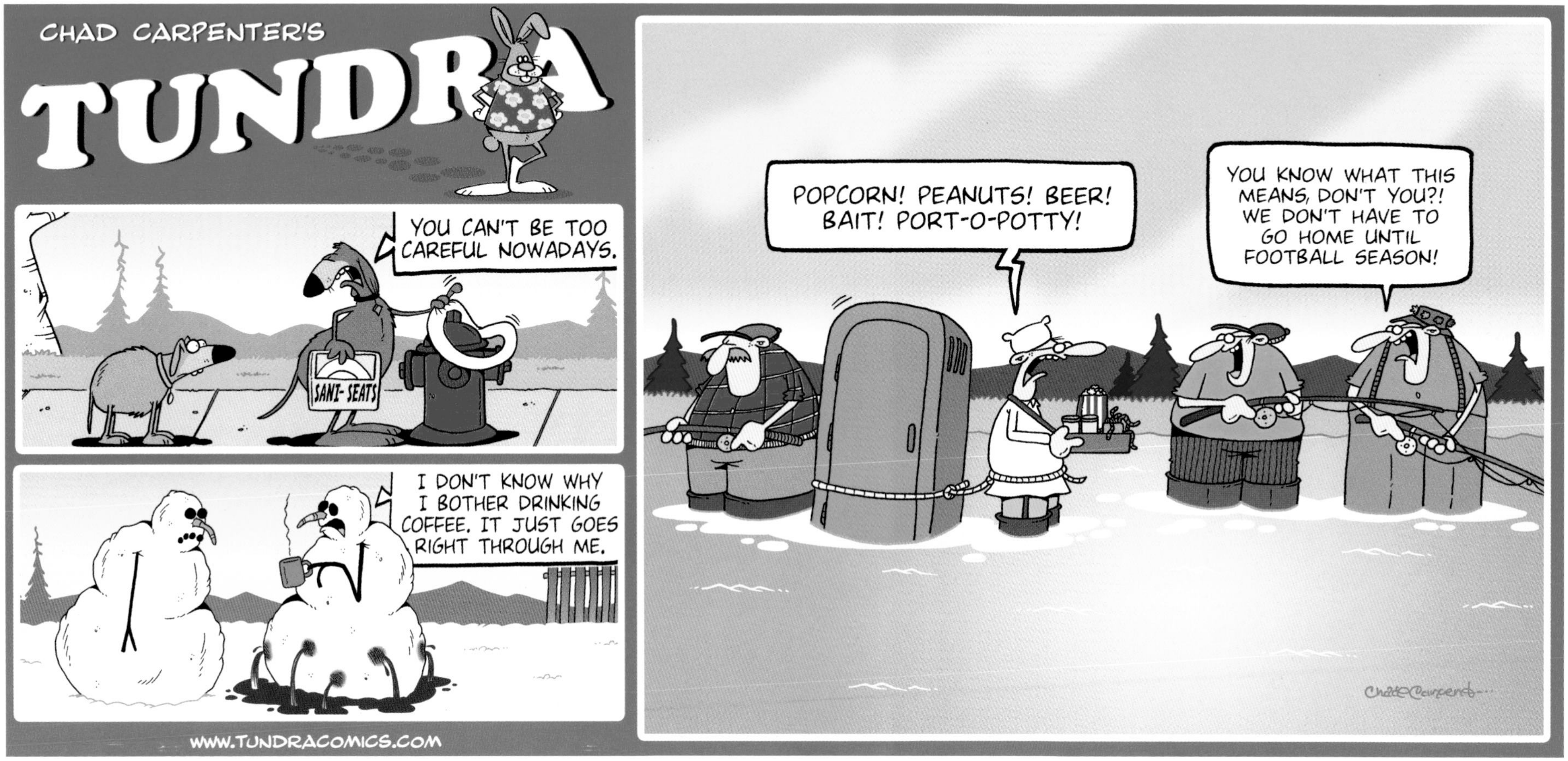
CHAD CARPENTER'S
TUNDRA
YOU CAN'T BE TOO CAREFUL NOWADAYS.
SANI-SEATS
I DON'T KNOW WHY I BOTHER DRINKING COFFEE. IT JUST GOES RIGHT THROUGH ME.
WWW.TUNDRACOMICS.COM
POPCORN! PEANUTS! BEER! BAIT! PORT-O-POTTY!
YOU KNOW WHAT THIS MEANS, DON'T YOU?! WE DON'T HAVE TO GO HOME UNTIL FOOTBALL SEASON!

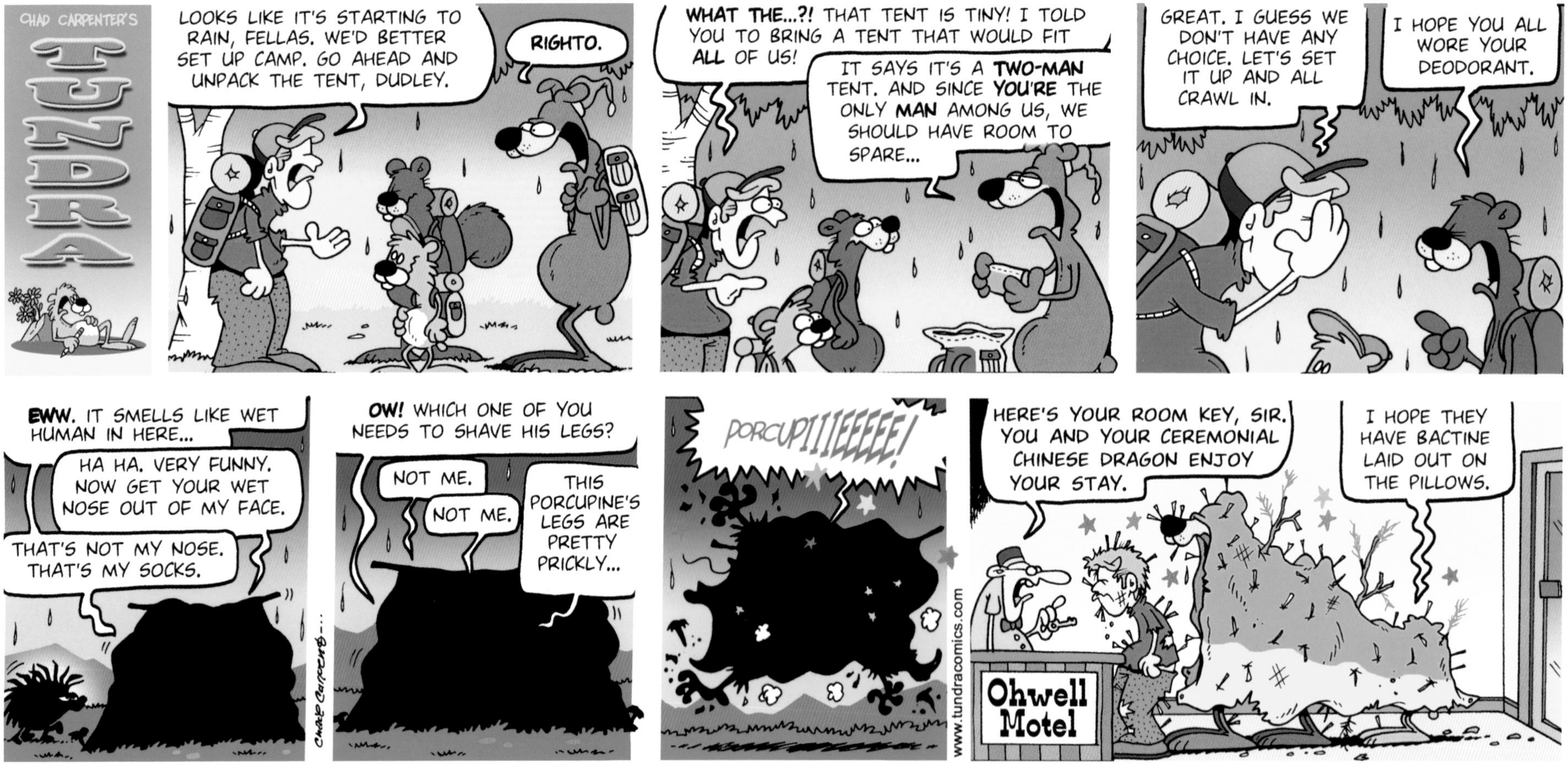
CHAD CARPENTER'S
TUNDRA
LOOKS LIKE IT'S STARTING TO RAIN, FELLAS. WE'D BETTER SET UP CAMP. GO AHEAD AND UNPACK THE TENT, DUDLEY.
RIGHTO.
WHAT THE...?! THAT TENT IS TINY! I TOLD YOU TO BRING A TENT THAT WOULD FIT ALL OF US!
IT SAYS IT'S A TWO-MAN TENT. AND SINCE YOU'RE THE ONLY MAN AMONG US, WE SHOULD HAVE ROOM TO SPARE...
GREAT. I GUESS WE DON'T HAVE ANY CHOICE. LET'S SET IT UP AND ALL CRAWL IN.
I HOPE YOU ALL WORE YOUR DEODORANT.
EWW. IT SMELLS LIKE WET HUMAN IN HERE...
HA HA. VERY FUNNY. NOW GET YOUR WET NOSE OUT OF MY FACE.
THAT'S NOT MY NOSE. THAT'S MY SOCKS.
OW! WHICH ONE OF YOU NEEDS TO SHAVE HIS LEGS?
NOT ME.
NOT ME.
THIS PORCUPINE'S LEGS ARE PRETTY PRICKLY...
PORCUPIIIEEEEE!
www.tundracomics.com
HERE'S YOUR ROOM KEY, SIR. YOU AND YOUR CEREMONIAL CHINESE DRAGON ENJOY YOUR STAY.
I HOPE THEY HAVE BACTINE LAID OUT ON THE PILLOWS.
Ohwell Motel

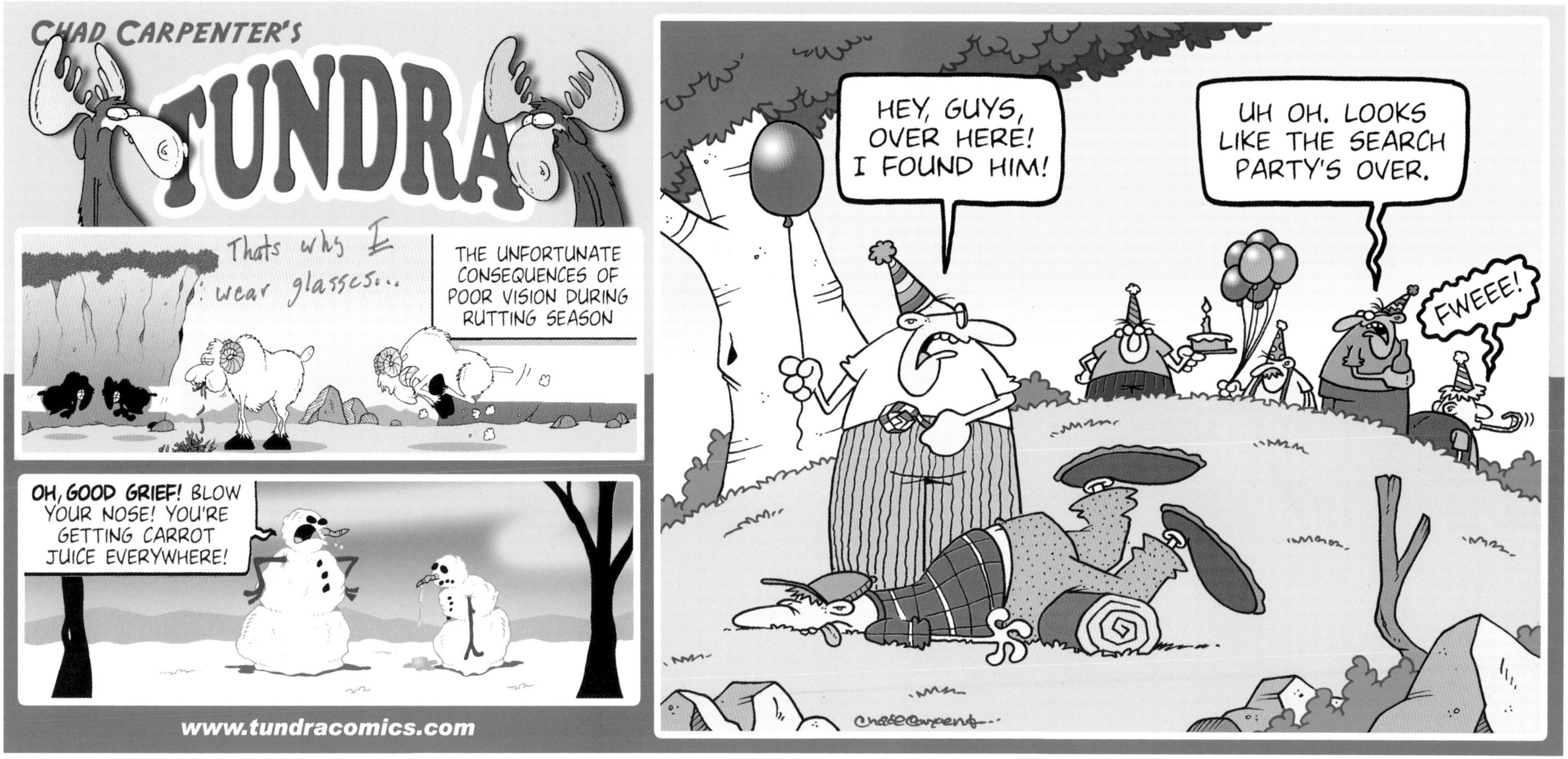
CHAD CARPENTER'S
TUNDRA
Thats why I wear glasses...
THE UNFORTUNATE CONSEQUENCES OF POOR VISION DURING RUTTING SEASON
OH, GOOD GRIEF! BLOW YOUR NOSE! YOU'RE GETTING CARROT JUICE EVERYWHERE!
www.tundracomics.com
HEY, GUYS, OVER HERE! I FOUND HIM!
UH OH. LOOKS LIKE THE SEARCH PARTY'S OVER.
FWEEE!

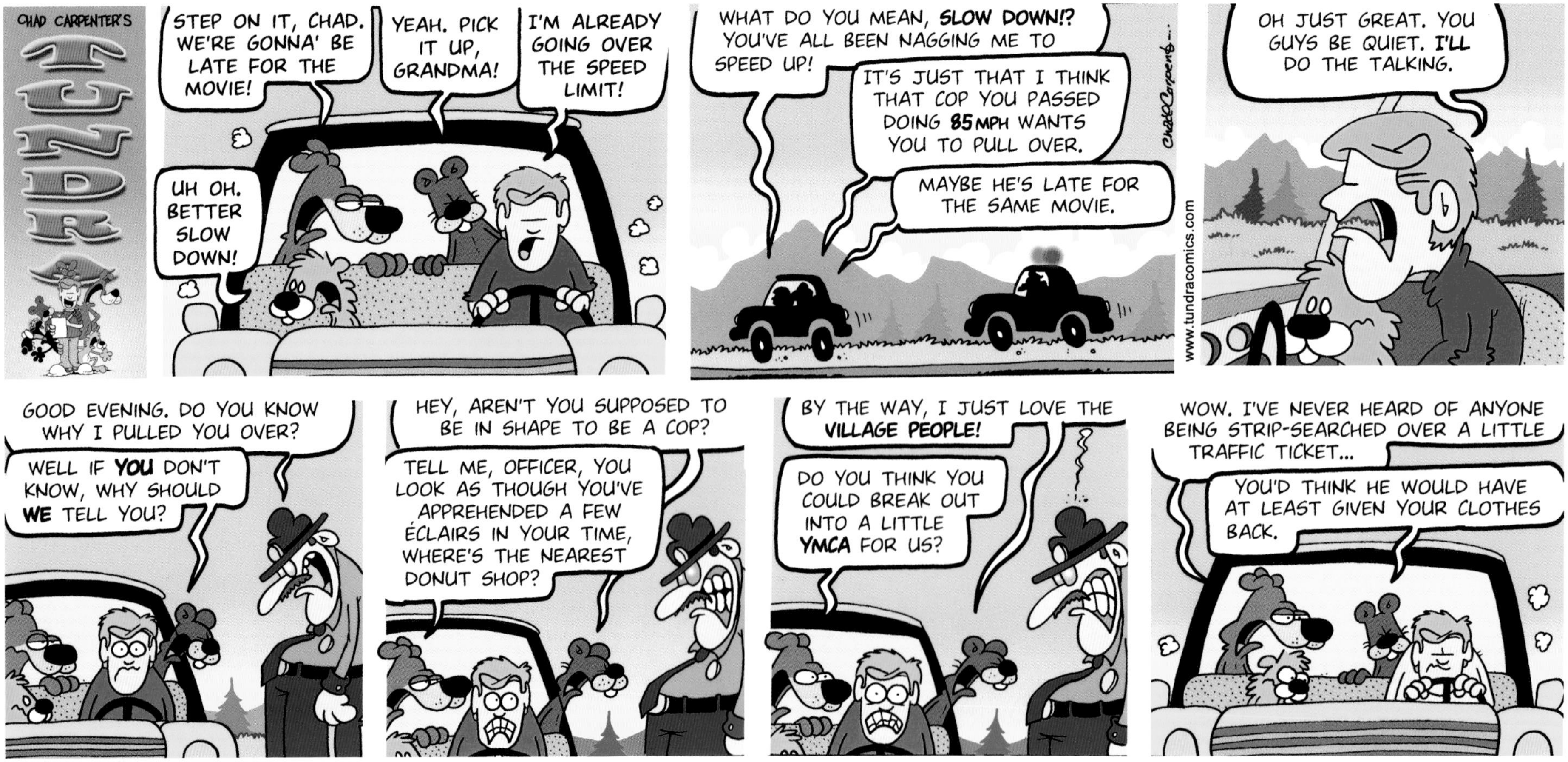
CHAD CARPENTER'S
TUNDRA
STEP ON IT, CHAD. WE'RE GONNA' BE LATE FOR THE MOVIE!
YEAH. PICK IT UP, GRANDMA!
I'M ALREADY GOING OVER THE SPEED LIMIT!
UH OH. BETTER SLOW DOWN!
WHAT DO YOU MEAN, **SLOW DOWN!?** YOU'VE ALL BEEN NAGGING ME TO SPEED UP!
IT'S JUST THAT I THINK THAT COP YOU PASSED DOING **85 MPH** WANTS YOU TO PULL OVER.
MAYBE HE'S LATE FOR THE SAME MOVIE.
www.tundracomics.com
OH JUST GREAT. YOU GUYS BE QUIET. **I'LL** DO THE TALKING.
GOOD EVENING. DO YOU KNOW WHY I PULLED YOU OVER?
WELL IF **YOU** DON'T KNOW, WHY SHOULD **WE** TELL YOU?
HEY, AREN'T YOU SUPPOSED TO BE IN SHAPE TO BE A COP?
TELL ME, OFFICER, YOU LOOK AS THOUGH YOU'VE APPREHENDED A FEW ÉCLAIRS IN YOUR TIME, WHERE'S THE NEAREST DONUT SHOP?
BY THE WAY, I JUST LOVE THE **VILLAGE PEOPLE!**
DO YOU THINK YOU COULD BREAK OUT INTO A LITTLE **YMCA** FOR US?
WOW. I'VE NEVER HEARD OF ANYONE BEING STRIP-SEARCHED OVER A LITTLE TRAFFIC TICKET...
YOU'D THINK HE WOULD HAVE AT LEAST GIVEN YOUR CLOTHES BACK.

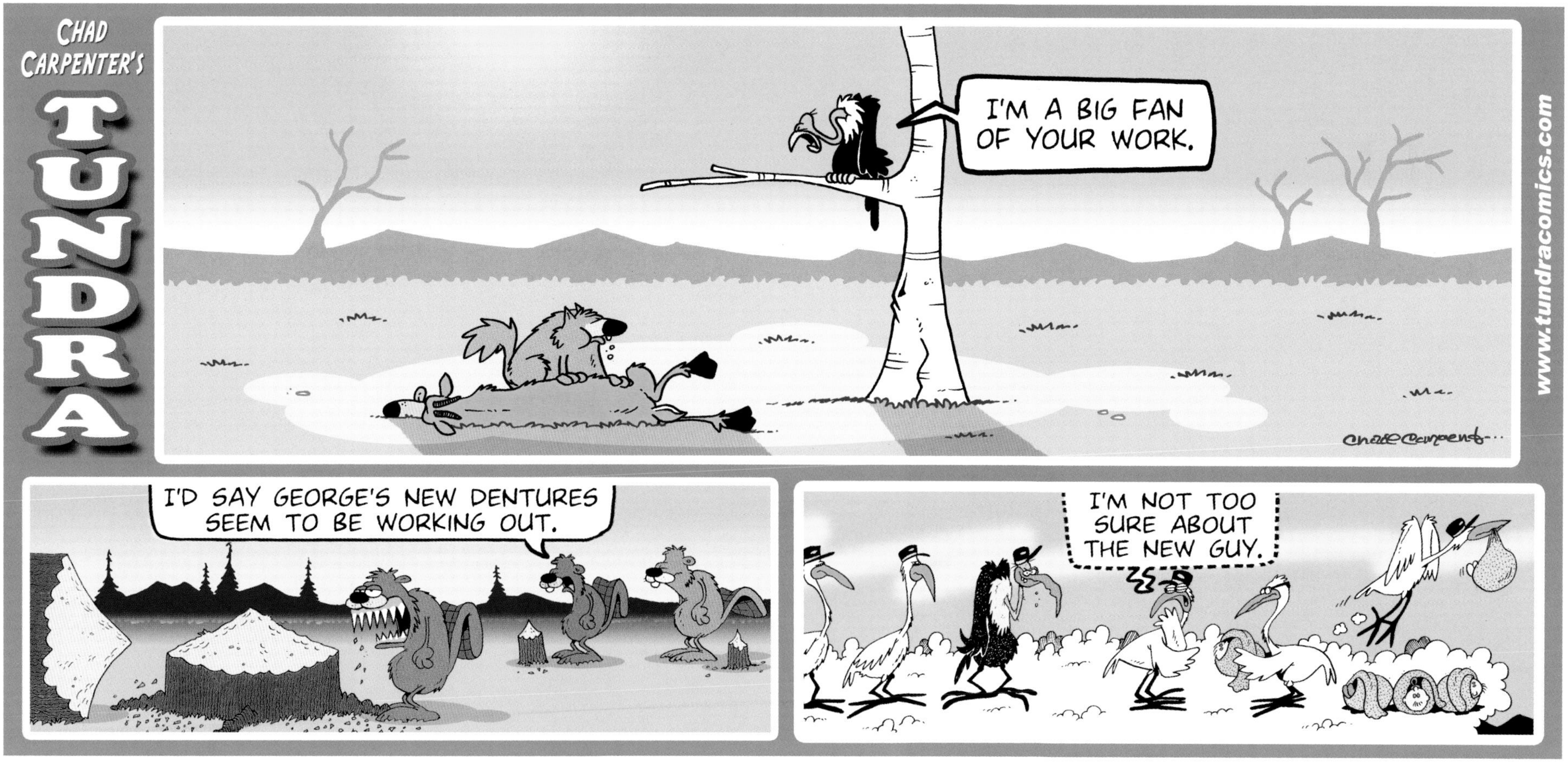
CHAD CARPENTER'S
TUNDRA
I'M A BIG FAN OF YOUR WORK.
I'D SAY GEORGE'S NEW DENTURES SEEM TO BE WORKING OUT.
I'M NOT TOO SURE ABOUT THE NEW GUY.
www.tundracomics.com

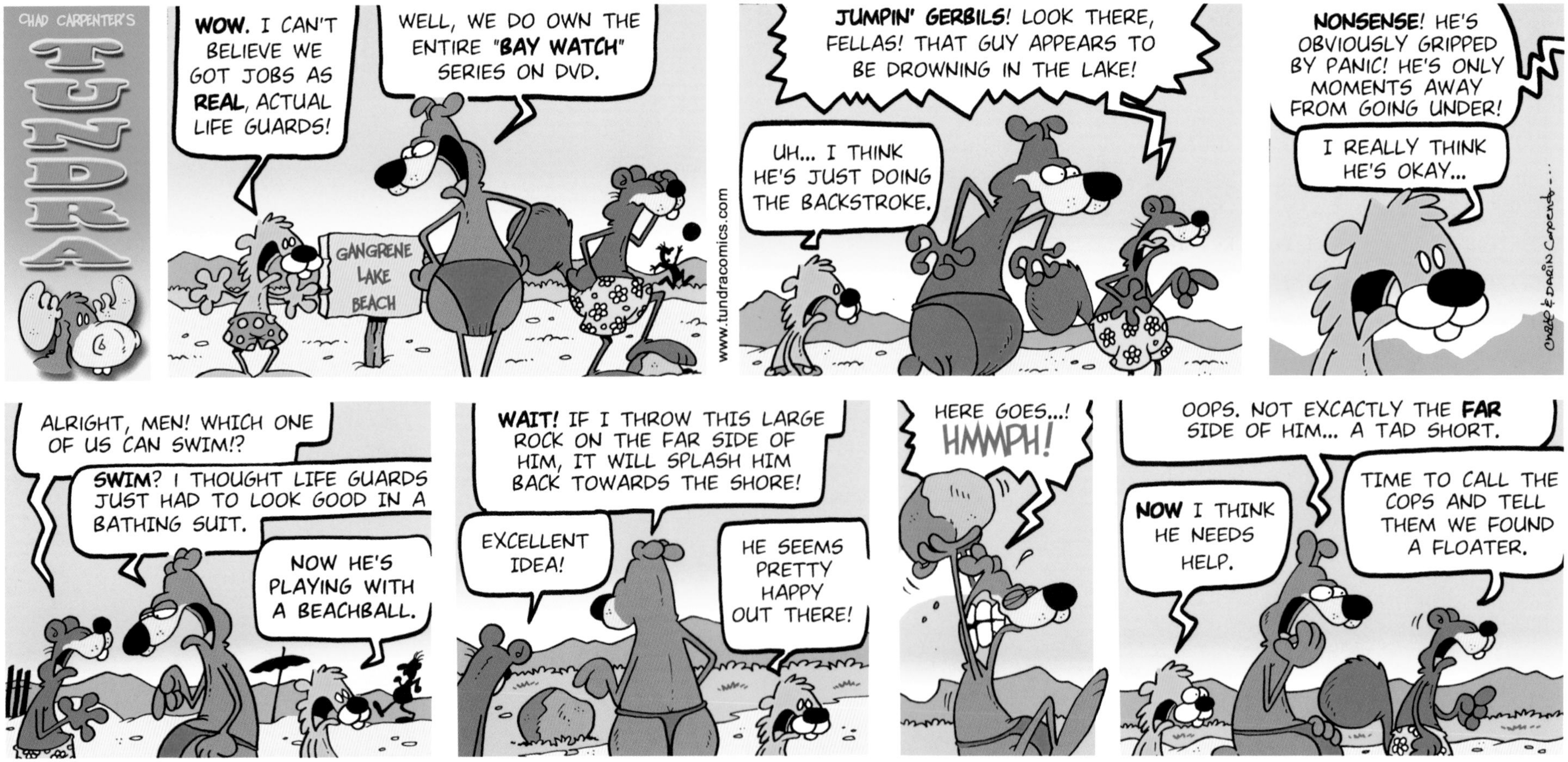
CHAD CARPENTER'S
TUNDRA
WOW. I CAN'T BELIEVE WE GOT JOBS AS REAL, ACTUAL LIFE GUARDS!
WELL, WE DO OWN THE ENTIRE "BAY WATCH" SERIES ON DVD.
GANGRENE LAKE BEACH
www.tundracomics.com
JUMPIN' GERBILS! LOOK THERE, FELLAS! THAT GUY APPEARS TO BE DROWNING IN THE LAKE!
UH... I THINK HE'S JUST DOING THE BACKSTROKE.
NONSENSE! HE'S OBVIOUSLY GRIPPED BY PANIC! HE'S ONLY MOMENTS AWAY FROM GOING UNDER!
I REALLY THINK HE'S OKAY...
ALRIGHT, MEN! WHICH ONE OF US CAN SWIM!?
SWIM? I THOUGHT LIFE GUARDS JUST HAD TO LOOK GOOD IN A BATHING SUIT.
NOW HE'S PLAYING WITH A BEACHBALL.
WAIT! IF I THROW THIS LARGE ROCK ON THE FAR SIDE OF HIM, IT WILL SPLASH HIM BACK TOWARDS THE SHORE!
EXCELLENT IDEA!
HE SEEMS PRETTY HAPPY OUT THERE!
HERE GOES...!
HMMPH!
OOPS. NOT EXCACTLY THE FAR SIDE OF HIM... A TAD SHORT.
NOW I THINK HE NEEDS HELP.
TIME TO CALL THE COPS AND TELL THEM WE FOUND A FLOATER.

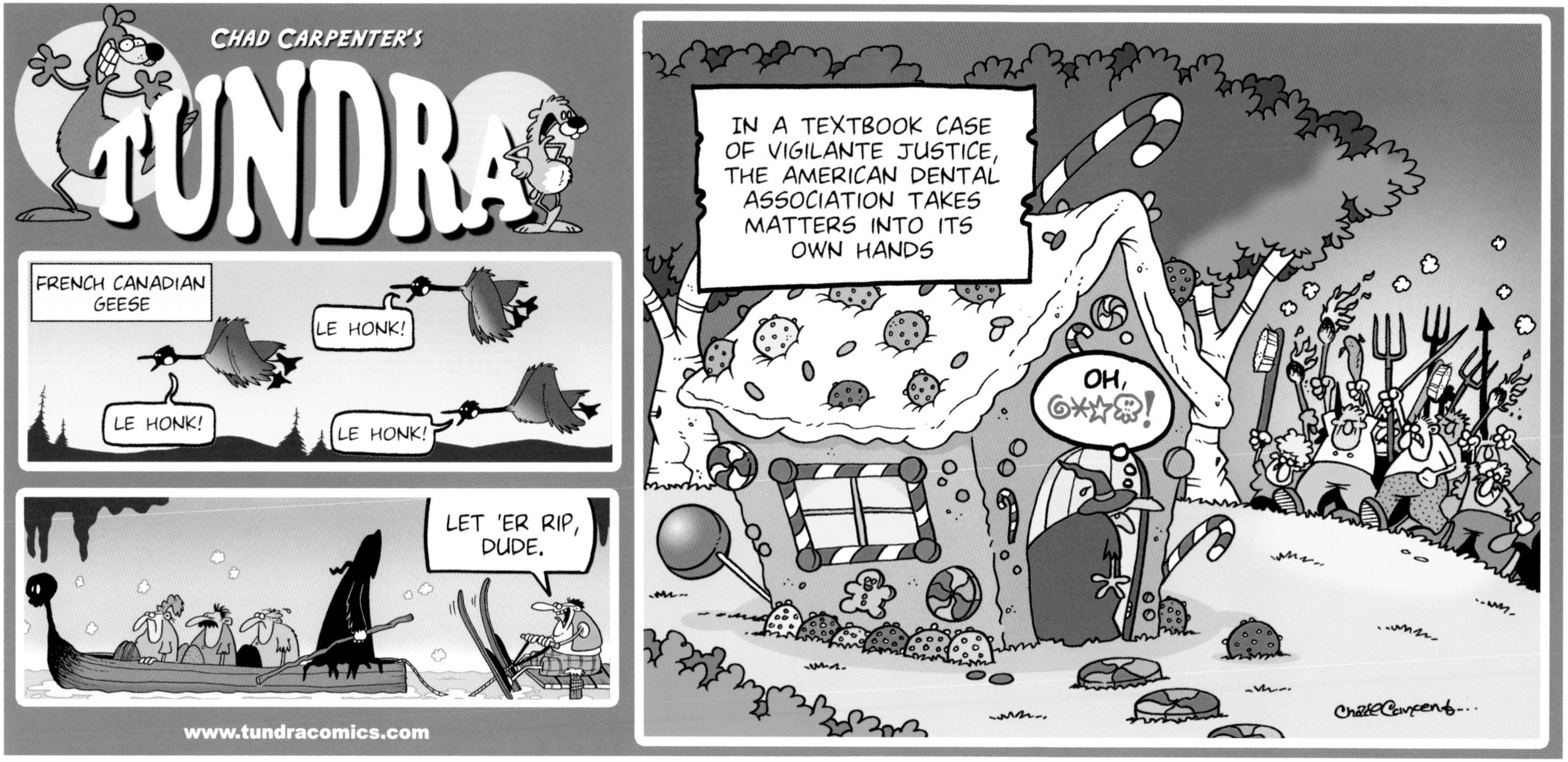
CHAD CARPENTER'S
TUNDRA
FRENCH CANADIAN GEESE
LE HONK!
LE HONK!
LE HONK!
LET 'ER RIP, DUDE.
www.tundracomics.com
IN A TEXTBOOK CASE OF VIGILANTE JUSTICE, THE AMERICAN DENTAL ASSOCIATION TAKES MATTERS INTO ITS OWN HANDS
OH,

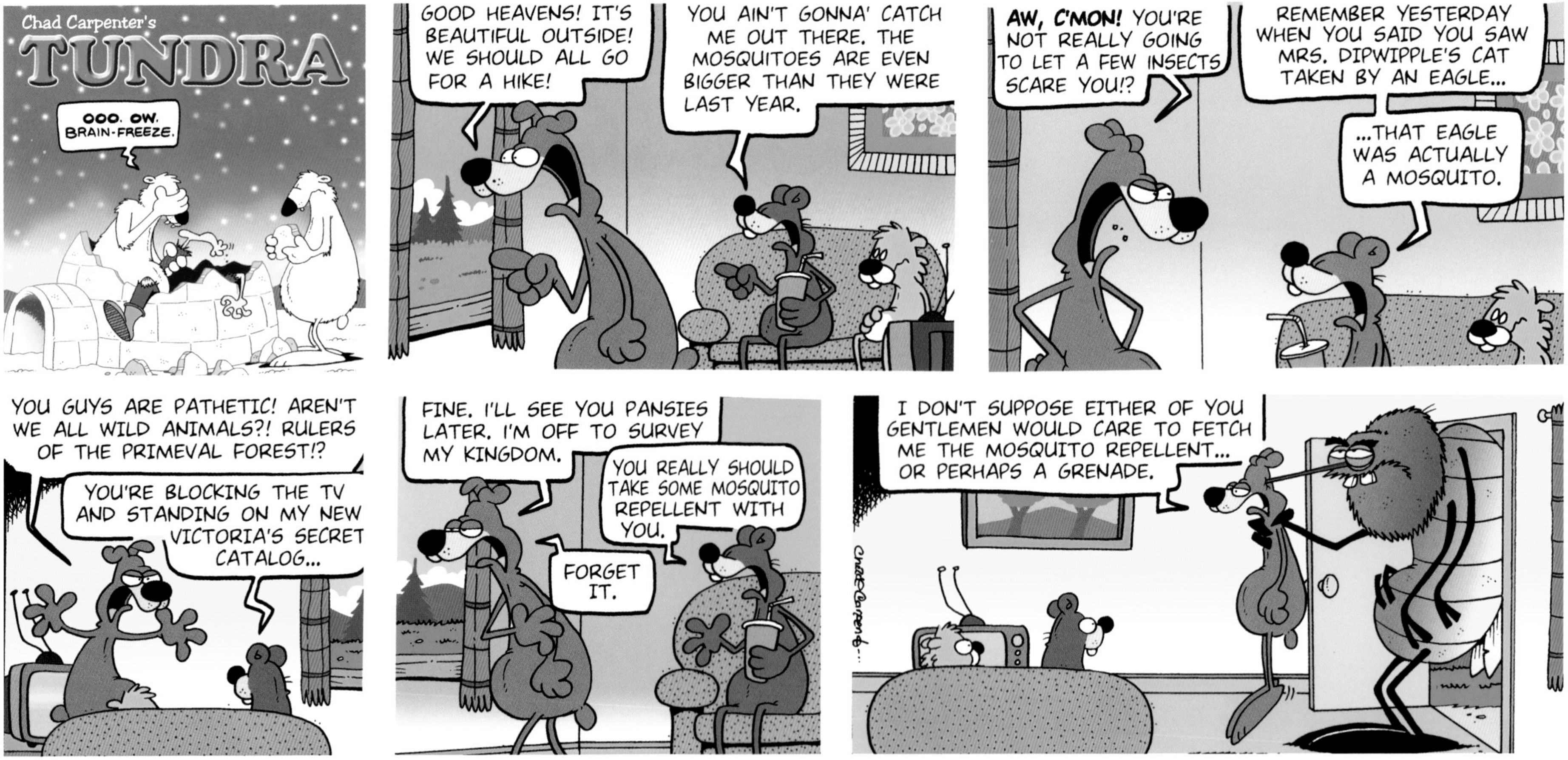
Chad Carpenter's
TUNDRA
OOO. OW. BRAIN-FREEZE.
GOOD HEAVENS! IT'S BEAUTIFUL OUTSIDE! WE SHOULD ALL GO FOR A HIKE!
YOU AIN'T GONNA' CATCH ME OUT THERE. THE MOSQUITOES ARE EVEN BIGGER THAN THEY WERE LAST YEAR.
AW, C'MON! YOU'RE NOT REALLY GOING TO LET A FEW INSECTS SCARE YOU!?
REMEMBER YESTERDAY WHEN YOU SAID YOU SAW MRS. DIPWIPPLE'S CAT TAKEN BY AN EAGLE...
...THAT EAGLE WAS ACTUALLY A MOSQUITO.
YOU GUYS ARE PATHETIC! AREN'T WE ALL WILD ANIMALS?! RULERS OF THE PRIMEVAL FOREST!?
YOU'RE BLOCKING THE TV AND STANDING ON MY NEW VICTORIA'S SECRET CATALOG...
FINE. I'LL SEE YOU PANSIES LATER. I'M OFF TO SURVEY MY KINGDOM.
YOU REALLY SHOULD TAKE SOME MOSQUITO REPELLENT WITH YOU.
FORGET IT.
I DON'T SUPPOSE EITHER OF YOU GENTLEMEN WOULD CARE TO FETCH ME THE MOSQUITO REPELLENT... OR PERHAPS A GRENADE.

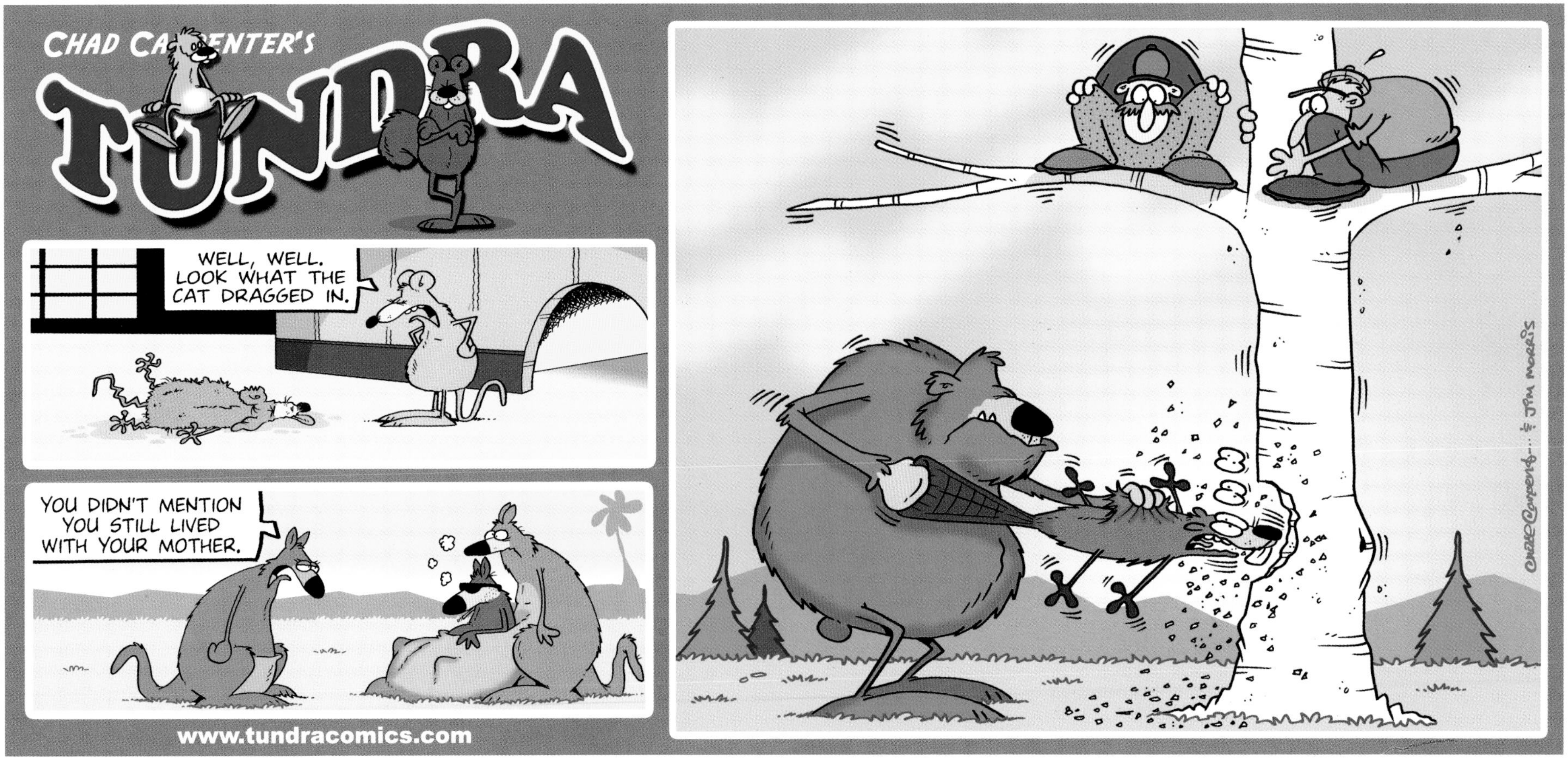
CHAD CARPENTER'S
TUNDRA
WELL, WELL. LOOK WHAT THE CAT DRAGGED IN.
YOU DIDN'T MENTION YOU STILL LIVED WITH YOUR MOTHER.
www.tundracomics.com

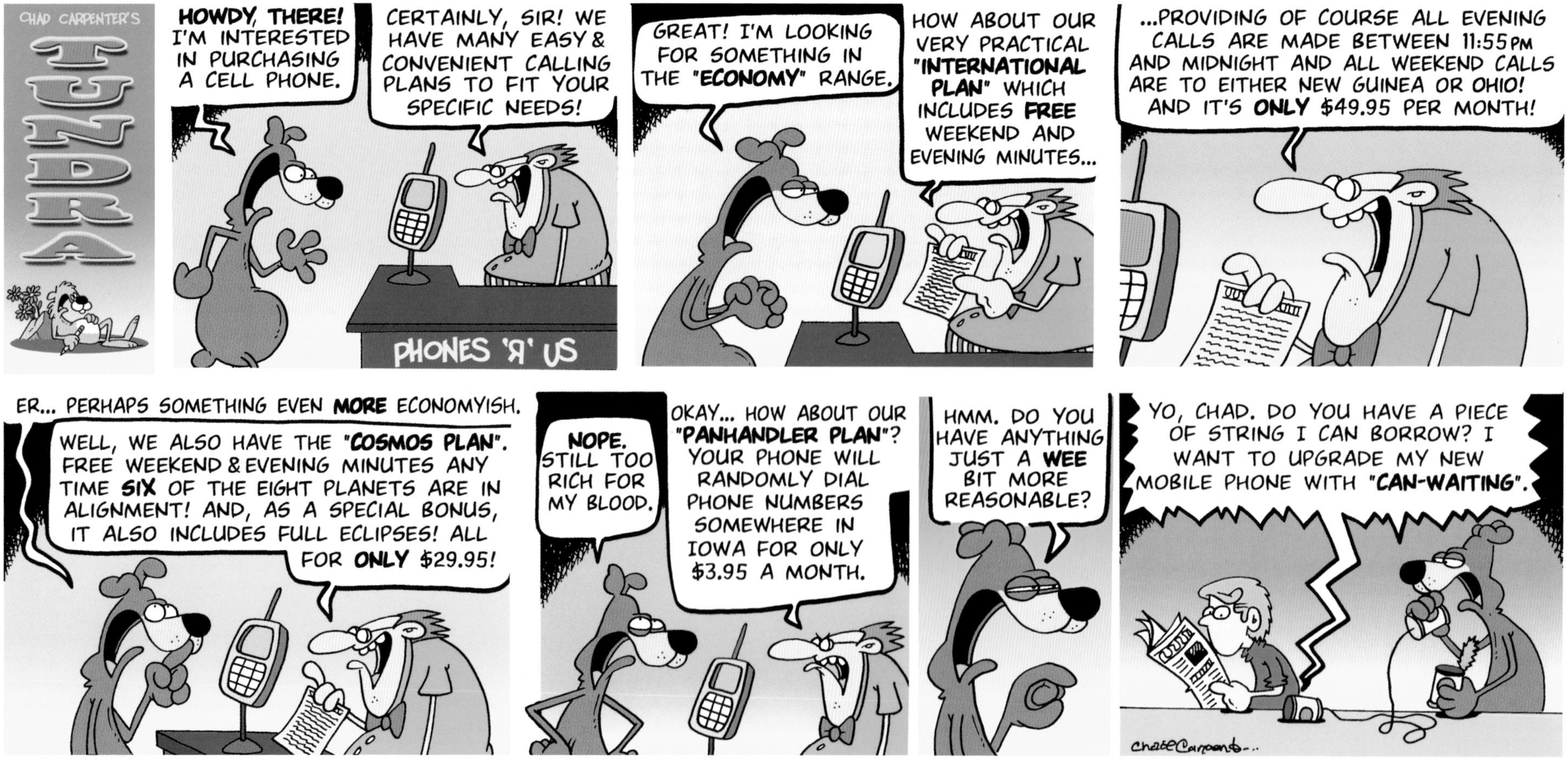
CHAD CARPENTER'S
TUNDRA
HOWDY, THERE! I'M INTERESTED IN PURCHASING A CELL PHONE.
CERTAINLY, SIR! WE HAVE MANY EASY & CONVENIENT CALLING PLANS TO FIT YOUR SPECIFIC NEEDS!
PHONES 'R' US
GREAT! I'M LOOKING FOR SOMETHING IN THE "ECONOMY" RANGE.
HOW ABOUT OUR VERY PRACTICAL "INTERNATIONAL PLAN" WHICH INCLUDES FREE WEEKEND AND EVENING MINUTES...
...PROVIDING OF COURSE ALL EVENING CALLS ARE MADE BETWEEN 11:55PM AND MIDNIGHT AND ALL WEEKEND CALLS ARE TO EITHER NEW GUINEA OR OHIO! AND IT'S ONLY $49.95 PER MONTH!
ER... PERHAPS SOMETHING EVEN MORE ECONOMYISH.
WELL, WE ALSO HAVE THE "COSMOS PLAN". FREE WEEKEND & EVENING MINUTES ANY TIME SIX OF THE EIGHT PLANETS ARE IN ALIGNMENT! AND, AS A SPECIAL BONUS, IT ALSO INCLUDES FULL ECLIPSES! ALL FOR ONLY $29.95!
NOPE. STILL TOO RICH FOR MY BLOOD.
OKAY... HOW ABOUT OUR "PANHANDLER PLAN"? YOUR PHONE WILL RANDOMLY DIAL PHONE NUMBERS SOMEWHERE IN IOWA FOR ONLY $3.95 A MONTH.
HMM. DO YOU HAVE ANYTHING JUST A WEE BIT MORE REASONABLE?
YO, CHAD. DO YOU HAVE A PIECE OF STRING I CAN BORROW? I WANT TO UPGRADE MY NEW MOBILE PHONE WITH "CAN-WAITING".

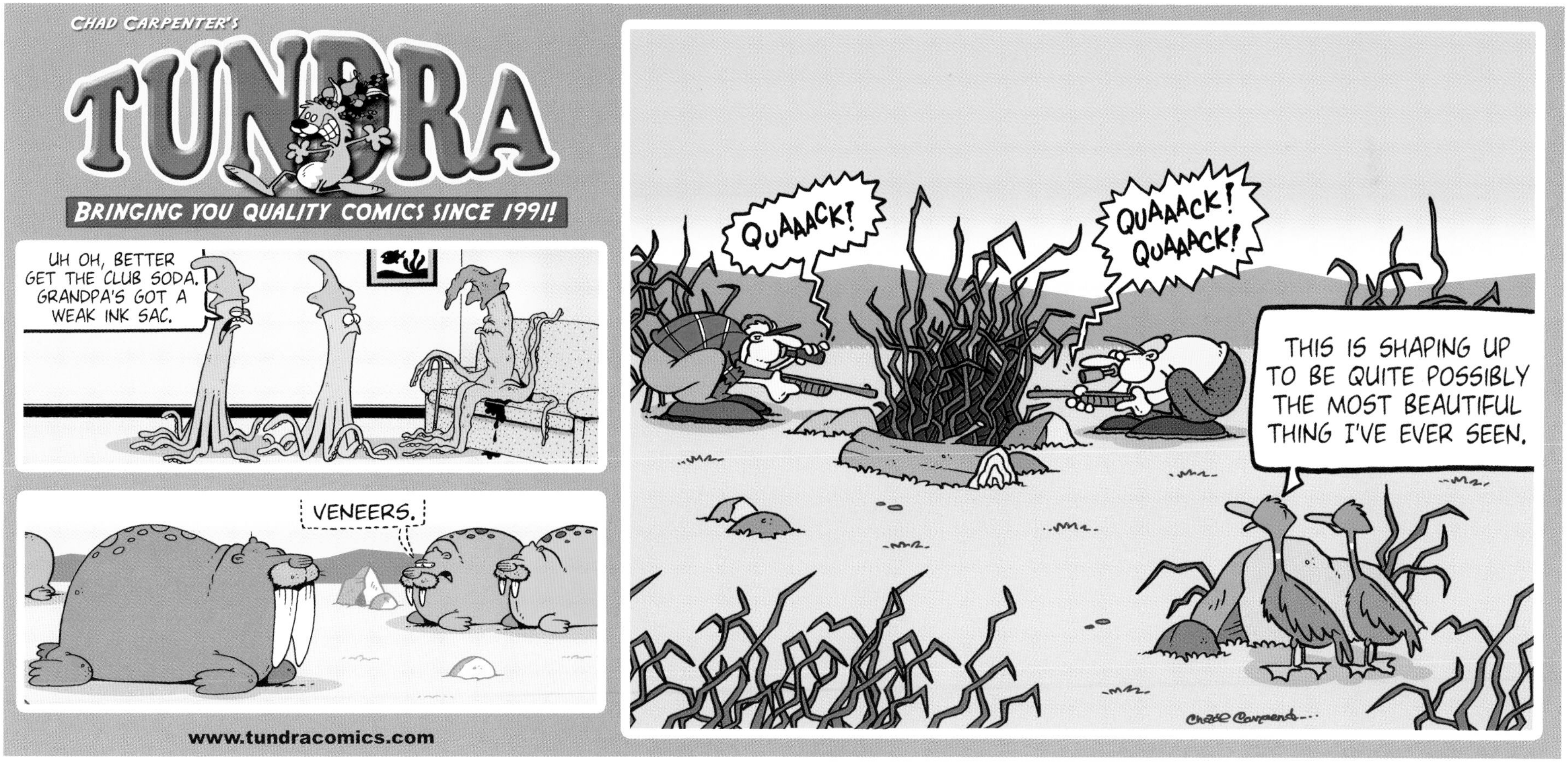
CHAD CARPENTER'S
TUNDRA
BRINGING YOU QUALITY COMICS SINCE 1991!
UH OH, BETTER GET THE CLUB SODA. GRANDPA'S GOT A WEAK INK SAC.
VENEERS.
QUAAACK!
QUAAACK! QUAAACK!
THIS IS SHAPING UP TO BE QUITE POSSIBLY THE MOST BEAUTIFUL THING I'VE EVER SEEN.
www.tundracomics.com

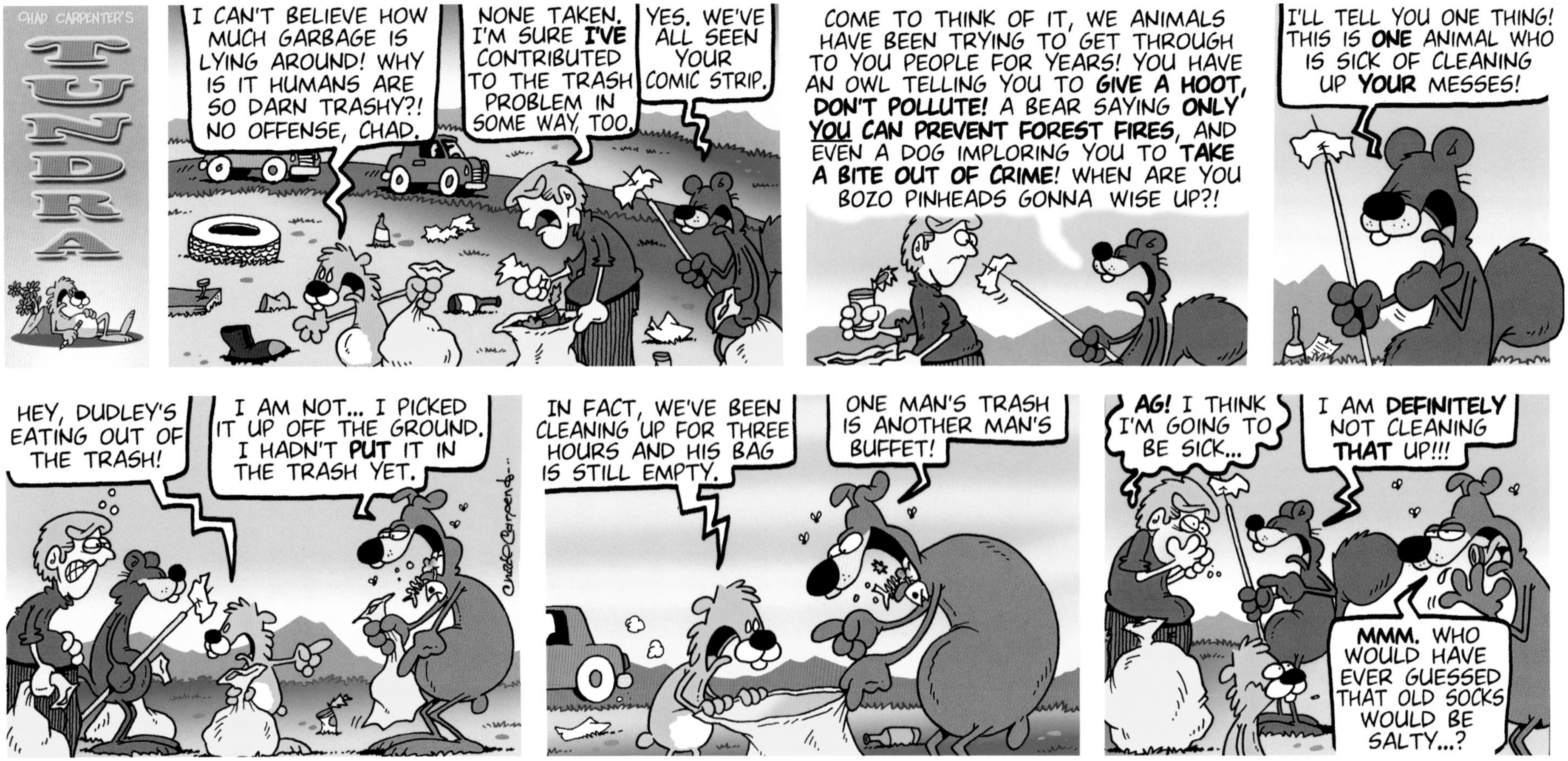
CHAD CARPENTER'S
TUNDRA
I CAN'T BELIEVE HOW MUCH GARBAGE IS LYING AROUND! WHY IS IT HUMANS ARE SO DARN TRASHY?! NO OFFENSE, CHAD.
NONE TAKEN. I'M SURE I'VE CONTRIBUTED TO THE TRASH PROBLEM IN SOME WAY, TOO.
YES. WE'VE ALL SEEN YOUR COMIC STRIP.
COME TO THINK OF IT, WE ANIMALS HAVE BEEN TRYING TO GET THROUGH TO YOU PEOPLE FOR YEARS! YOU HAVE AN OWL TELLING YOU TO GIVE A HOOT, DON'T POLLUTE! A BEAR SAYING ONLY YOU CAN PREVENT FOREST FIRES, AND EVEN A DOG IMPLORING YOU TO TAKE A BITE OUT OF CRIME! WHEN ARE YOU BOZO PINHEADS GONNA WISE UP?!
I'LL TELL YOU ONE THING! THIS IS ONE ANIMAL WHO IS SICK OF CLEANING UP YOUR MESSES!
HEY, DUDLEY'S EATING OUT OF THE TRASH!
I AM NOT... I PICKED IT UP OFF THE GROUND. I HADN'T PUT IT IN THE TRASH YET.
IN FACT, WE'VE BEEN CLEANING UP FOR THREE HOURS AND HIS BAG IS STILL EMPTY.
ONE MAN'S TRASH IS ANOTHER MAN'S BUFFET!
AG! I THINK I'M GOING TO BE SICK...
I AM DEFINITELY NOT CLEANING THAT UP!!!
MMM. WHO WOULD HAVE EVER GUESSED THAT OLD SOCKS WOULD BE SALTY...?

...makes me laugh...*

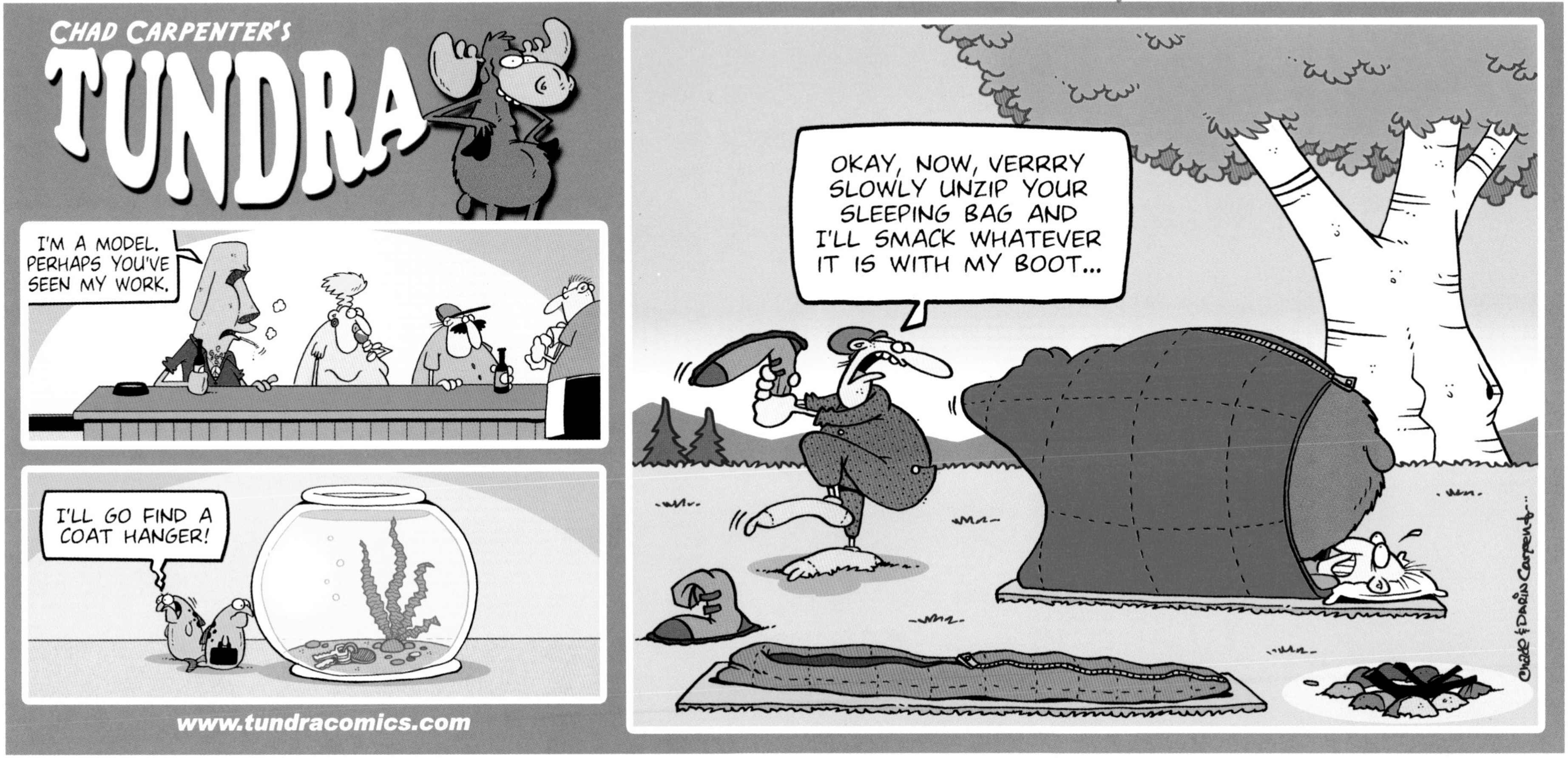

CHAD CARPENTER'S
TUNDRA
I'M A MODEL. PERHAPS YOU'VE SEEN MY WORK.
I'LL GO FIND A COAT HANGER!
www.tundracomics.com
OKAY, NOW, VERRRY SLOWLY UNZIP YOUR SLEEPING BAG AND I'LL SMACK WHATEVER IT IS WITH MY BOOT...

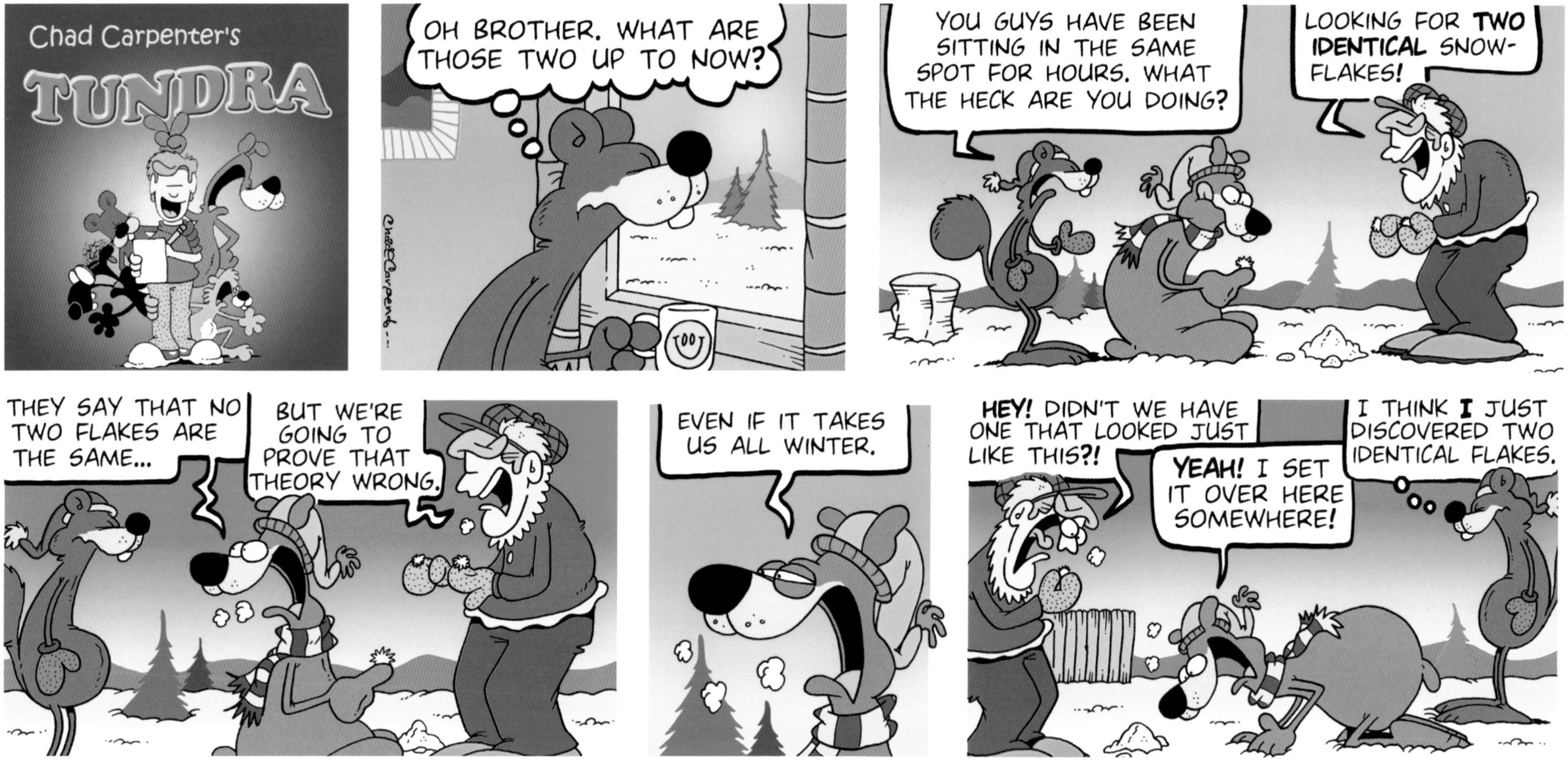
Chad Carpenter's
TUNDRA
OH BROTHER. WHAT ARE THOSE TWO UP TO NOW?
Chad Carpenter
YOU GUYS HAVE BEEN SITTING IN THE SAME SPOT FOR HOURS. WHAT THE HECK ARE YOU DOING?
LOOKING FOR **TWO IDENTICAL** SNOW-FLAKES!
THEY SAY THAT NO TWO FLAKES ARE THE SAME...
BUT WE'RE GOING TO PROVE THAT THEORY WRONG.
EVEN IF IT TAKES US ALL WINTER.
HEY! DIDN'T WE HAVE ONE THAT LOOKED JUST LIKE THIS?!
YEAH! I SET IT OVER HERE SOMEWHERE!
I THINK **I** JUST DISCOVERED TWO IDENTICAL FLAKES.

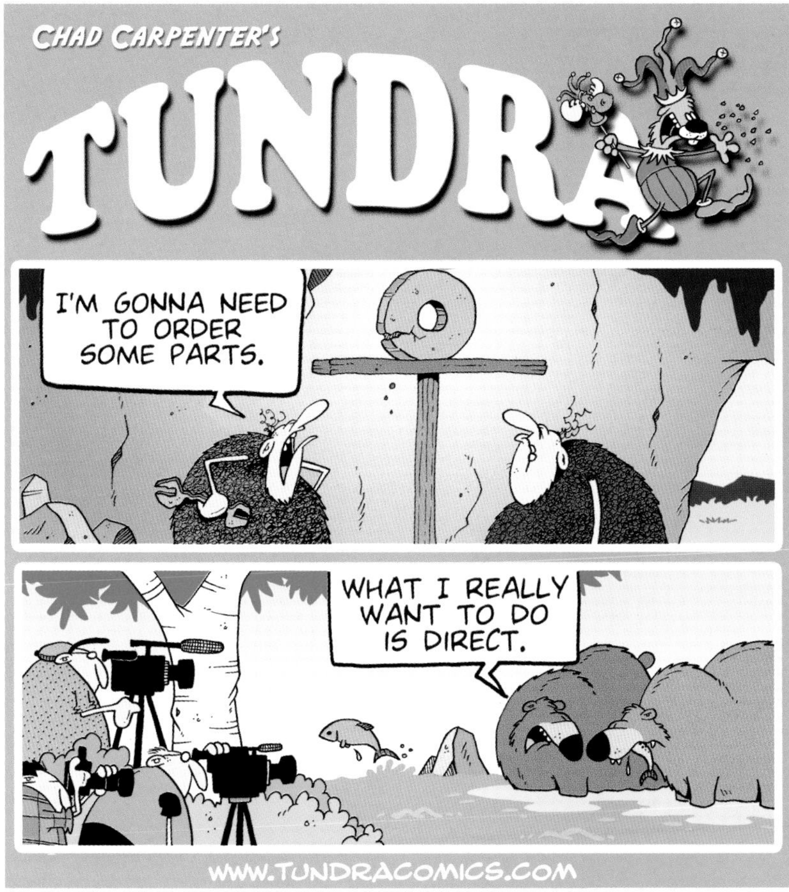
CHAD CARPENTER'S
TUNDRA
I'M GONNA NEED TO ORDER SOME PARTS.
WHAT I REALLY WANT TO DO IS DIRECT.
WWW.TUNDRACOMICS.COM

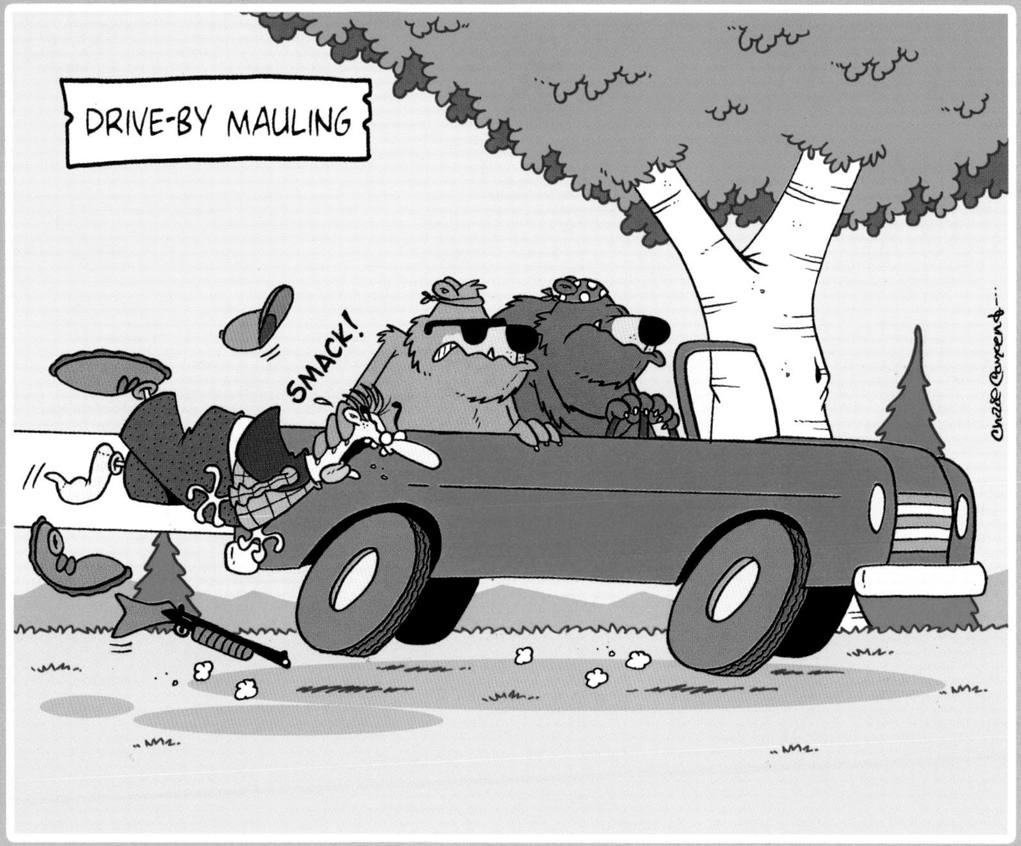
DRIVE-BY MAULING
SMACK!

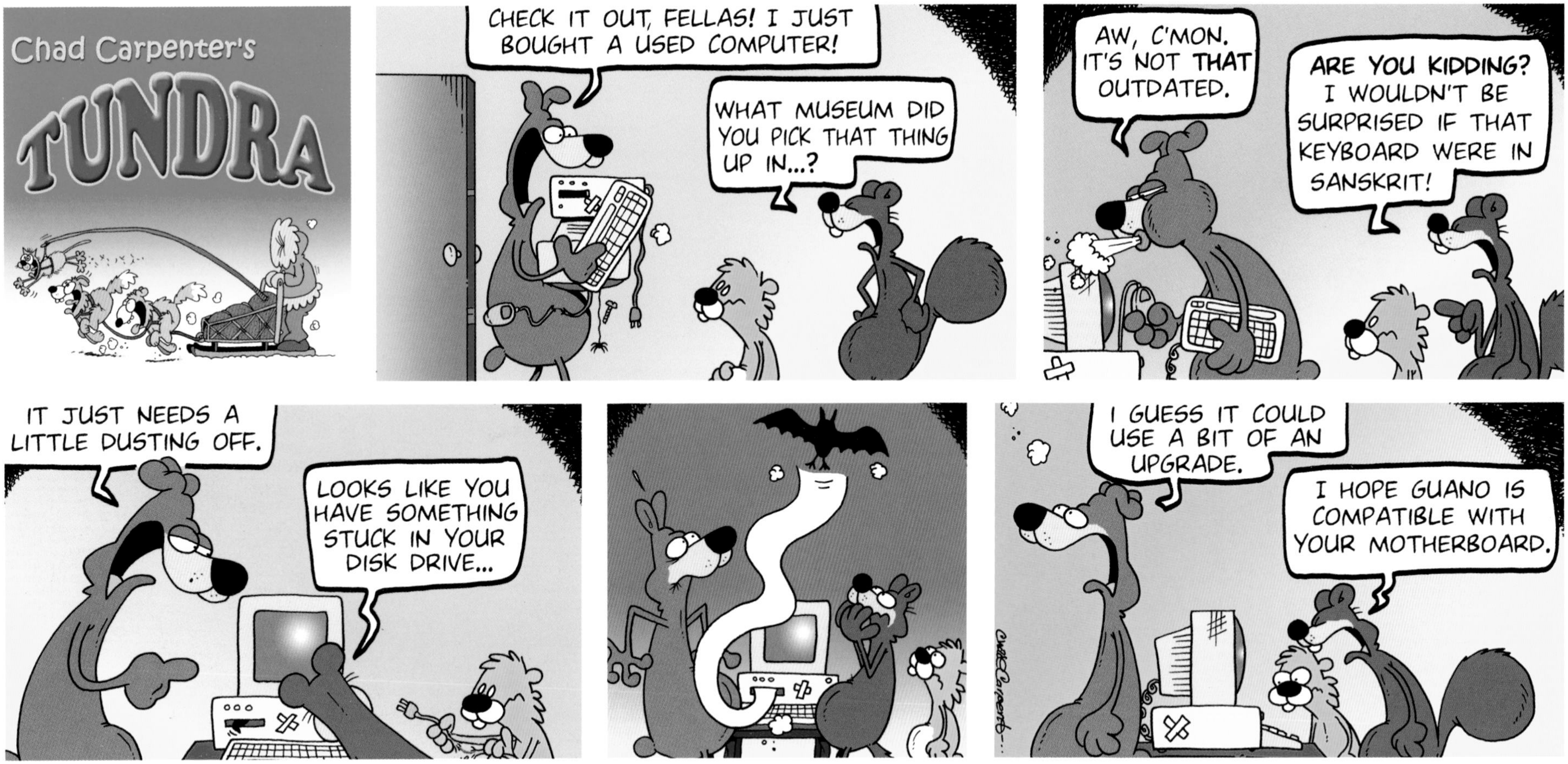
Chad Carpenter's
TUNDRA
CHECK IT OUT, FELLAS! I JUST BOUGHT A USED COMPUTER!
WHAT MUSEUM DID YOU PICK THAT THING UP IN...?
AW, C'MON. IT'S NOT THAT OUTDATED.
ARE YOU KIDDING? I WOULDN'T BE SURPRISED IF THAT KEYBOARD WERE IN SANSKRIT!
IT JUST NEEDS A LITTLE DUSTING OFF.
LOOKS LIKE YOU HAVE SOMETHING STUCK IN YOUR DISK DRIVE...
I GUESS IT COULD USE A BIT OF AN UPGRADE.
I HOPE GUANO IS COMPATIBLE WITH YOUR MOTHERBOARD.

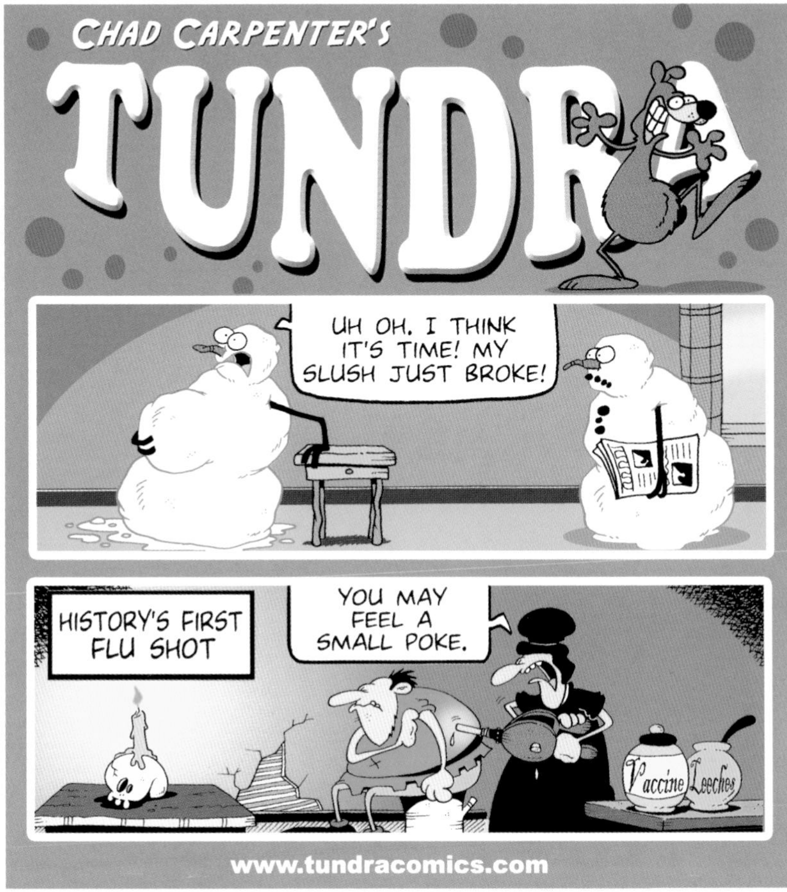
CHAD CARPENTER'S
TUNDRA
UH OH. I THINK IT'S TIME! MY SLUSH JUST BROKE!
HISTORY'S FIRST FLU SHOT
YOU MAY FEEL A SMALL POKE.
Vaccine
Leeches
www.tundracomics.com

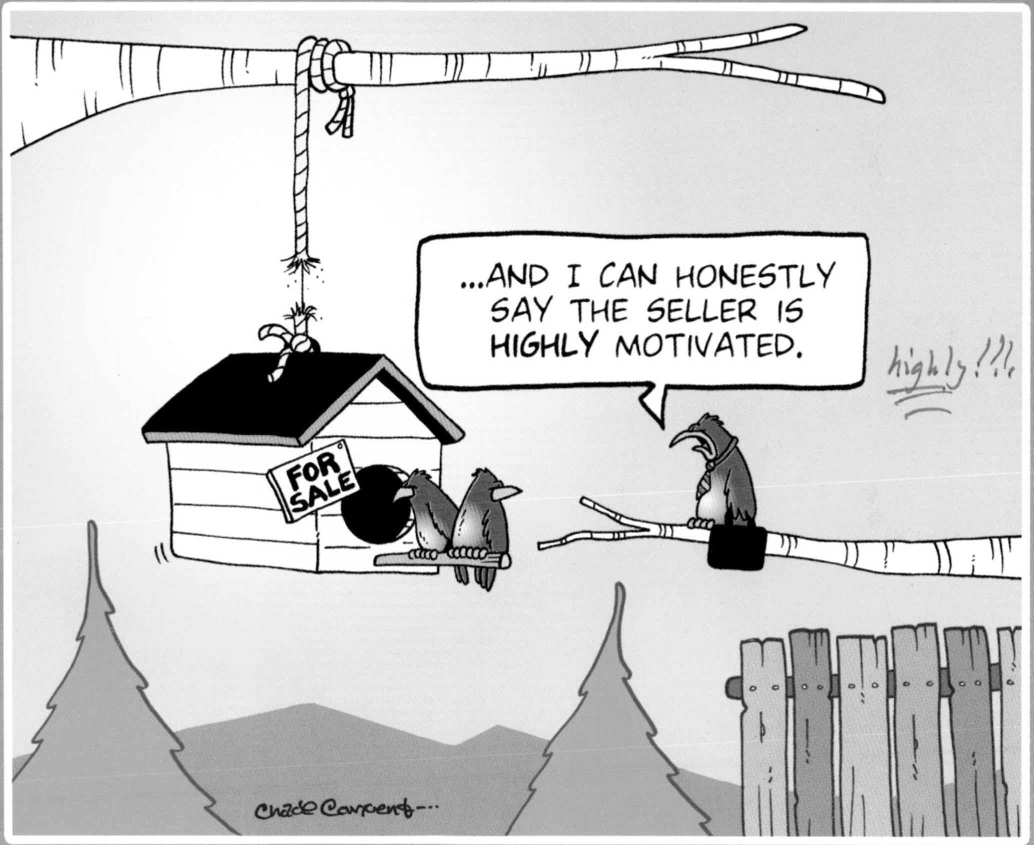
FOR SALE
...AND I CAN HONESTLY SAY THE SELLER IS HIGHLY MOTIVATED.
highly!?!

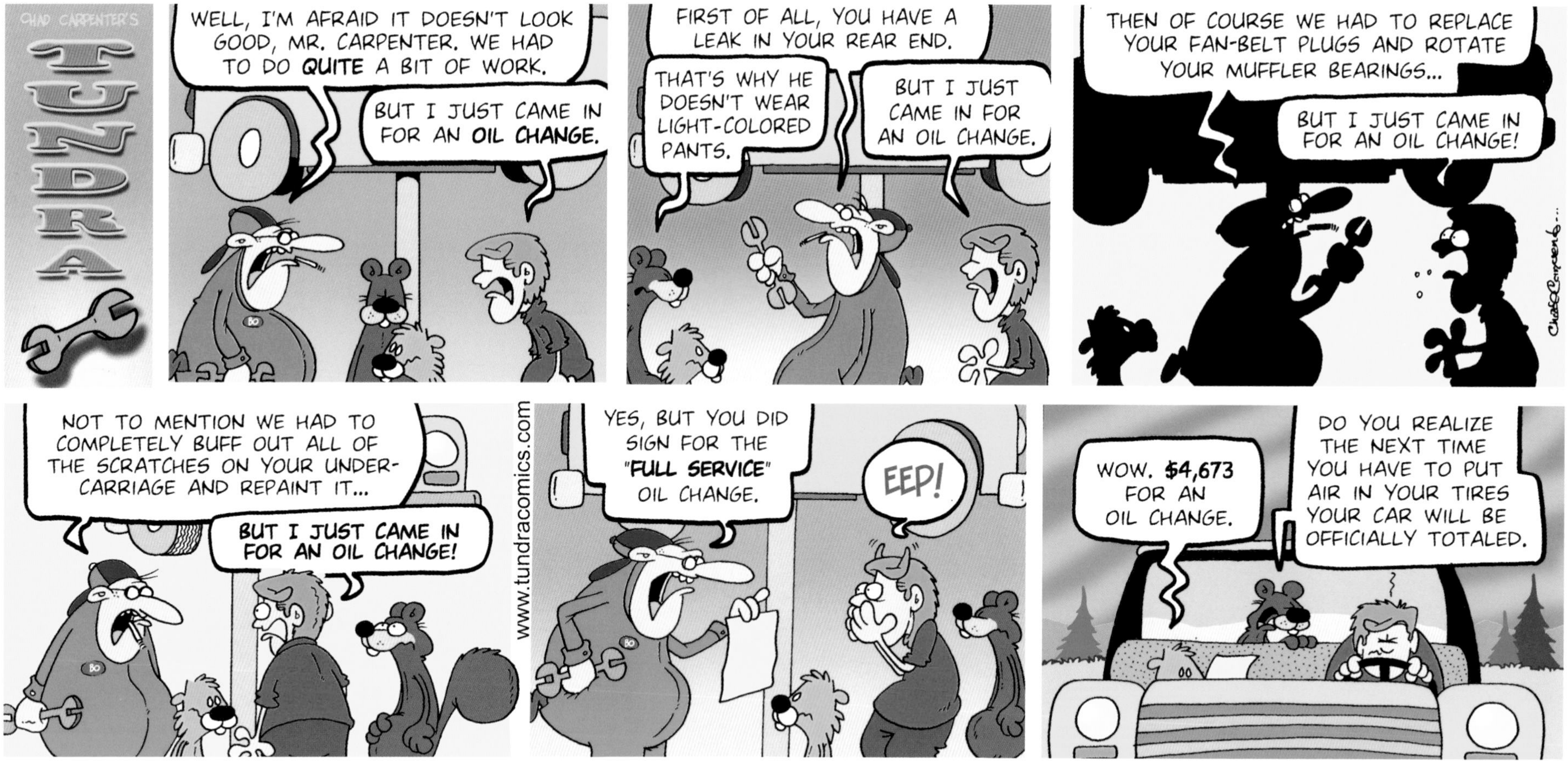
CHAD CARPENTER'S
TUNDRA
WELL, I'M AFRAID IT DOESN'T LOOK GOOD, MR. CARPENTER. WE HAD TO DO **QUITE** A BIT OF WORK.
BUT I JUST CAME IN FOR AN **OIL CHANGE.**
FIRST OF ALL, YOU HAVE A LEAK IN YOUR REAR END.
THAT'S WHY HE DOESN'T WEAR LIGHT-COLORED PANTS.
BUT I JUST CAME IN FOR AN OIL CHANGE.
THEN OF COURSE WE HAD TO REPLACE YOUR FAN-BELT PLUGS AND ROTATE YOUR MUFFLER BEARINGS...
BUT I JUST CAME IN FOR AN OIL CHANGE!
NOT TO MENTION WE HAD TO COMPLETELY BUFF OUT ALL OF THE SCRATCHES ON YOUR UNDER-CARRIAGE AND REPAINT IT...
BUT I JUST CAME IN FOR AN OIL CHANGE!
www.tundracomics.com
YES, BUT YOU DID SIGN FOR THE "**FULL SERVICE**" OIL CHANGE.
EEP!
WOW. **$4,673** FOR AN OIL CHANGE.
DO YOU REALIZE THE NEXT TIME YOU HAVE TO PUT AIR IN YOUR TIRES YOUR CAR WILL BE OFFICIALLY TOTALED.

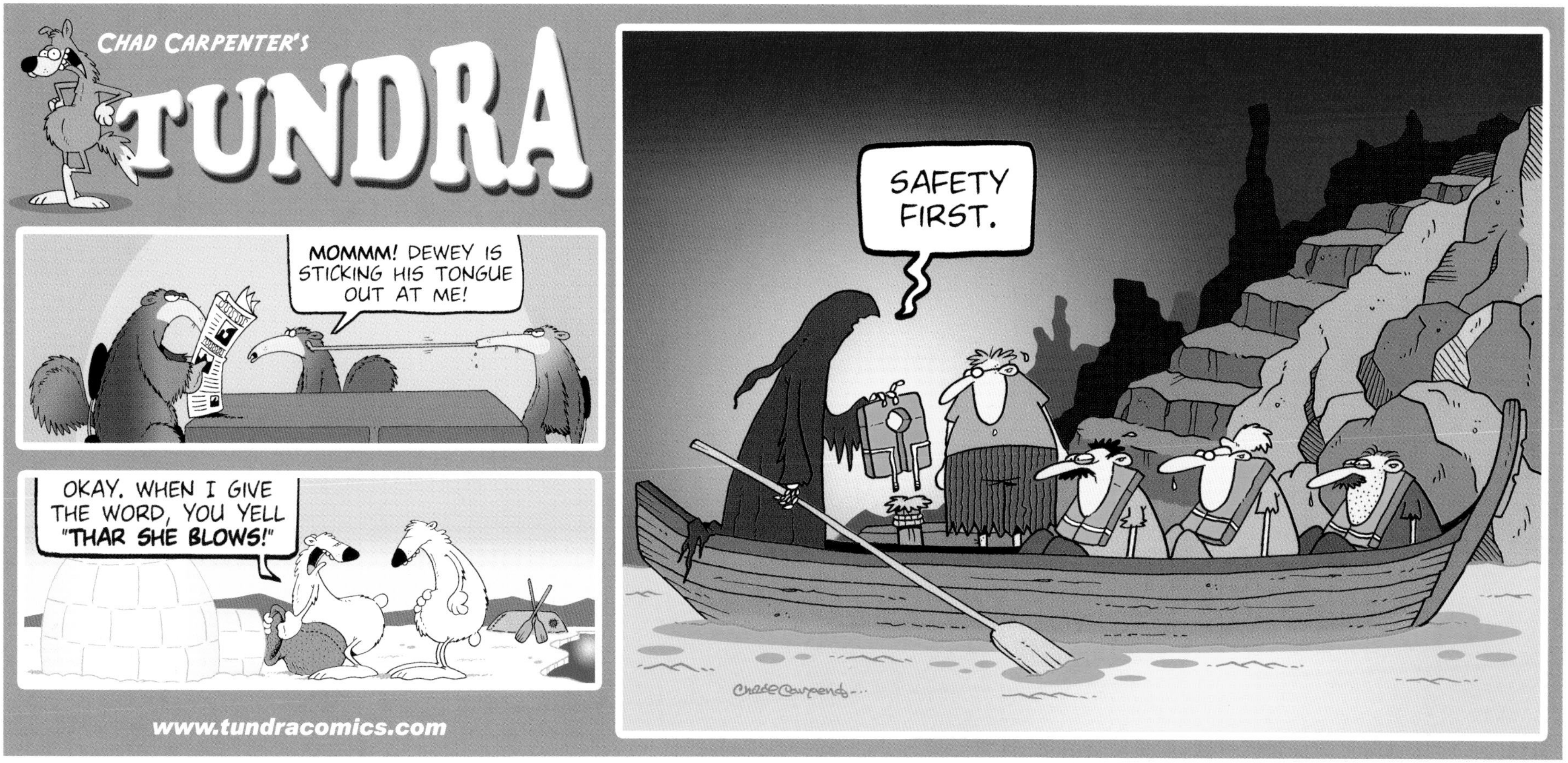
CHAD CARPENTER'S
TUNDRA
MOMMM! DEWEY IS STICKING HIS TONGUE OUT AT ME!
OKAY. WHEN I GIVE THE WORD, YOU YELL "THAR SHE BLOWS!"
www.tundracomics.com
SAFETY FIRST.

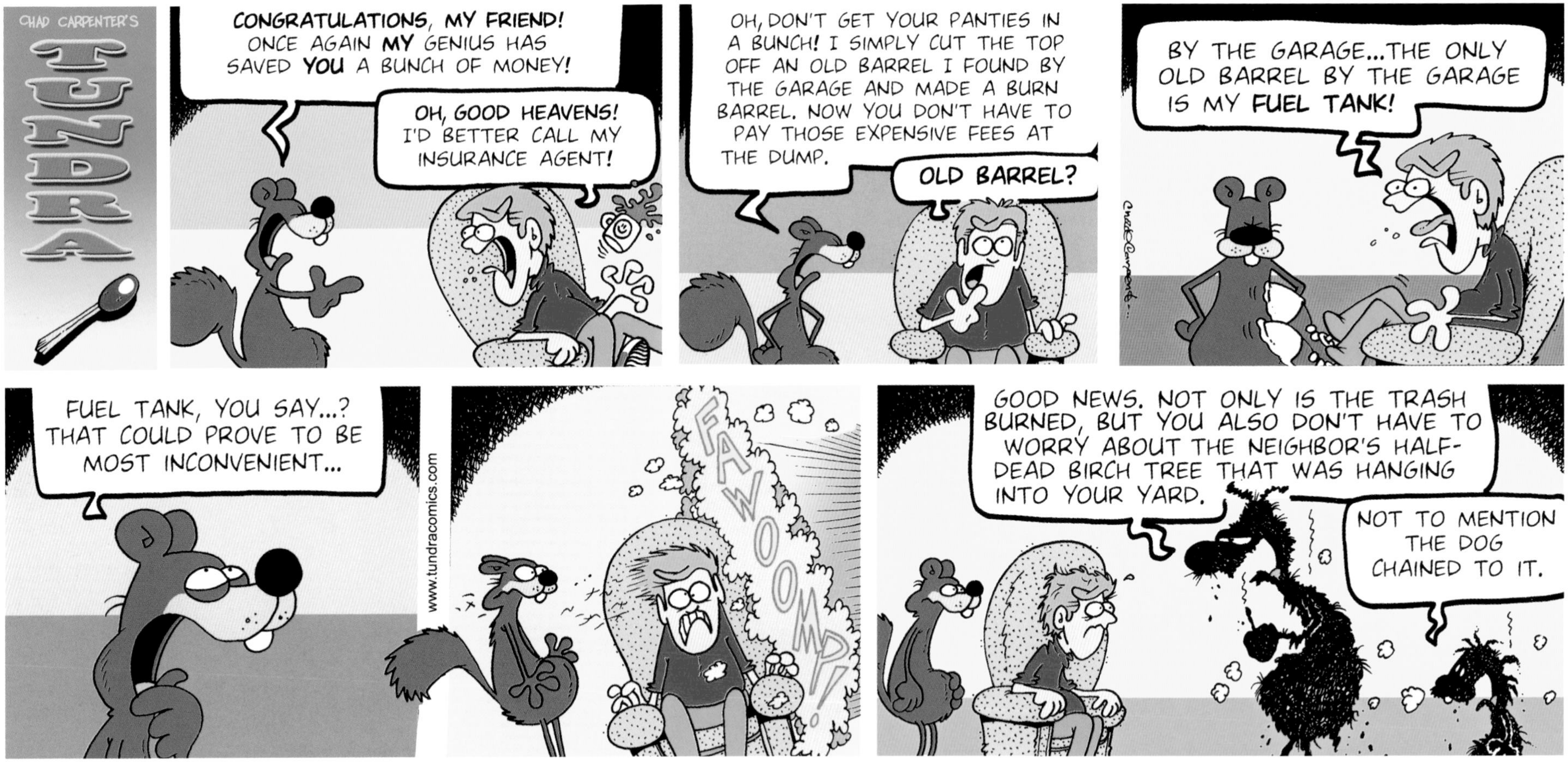
CHAD CARPENTER'S
TUNDRA
CONGRATULATIONS, MY FRIEND! ONCE AGAIN MY GENIUS HAS SAVED YOU A BUNCH OF MONEY!
OH, GOOD HEAVENS! I'D BETTER CALL MY INSURANCE AGENT!
OH, DON'T GET YOUR PANTIES IN A BUNCH! I SIMPLY CUT THE TOP OFF AN OLD BARREL I FOUND BY THE GARAGE AND MADE A BURN BARREL. NOW YOU DON'T HAVE TO PAY THOSE EXPENSIVE FEES AT THE DUMP.
OLD BARREL?
BY THE GARAGE...THE ONLY OLD BARREL BY THE GARAGE IS MY FUEL TANK!
FUEL TANK, YOU SAY...? THAT COULD PROVE TO BE MOST INCONVENIENT...
www.tundracomics.com
FAWOOOMP!
GOOD NEWS. NOT ONLY IS THE TRASH BURNED, BUT YOU ALSO DON'T HAVE TO WORRY ABOUT THE NEIGHBOR'S HALF-DEAD BIRCH TREE THAT WAS HANGING INTO YOUR YARD.
NOT TO MENTION THE DOG CHAINED TO IT.

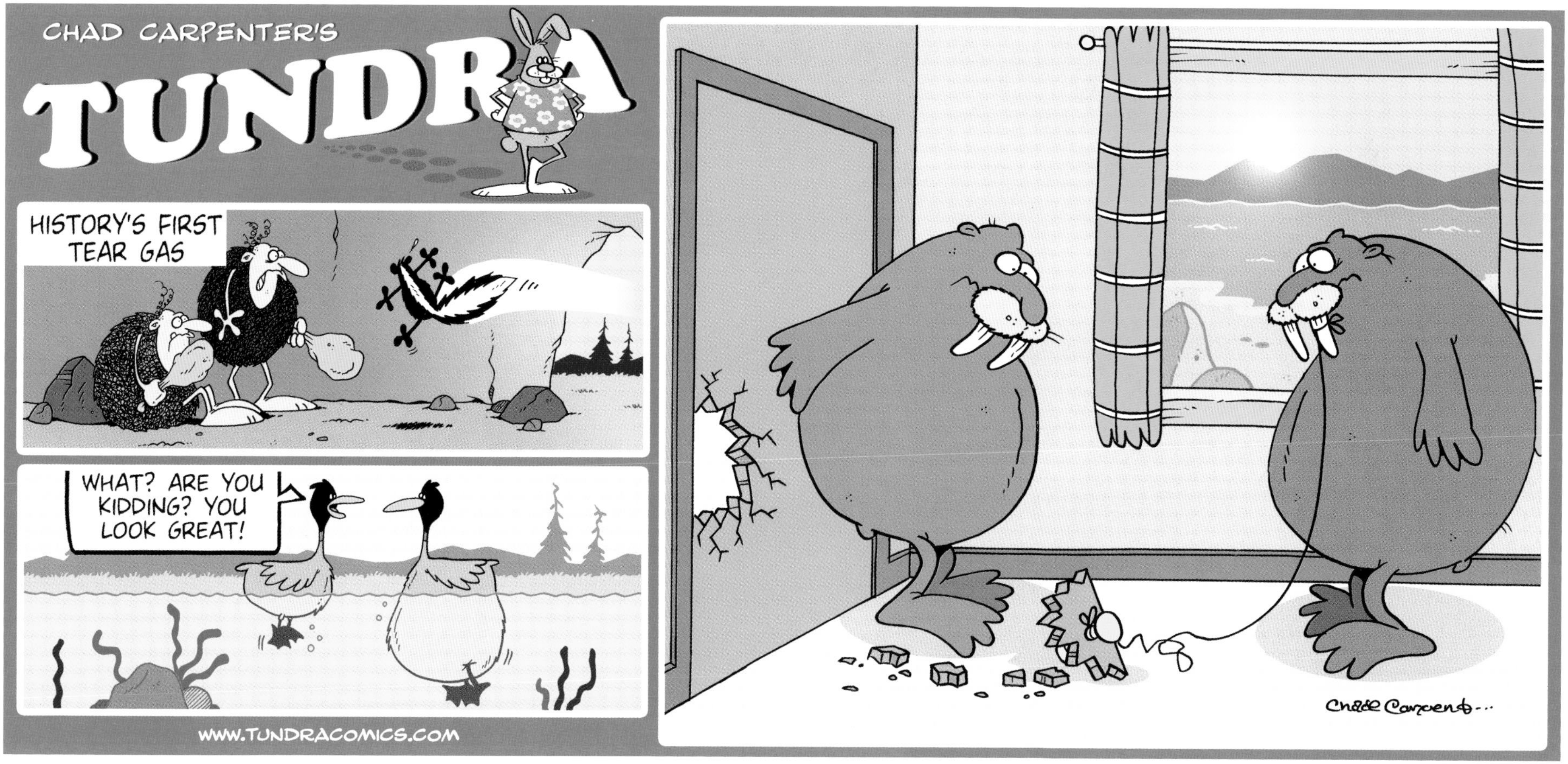
CHAD CARPENTER'S
TUNDRA
HISTORY'S FIRST TEAR GAS
WHAT? ARE YOU KIDDING? YOU LOOK GREAT!
WWW.TUNDRACOMICS.COM

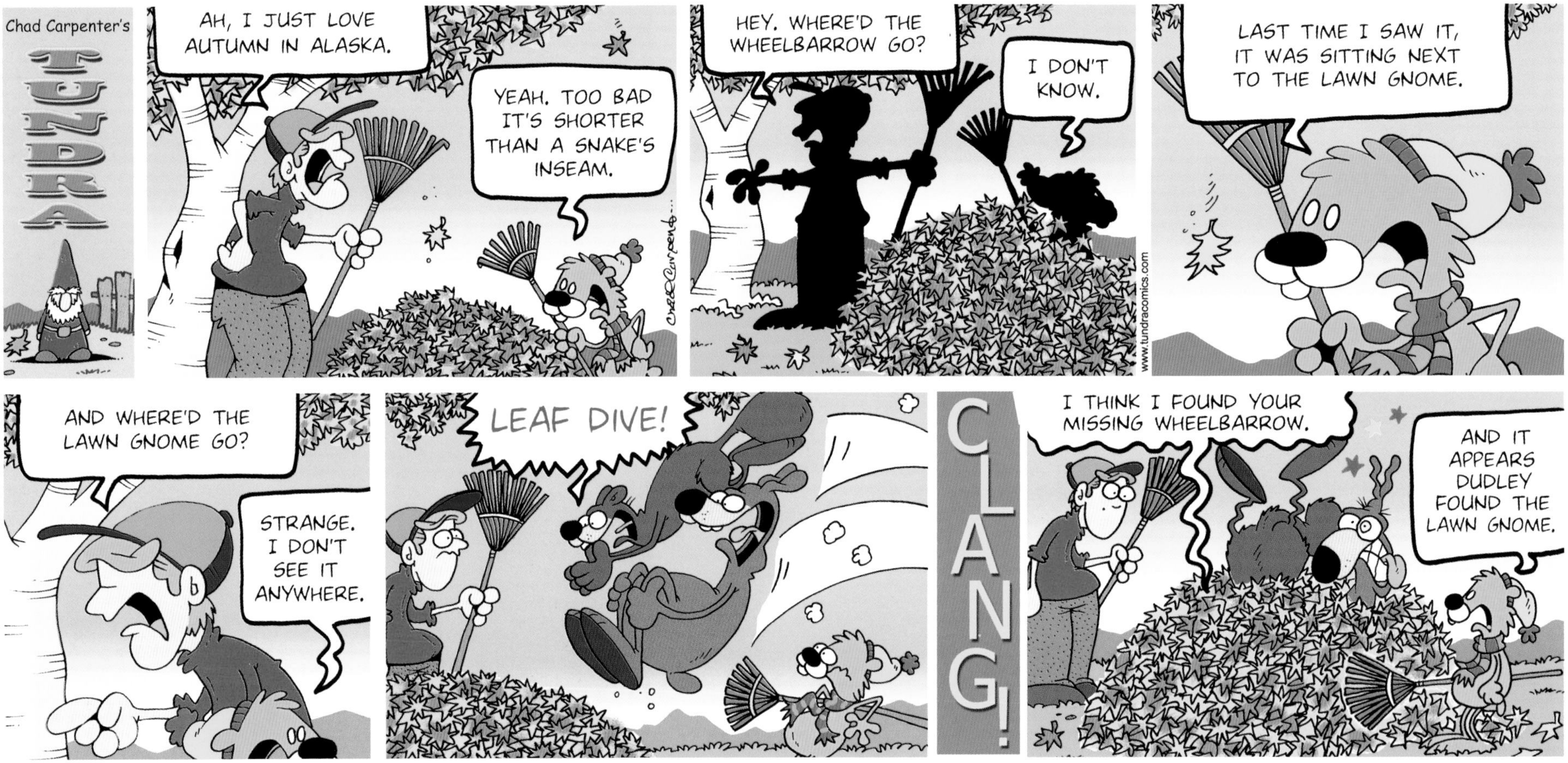
Chad Carpenter's
TUNDRA
AH, I JUST LOVE AUTUMN IN ALASKA.
YEAH. TOO BAD IT'S SHORTER THAN A SNAKE'S INSEAM.
HEY. WHERE'D THE WHEELBARROW GO?
I DON'T KNOW.
www.tundracomics.com
LAST TIME I SAW IT, IT WAS SITTING NEXT TO THE LAWN GNOME.
AND WHERE'D THE LAWN GNOME GO?
STRANGE. I DON'T SEE IT ANYWHERE.
LEAF DIVE!
CLANG!
I THINK I FOUND YOUR MISSING WHEELBARROW.
AND IT APPEARS DUDLEY FOUND THE LAWN GNOME.

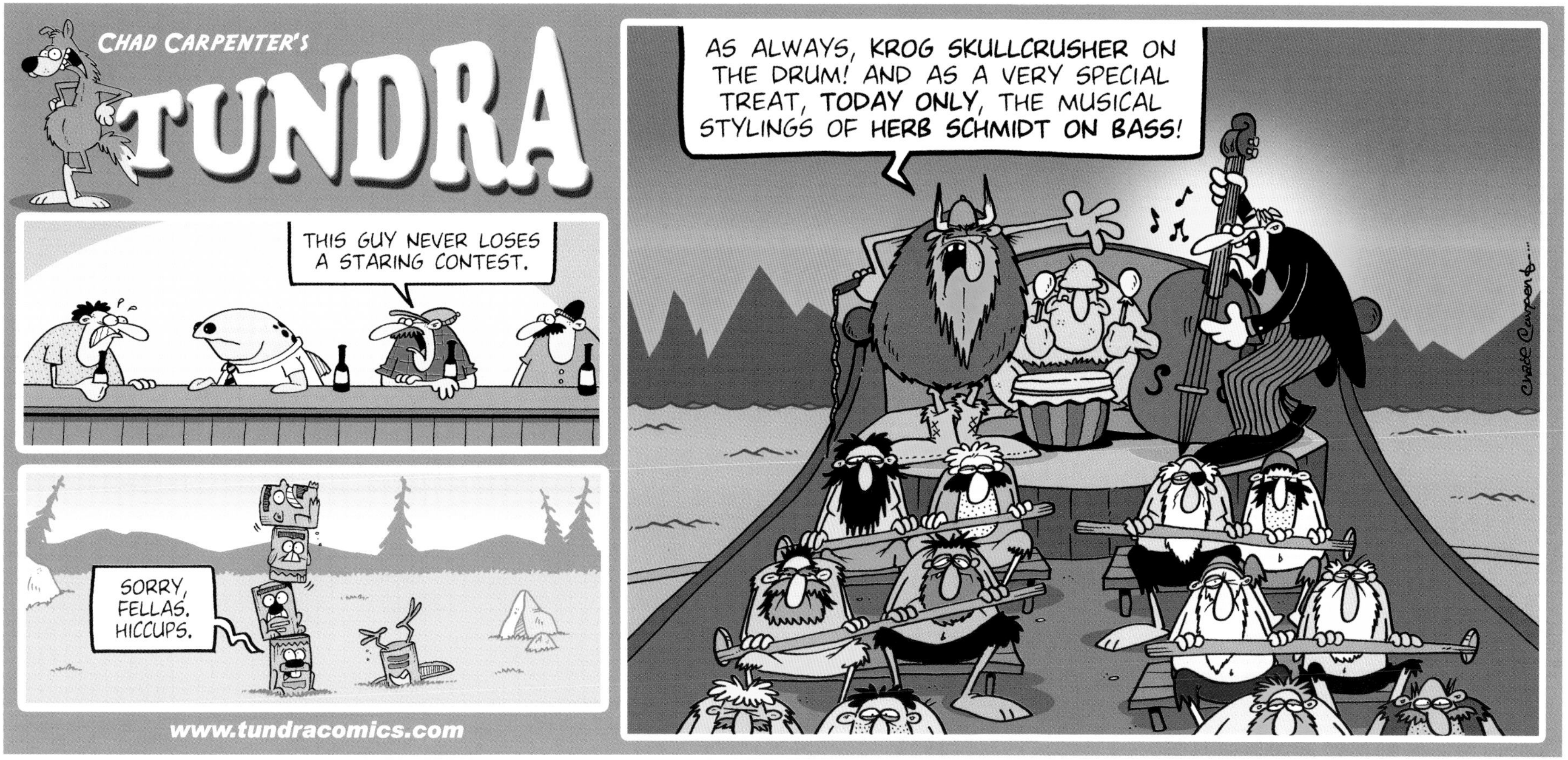
CHAD CARPENTER'S
TUNDRA
THIS GUY NEVER LOSES A STARING CONTEST.
SORRY, FELLAS. HICCUPS.
www.tundracomics.com
AS ALWAYS, KROG SKULLCRUSHER ON THE DRUM! AND AS A VERY SPECIAL TREAT, TODAY ONLY, THE MUSICAL STYLINGS OF HERB SCHMIDT ON BASS!

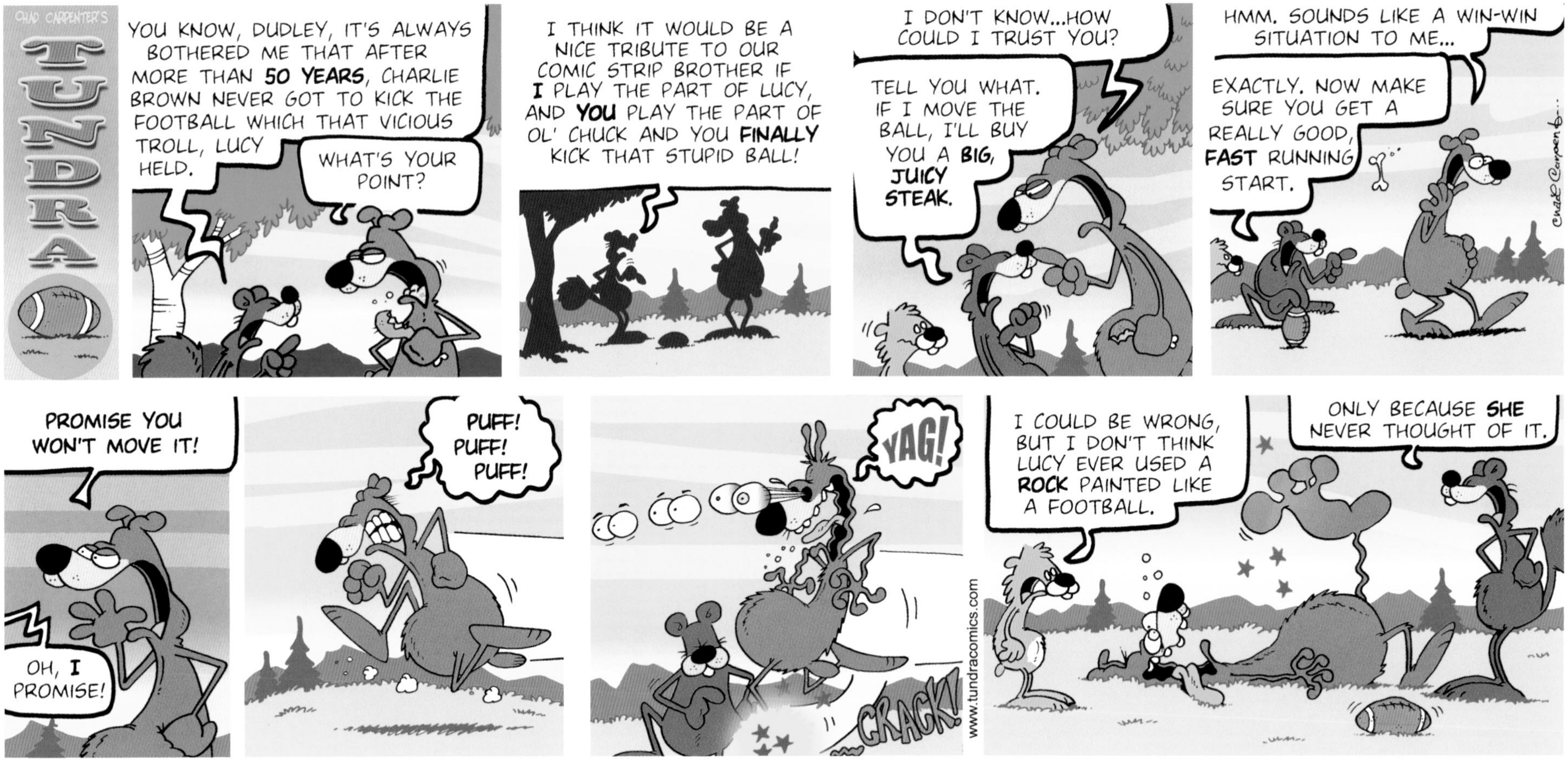
CHAD CARPENTER'S
TUNDRA
YOU KNOW, DUDLEY, IT'S ALWAYS BOTHERED ME THAT AFTER MORE THAN 50 YEARS, CHARLIE BROWN NEVER GOT TO KICK THE FOOTBALL WHICH THAT VICIOUS TROLL, LUCY HELD.
WHAT'S YOUR POINT?
I THINK IT WOULD BE A NICE TRIBUTE TO OUR COMIC STRIP BROTHER IF I PLAY THE PART OF LUCY, AND YOU PLAY THE PART OF OL' CHUCK AND YOU FINALLY KICK THAT STUPID BALL!
I DON'T KNOW...HOW COULD I TRUST YOU?
TELL YOU WHAT. IF I MOVE THE BALL, I'LL BUY YOU A BIG, JUICY STEAK.
HMM. SOUNDS LIKE A WIN-WIN SITUATION TO ME...
EXACTLY. NOW MAKE SURE YOU GET A REALLY GOOD, FAST RUNNING START.
PROMISE YOU WON'T MOVE IT!
OH, I PROMISE!
PUFF! PUFF! PUFF!
YAG!
CRACK!
www.tundracomics.com
I COULD BE WRONG, BUT I DON'T THINK LUCY EVER USED A ROCK PAINTED LIKE A FOOTBALL.
ONLY BECAUSE SHE NEVER THOUGHT OF IT.

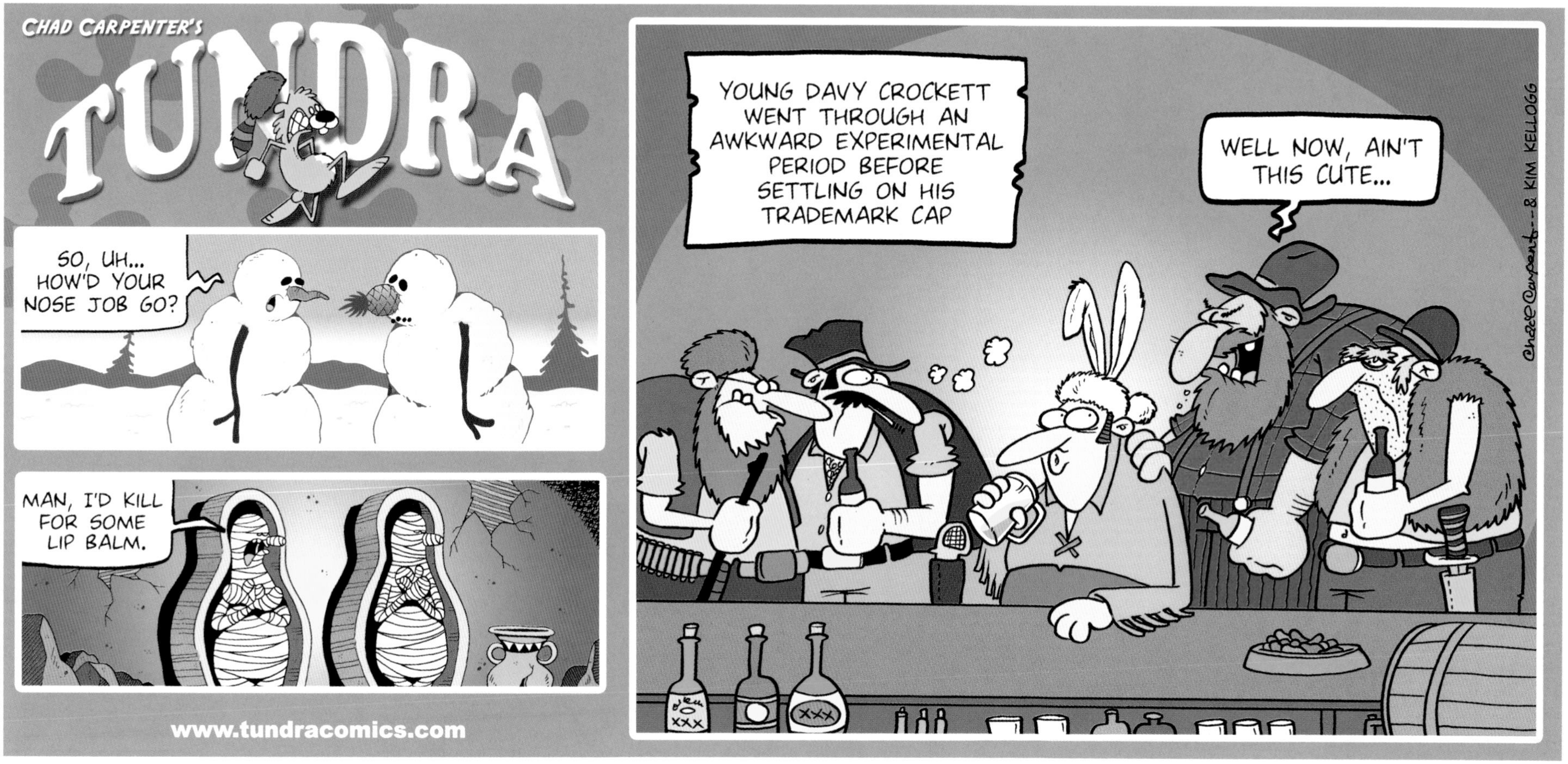
CHAD CARPENTER'S
TUNDRA
SO, UH... HOW'D YOUR NOSE JOB GO?
MAN, I'D KILL FOR SOME LIP BALM.
www.tundracomics.com
YOUNG DAVY CROCKETT WENT THROUGH AN AWKWARD EXPERIMENTAL PERIOD BEFORE SETTLING ON HIS TRADEMARK CAP
WELL NOW, AIN'T THIS CUTE...
& KIM KELLOGG
XXX
XXX

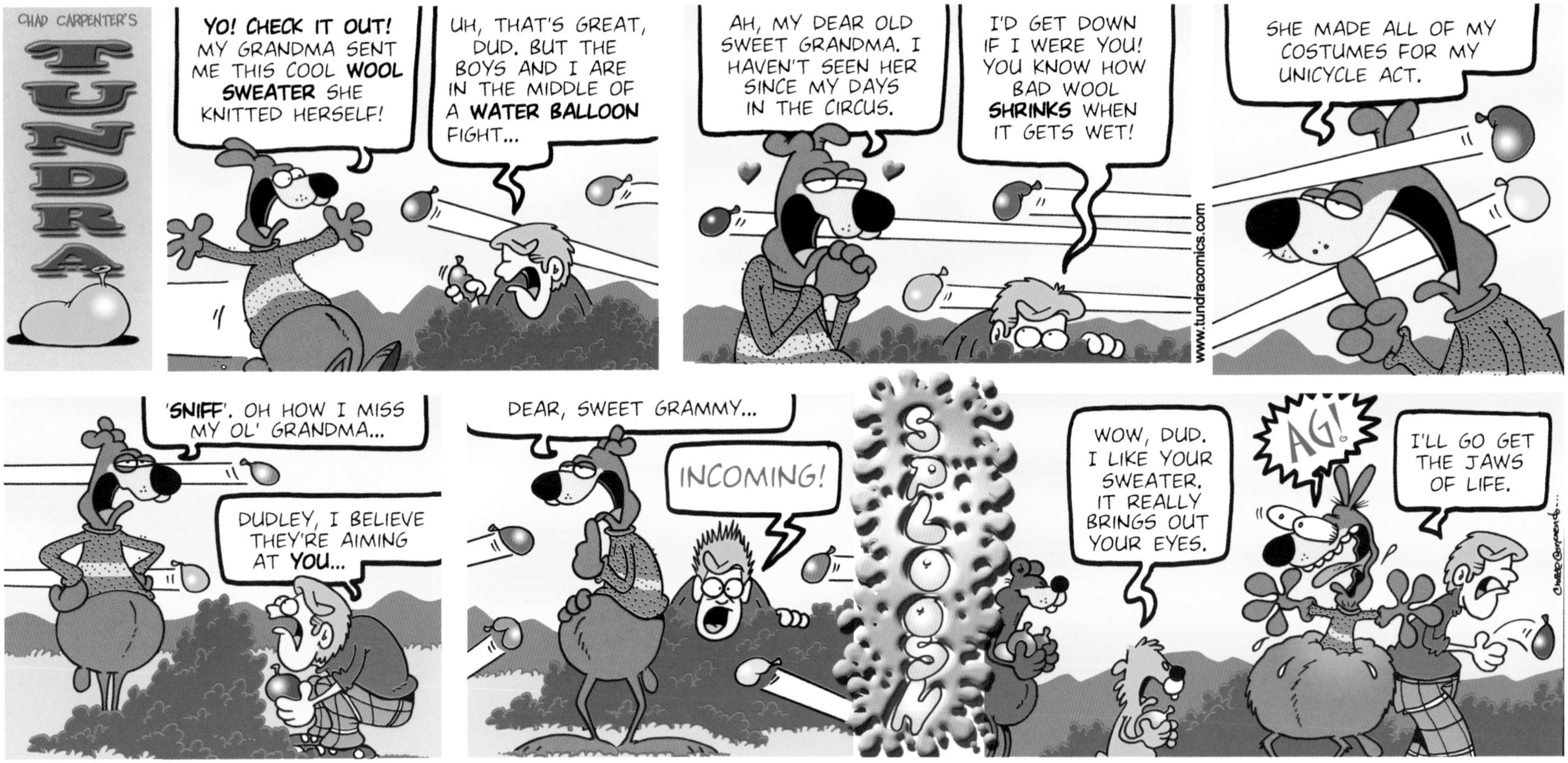
CHAD CARPENTER'S
TUNDRA
YO! CHECK IT OUT! MY GRANDMA SENT ME THIS COOL WOOL SWEATER SHE KNITTED HERSELF!
UH, THAT'S GREAT, DUD. BUT THE BOYS AND I ARE IN THE MIDDLE OF A WATER BALLOON FIGHT...
AH, MY DEAR OLD SWEET GRANDMA. I HAVEN'T SEEN HER SINCE MY DAYS IN THE CIRCUS.
I'D GET DOWN IF I WERE YOU! YOU KNOW HOW BAD WOOL SHRINKS WHEN IT GETS WET!
www.tundracomics.com
SHE MADE ALL OF MY COSTUMES FOR MY UNICYCLE ACT.
'SNIFF'. OH HOW I MISS MY OL' GRANDMA...
DUDLEY, I BELIEVE THEY'RE AIMING AT YOU...
DEAR, SWEET GRAMMY...
INCOMING!
SPLOOSH
WOW, DUD. I LIKE YOUR SWEATER. IT REALLY BRINGS OUT YOUR EYES.
AG!
I'LL GO GET THE JAWS OF LIFE.

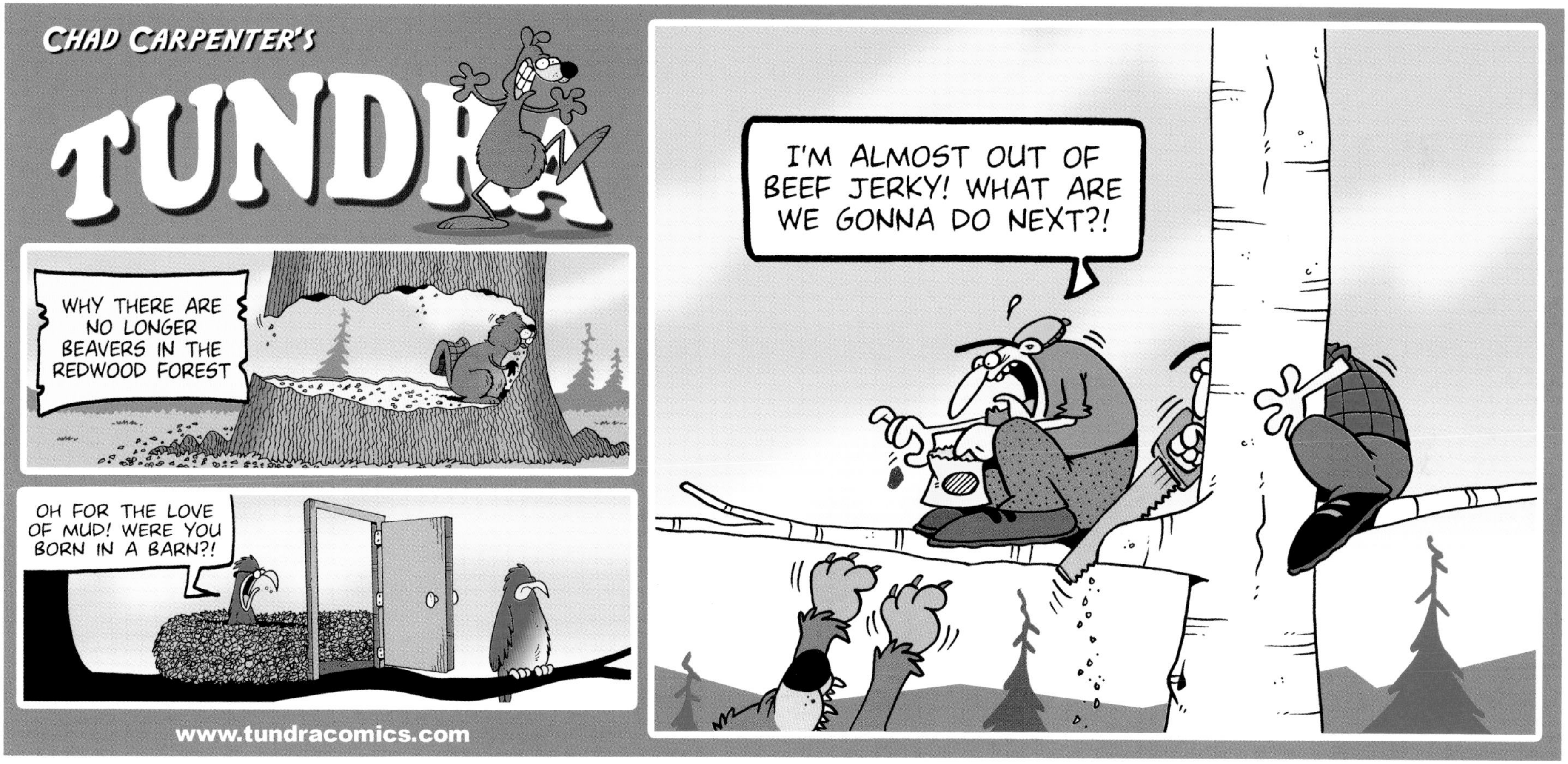
CHAD CARPENTER'S
TUNDRA
WHY THERE ARE NO LONGER BEAVERS IN THE REDWOOD FOREST
OH FOR THE LOVE OF MUD! WERE YOU BORN IN A BARN?!
I'M ALMOST OUT OF BEEF JERKY! WHAT ARE WE GONNA DO NEXT?!
www.tundracomics.com

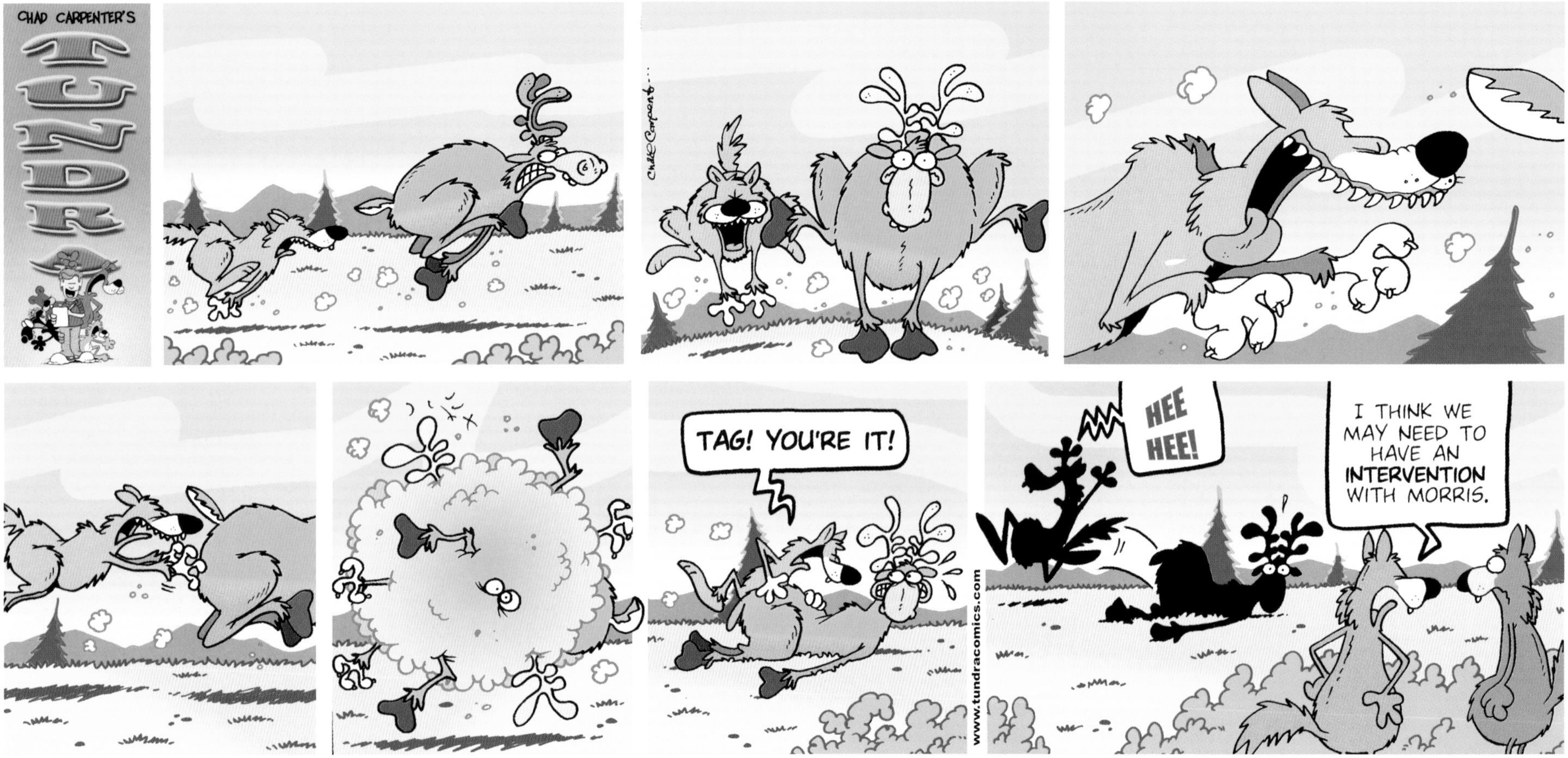
CHAD CARPENTER'S
TUNDRA
TAG! YOU'RE IT!
www.tundracomics.com
HEE HEE!
I THINK WE MAY NEED TO HAVE AN **INTERVENTION** WITH MORRIS.

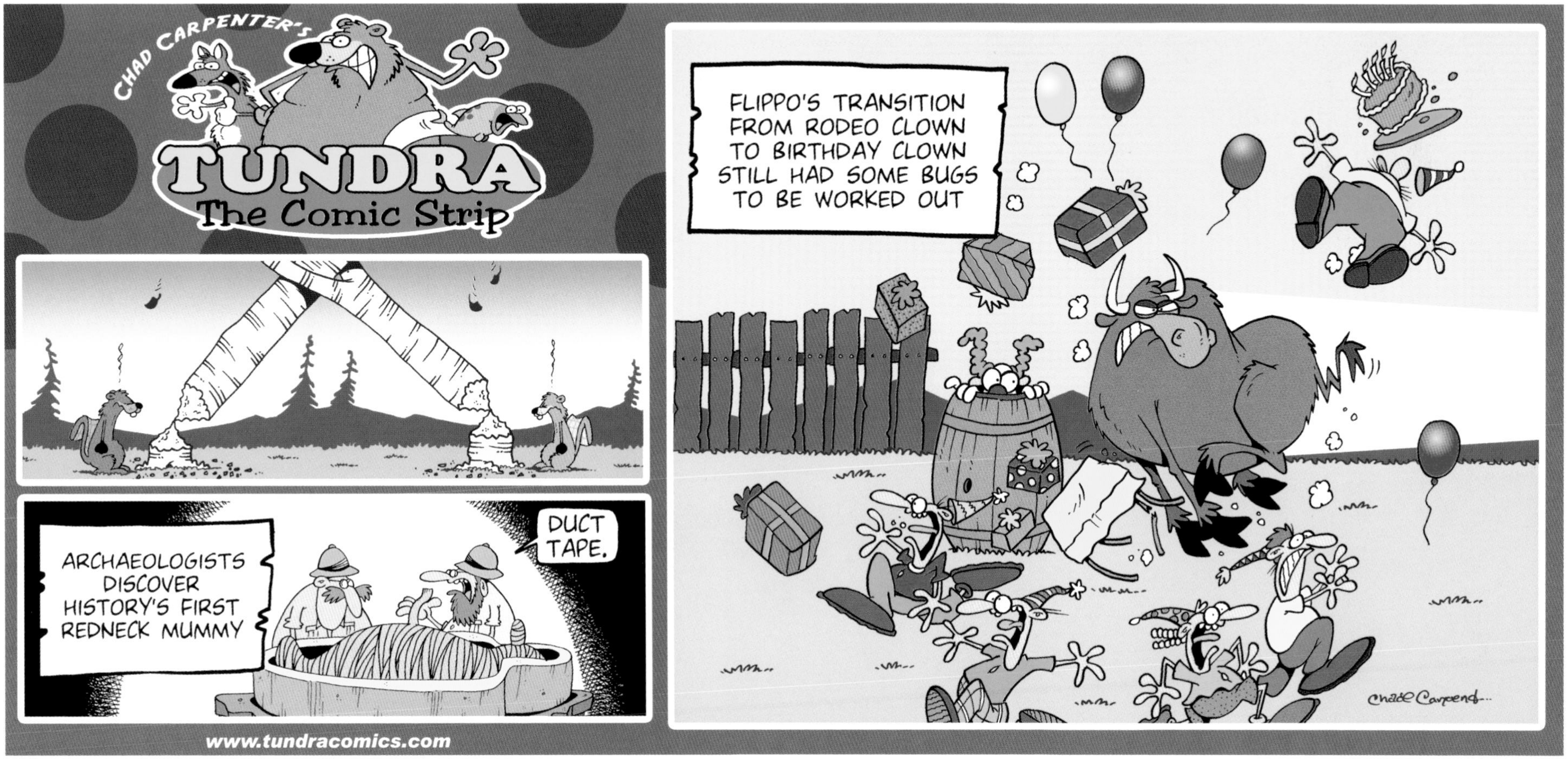
CHAD CARPENTER'S
TUNDRA
The Comic Strip
ARCHAEOLOGISTS DISCOVER HISTORY'S FIRST REDNECK MUMMY
DUCT TAPE.
www.tundracomics.com
FLIPPO'S TRANSITION FROM RODEO CLOWN TO BIRTHDAY CLOWN STILL HAD SOME BUGS TO BE WORKED OUT

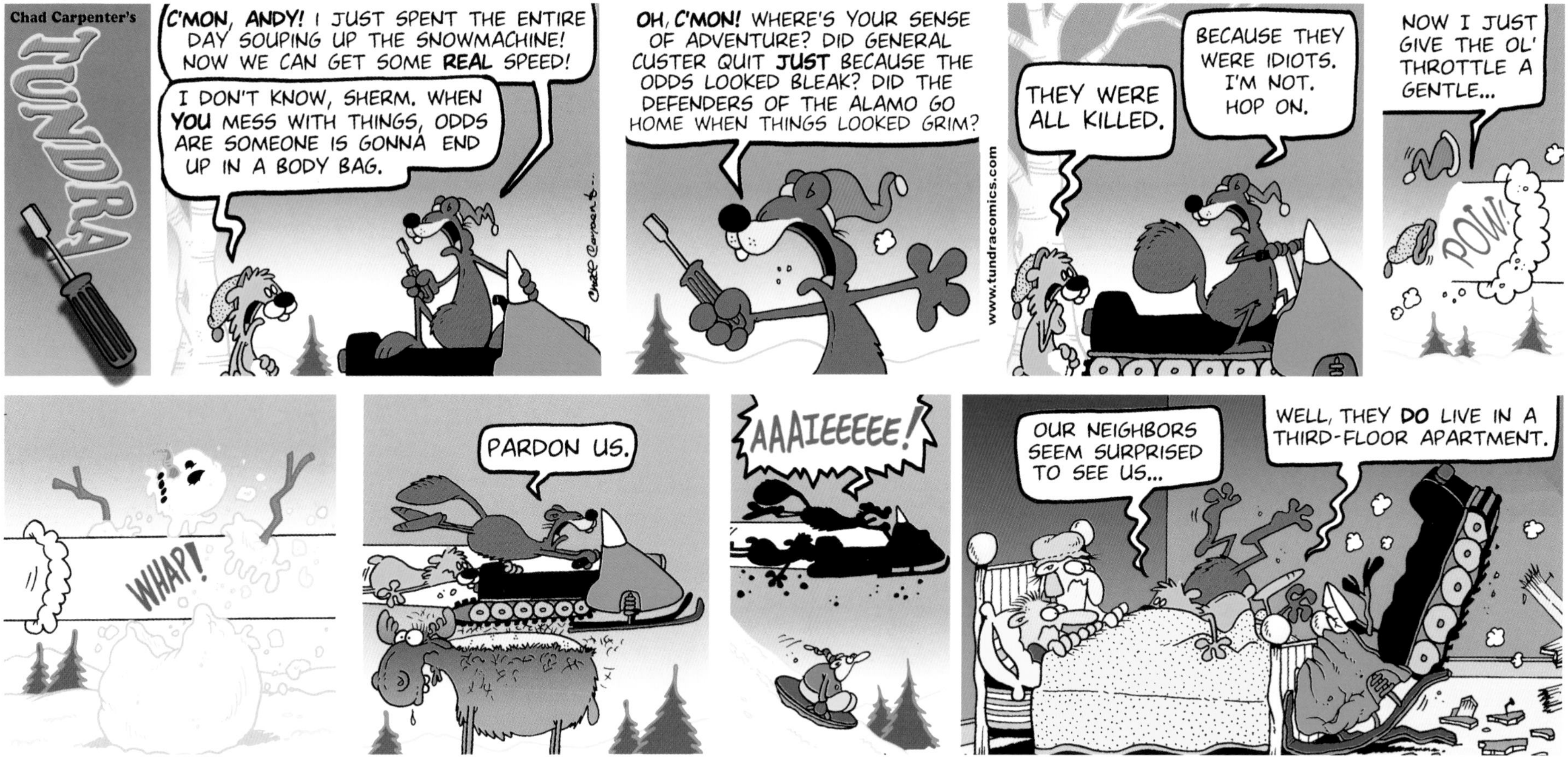
Chad Carpenter's
TUNDRA
C'MON, ANDY! I JUST SPENT THE ENTIRE DAY SOUPING UP THE SNOWMACHINE! NOW WE CAN GET SOME REAL SPEED!
I DON'T KNOW, SHERM. WHEN YOU MESS WITH THINGS, ODDS ARE SOMEONE IS GONNA END UP IN A BODY BAG.
OH, C'MON! WHERE'S YOUR SENSE OF ADVENTURE? DID GENERAL CUSTER QUIT JUST BECAUSE THE ODDS LOOKED BLEAK? DID THE DEFENDERS OF THE ALAMO GO HOME WHEN THINGS LOOKED GRIM?
www.tundracomics.com
THEY WERE ALL KILLED.
BECAUSE THEY WERE IDIOTS. I'M NOT. HOP ON.
NOW I JUST GIVE THE OL' THROTTLE A GENTLE...
POW!
WHAP!
PARDON US.
AAAIEEEEE!
OUR NEIGHBORS SEEM SURPRISED TO SEE US...
WELL, THEY DO LIVE IN A THIRD-FLOOR APARTMENT.

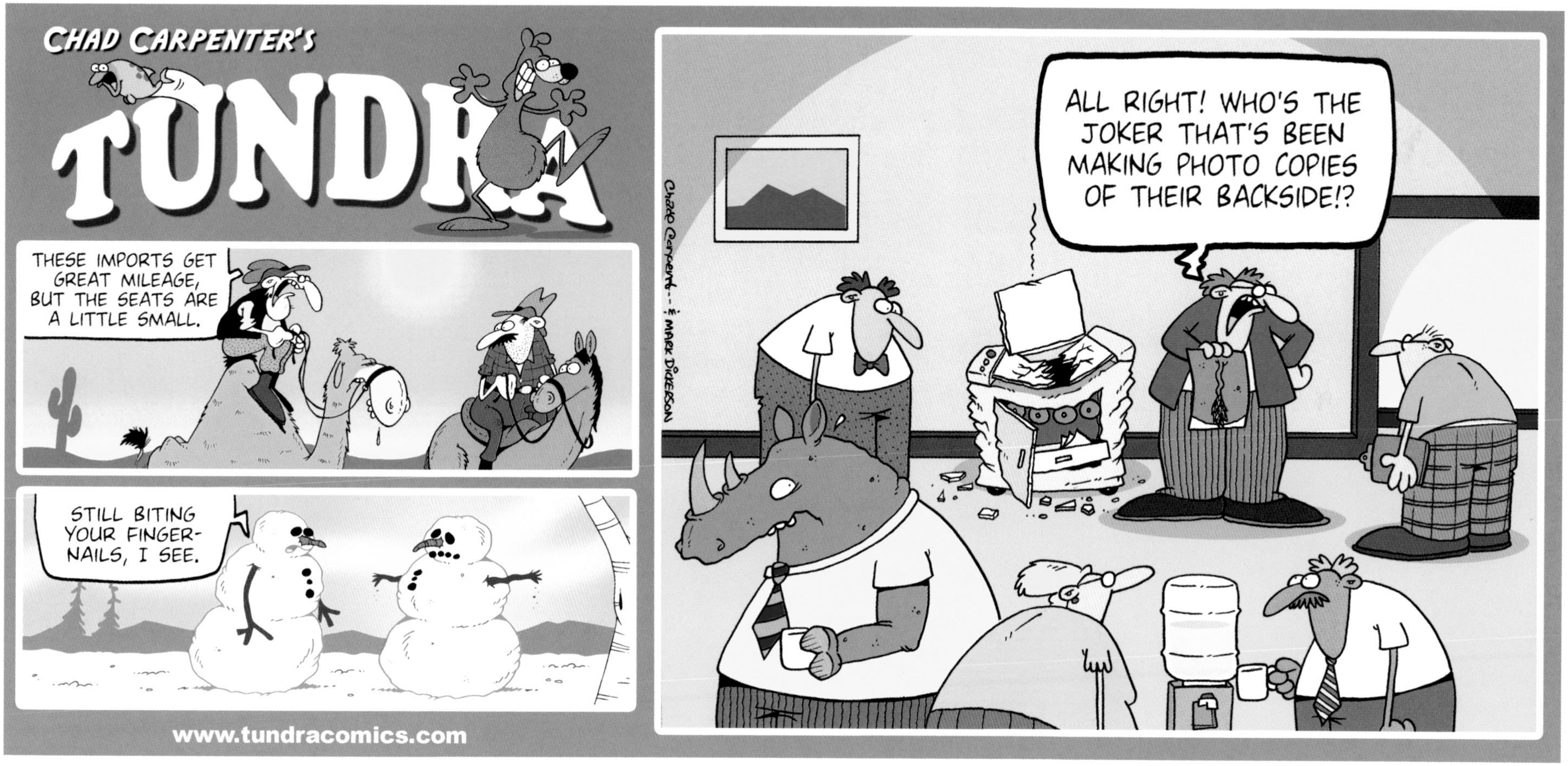
CHAD CARPENTER'S
TUNDRA
THESE IMPORTS GET GREAT MILEAGE, BUT THE SEATS ARE A LITTLE SMALL.
STILL BITING YOUR FINGER-NAILS, I SEE.
www.tundracomics.com
ALL RIGHT! WHO'S THE JOKER THAT'S BEEN MAKING PHOTO COPIES OF THEIR BACKSIDE!?
CHAD CARPENTER ... & MARK DICKERSON

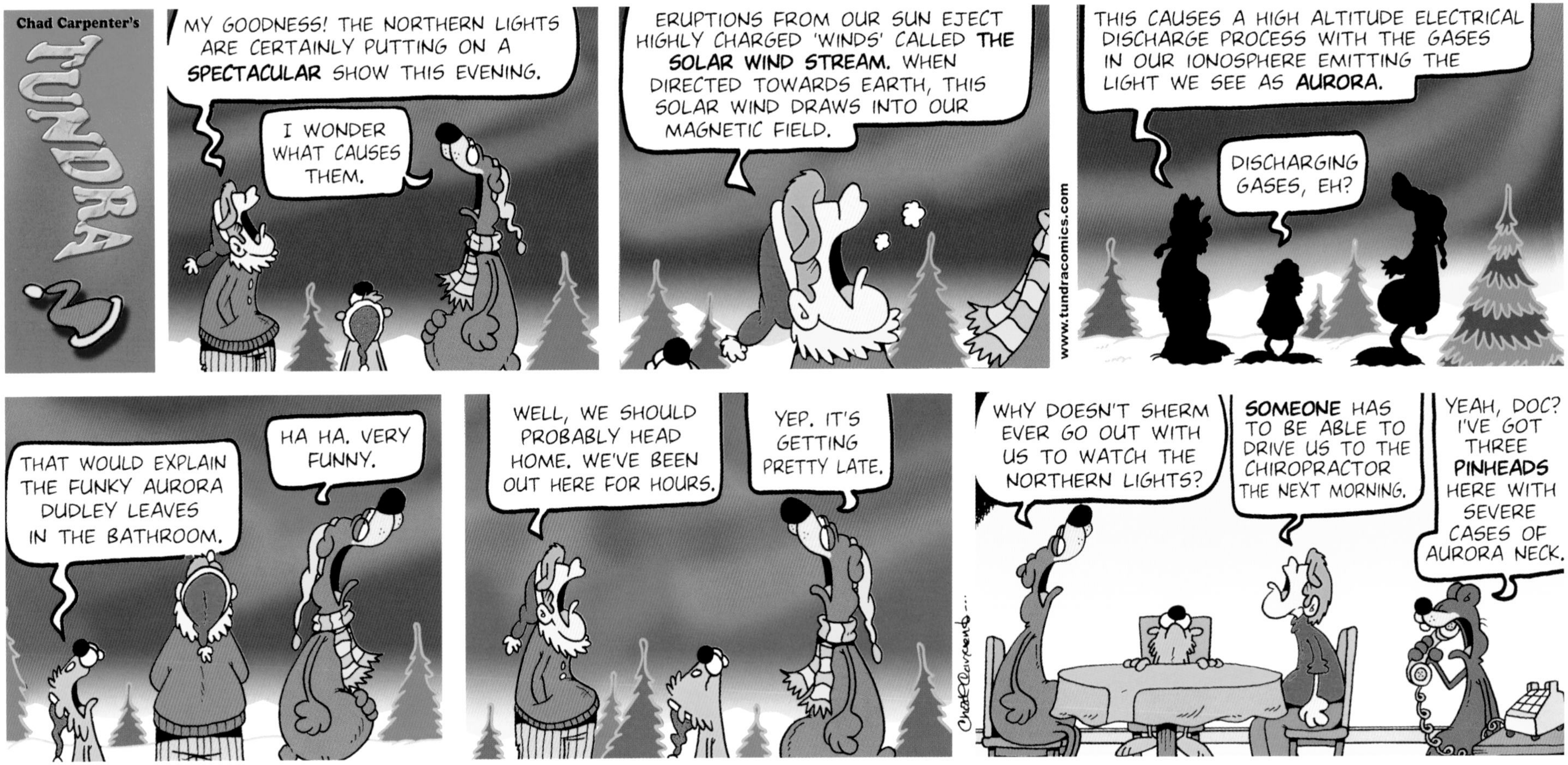
Chad Carpenter's
TUNDRA
MY GOODNESS! THE NORTHERN LIGHTS ARE CERTAINLY PUTTING ON A SPECTACULAR SHOW THIS EVENING.
I WONDER WHAT CAUSES THEM.
ERUPTIONS FROM OUR SUN EJECT HIGHLY CHARGED 'WINDS' CALLED THE SOLAR WIND STREAM. WHEN DIRECTED TOWARDS EARTH, THIS SOLAR WIND DRAWS INTO OUR MAGNETIC FIELD.
www.tundracomics.com
THIS CAUSES A HIGH ALTITUDE ELECTRICAL DISCHARGE PROCESS WITH THE GASES IN OUR IONOSPHERE EMITTING THE LIGHT WE SEE AS AURORA.
DISCHARGING GASES, EH?
THAT WOULD EXPLAIN THE FUNKY AURORA DUDLEY LEAVES IN THE BATHROOM.
HA HA. VERY FUNNY.
WELL, WE SHOULD PROBABLY HEAD HOME. WE'VE BEEN OUT HERE FOR HOURS.
YEP. IT'S GETTING PRETTY LATE.
WHY DOESN'T SHERM EVER GO OUT WITH US TO WATCH THE NORTHERN LIGHTS?
SOMEONE HAS TO BE ABLE TO DRIVE US TO THE CHIROPRACTOR THE NEXT MORNING.
YEAH, DOC? I'VE GOT THREE PINHEADS HERE WITH SEVERE CASES OF AURORA NECK.

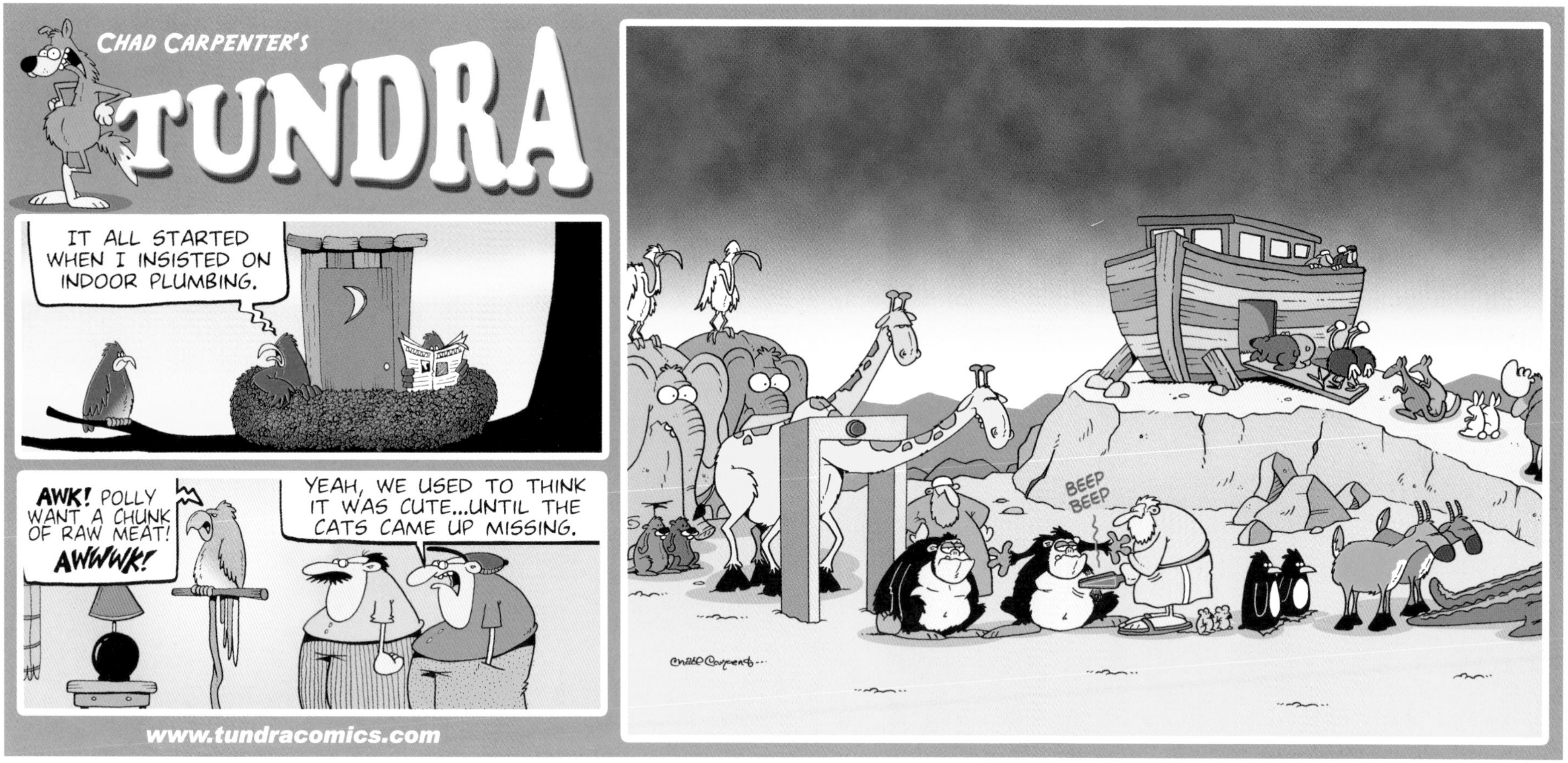
CHAD CARPENTER'S
TUNDRA
IT ALL STARTED WHEN I INSISTED ON INDOOR PLUMBING.
AWK! POLLY WANT A CHUNK OF RAW MEAT! AWWWK!
YEAH, WE USED TO THINK IT WAS CUTE...UNTIL THE CATS CAME UP MISSING.
BEEP BEEP
www.tundracomics.com

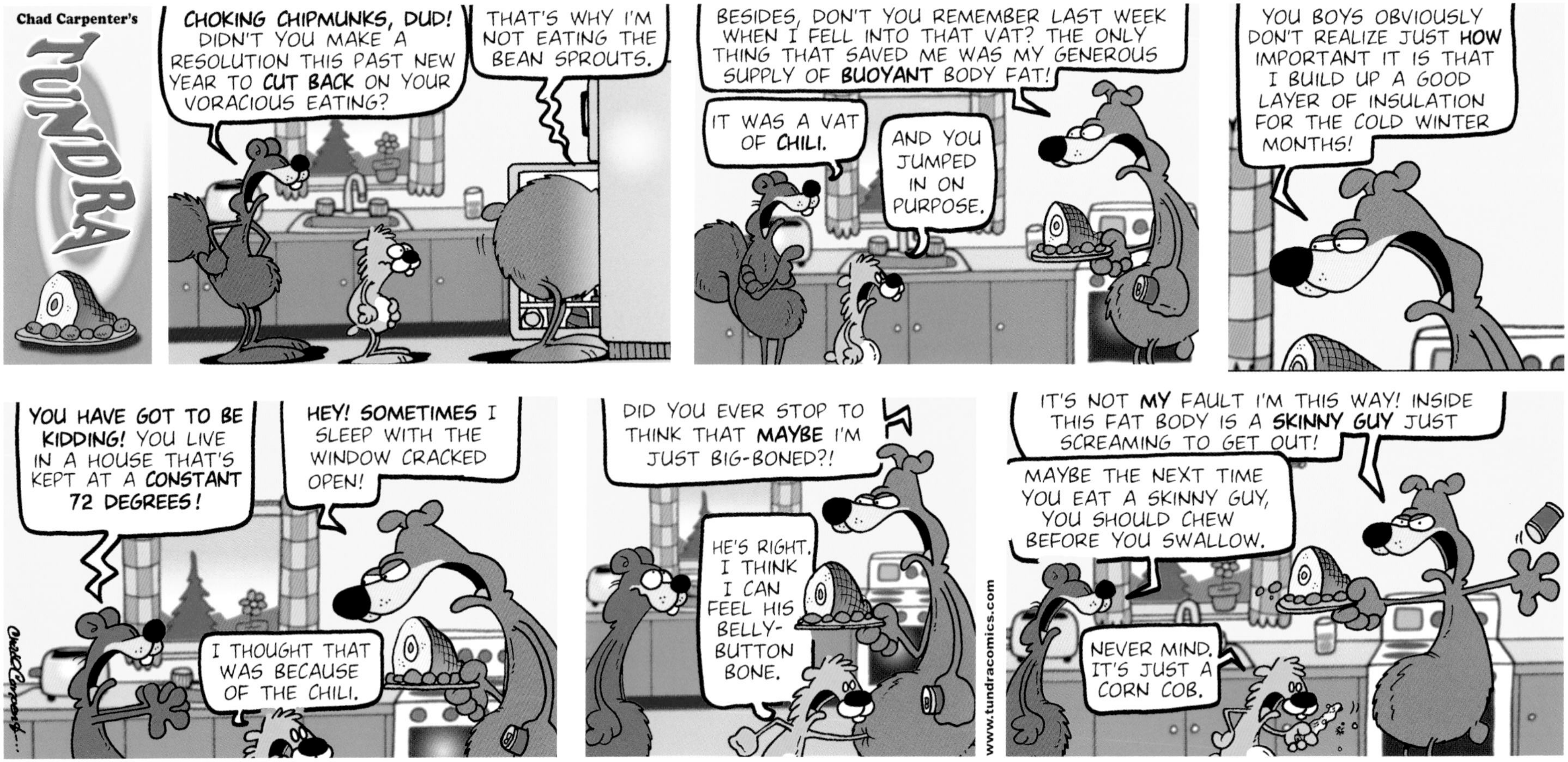
Chad Carpenter's
TUNDRA
CHOKING CHIPMUNKS, DUD! DIDN'T YOU MAKE A RESOLUTION THIS PAST NEW YEAR TO CUT BACK ON YOUR VORACIOUS EATING?
THAT'S WHY I'M NOT EATING THE BEAN SPROUTS.
BESIDES, DON'T YOU REMEMBER LAST WEEK WHEN I FELL INTO THAT VAT? THE ONLY THING THAT SAVED ME WAS MY GENEROUS SUPPLY OF BUOYANT BODY FAT!
IT WAS A VAT OF CHILI.
AND YOU JUMPED IN ON PURPOSE.
YOU BOYS OBVIOUSLY DON'T REALIZE JUST HOW IMPORTANT IT IS THAT I BUILD UP A GOOD LAYER OF INSULATION FOR THE COLD WINTER MONTHS!
YOU HAVE GOT TO BE KIDDING! YOU LIVE IN A HOUSE THAT'S KEPT AT A CONSTANT 72 DEGREES!
HEY! SOMETIMES I SLEEP WITH THE WINDOW CRACKED OPEN!
I THOUGHT THAT WAS BECAUSE OF THE CHILI.
DID YOU EVER STOP TO THINK THAT MAYBE I'M JUST BIG-BONED?!
HE'S RIGHT. I THINK I CAN FEEL HIS BELLY-BUTTON BONE.
www.tundracomics.com
IT'S NOT MY FAULT I'M THIS WAY! INSIDE THIS FAT BODY IS A SKINNY GUY JUST SCREAMING TO GET OUT!
MAYBE THE NEXT TIME YOU EAT A SKINNY GUY, YOU SHOULD CHEW BEFORE YOU SWALLOW.
NEVER MIND. IT'S JUST A CORN COB.

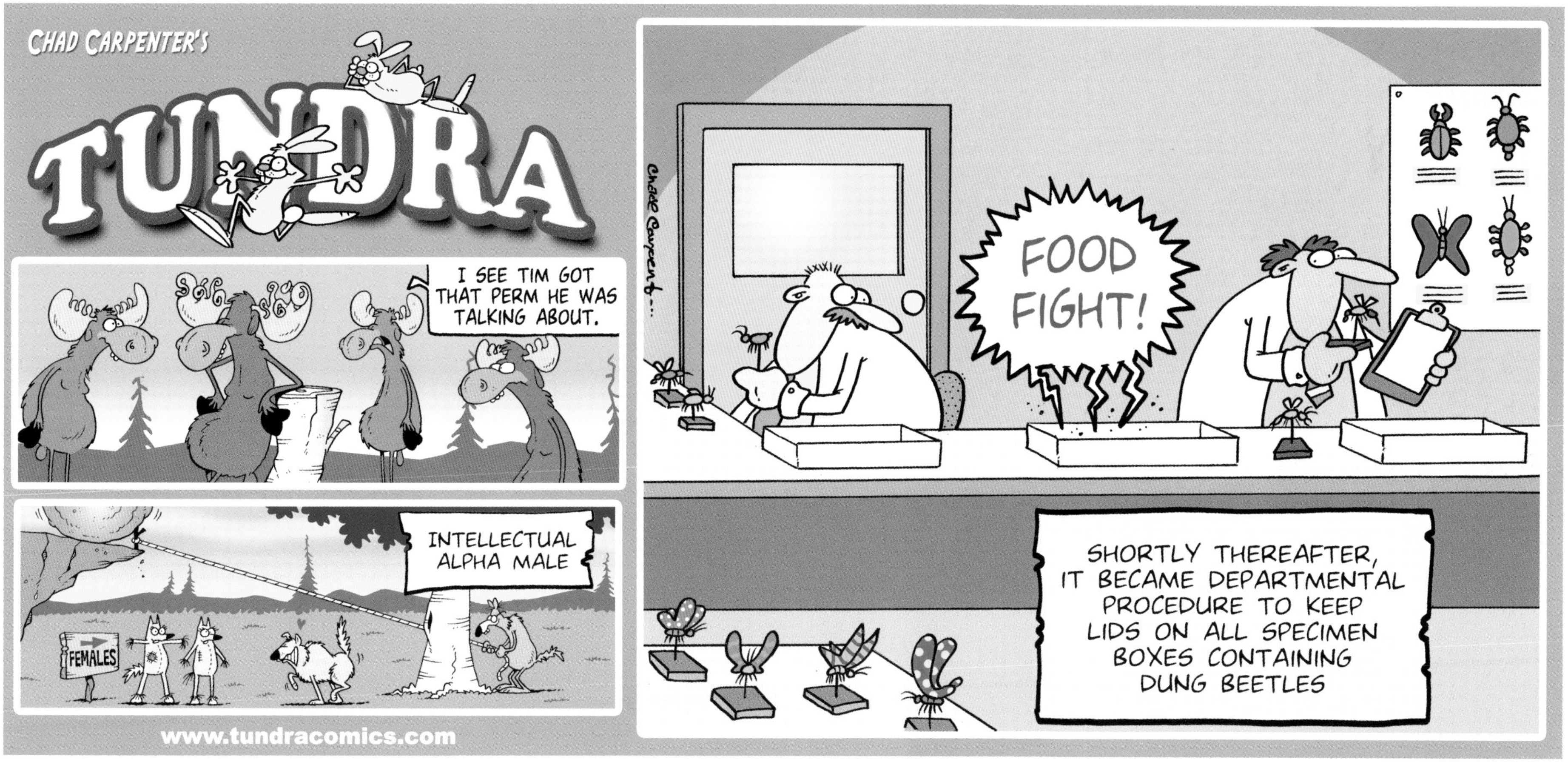
CHAD CARPENTER'S
TUNDRA
I SEE TIM GOT THAT PERM HE WAS TALKING ABOUT.
INTELLECTUAL ALPHA MALE
FEMALES
www.tundracomics.com
FOOD FIGHT!
SHORTLY THEREAFTER, IT BECAME DEPARTMENTAL PROCEDURE TO KEEP LIDS ON ALL SPECIMEN BOXES CONTAINING DUNG BEETLES

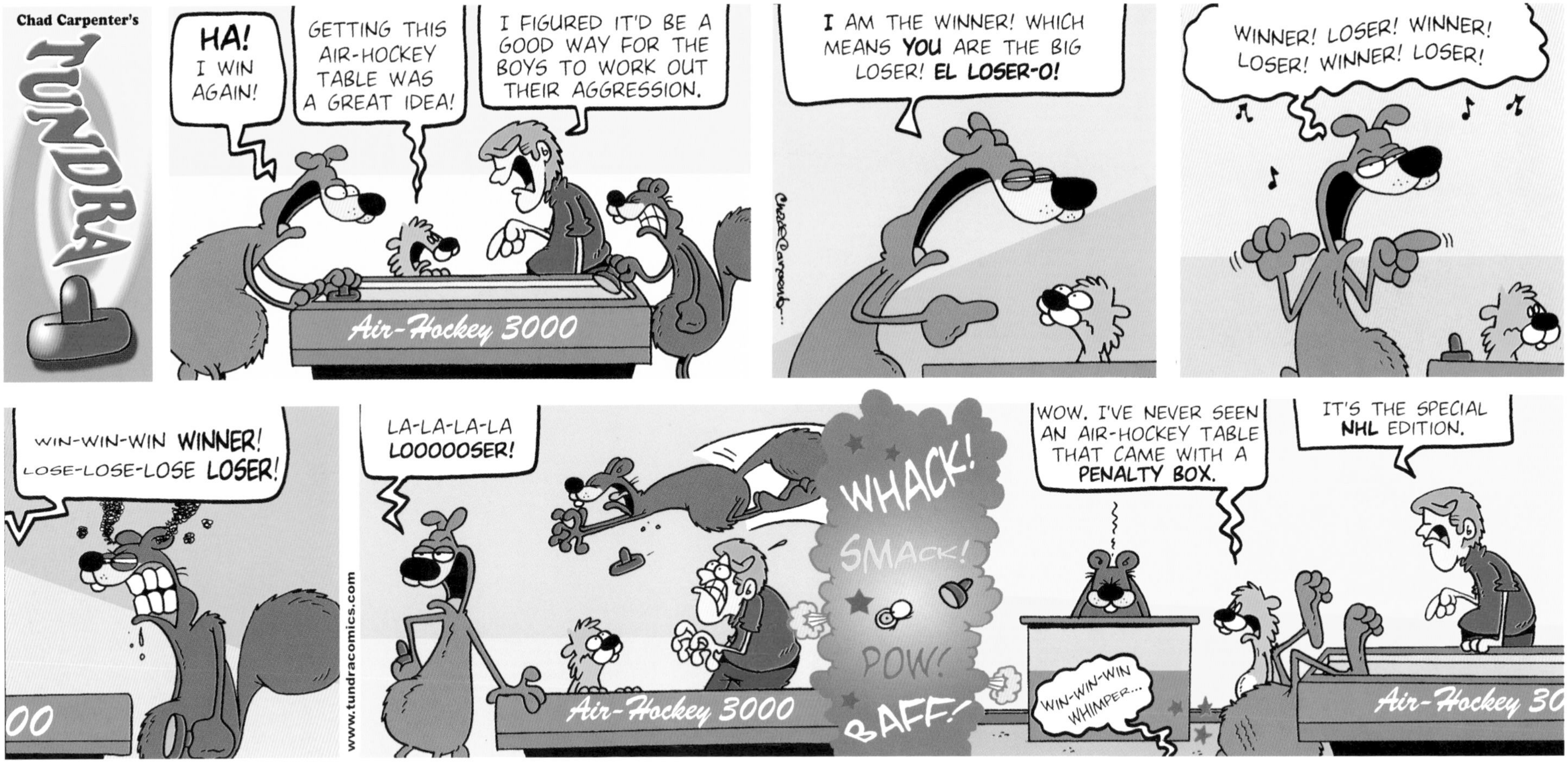
Chad Carpenter's
TUNDRA
HA! I WIN AGAIN!
GETTING THIS AIR-HOCKEY TABLE WAS A GREAT IDEA!
I FIGURED IT'D BE A GOOD WAY FOR THE BOYS TO WORK OUT THEIR AGGRESSION.
Air-Hockey 3000
I AM THE WINNER! WHICH MEANS YOU ARE THE BIG LOSER! EL LOSER-O!
WINNER! LOSER! WINNER! LOSER! WINNER! LOSER!
WIN-WIN-WIN WINNER! LOSE-LOSE-LOSE LOSER!
LA-LA-LA-LA LOOOOOSER!
www.tundracomics.com
WHACK! SMACK! POW! BAFF!
WOW. I'VE NEVER SEEN AN AIR-HOCKEY TABLE THAT CAME WITH A PENALTY BOX.
IT'S THE SPECIAL NHL EDITION.
WIN-WIN-WIN WHIMPER...

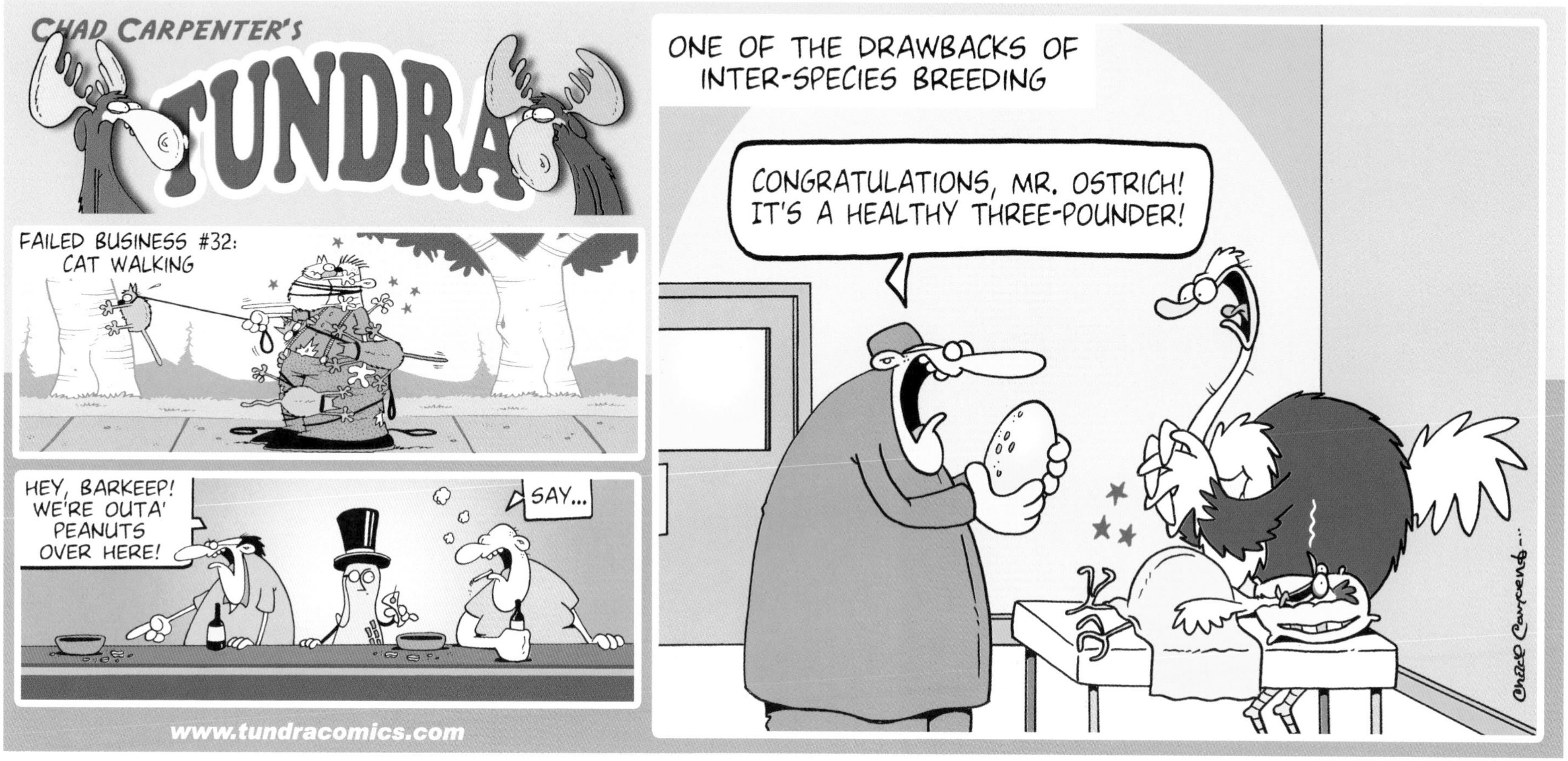
CHAD CARPENTER'S
TUNDRA
FAILED BUSINESS #32: CAT WALKING
HEY, BARKEEP! WE'RE OUTA' PEANUTS OVER HERE!
SAY...
www.tundracomics.com
ONE OF THE DRAWBACKS OF INTER-SPECIES BREEDING
CONGRATULATIONS, MR. OSTRICH! IT'S A HEALTHY THREE-POUNDER!

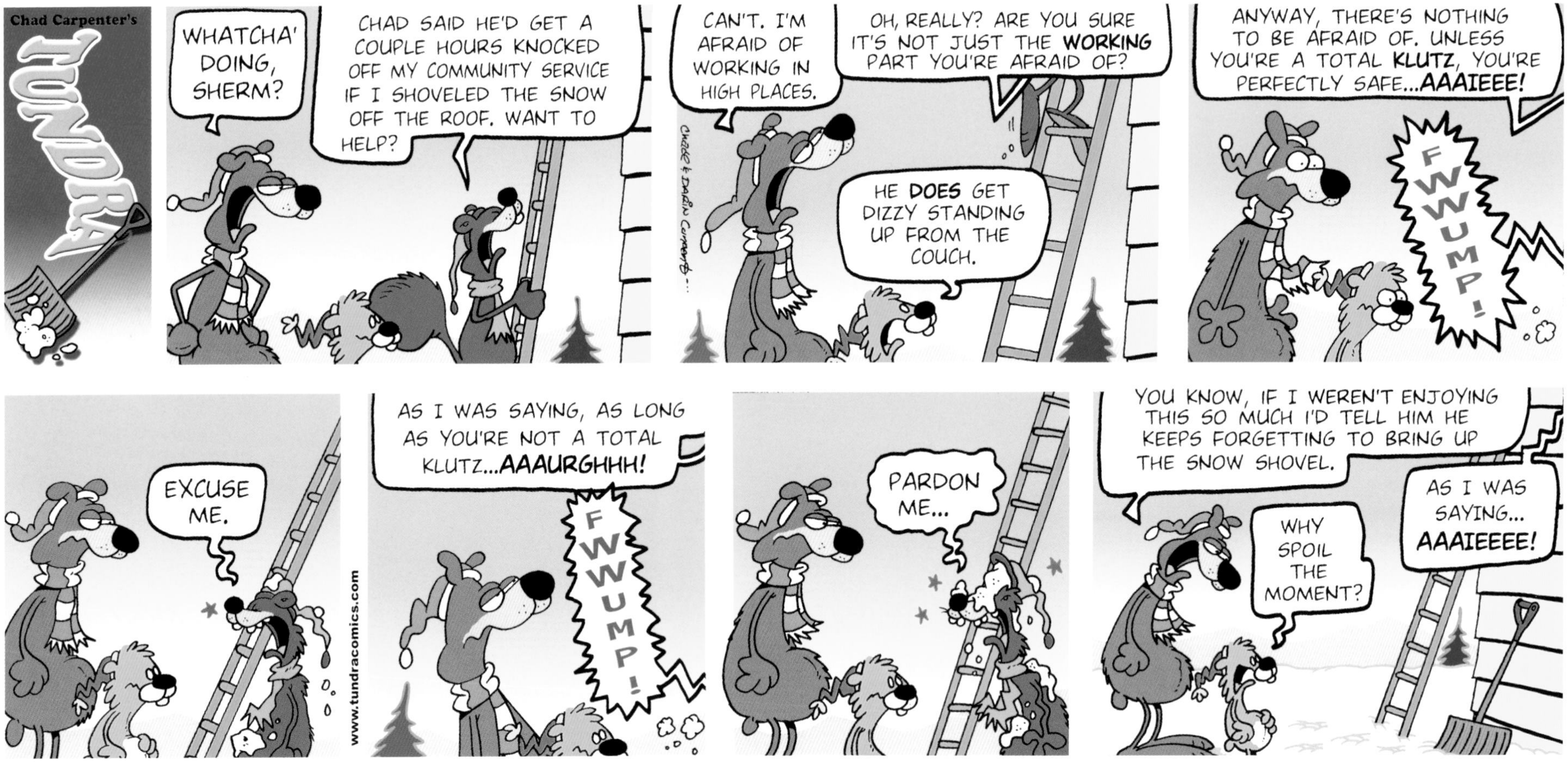
Chad Carpenter's
TUNDRA
WHATCHA' DOING, SHERM?
CHAD SAID HE'D GET A COUPLE HOURS KNOCKED OFF MY COMMUNITY SERVICE IF I SHOVELED THE SNOW OFF THE ROOF. WANT TO HELP?
CAN'T. I'M AFRAID OF WORKING IN HIGH PLACES.
OH, REALLY? ARE YOU SURE IT'S NOT JUST THE WORKING PART YOU'RE AFRAID OF?
HE DOES GET DIZZY STANDING UP FROM THE COUCH.
ANYWAY, THERE'S NOTHING TO BE AFRAID OF. UNLESS YOU'RE A TOTAL KLUTZ, YOU'RE PERFECTLY SAFE...AAAIEEE!
FWWUMP!
EXCUSE ME.
www.tundracomics.com
AS I WAS SAYING, AS LONG AS YOU'RE NOT A TOTAL KLUTZ...AAAURGHHH!
FWWUMP!
PARDON ME...
YOU KNOW, IF I WEREN'T ENJOYING THIS SO MUCH I'D TELL HIM HE KEEPS FORGETTING TO BRING UP THE SNOW SHOVEL.
WHY SPOIL THE MOMENT?
AS I WAS SAYING... AAAIEEEE!

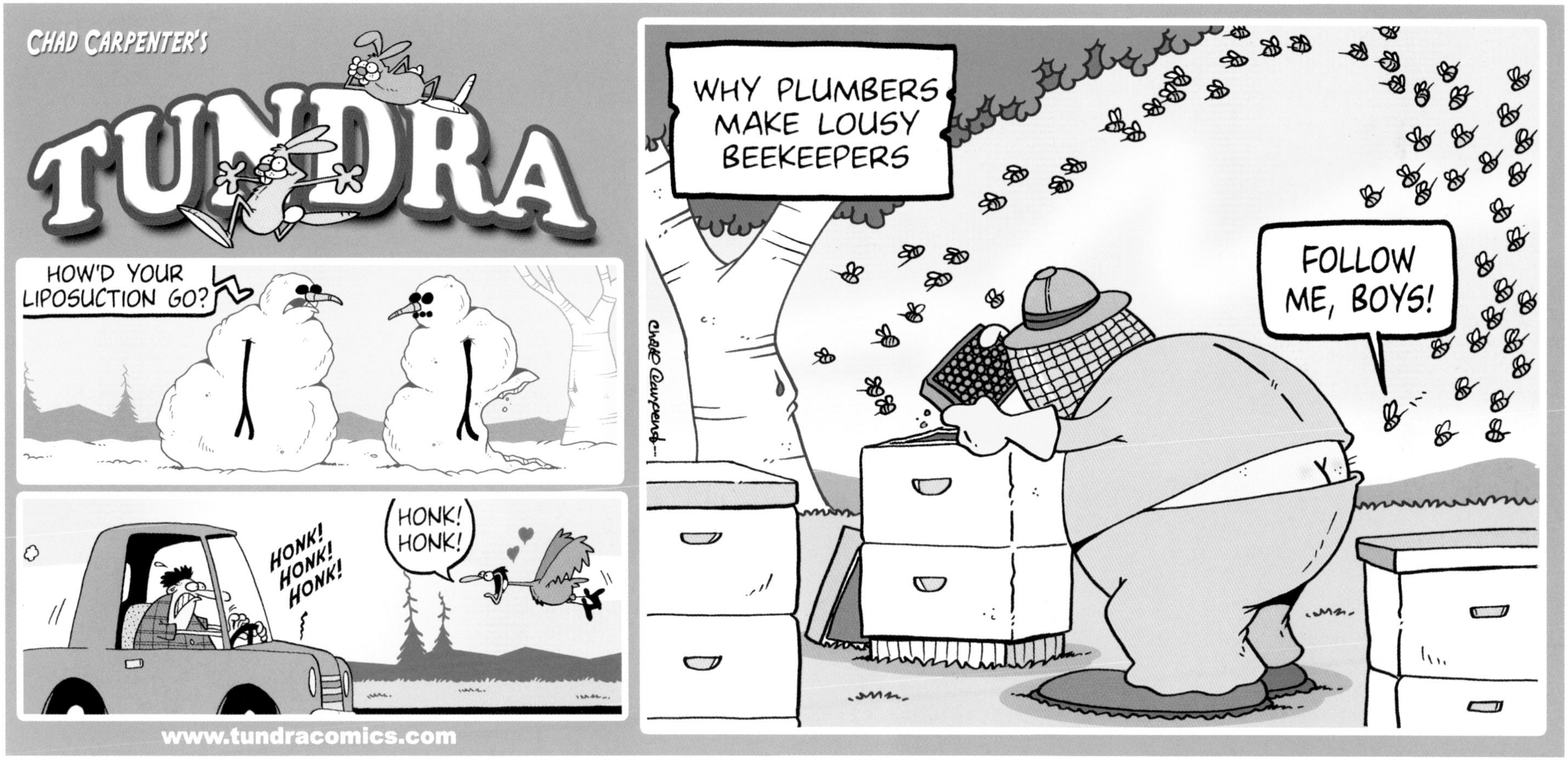
CHAD CARPENTER'S
TUNDRA
HOW'D YOUR LIPOSUCTION GO?
HONK! HONK! HONK!
HONK! HONK!
www.tundracomics.com
WHY PLUMBERS MAKE LOUSY BEEKEEPERS
FOLLOW ME, BOYS!

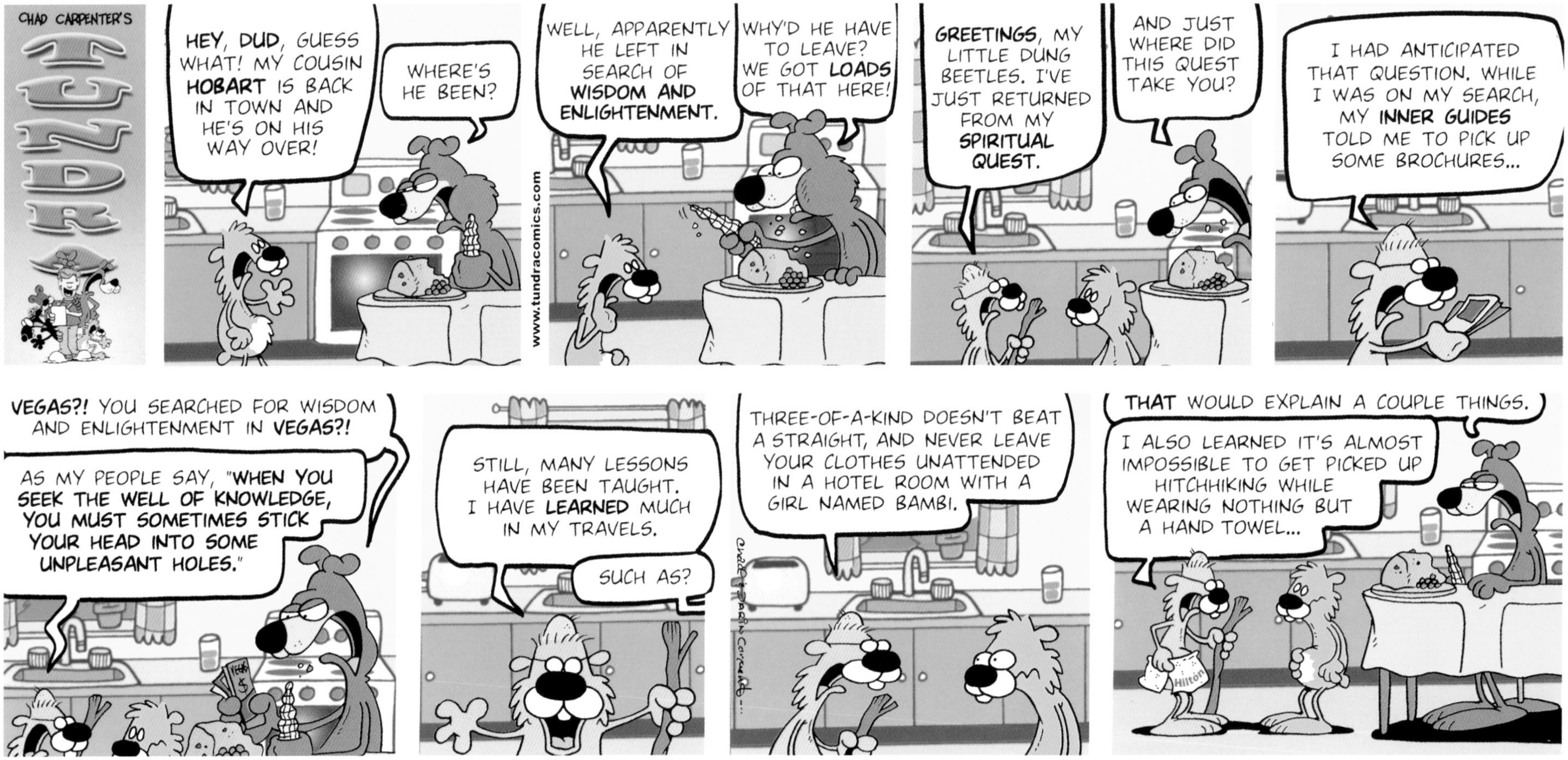
CHAD CARPENTER'S
TUNDRA
HEY, DUD, GUESS WHAT! MY COUSIN HOBART IS BACK IN TOWN AND HE'S ON HIS WAY OVER!
WHERE'S HE BEEN?
www.tundracomics.com
WELL, APPARENTLY HE LEFT IN SEARCH OF WISDOM AND ENLIGHTENMENT.
WHY'D HE HAVE TO LEAVE? WE GOT LOADS OF THAT HERE!
GREETINGS, MY LITTLE DUNG BEETLES. I'VE JUST RETURNED FROM MY SPIRITUAL QUEST.
AND JUST WHERE DID THIS QUEST TAKE YOU?
I HAD ANTICIPATED THAT QUESTION. WHILE I WAS ON MY SEARCH, MY INNER GUIDES TOLD ME TO PICK UP SOME BROCHURES...
VEGAS?! YOU SEARCHED FOR WISDOM AND ENLIGHTENMENT IN VEGAS?!
AS MY PEOPLE SAY, "WHEN YOU SEEK THE WELL OF KNOWLEDGE, YOU MUST SOMETIMES STICK YOUR HEAD INTO SOME UNPLEASANT HOLES."
STILL, MANY LESSONS HAVE BEEN TAUGHT. I HAVE LEARNED MUCH IN MY TRAVELS.
SUCH AS?
THREE-OF-A-KIND DOESN'T BEAT A STRAIGHT, AND NEVER LEAVE YOUR CLOTHES UNATTENDED IN A HOTEL ROOM WITH A GIRL NAMED BAMBI.
THAT WOULD EXPLAIN A COUPLE THINGS.
I ALSO LEARNED IT'S ALMOST IMPOSSIBLE TO GET PICKED UP HITCHHIKING WHILE WEARING NOTHING BUT A HAND TOWEL...
Hilton

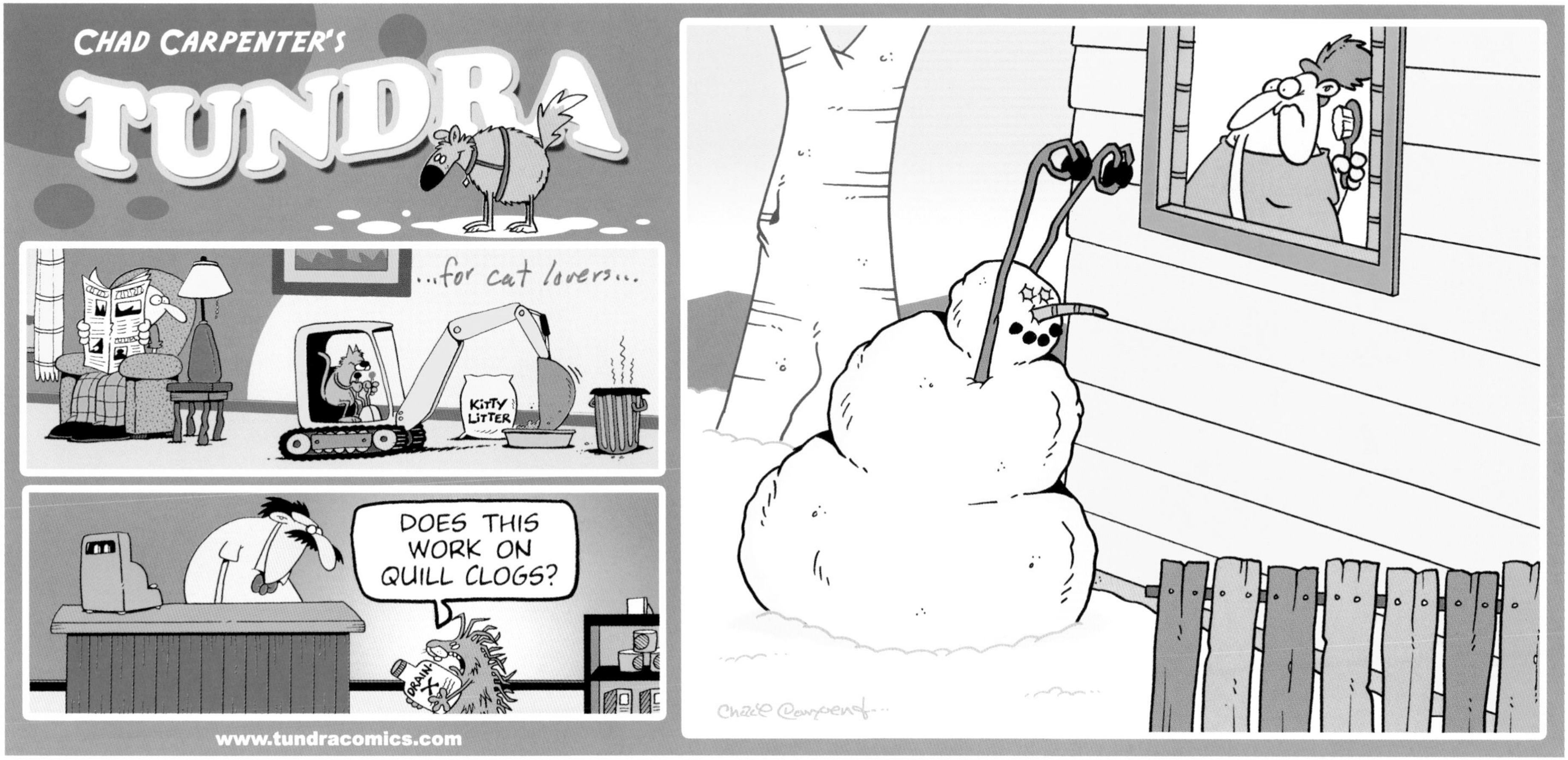
CHAD CARPENTER'S
TUNDRA
...for cat lovers...
KITTY LITTER
DOES THIS WORK ON QUILL CLOGS?
DRAIN-X
www.tundracomics.com

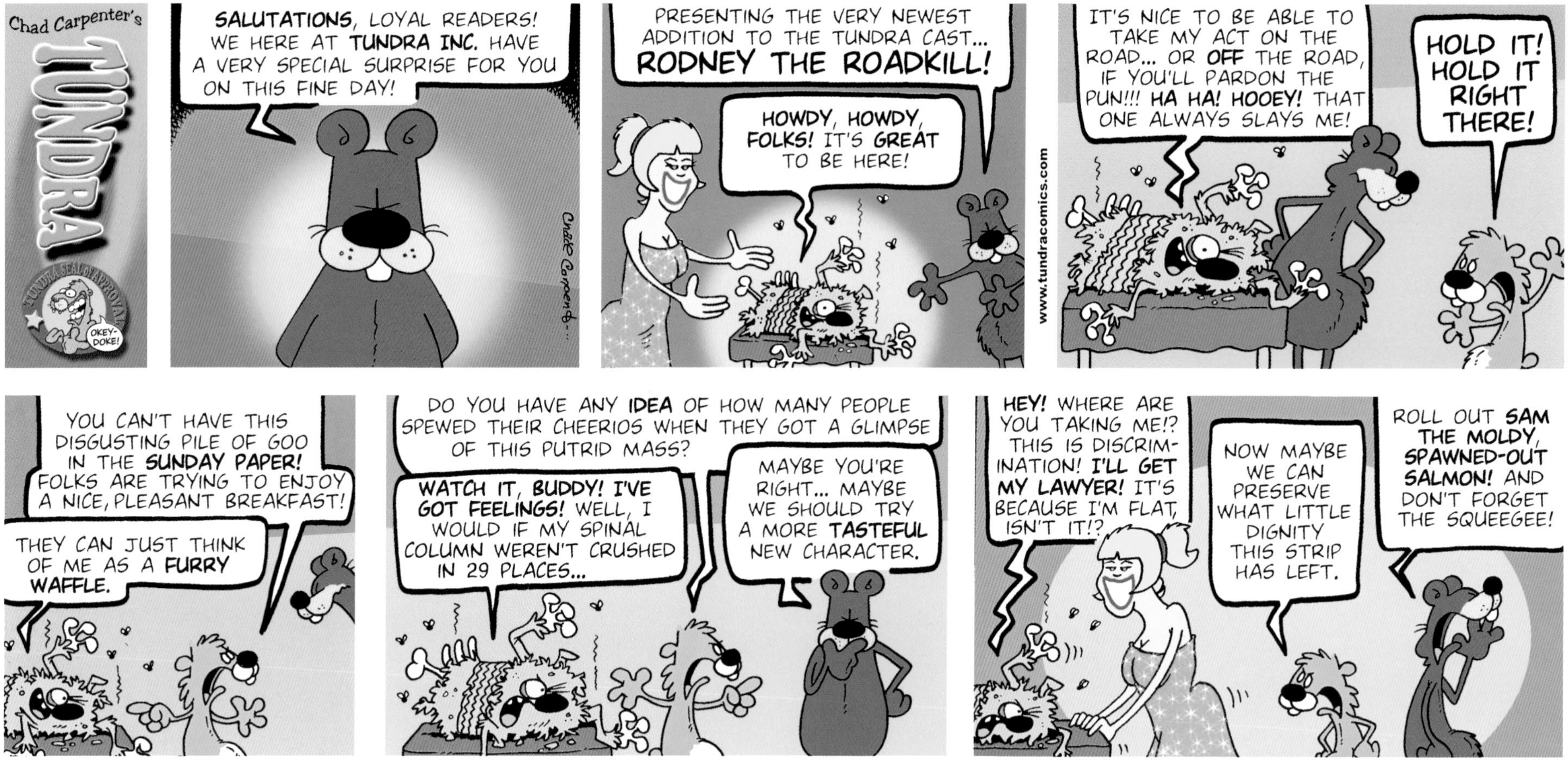
Chad Carpenter's
TUNDRA
TUNDRA SEAL OF APPROVAL
OKEY-DOKE!
SALUTATIONS, LOYAL READERS! WE HERE AT TUNDRA INC. HAVE A VERY SPECIAL SURPRISE FOR YOU ON THIS FINE DAY!
Chad Carpenter
PRESENTING THE VERY NEWEST ADDITION TO THE TUNDRA CAST... RODNEY THE ROADKILL!
HOWDY, HOWDY, FOLKS! IT'S GREAT TO BE HERE!
www.tundracomics.com
IT'S NICE TO BE ABLE TO TAKE MY ACT ON THE ROAD... OR OFF THE ROAD, IF YOU'LL PARDON THE PUN!!! HA HA! HOOEY! THAT ONE ALWAYS SLAYS ME!
HOLD IT! HOLD IT RIGHT THERE!
YOU CAN'T HAVE THIS DISGUSTING PILE OF GOO IN THE SUNDAY PAPER! FOLKS ARE TRYING TO ENJOY A NICE, PLEASANT BREAKFAST!
THEY CAN JUST THINK OF ME AS A FURRY WAFFLE.
DO YOU HAVE ANY IDEA OF HOW MANY PEOPLE SPEWED THEIR CHEERIOS WHEN THEY GOT A GLIMPSE OF THIS PUTRID MASS?
WATCH IT, BUDDY! I'VE GOT FEELINGS! WELL, I WOULD IF MY SPINAL COLUMN WEREN'T CRUSHED IN 29 PLACES...
MAYBE YOU'RE RIGHT... MAYBE WE SHOULD TRY A MORE TASTEFUL NEW CHARACTER.
HEY! WHERE ARE YOU TAKING ME!? THIS IS DISCRIMINATION! I'LL GET MY LAWYER! IT'S BECAUSE I'M FLAT, ISN'T IT!?
NOW MAYBE WE CAN PRESERVE WHAT LITTLE DIGNITY THIS STRIP HAS LEFT.
ROLL OUT SAM THE MOLDY, SPAWNED-OUT SALMON! AND DON'T FORGET THE SQUEEGEE!

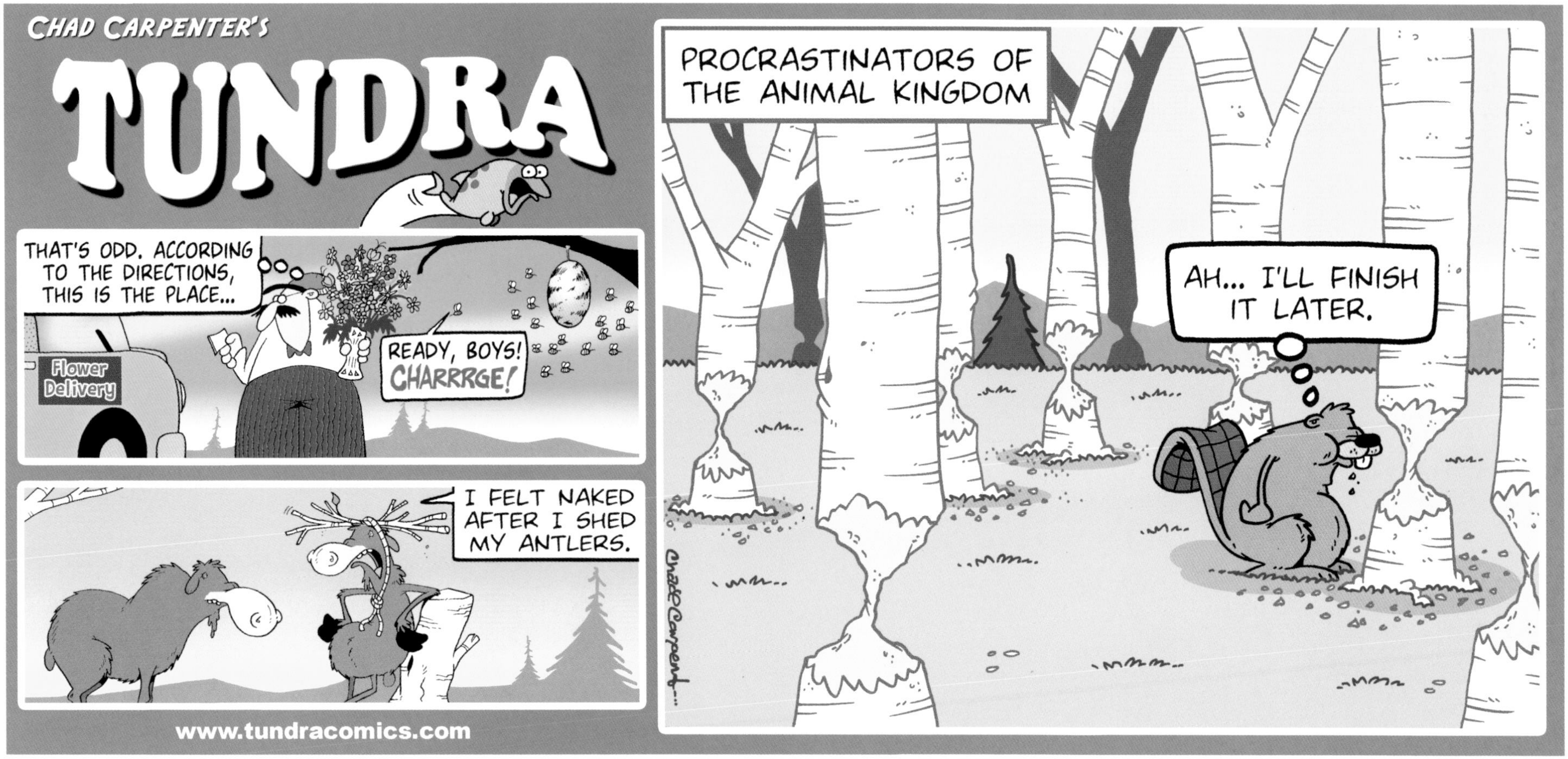
CHAD CARPENTER'S
TUNDRA
THAT'S ODD. ACCORDING TO THE DIRECTIONS, THIS IS THE PLACE...
Flower Delivery
READY, BOYS! CHARRRGE!
I FELT NAKED AFTER I SHED MY ANTLERS.
www.tundracomics.com
PROCRASTINATORS OF THE ANIMAL KINGDOM
AH... I'LL FINISH IT LATER.

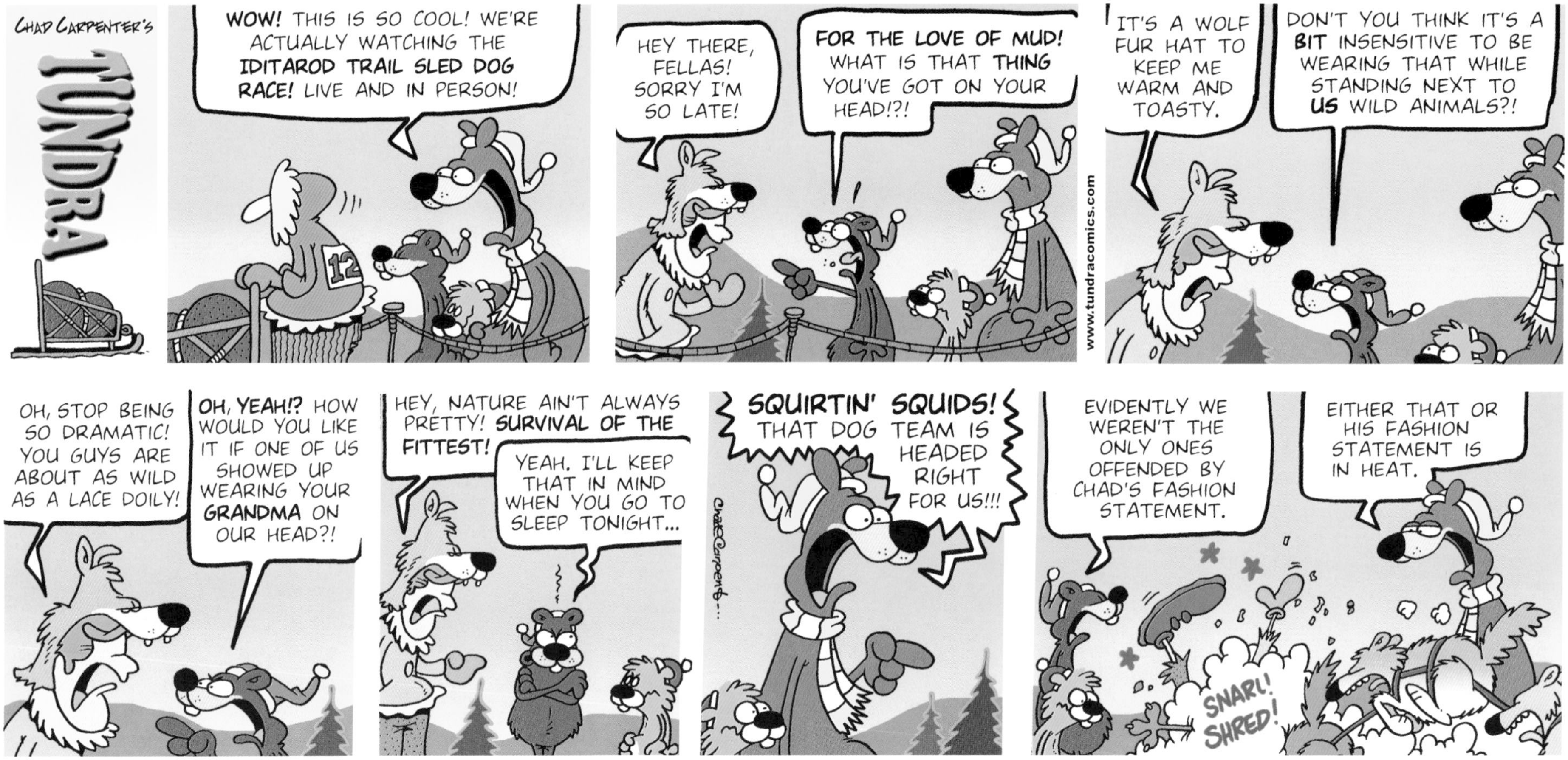
CHAD CARPENTER'S
TUNDRA
WOW! THIS IS SO COOL! WE'RE ACTUALLY WATCHING THE IDITAROD TRAIL SLED DOG RACE! LIVE AND IN PERSON!
HEY THERE, FELLAS! SORRY I'M SO LATE!
FOR THE LOVE OF MUD! WHAT IS THAT THING YOU'VE GOT ON YOUR HEAD!?!
www.tundracomics.com
IT'S A WOLF FUR HAT TO KEEP ME WARM AND TOASTY.
DON'T YOU THINK IT'S A BIT INSENSITIVE TO BE WEARING THAT WHILE STANDING NEXT TO US WILD ANIMALS?!
OH, STOP BEING SO DRAMATIC! YOU GUYS ARE ABOUT AS WILD AS A LACE DOILY!
OH, YEAH!? HOW WOULD YOU LIKE IT IF ONE OF US SHOWED UP WEARING YOUR GRANDMA ON OUR HEAD?!
HEY, NATURE AIN'T ALWAYS PRETTY! SURVIVAL OF THE FITTEST!
YEAH. I'LL KEEP THAT IN MIND WHEN YOU GO TO SLEEP TONIGHT...
SQUIRTIN' SQUIDS! THAT DOG TEAM IS HEADED RIGHT FOR US!!!
EVIDENTLY WE WEREN'T THE ONLY ONES OFFENDED BY CHAD'S FASHION STATEMENT.
EITHER THAT OR HIS FASHION STATEMENT IS IN HEAT.
SNARL! SHRED!

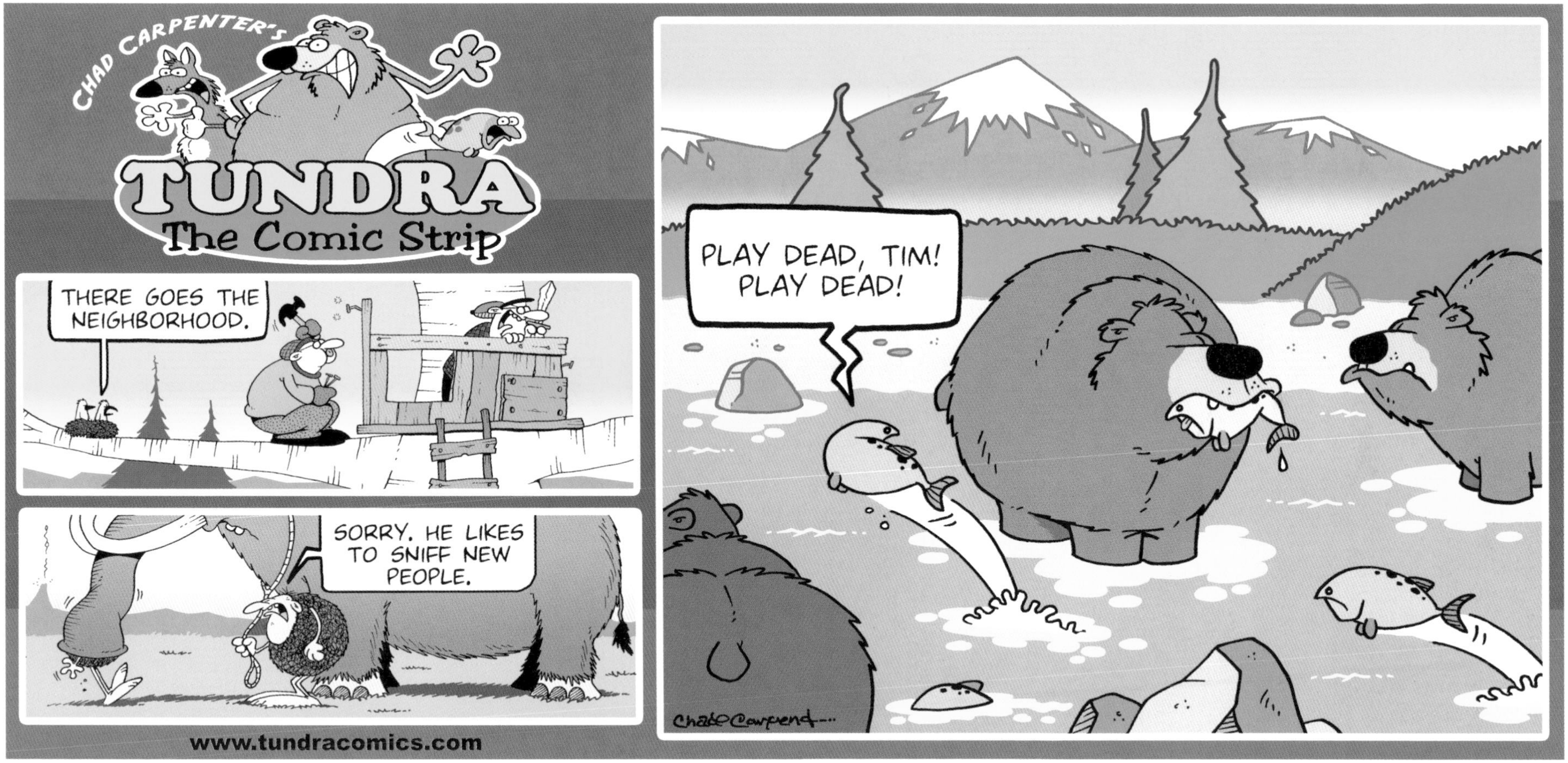
CHAD CARPENTER'S
TUNDRA
The Comic Strip
THERE GOES THE NEIGHBORHOOD.
SORRY. HE LIKES TO SNIFF NEW PEOPLE.
www.tundracomics.com
PLAY DEAD, TIM! PLAY DEAD!

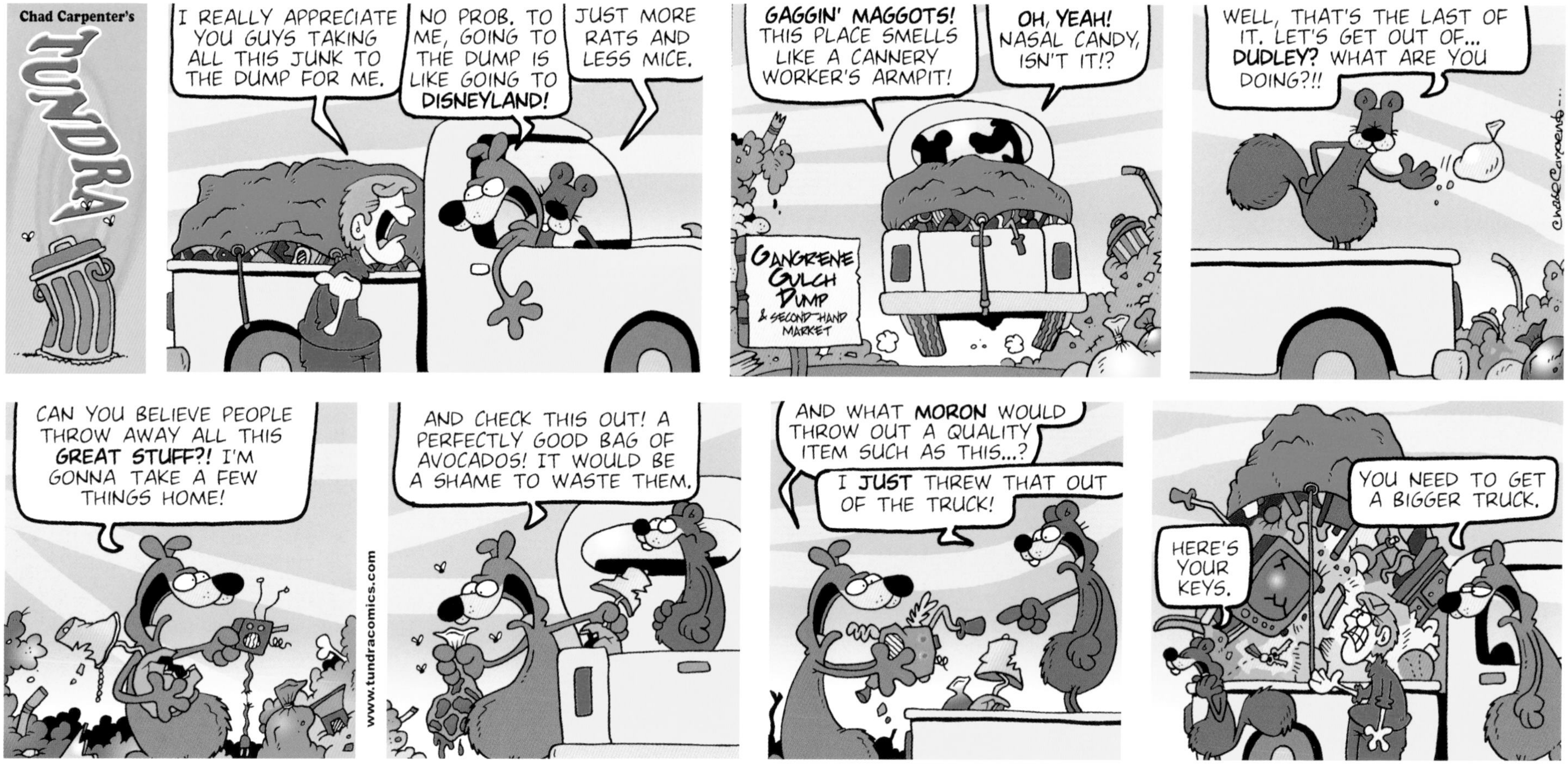
Chad Carpenter's
TUNDRA
I REALLY APPRECIATE YOU GUYS TAKING ALL THIS JUNK TO THE DUMP FOR ME.
NO PROB. TO ME, GOING TO THE DUMP IS LIKE GOING TO DISNEYLAND!
JUST MORE RATS AND LESS MICE.
GAGGIN' MAGGOTS! THIS PLACE SMELLS LIKE A CANNERY WORKER'S ARMPIT!
OH, YEAH! NASAL CANDY, ISN'T IT!?
GANGRENE GULCH DUMP & SECOND-HAND MARKET
WELL, THAT'S THE LAST OF IT. LET'S GET OUT OF... DUDLEY? WHAT ARE YOU DOING?!!
CAN YOU BELIEVE PEOPLE THROW AWAY ALL THIS GREAT STUFF?! I'M GONNA TAKE A FEW THINGS HOME!
www.tundracomics.com
AND CHECK THIS OUT! A PERFECTLY GOOD BAG OF AVOCADOS! IT WOULD BE A SHAME TO WASTE THEM.
AND WHAT MORON WOULD THROW OUT A QUALITY ITEM SUCH AS THIS...?
I JUST THREW THAT OUT OF THE TRUCK!
HERE'S YOUR KEYS.
YOU NEED TO GET A BIGGER TRUCK.

He does a great "bear drawing"...

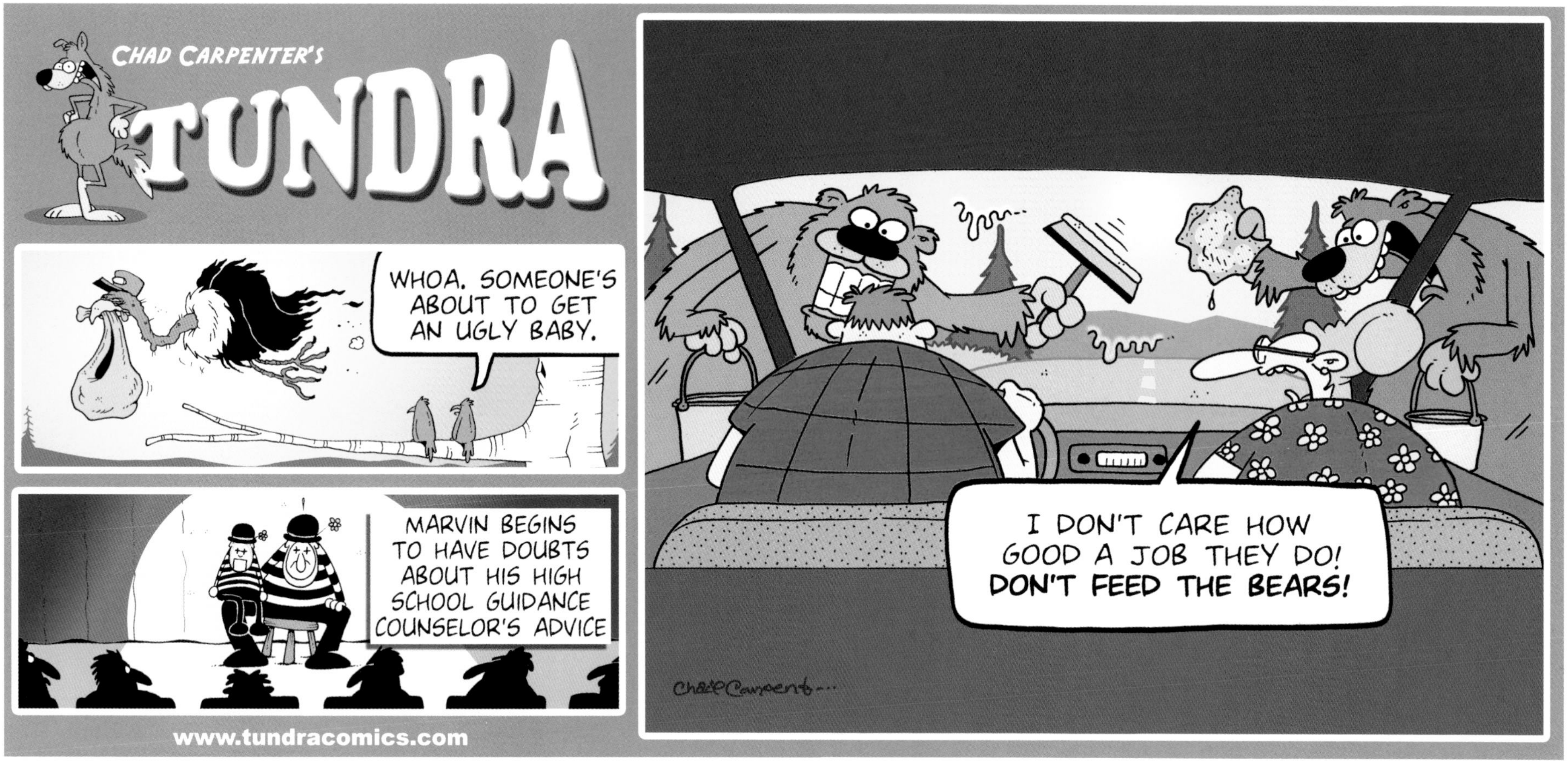
CHAD CARPENTER'S
TUNDRA
WHOA. SOMEONE'S ABOUT TO GET AN UGLY BABY.
MARVIN BEGINS TO HAVE DOUBTS ABOUT HIS HIGH SCHOOL GUIDANCE COUNSELOR'S ADVICE
www.tundracomics.com
I DON'T CARE HOW GOOD A JOB THEY DO! **DON'T FEED THE BEARS!**

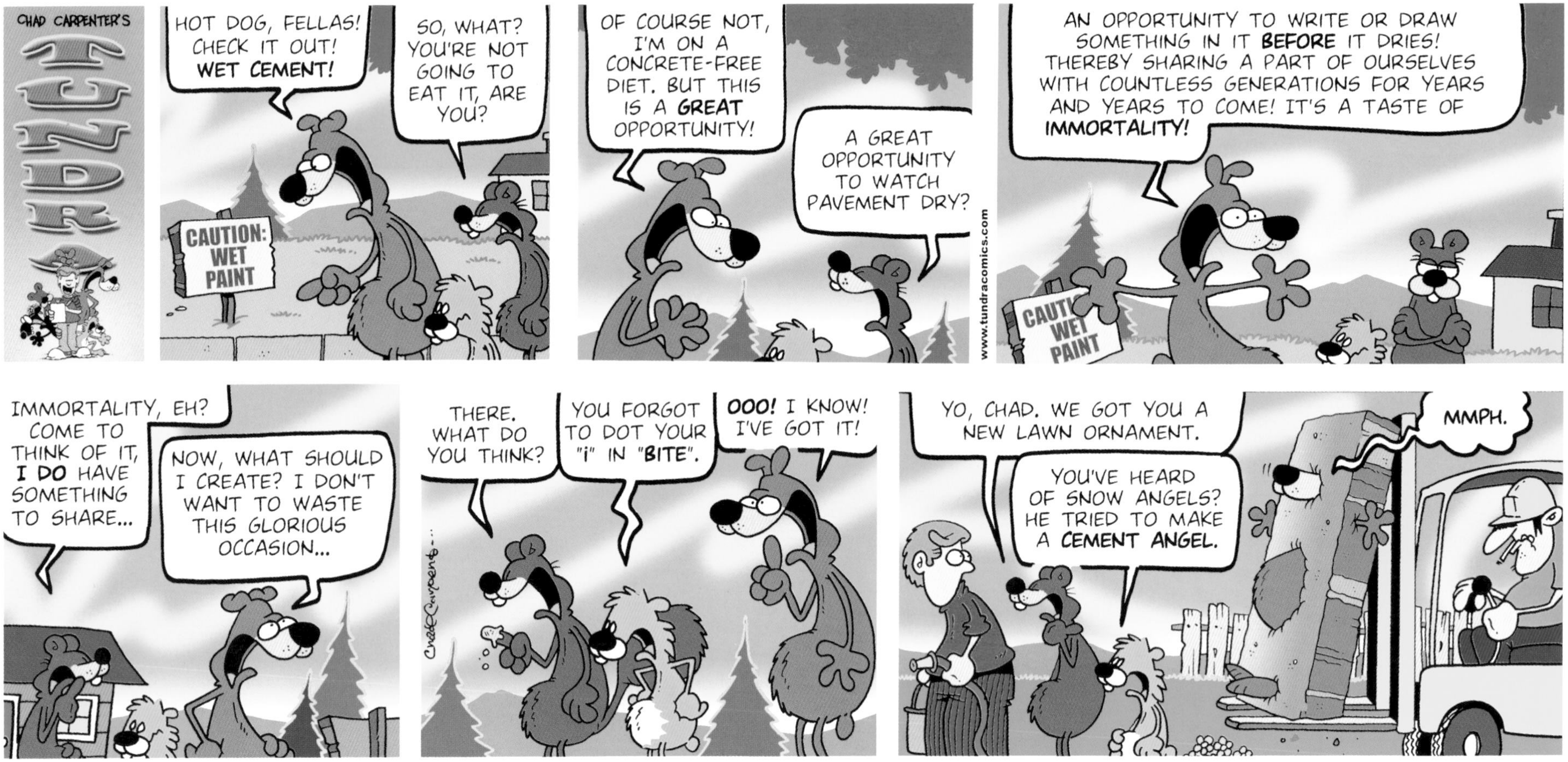
CHAD CARPENTER'S
TUNDRA
HOT DOG, FELLAS! CHECK IT OUT! WET CEMENT!
CAUTION: WET PAINT
SO, WHAT? YOU'RE NOT GOING TO EAT IT, ARE YOU?
OF COURSE NOT, I'M ON A CONCRETE-FREE DIET. BUT THIS IS A GREAT OPPORTUNITY!
A GREAT OPPORTUNITY TO WATCH PAVEMENT DRY?
www.tundracomics.com
AN OPPORTUNITY TO WRITE OR DRAW SOMETHING IN IT BEFORE IT DRIES! THEREBY SHARING A PART OF OURSELVES WITH COUNTLESS GENERATIONS FOR YEARS AND YEARS TO COME! IT'S A TASTE OF IMMORTALITY!
IMMORTALITY, EH? COME TO THINK OF IT, I DO HAVE SOMETHING TO SHARE...
NOW, WHAT SHOULD I CREATE? I DON'T WANT TO WASTE THIS GLORIOUS OCCASION...
THERE. WHAT DO YOU THINK?
YOU FORGOT TO DOT YOUR "i" IN "BITE".
OOO! I KNOW! I'VE GOT IT!
YO, CHAD. WE GOT YOU A NEW LAWN ORNAMENT.
MMPH.
YOU'VE HEARD OF SNOW ANGELS? HE TRIED TO MAKE A CEMENT ANGEL.

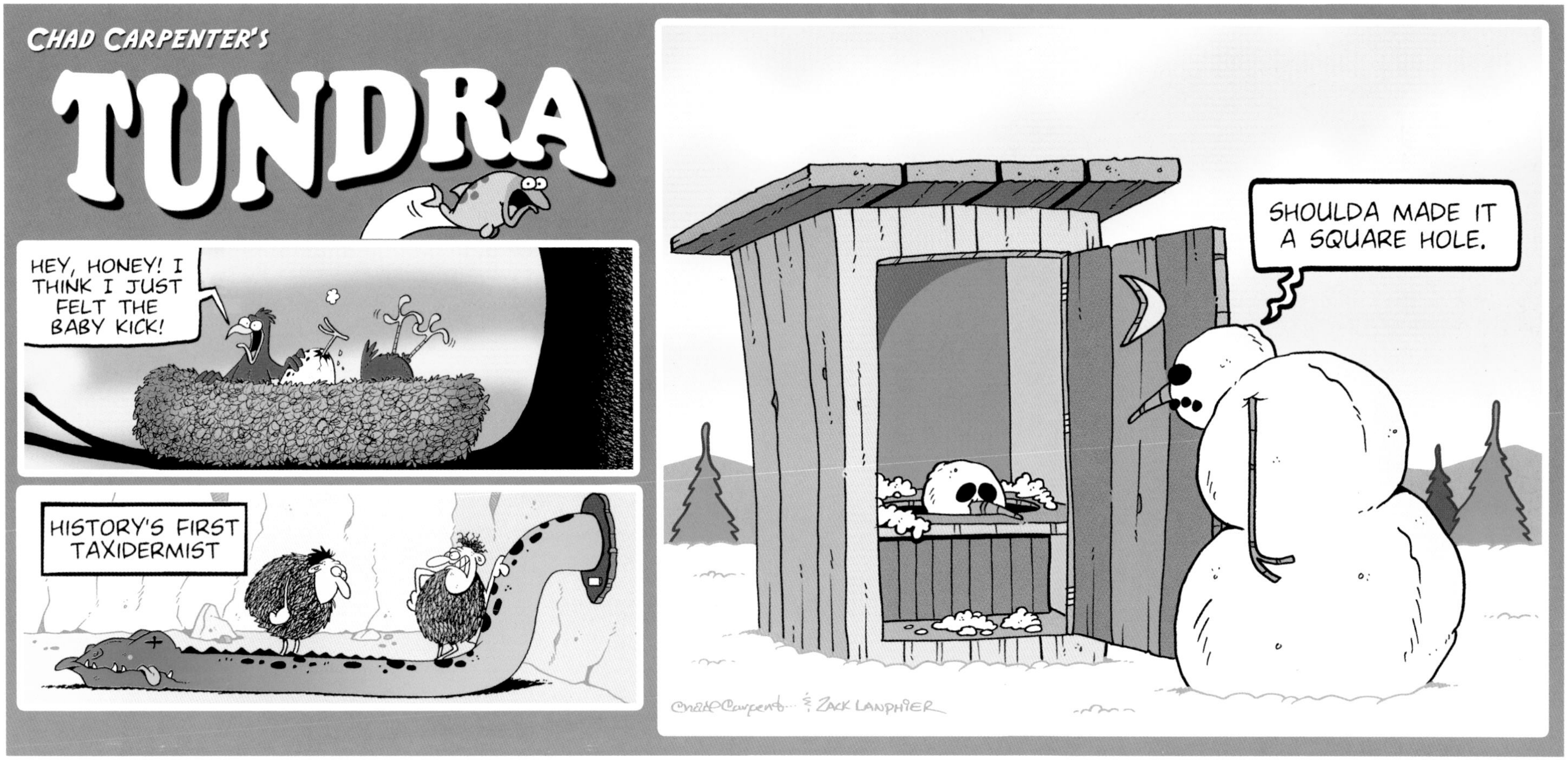
CHAD CARPENTER'S
TUNDRA
HEY, HONEY! I THINK I JUST FELT THE BABY KICK!
HISTORY'S FIRST TAXIDERMIST
SHOULDA MADE IT A SQUARE HOLE.
ZACK LANPHIER

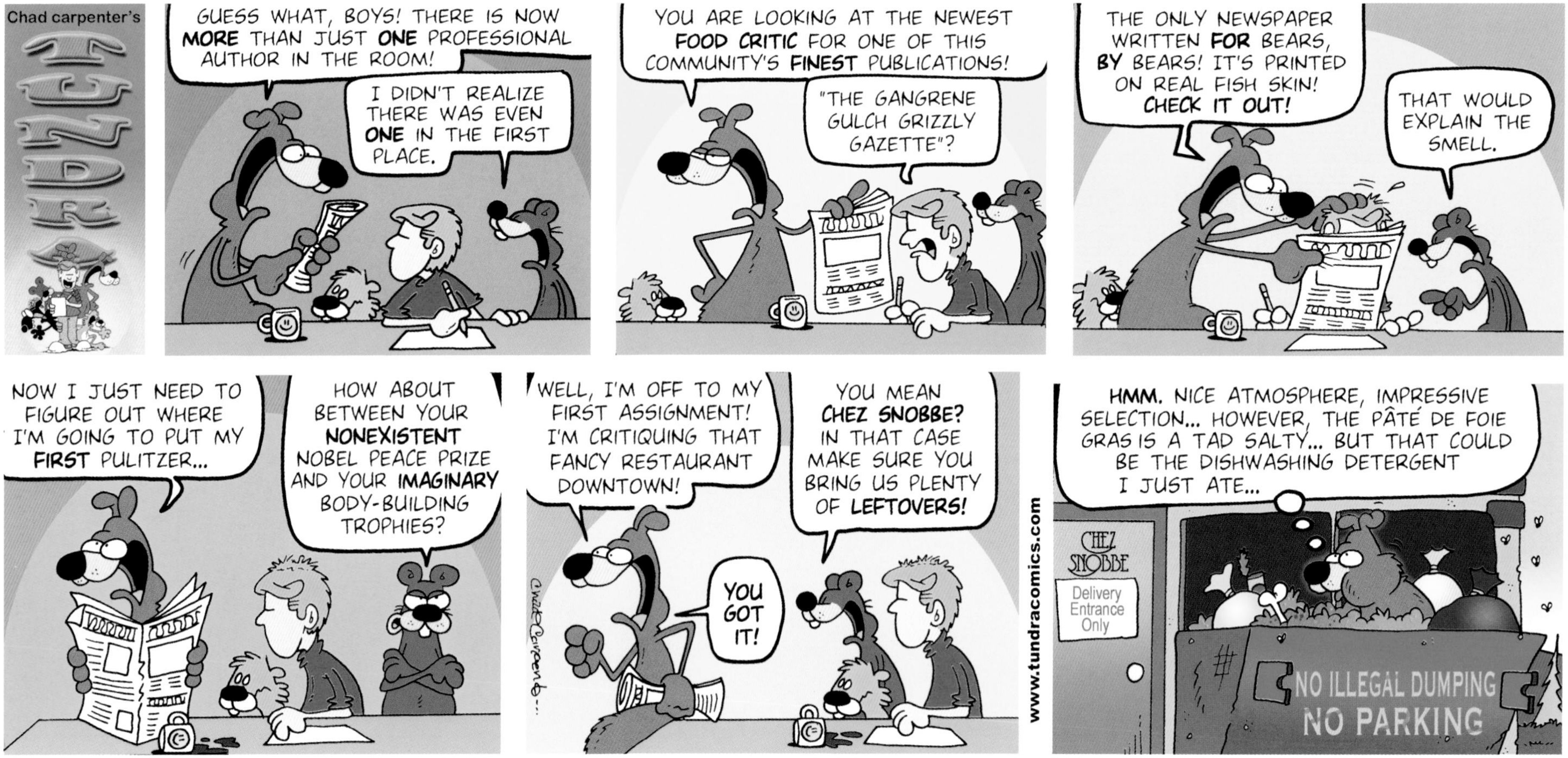
Chad carpenter's
TUNDRA
GUESS WHAT, BOYS! THERE IS NOW MORE THAN JUST ONE PROFESSIONAL AUTHOR IN THE ROOM!
I DIDN'T REALIZE THERE WAS EVEN ONE IN THE FIRST PLACE.
YOU ARE LOOKING AT THE NEWEST FOOD CRITIC FOR ONE OF THIS COMMUNITY'S FINEST PUBLICATIONS!
"THE GANGRENE GULCH GRIZZLY GAZETTE"?
THE ONLY NEWSPAPER WRITTEN FOR BEARS, BY BEARS! IT'S PRINTED ON REAL FISH SKIN! CHECK IT OUT!
THAT WOULD EXPLAIN THE SMELL.
NOW I JUST NEED TO FIGURE OUT WHERE I'M GOING TO PUT MY FIRST PULITZER...
HOW ABOUT BETWEEN YOUR NONEXISTENT NOBEL PEACE PRIZE AND YOUR IMAGINARY BODY-BUILDING TROPHIES?
WELL, I'M OFF TO MY FIRST ASSIGNMENT! I'M CRITIQUING THAT FANCY RESTAURANT DOWNTOWN!
YOU MEAN CHEZ SNOBBE? IN THAT CASE MAKE SURE YOU BRING US PLENTY OF LEFTOVERS!
YOU GOT IT!
www.tundracomics.com
HMM. NICE ATMOSPHERE, IMPRESSIVE SELECTION... HOWEVER, THE PÂTÉ DE FOIE GRAS IS A TAD SALTY... BUT THAT COULD BE THE DISHWASHING DETERGENT I JUST ATE...
CHEZ SNOBBE
Delivery Entrance Only
NO ILLEGAL DUMPING
NO PARKING

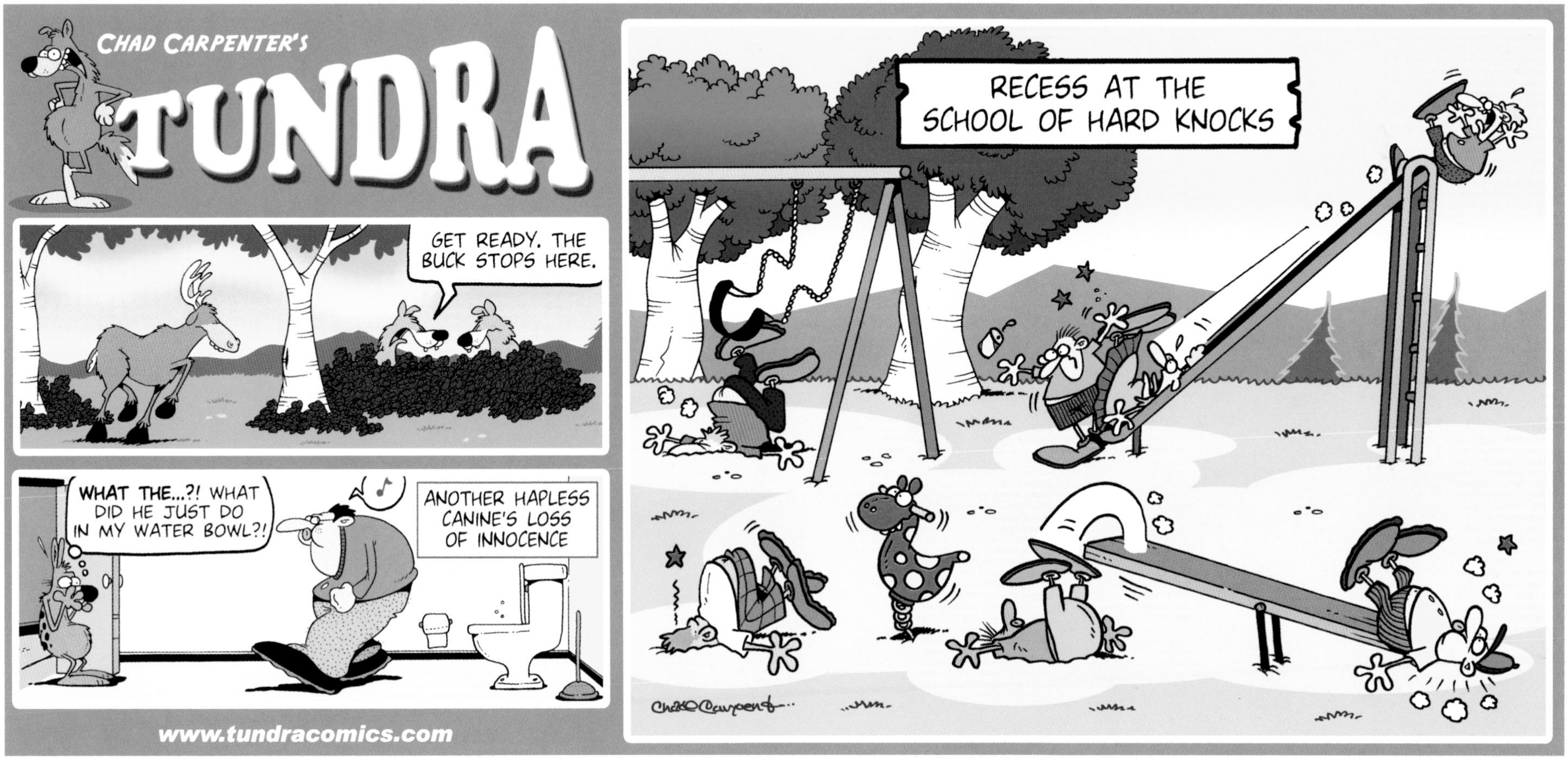
CHAD CARPENTER'S
TUNDRA
GET READY. THE BUCK STOPS HERE.
WHAT THE...?! WHAT DID HE JUST DO IN MY WATER BOWL?!
ANOTHER HAPLESS CANINE'S LOSS OF INNOCENCE
www.tundracomics.com
RECESS AT THE SCHOOL OF HARD KNOCKS

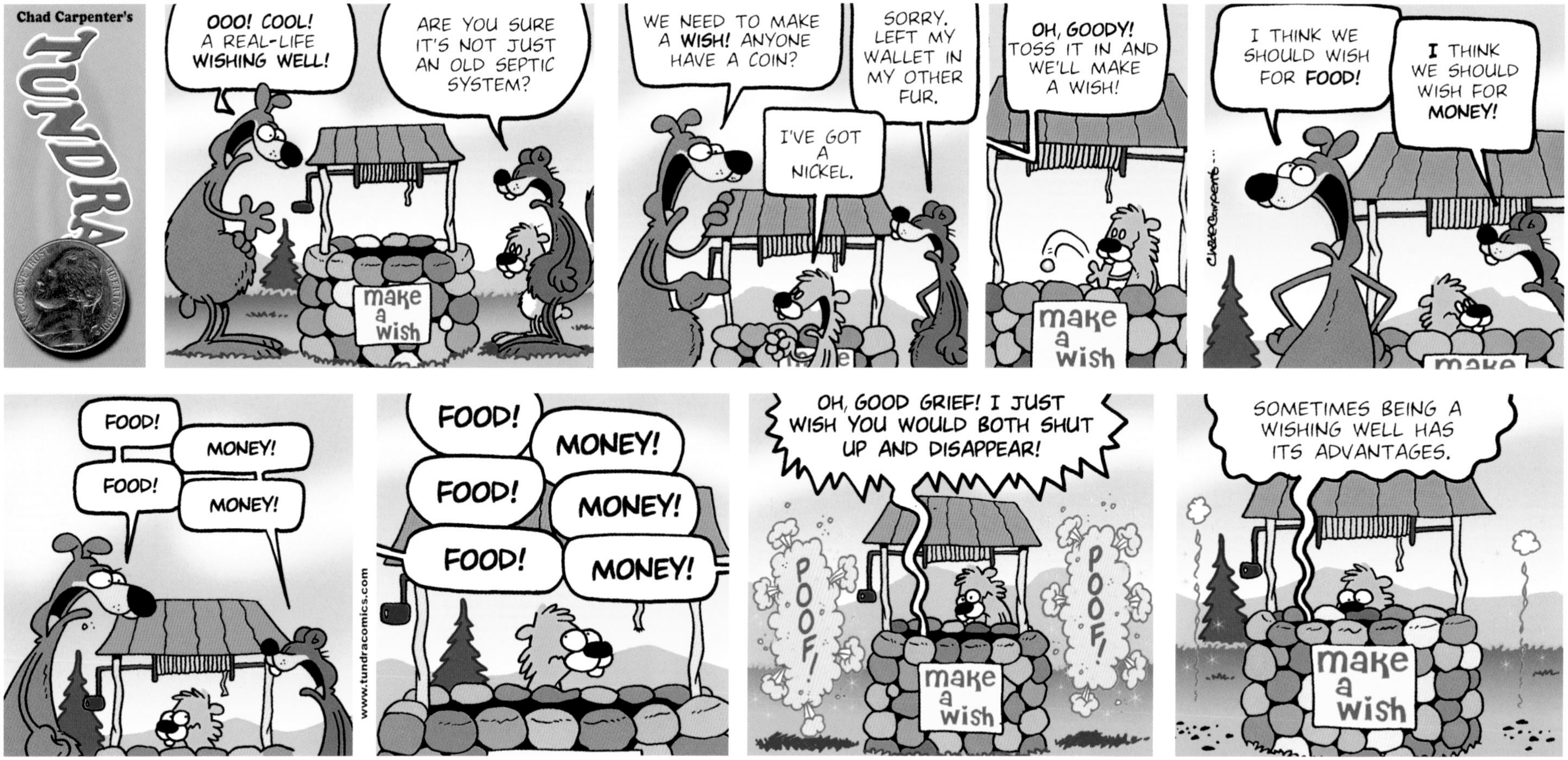
Chad Carpenter's
TUNDRA
OOO! COOL! A REAL-LIFE WISHING WELL!
ARE YOU SURE IT'S NOT JUST AN OLD SEPTIC SYSTEM?
make a wish
WE NEED TO MAKE A WISH! ANYONE HAVE A COIN?
I'VE GOT A NICKEL.
SORRY. LEFT MY WALLET IN MY OTHER FUR.
OH, GOODY! TOSS IT IN AND WE'LL MAKE A WISH!
make a wish
I THINK WE SHOULD WISH FOR FOOD!
I THINK WE SHOULD WISH FOR MONEY!
FOOD!
MONEY!
FOOD!
MONEY!
www.tundracomics.com
FOOD!
MONEY!
FOOD!
MONEY!
FOOD!
MONEY!
OH, GOOD GRIEF! I JUST WISH YOU WOULD BOTH SHUT UP AND DISAPPEAR!
POOF!
POOF!
make a wish
SOMETIMES BEING A WISHING WELL HAS ITS ADVANTAGES.
make a wish

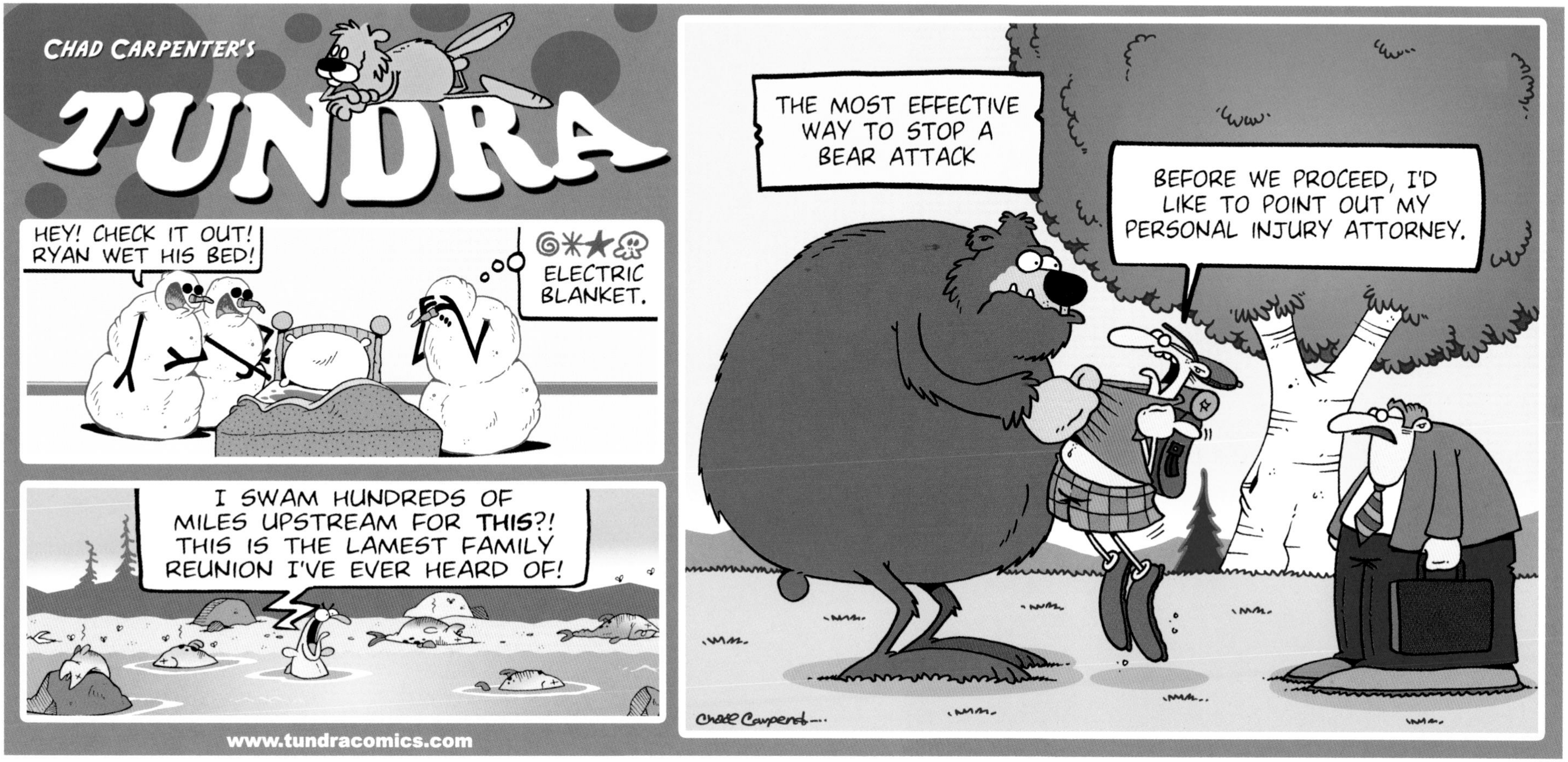
CHAD CARPENTER'S
TUNDRA
HEY! CHECK IT OUT! RYAN WET HIS BED!
ELECTRIC BLANKET.
I SWAM HUNDREDS OF MILES UPSTREAM FOR THIS?! THIS IS THE LAMEST FAMILY REUNION I'VE EVER HEARD OF!
www.tundracomics.com
THE MOST EFFECTIVE WAY TO STOP A BEAR ATTACK
BEFORE WE PROCEED, I'D LIKE TO POINT OUT MY PERSONAL INJURY ATTORNEY.

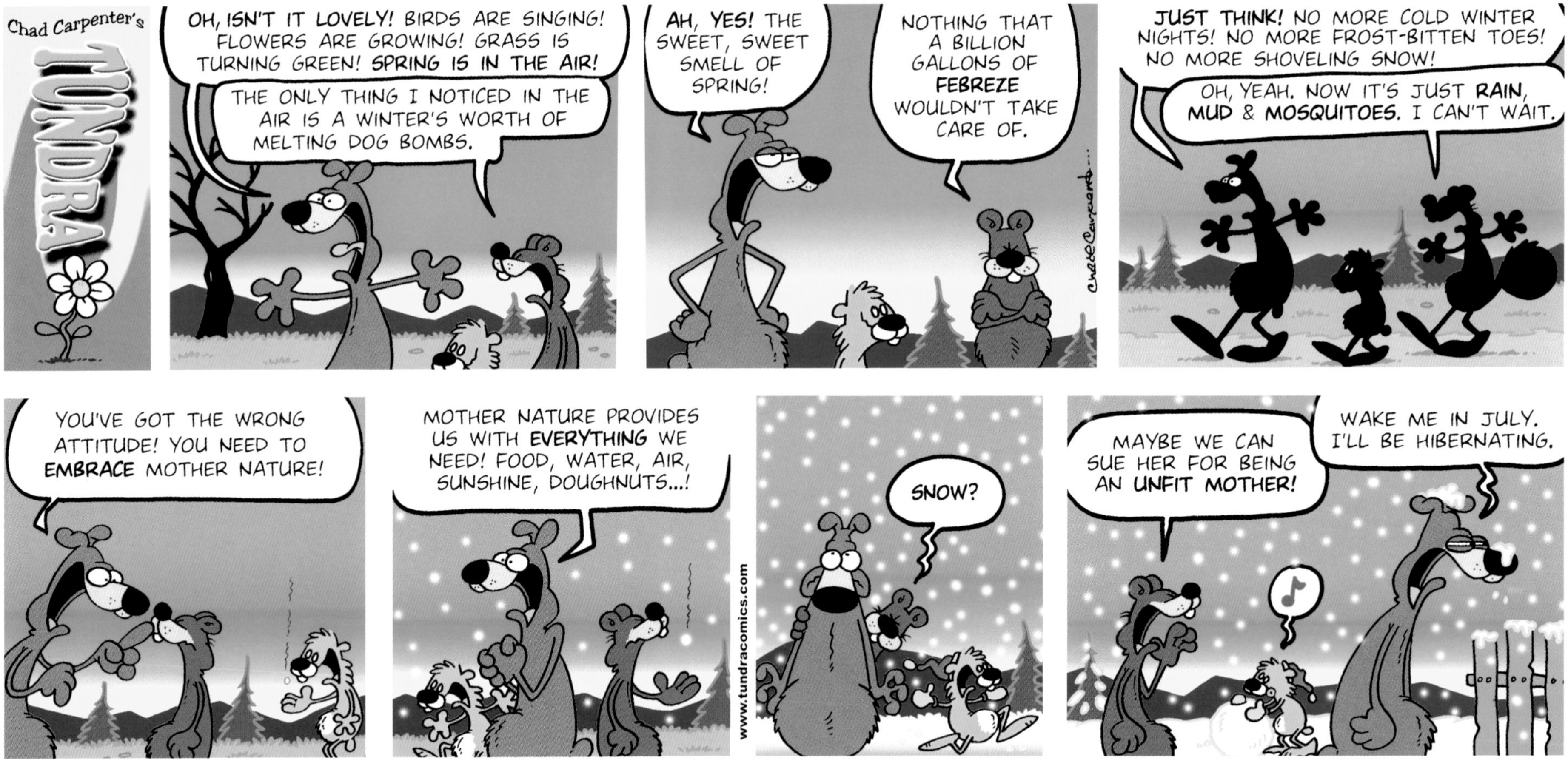
Chad Carpenter's
TUNDRA
OH, ISN'T IT LOVELY! BIRDS ARE SINGING! FLOWERS ARE GROWING! GRASS IS TURNING GREEN! SPRING IS IN THE AIR!
THE ONLY THING I NOTICED IN THE AIR IS A WINTER'S WORTH OF MELTING DOG BOMBS.
AH, YES! THE SWEET, SWEET SMELL OF SPRING!
NOTHING THAT A BILLION GALLONS OF FEBREZE WOULDN'T TAKE CARE OF.
JUST THINK! NO MORE COLD WINTER NIGHTS! NO MORE FROST-BITTEN TOES! NO MORE SHOVELING SNOW!
OH, YEAH. NOW IT'S JUST RAIN, MUD & MOSQUITOES. I CAN'T WAIT.
YOU'VE GOT THE WRONG ATTITUDE! YOU NEED TO EMBRACE MOTHER NATURE!
MOTHER NATURE PROVIDES US WITH EVERYTHING WE NEED! FOOD, WATER, AIR, SUNSHINE, DOUGHNUTS...!
www.tundracomics.com
SNOW?
MAYBE WE CAN SUE HER FOR BEING AN UNFIT MOTHER!
WAKE ME IN JULY. I'LL BE HIBERNATING.

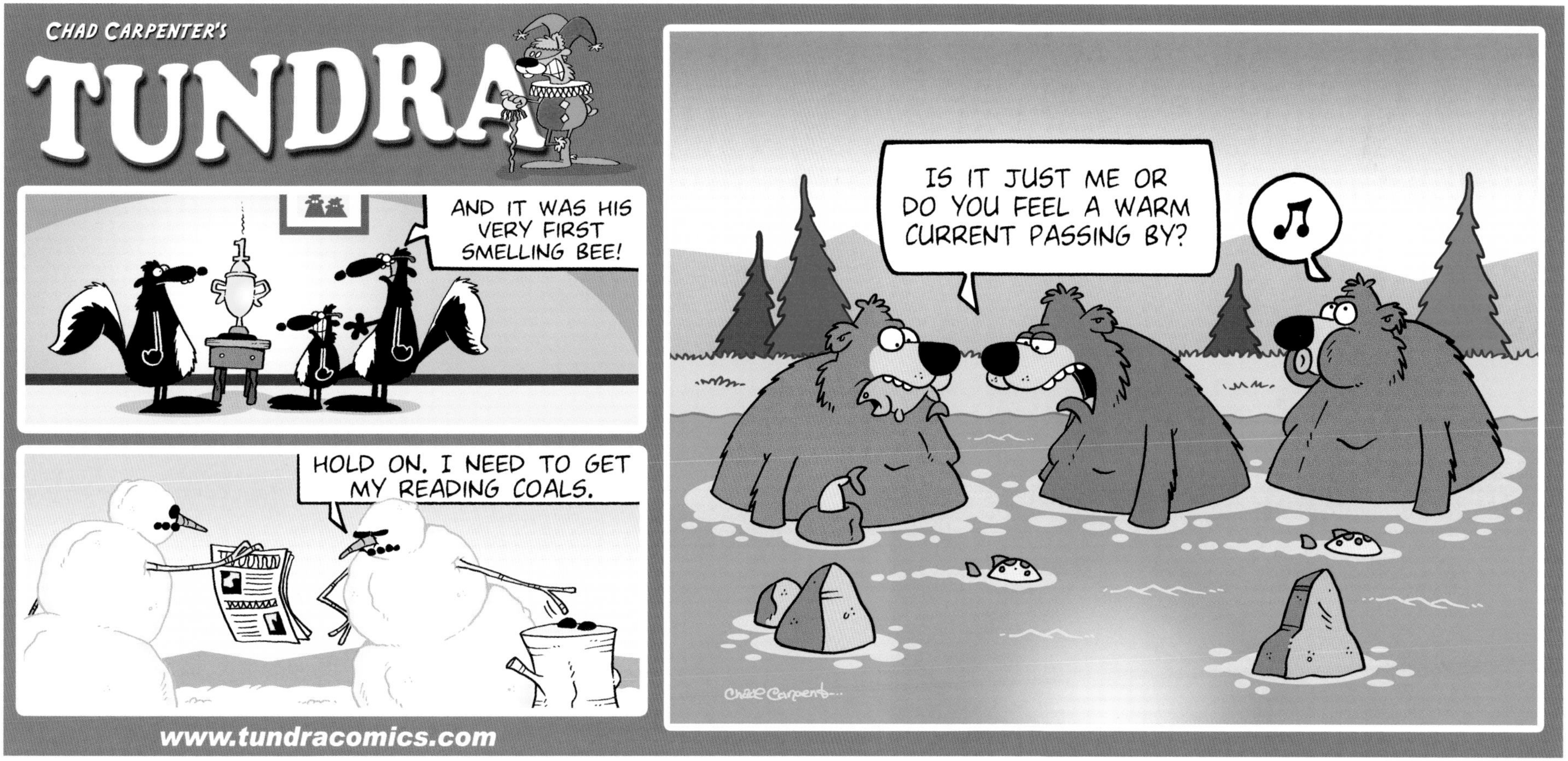
CHAD CARPENTER'S
TUNDRA
AND IT WAS HIS VERY FIRST SMELLING BEE!
HOLD ON. I NEED TO GET MY READING COALS.
IS IT JUST ME OR DO YOU FEEL A WARM CURRENT PASSING BY?
www.tundracomics.com

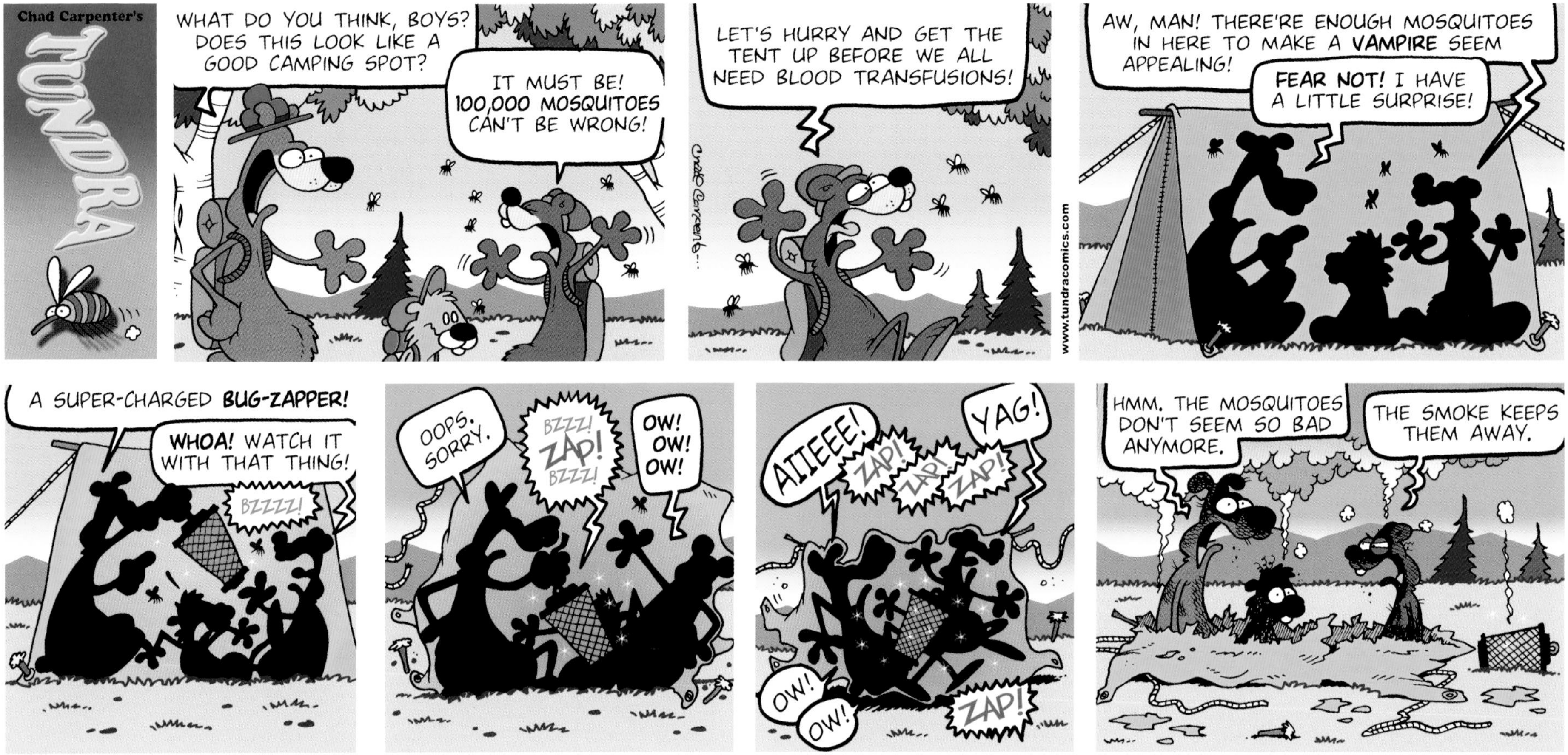
Chad Carpenter's
TUNDRA
WHAT DO YOU THINK, BOYS? DOES THIS LOOK LIKE A GOOD CAMPING SPOT?
IT MUST BE! 100,000 MOSQUITOES CAN'T BE WRONG!
LET'S HURRY AND GET THE TENT UP BEFORE WE ALL NEED BLOOD TRANSFUSIONS!
www.tundracomics.com
AW, MAN! THERE'RE ENOUGH MOSQUITOES IN HERE TO MAKE A VAMPIRE SEEM APPEALING!
FEAR NOT! I HAVE A LITTLE SURPRISE!
A SUPER-CHARGED BUG-ZAPPER!
WHOA! WATCH IT WITH THAT THING!
BZZZZ!
OOPS. SORRY.
BZZZ! ZAP! BZZZ!
OW! OW! OW!
AIIEEE!
ZAP! ZAP! ZAP!
YAG!
OW! OW!
ZAP!
HMM. THE MOSQUITOES DON'T SEEM SO BAD ANYMORE.
THE SMOKE KEEPS THEM AWAY.

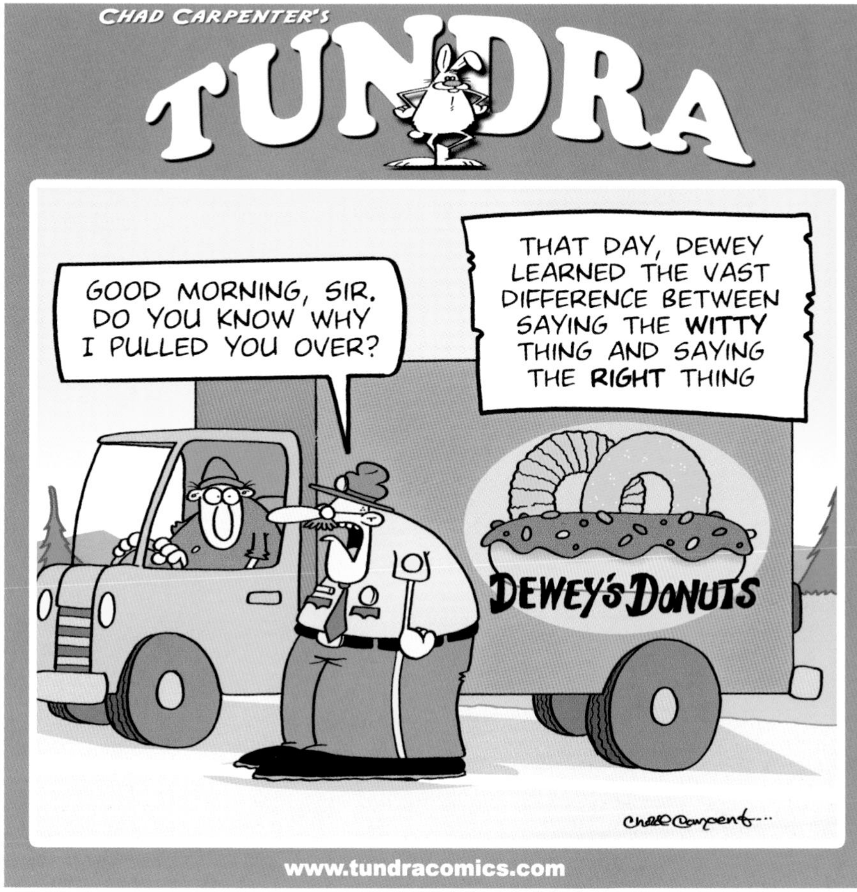
CHAD CARPENTER'S
TUNDRA
GOOD MORNING, SIR. DO YOU KNOW WHY I PULLED YOU OVER?
THAT DAY, DEWEY LEARNED THE VAST DIFFERENCE BETWEEN SAYING THE **WITTY** THING AND SAYING THE **RIGHT** THING
DEWEY'S DONUTS
www.tundracomics.com

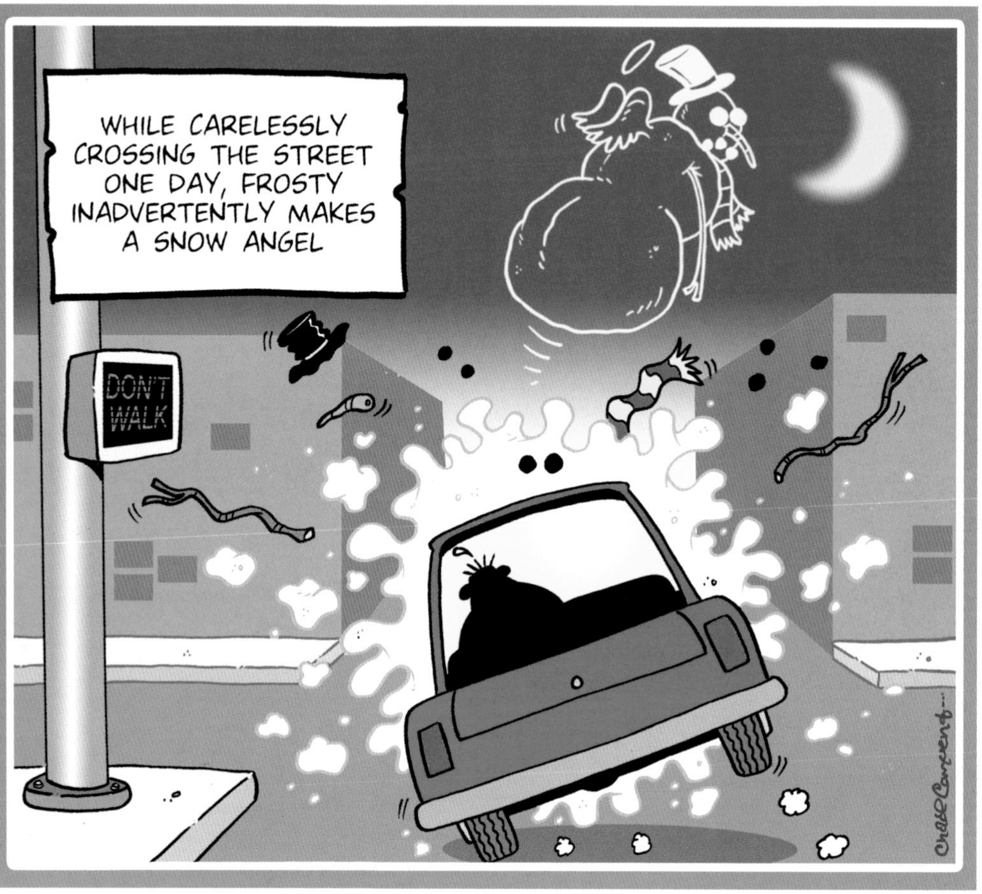
WHILE CARELESSLY CROSSING THE STREET ONE DAY, FROSTY INADVERTENTLY MAKES A SNOW ANGEL
DON'T WALK

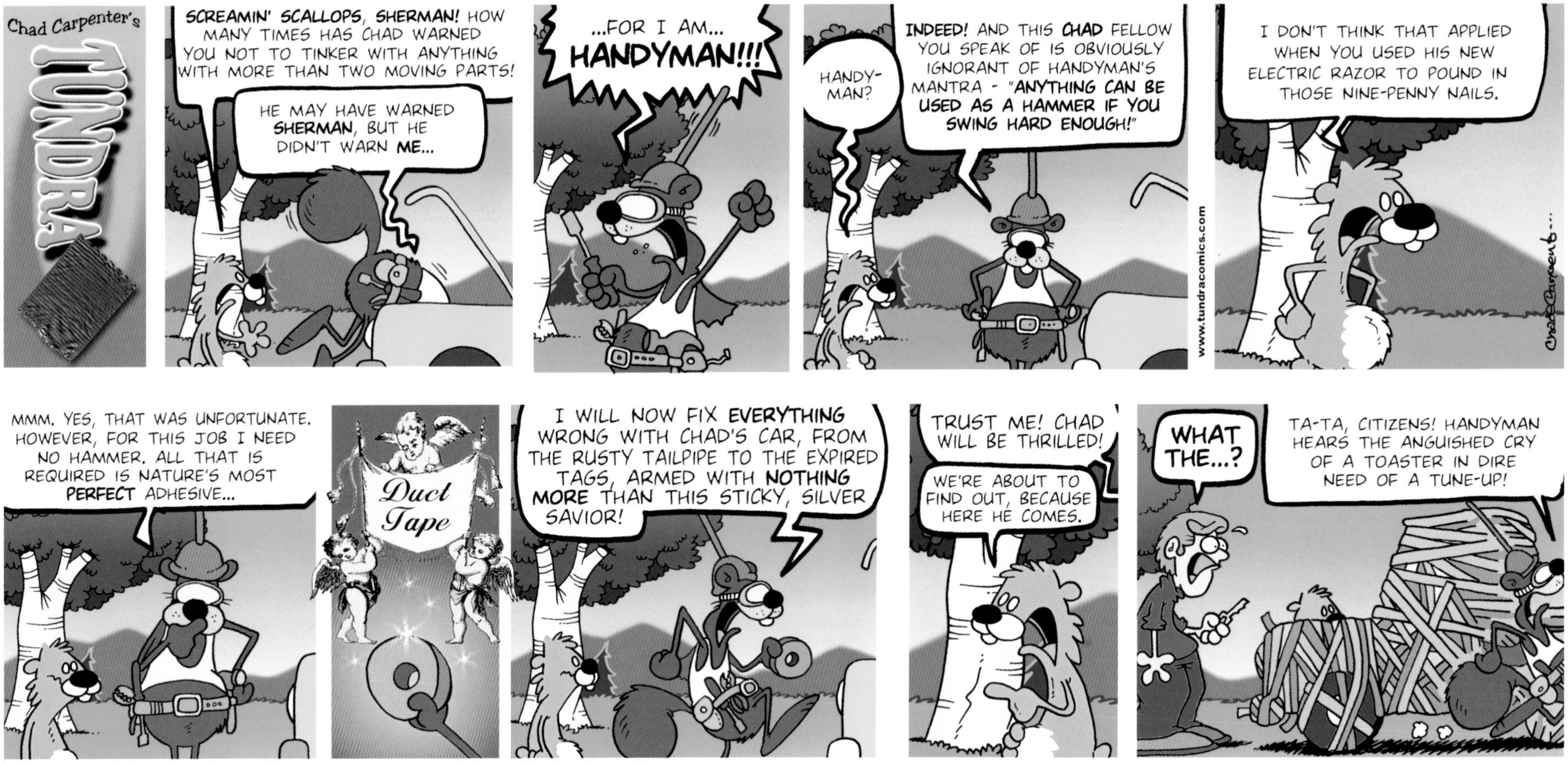
Chad Carpenter's
TUNDRA
SCREAMIN' SCALLOPS, SHERMAN! HOW MANY TIMES HAS CHAD WARNED YOU NOT TO TINKER WITH ANYTHING WITH MORE THAN TWO MOVING PARTS!
HE MAY HAVE WARNED SHERMAN, BUT HE DIDN'T WARN ME...
...FOR I AM... HANDYMAN!!!
HANDY-MAN?
INDEED! AND THIS CHAD FELLOW YOU SPEAK OF IS OBVIOUSLY IGNORANT OF HANDYMAN'S MANTRA - "ANYTHING CAN BE USED AS A HAMMER IF YOU SWING HARD ENOUGH!"
www.tundracomics.com
I DON'T THINK THAT APPLIED WHEN YOU USED HIS NEW ELECTRIC RAZOR TO POUND IN THOSE NINE-PENNY NAILS.
MMM. YES, THAT WAS UNFORTUNATE. HOWEVER, FOR THIS JOB I NEED NO HAMMER. ALL THAT IS REQUIRED IS NATURE'S MOST PERFECT ADHESIVE...
Duct Tape
I WILL NOW FIX EVERYTHING WRONG WITH CHAD'S CAR, FROM THE RUSTY TAILPIPE TO THE EXPIRED TAGS, ARMED WITH NOTHING MORE THAN THIS STICKY, SILVER SAVIOR!
TRUST ME! CHAD WILL BE THRILLED!
WE'RE ABOUT TO FIND OUT, BECAUSE HERE HE COMES.
WHAT THE...?
TA-TA, CITIZENS! HANDYMAN HEARS THE ANGUISHED CRY OF A TOASTER IN DIRE NEED OF A TUNE-UP!

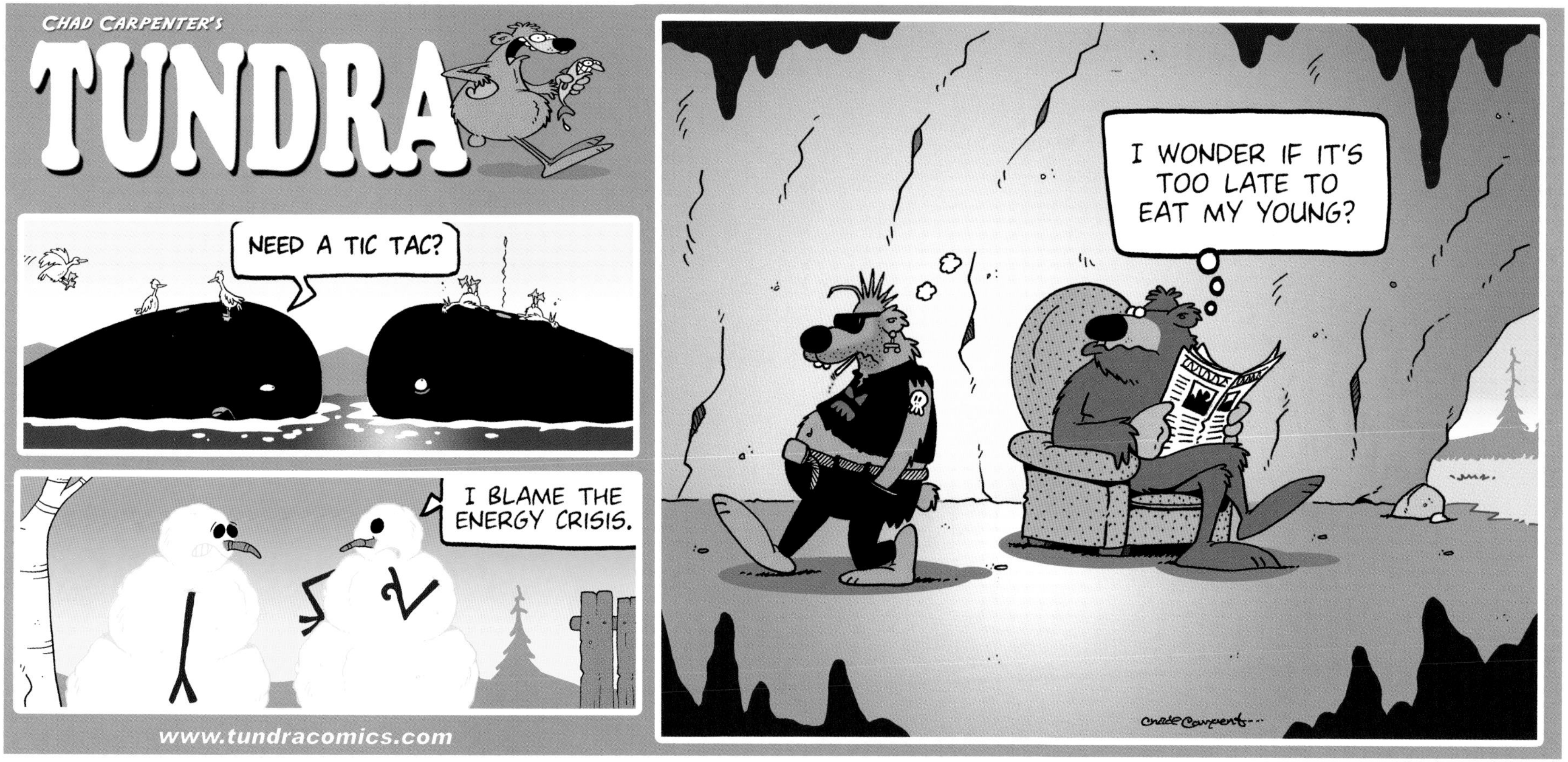
CHAD CARPENTER'S
TUNDRA
NEED A TIC TAC?
I BLAME THE ENERGY CRISIS.
I WONDER IF IT'S TOO LATE TO EAT MY YOUNG?
www.tundracomics.com

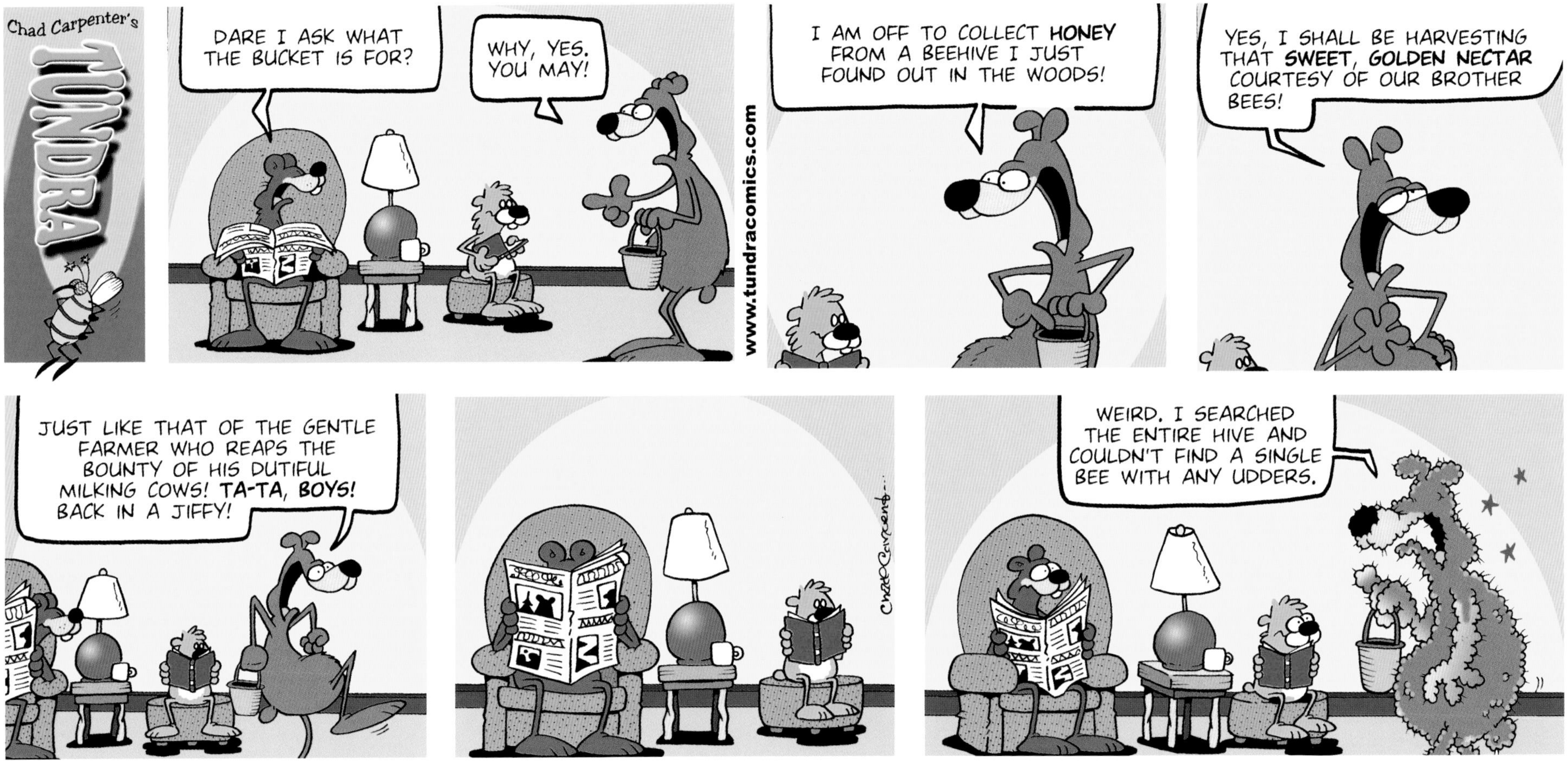
Chad Carpenter's
TUNDRA
DARE I ASK WHAT THE BUCKET IS FOR?
WHY, YES. YOU MAY!
www.tundracomics.com
I AM OFF TO COLLECT **HONEY** FROM A BEEHIVE I JUST FOUND OUT IN THE WOODS!
YES, I SHALL BE HARVESTING THAT **SWEET, GOLDEN NECTAR** COURTESY OF OUR BROTHER BEES!
JUST LIKE THAT OF THE GENTLE FARMER WHO REAPS THE BOUNTY OF HIS DUTIFUL MILKING COWS! **TA-TA, BOYS!** BACK IN A JIFFY!
WEIRD. I SEARCHED THE ENTIRE HIVE AND COULDN'T FIND A SINGLE BEE WITH ANY UDDERS.

...in my "Top 3" ☺

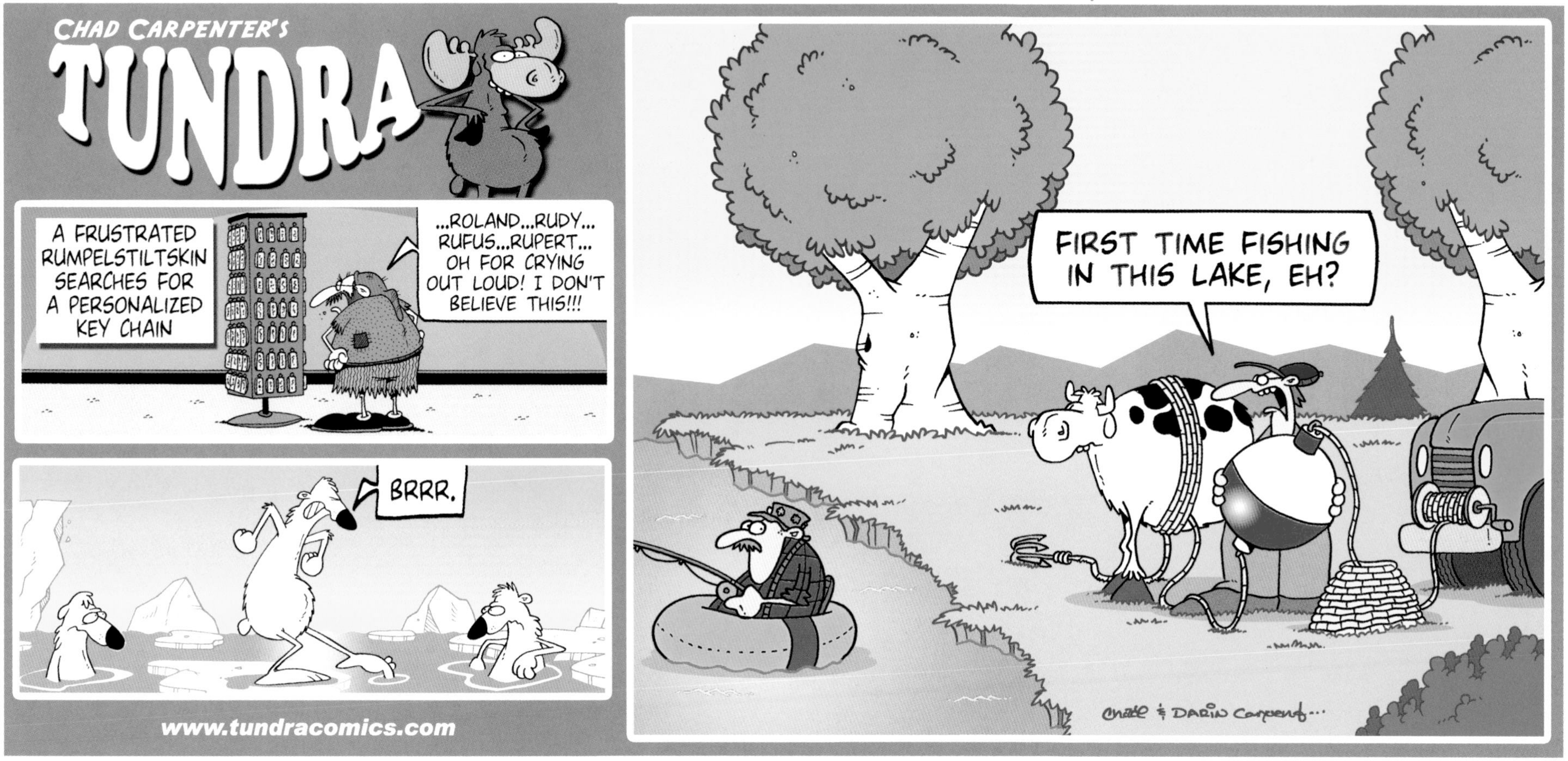
CHAD CARPENTER'S
TUNDRA
A FRUSTRATED RUMPELSTILTSKIN SEARCHES FOR A PERSONALIZED KEY CHAIN
...ROLAND...RUDY... RUFUS...RUPERT... OH FOR CRYING OUT LOUD! I DON'T BELIEVE THIS!!!
BRRR.
www.tundracomics.com
FIRST TIME FISHING IN THIS LAKE, EH?
Chad & Darin Carpenter...

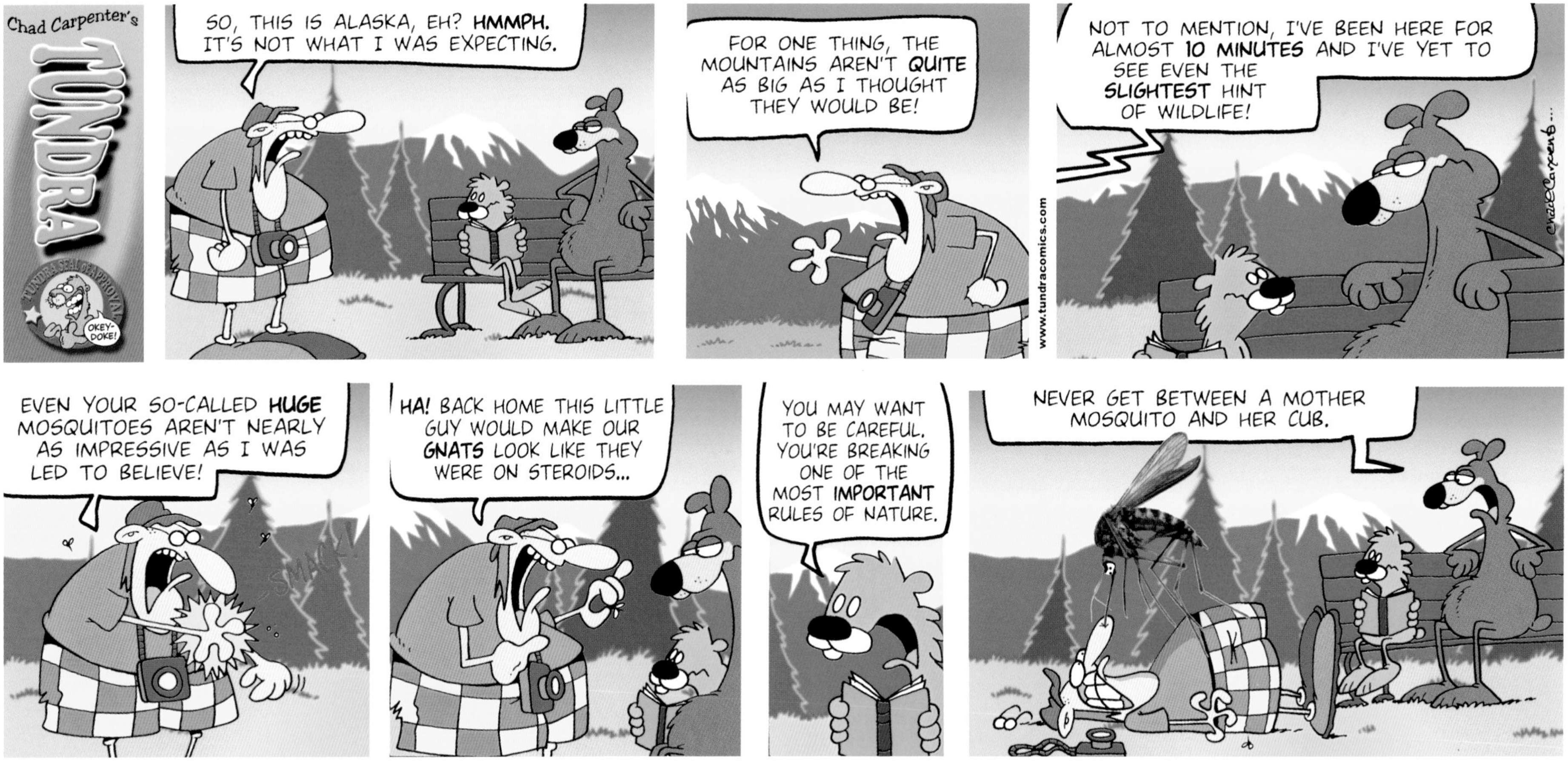
Chad Carpenter's
TUNDRA
TUNDRA SEAL OF APPROVAL
OKEY-DOKE!
SO, THIS IS ALASKA, EH? HMMPH. IT'S NOT WHAT I WAS EXPECTING.
FOR ONE THING, THE MOUNTAINS AREN'T QUITE AS BIG AS I THOUGHT THEY WOULD BE!
www.tundracomics.com
NOT TO MENTION, I'VE BEEN HERE FOR ALMOST 10 MINUTES AND I'VE YET TO SEE EVEN THE SLIGHTEST HINT OF WILDLIFE!
EVEN YOUR SO-CALLED HUGE MOSQUITOES AREN'T NEARLY AS IMPRESSIVE AS I WAS LED TO BELIEVE!
SMACK!
HA! BACK HOME THIS LITTLE GUY WOULD MAKE OUR GNATS LOOK LIKE THEY WERE ON STEROIDS...
YOU MAY WANT TO BE CAREFUL. YOU'RE BREAKING ONE OF THE MOST IMPORTANT RULES OF NATURE.
NEVER GET BETWEEN A MOTHER MOSQUITO AND HER CUB.

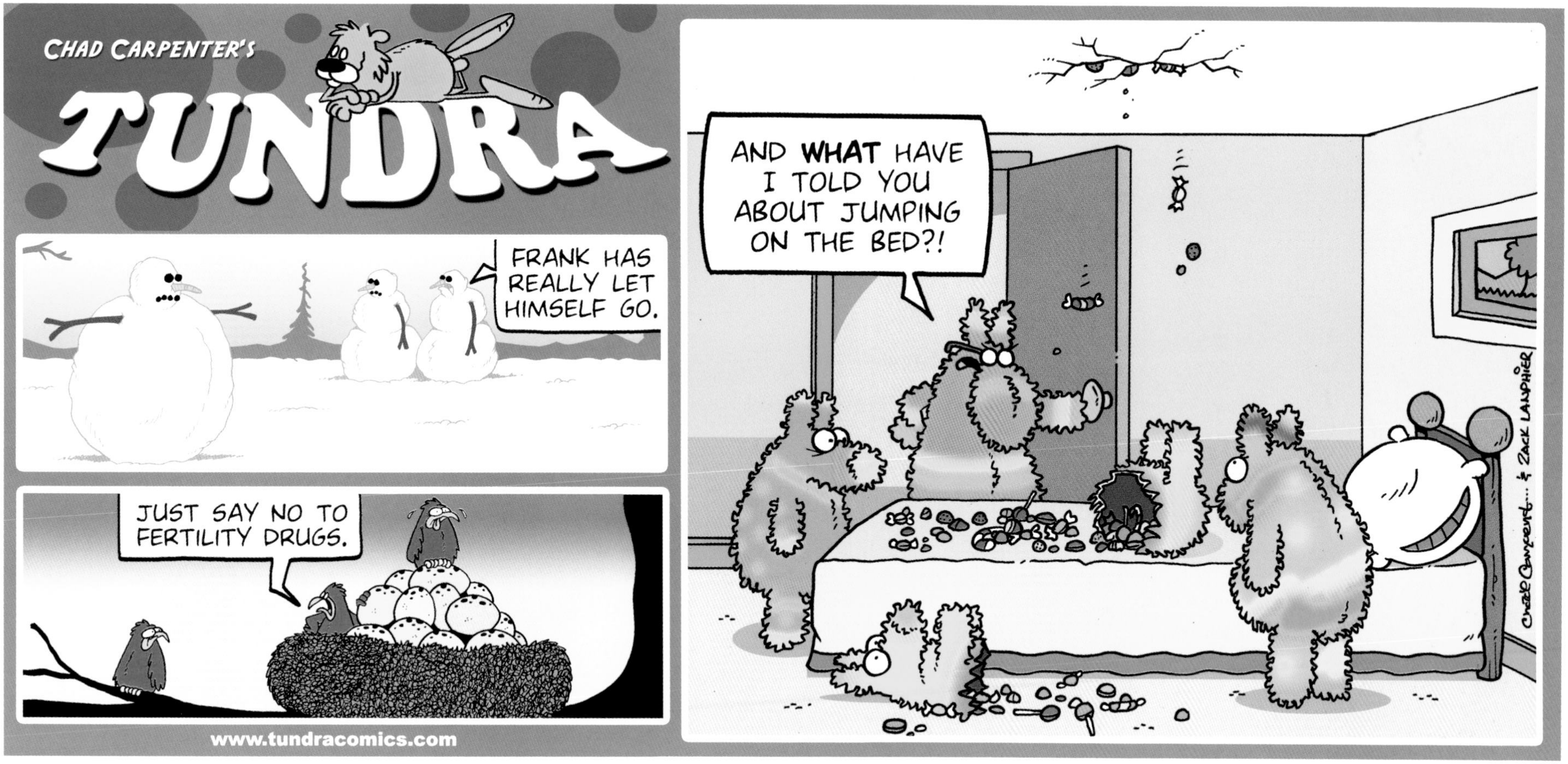
CHAD CARPENTER'S
TUNDRA
FRANK HAS REALLY LET HIMSELF GO.
JUST SAY NO TO FERTILITY DRUGS.
AND **WHAT** HAVE I TOLD YOU ABOUT JUMPING ON THE BED?!
www.tundracomics.com

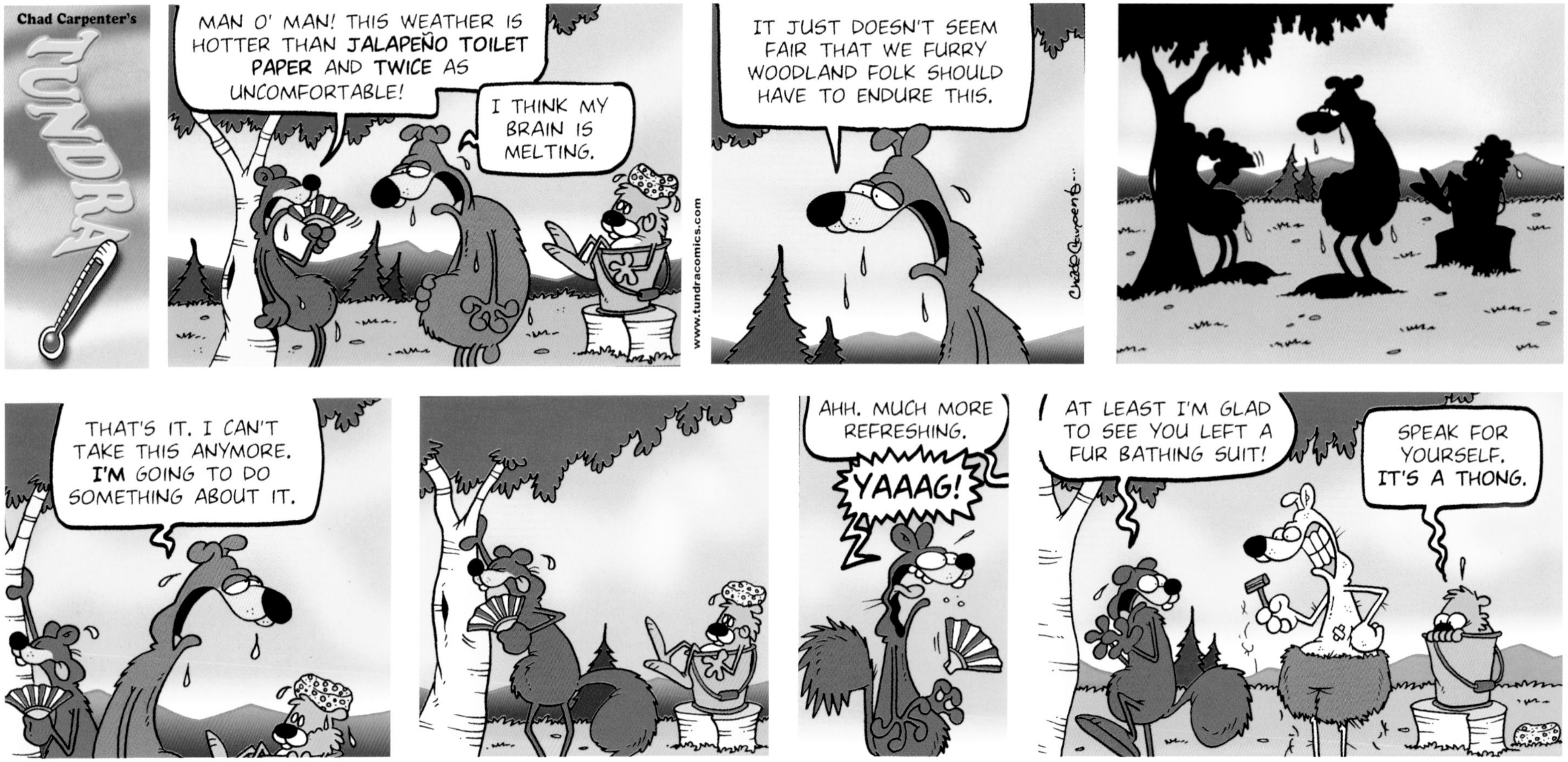
Chad Carpenter's
TUNDRA
MAN O' MAN! THIS WEATHER IS HOTTER THAN JALAPEÑO TOILET PAPER AND TWICE AS UNCOMFORTABLE!
I THINK MY BRAIN IS MELTING.
www.tundracomics.com
IT JUST DOESN'T SEEM FAIR THAT WE FURRY WOODLAND FOLK SHOULD HAVE TO ENDURE THIS.
THAT'S IT. I CAN'T TAKE THIS ANYMORE. I'M GOING TO DO SOMETHING ABOUT IT.
AHH. MUCH MORE REFRESHING.
YAAAG!
AT LEAST I'M GLAD TO SEE YOU LEFT A FUR BATHING SUIT!
SPEAK FOR YOURSELF. IT'S A THONG.

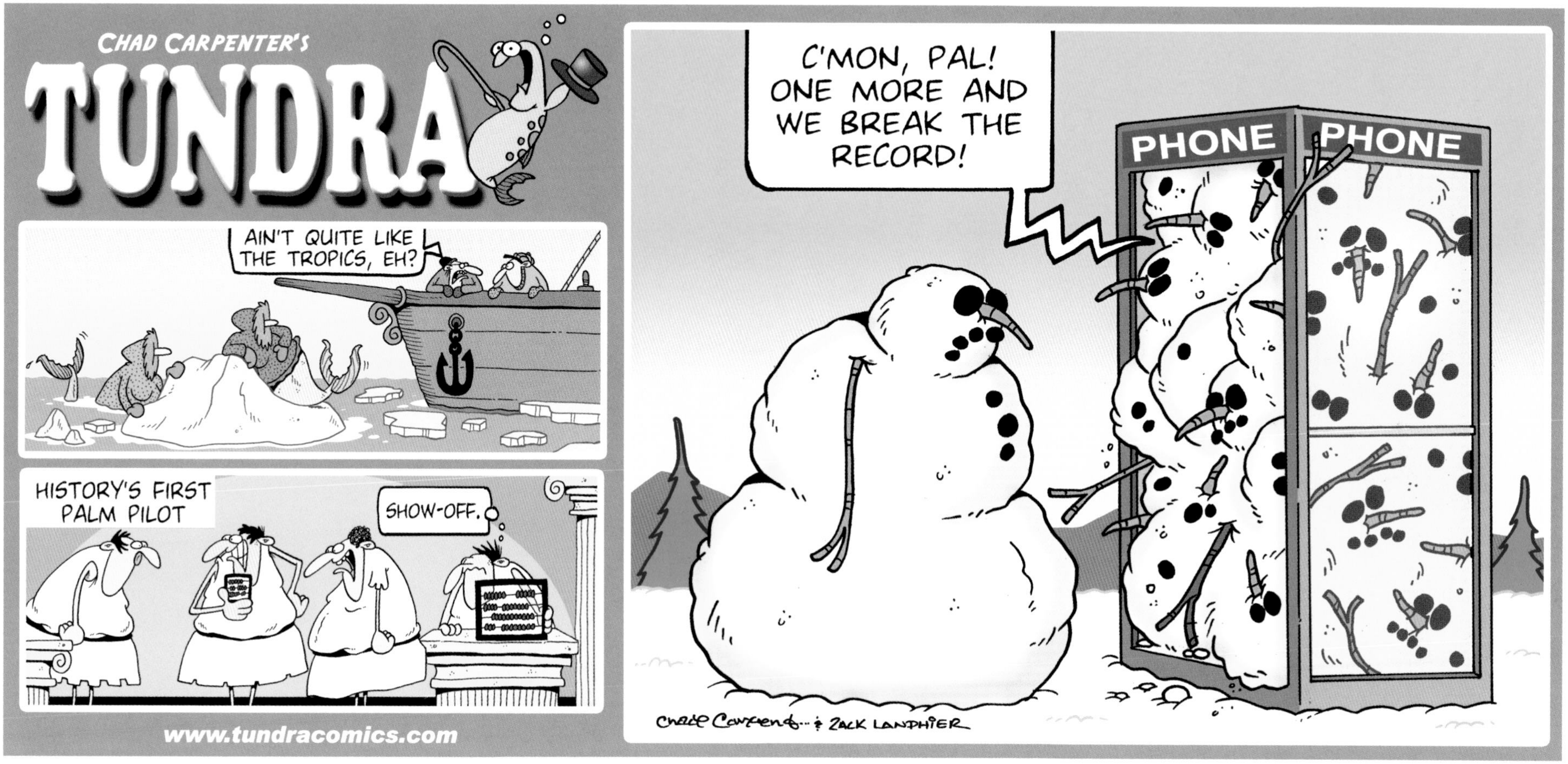
CHAD CARPENTER'S
TUNDRA
AIN'T QUITE LIKE THE TROPICS, EH?
HISTORY'S FIRST PALM PILOT
SHOW-OFF.
www.tundracomics.com
C'MON, PAL! ONE MORE AND WE BREAK THE RECORD!
PHONE
PHONE

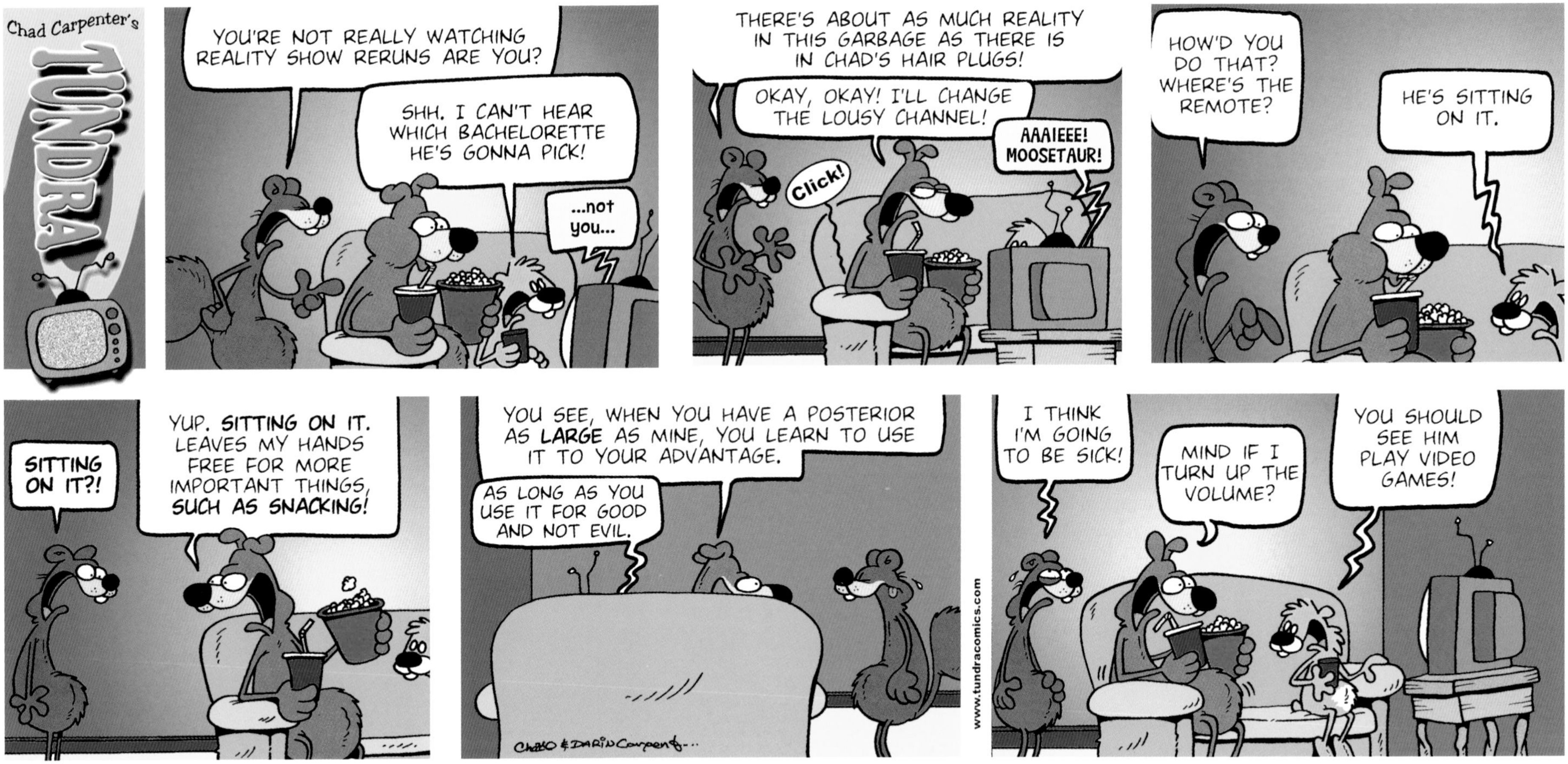
Chad Carpenter's
TUNDRA
YOU'RE NOT REALLY WATCHING REALITY SHOW RERUNS ARE YOU?
SHH. I CAN'T HEAR WHICH BACHELORETTE HE'S GONNA PICK!
...not you...
THERE'S ABOUT AS MUCH REALITY IN THIS GARBAGE AS THERE IS IN CHAD'S HAIR PLUGS!
OKAY, OKAY! I'LL CHANGE THE LOUSY CHANNEL!
Click!
AAAIEEE! MOOSETAUR!
HOW'D YOU DO THAT? WHERE'S THE REMOTE?
HE'S SITTING ON IT.
SITTING ON IT?!
YUP. SITTING ON IT. LEAVES MY HANDS FREE FOR MORE IMPORTANT THINGS, SUCH AS SNACKING!
YOU SEE, WHEN YOU HAVE A POSTERIOR AS LARGE AS MINE, YOU LEARN TO USE IT TO YOUR ADVANTAGE.
AS LONG AS YOU USE IT FOR GOOD AND NOT EVIL.
www.tundracomics.com
I THINK I'M GOING TO BE SICK!
MIND IF I TURN UP THE VOLUME?
YOU SHOULD SEE HIM PLAY VIDEO GAMES!

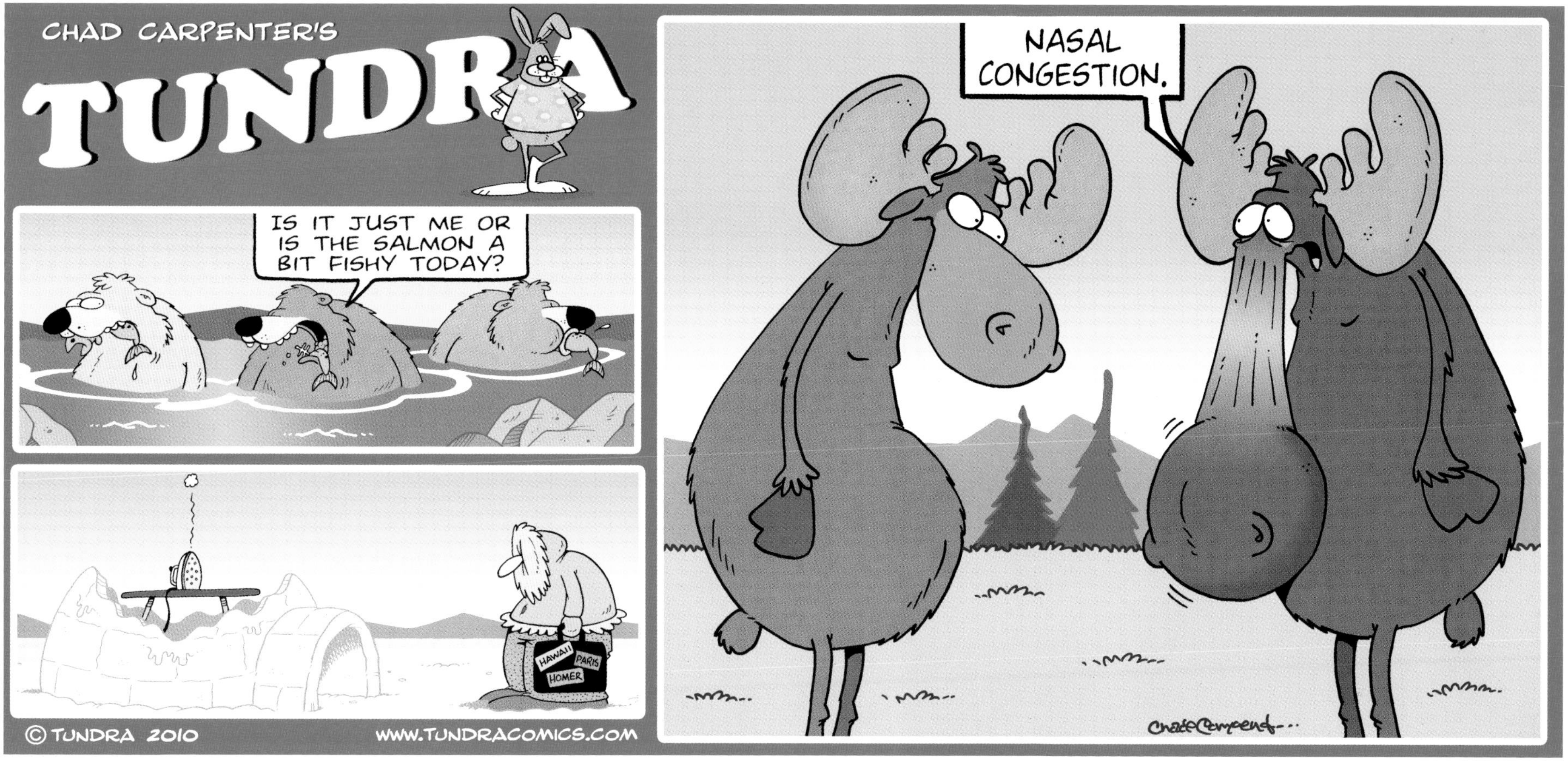
CHAD CARPENTER'S
TUNDRA
IS IT JUST ME OR IS THE SALMON A BIT FISHY TODAY?
HAWAII
PARIS
HOMER
NASAL CONGESTION.
© TUNDRA 2010
WWW.TUNDRACOMICS.COM

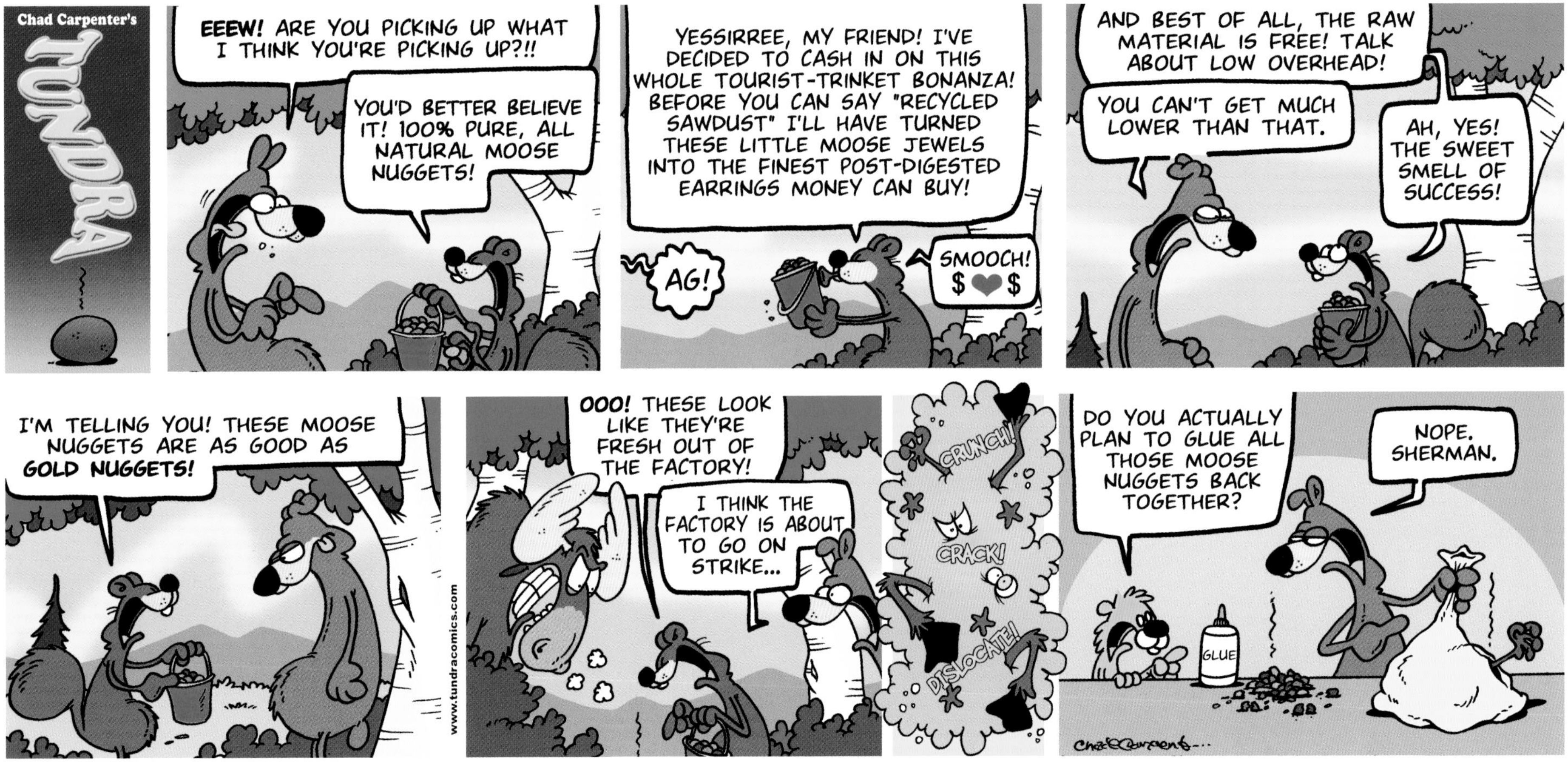
Chad Carpenter's
TUNDRA
EEEW! ARE YOU PICKING UP WHAT I THINK YOU'RE PICKING UP?!!
YOU'D BETTER BELIEVE IT! 100% PURE, ALL NATURAL MOOSE NUGGETS!
YESSIRREE, MY FRIEND! I'VE DECIDED TO CASH IN ON THIS WHOLE TOURIST-TRINKET BONANZA! BEFORE YOU CAN SAY "RECYCLED SAWDUST" I'LL HAVE TURNED THESE LITTLE MOOSE JEWELS INTO THE FINEST POST-DIGESTED EARRINGS MONEY CAN BUY!
AG!
SMOOCH!
$ $
AND BEST OF ALL, THE RAW MATERIAL IS FREE! TALK ABOUT LOW OVERHEAD!
YOU CAN'T GET MUCH LOWER THAN THAT.
AH, YES! THE SWEET SMELL OF SUCCESS!
I'M TELLING YOU! THESE MOOSE NUGGETS ARE AS GOOD AS GOLD NUGGETS!
www.tundracomics.com
OOO! THESE LOOK LIKE THEY'RE FRESH OUT OF THE FACTORY!
I THINK THE FACTORY IS ABOUT TO GO ON STRIKE...
CRUNCH!
CRACK!
DISLOCATE!
DO YOU ACTUALLY PLAN TO GLUE ALL THOSE MOOSE NUGGETS BACK TOGETHER?
NOPE. SHERMAN.
GLUE

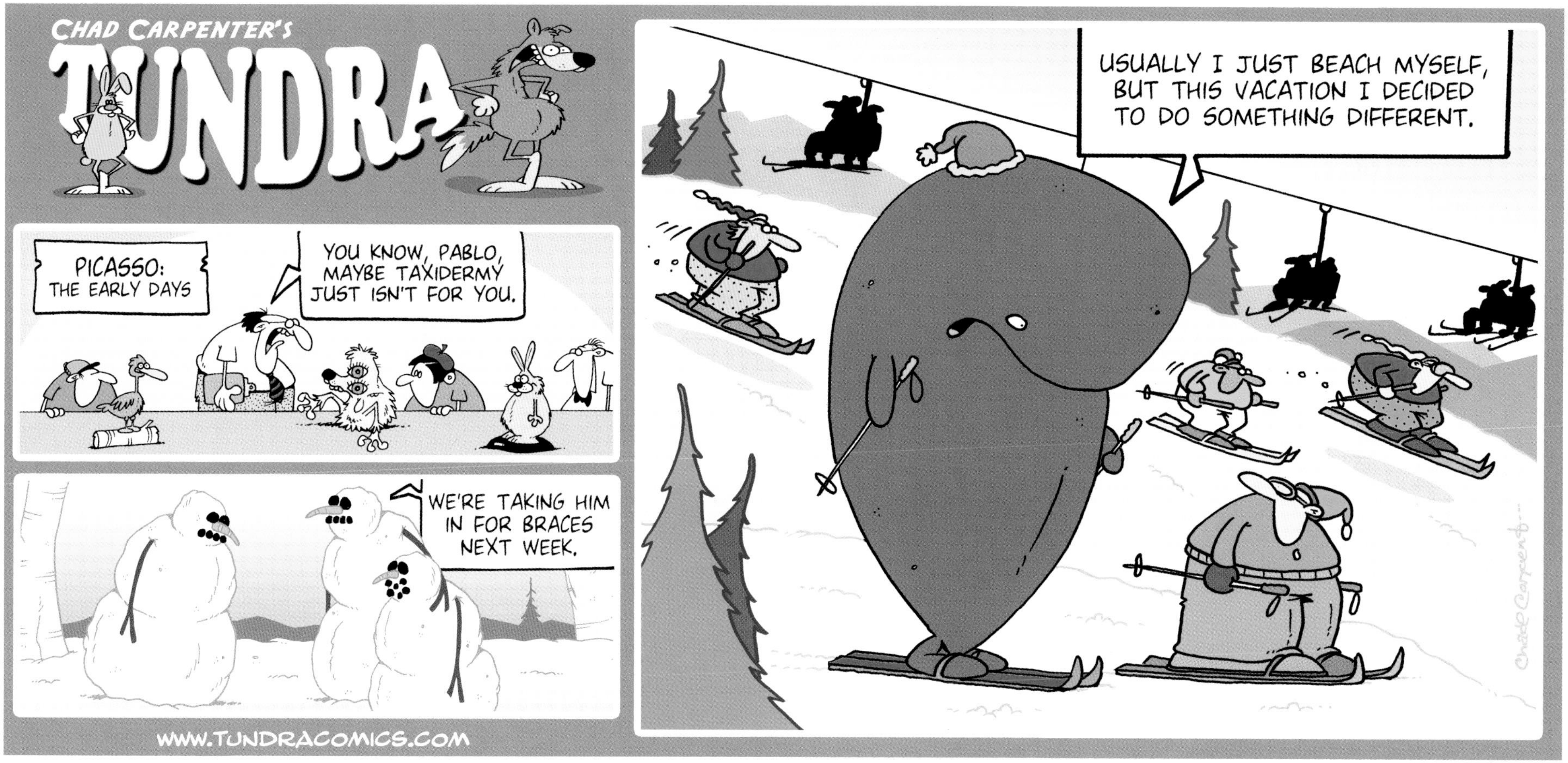
CHAD CARPENTER'S
TUNDRA
PICASSO: THE EARLY DAYS
YOU KNOW, PABLO, MAYBE TAXIDERMY JUST ISN'T FOR YOU.
WE'RE TAKING HIM IN FOR BRACES NEXT WEEK.
WWW.TUNDRACOMICS.COM
USUALLY I JUST BEACH MYSELF, BUT THIS VACATION I DECIDED TO DO SOMETHING DIFFERENT.

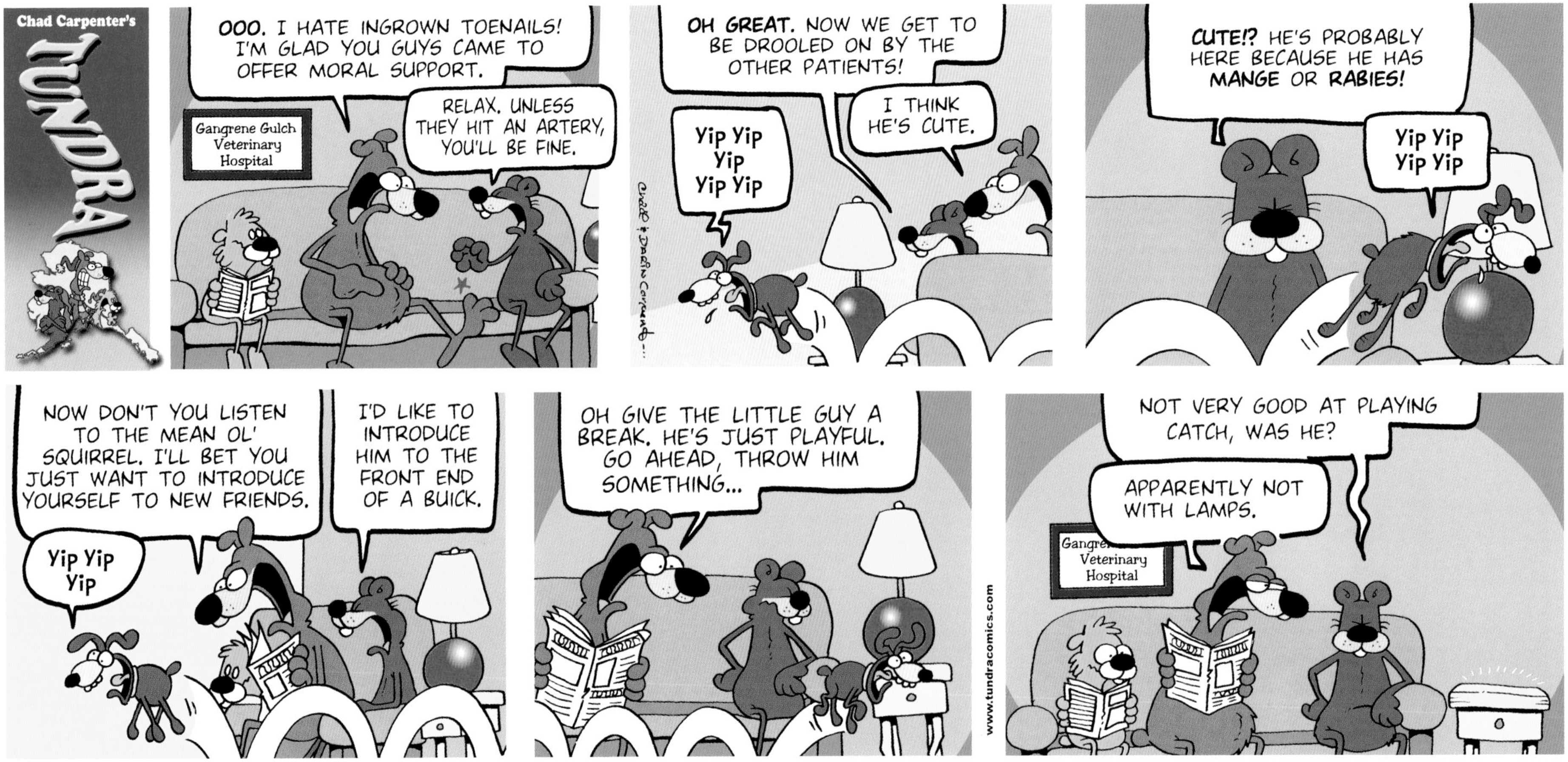
Chad Carpenter's
TUNDRA
OOO. I HATE INGROWN TOENAILS! I'M GLAD YOU GUYS CAME TO OFFER MORAL SUPPORT.
Gangrene Gulch Veterinary Hospital
RELAX. UNLESS THEY HIT AN ARTERY, YOU'LL BE FINE.
OH GREAT. NOW WE GET TO BE DROOLED ON BY THE OTHER PATIENTS!
Yip Yip Yip Yip Yip
I THINK HE'S CUTE.
CUTE!? HE'S PROBABLY HERE BECAUSE HE HAS MANGE OR RABIES!
Yip Yip Yip Yip
NOW DON'T YOU LISTEN TO THE MEAN OL' SQUIRREL. I'LL BET YOU JUST WANT TO INTRODUCE YOURSELF TO NEW FRIENDS.
Yip Yip Yip
I'D LIKE TO INTRODUCE HIM TO THE FRONT END OF A BUICK.
OH GIVE THE LITTLE GUY A BREAK. HE'S JUST PLAYFUL. GO AHEAD, THROW HIM SOMETHING...
www.tundracomics.com
NOT VERY GOOD AT PLAYING CATCH, WAS HE?
APPARENTLY NOT WITH LAMPS.
Veterinary Hospital

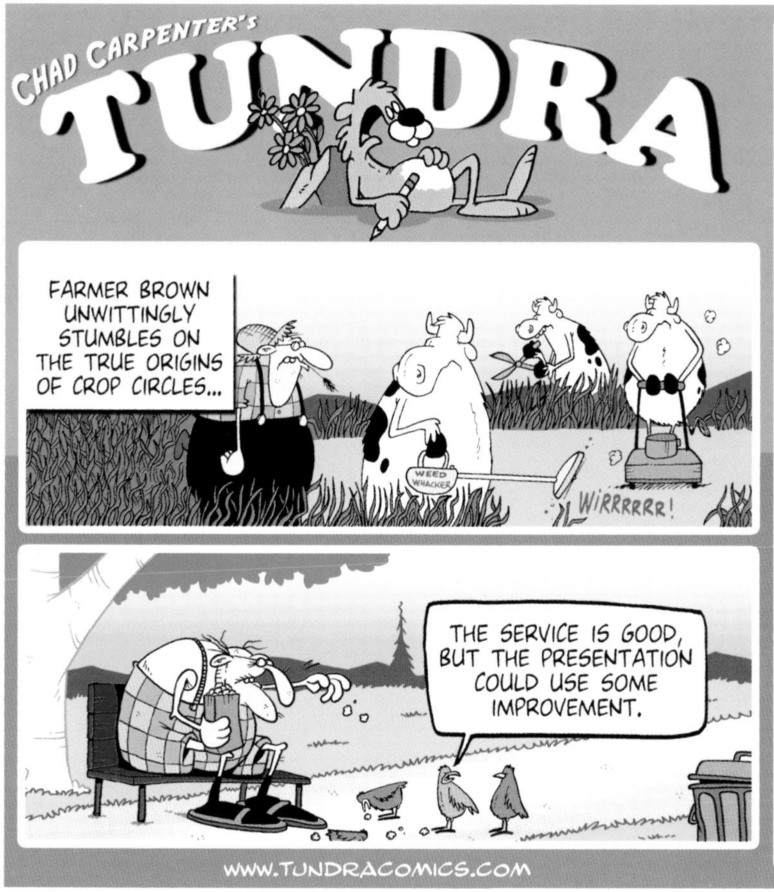
CHAD CARPENTER'S
TUNDRA
FARMER BROWN UNWITTINGLY STUMBLES ON THE TRUE ORIGINS OF CROP CIRCLES...
WEED WHACKER
WIRRRRRR!
THE SERVICE IS GOOD, BUT THE PRESENTATION COULD USE SOME IMPROVEMENT.
WWW.TUNDRACOMICS.COM

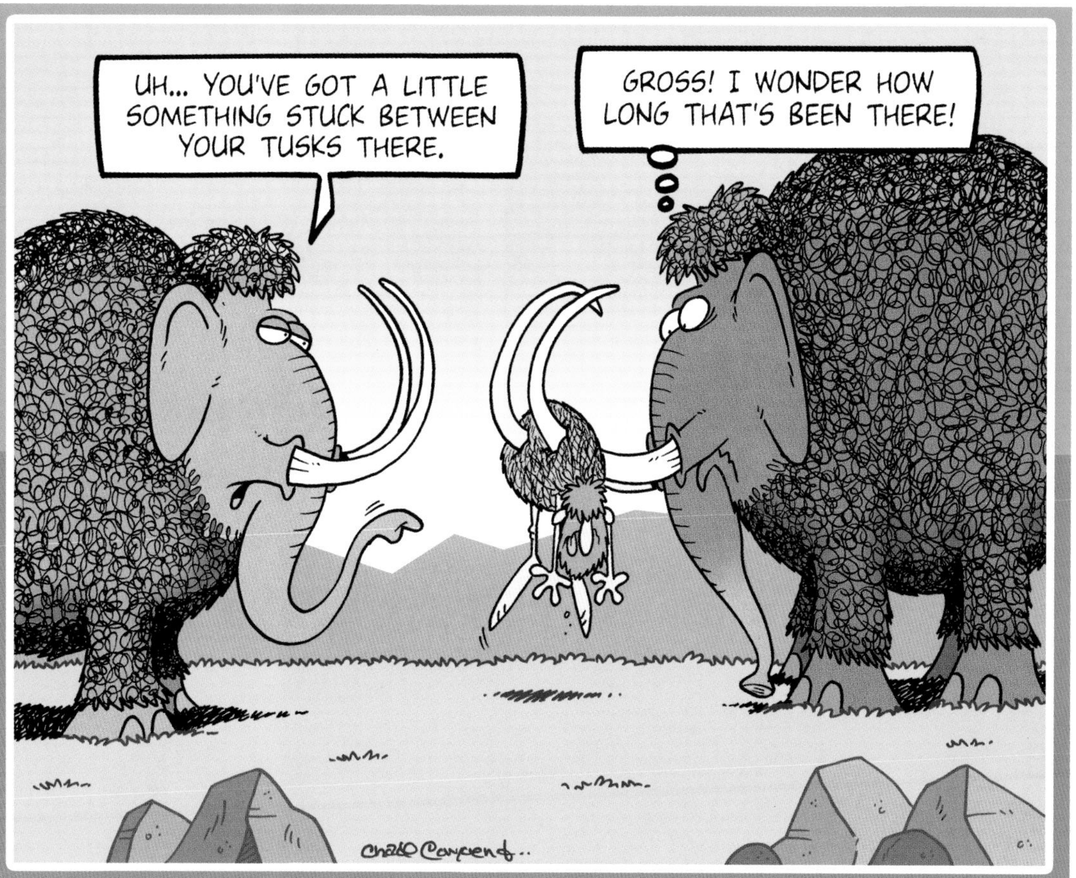
UH... YOU'VE GOT A LITTLE SOMETHING STUCK BETWEEN YOUR TUSKS THERE.
GROSS! I WONDER HOW LONG THAT'S BEEN THERE!
Chad Carpenter

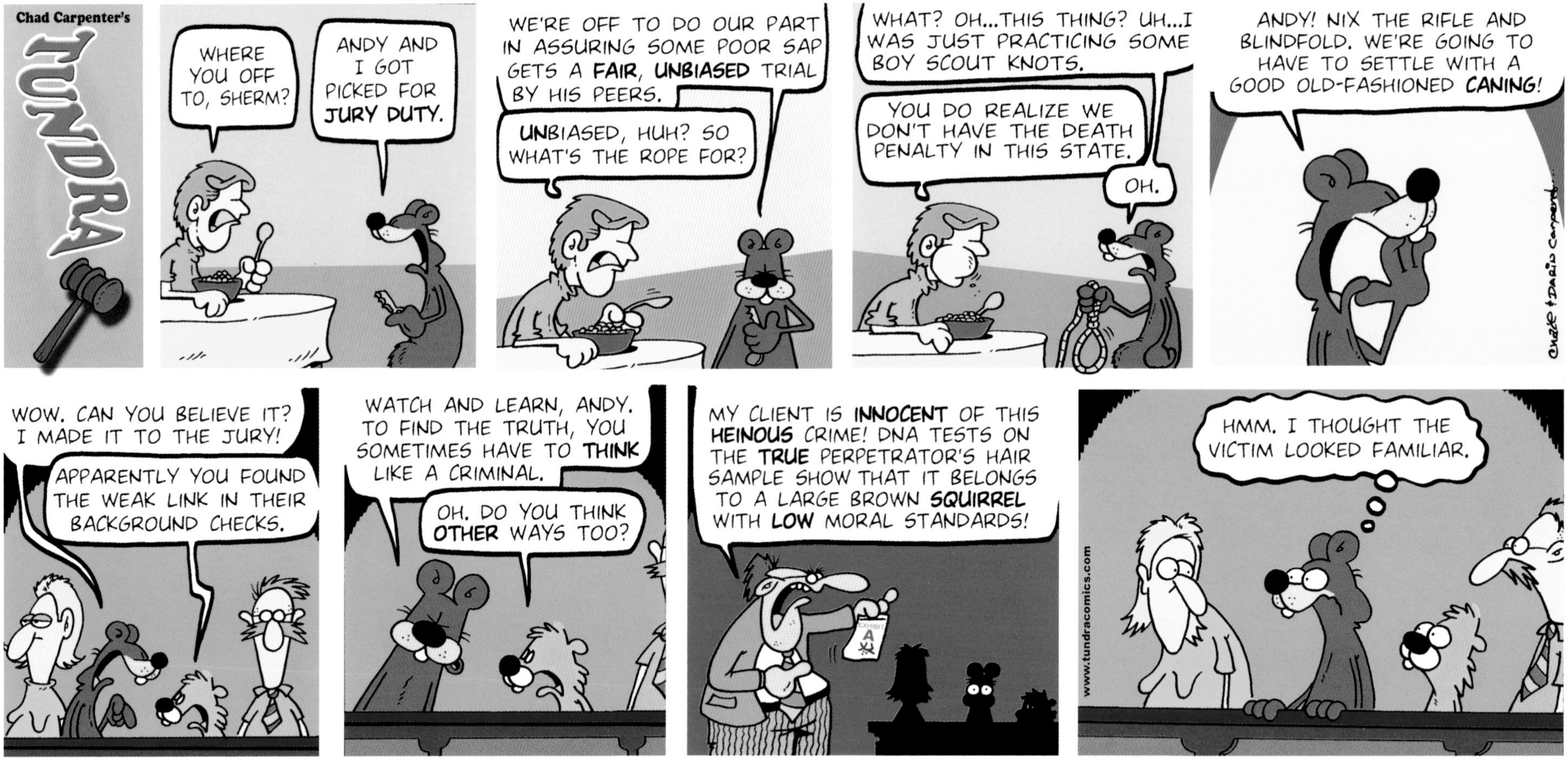
Chad Carpenter's
TUNDRA
WHERE YOU OFF TO, SHERM?
ANDY AND I GOT PICKED FOR JURY DUTY.
WE'RE OFF TO DO OUR PART IN ASSURING SOME POOR SAP GETS A FAIR, UNBIASED TRIAL BY HIS PEERS.
UNBIASED, HUH? SO WHAT'S THE ROPE FOR?
WHAT? OH...THIS THING? UH...I WAS JUST PRACTICING SOME BOY SCOUT KNOTS.
YOU DO REALIZE WE DON'T HAVE THE DEATH PENALTY IN THIS STATE.
OH.
ANDY! NIX THE RIFLE AND BLINDFOLD. WE'RE GOING TO HAVE TO SETTLE WITH A GOOD OLD-FASHIONED CANING!
WOW. CAN YOU BELIEVE IT? I MADE IT TO THE JURY!
APPARENTLY YOU FOUND THE WEAK LINK IN THEIR BACKGROUND CHECKS.
WATCH AND LEARN, ANDY. TO FIND THE TRUTH, YOU SOMETIMES HAVE TO THINK LIKE A CRIMINAL.
OH. DO YOU THINK OTHER WAYS TOO?
MY CLIENT IS INNOCENT OF THIS HEINOUS CRIME! DNA TESTS ON THE TRUE PERPETRATOR'S HAIR SAMPLE SHOW THAT IT BELONGS TO A LARGE BROWN SQUIRREL WITH LOW MORAL STANDARDS!
EXHIBIT A
www.tundracomics.com
HMM. I THOUGHT THE VICTIM LOOKED FAMILIAR.

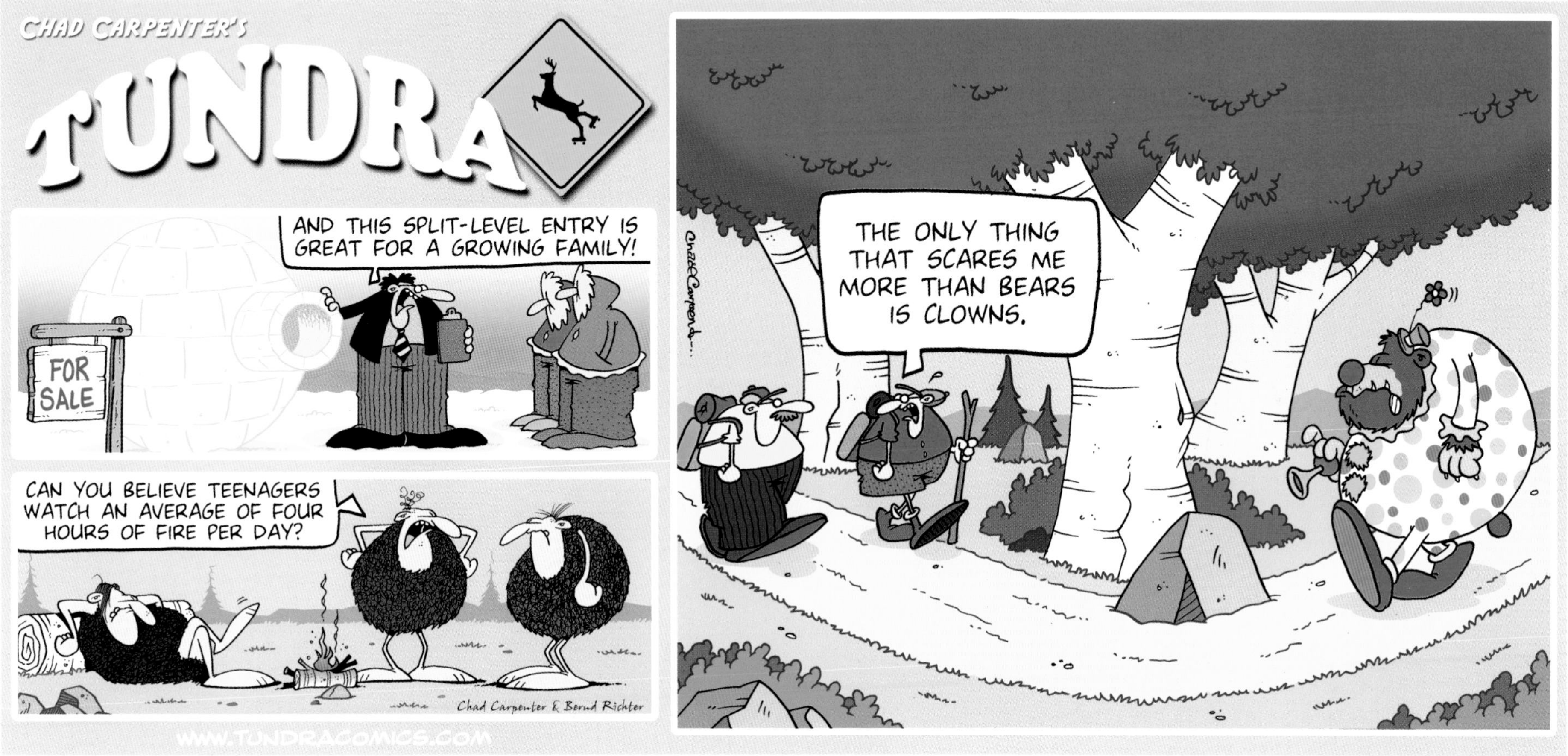
CHAD CARPENTER'S
TUNDRA
AND THIS SPLIT-LEVEL ENTRY IS GREAT FOR A GROWING FAMILY!
FOR SALE
CAN YOU BELIEVE TEENAGERS WATCH AN AVERAGE OF FOUR HOURS OF FIRE PER DAY?
Chad Carpenter & Bernd Richter
WWW.TUNDRACOMICS.COM
THE ONLY THING THAT SCARES ME MORE THAN BEARS IS CLOWNS.

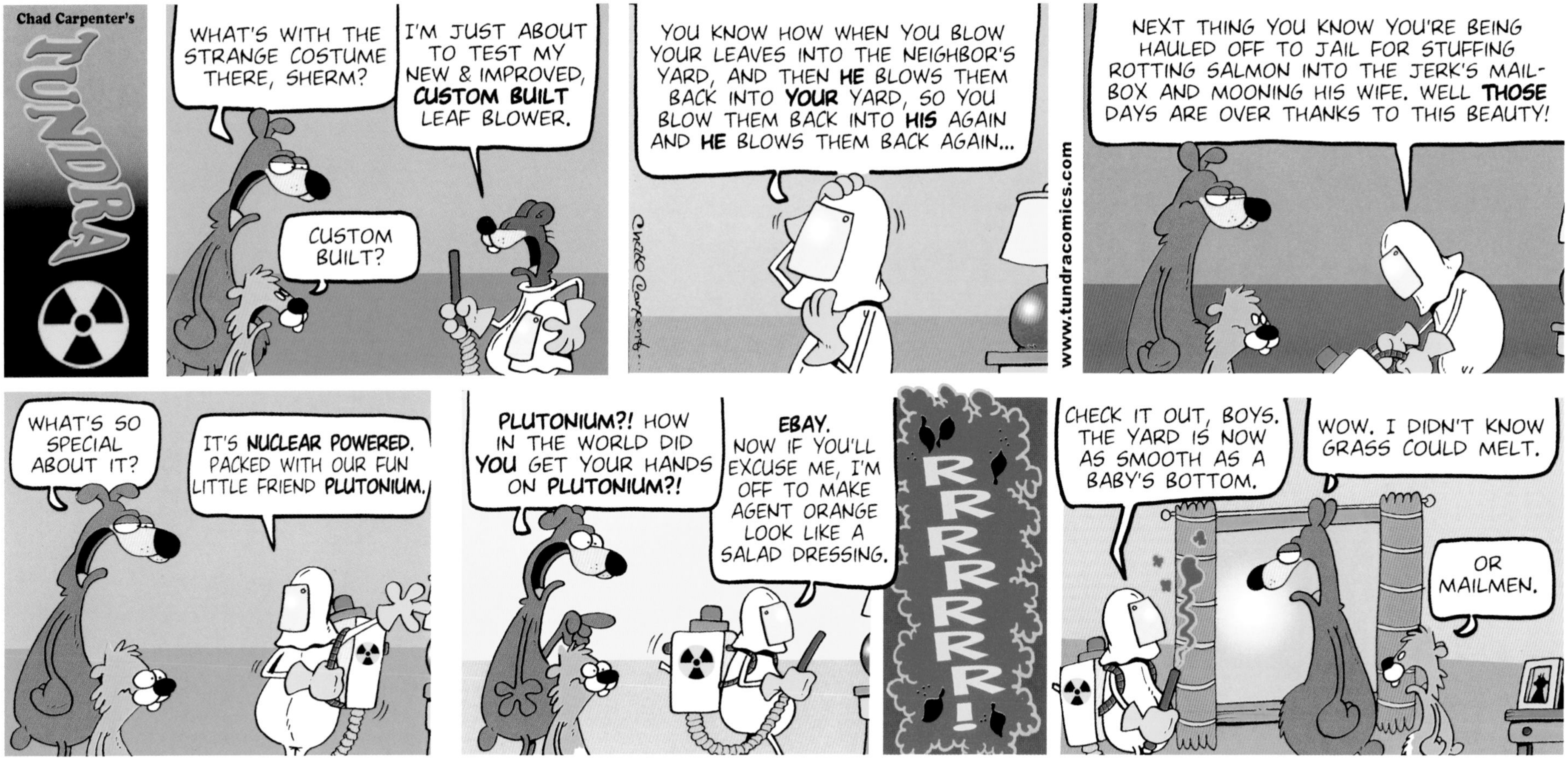
Chad Carpenter's
TUNDRA
WHAT'S WITH THE STRANGE COSTUME THERE, SHERM?
I'M JUST ABOUT TO TEST MY NEW & IMPROVED, **CUSTOM BUILT** LEAF BLOWER.
CUSTOM BUILT?
YOU KNOW HOW WHEN YOU BLOW YOUR LEAVES INTO THE NEIGHBOR'S YARD, AND THEN **HE** BLOWS THEM BACK INTO **YOUR** YARD, SO YOU BLOW THEM BACK INTO **HIS** AGAIN AND **HE** BLOWS THEM BACK AGAIN...
www.tundracomics.com
NEXT THING YOU KNOW YOU'RE BEING HAULED OFF TO JAIL FOR STUFFING ROTTING SALMON INTO THE JERK'S MAIL-BOX AND MOONING HIS WIFE. WELL **THOSE** DAYS ARE OVER THANKS TO THIS BEAUTY!
WHAT'S SO SPECIAL ABOUT IT?
IT'S **NUCLEAR POWERED.** PACKED WITH OUR FUN LITTLE FRIEND **PLUTONIUM.**
PLUTONIUM?! HOW IN THE WORLD DID **YOU** GET YOUR HANDS ON **PLUTONIUM?!**
EBAY. NOW IF YOU'LL EXCUSE ME, I'M OFF TO MAKE AGENT ORANGE LOOK LIKE A SALAD DRESSING.
RRRRRR!
CHECK IT OUT, BOYS. THE YARD IS NOW AS SMOOTH AS A BABY'S BOTTOM.
WOW. I DIDN'T KNOW GRASS COULD MELT.
OR MAILMEN.

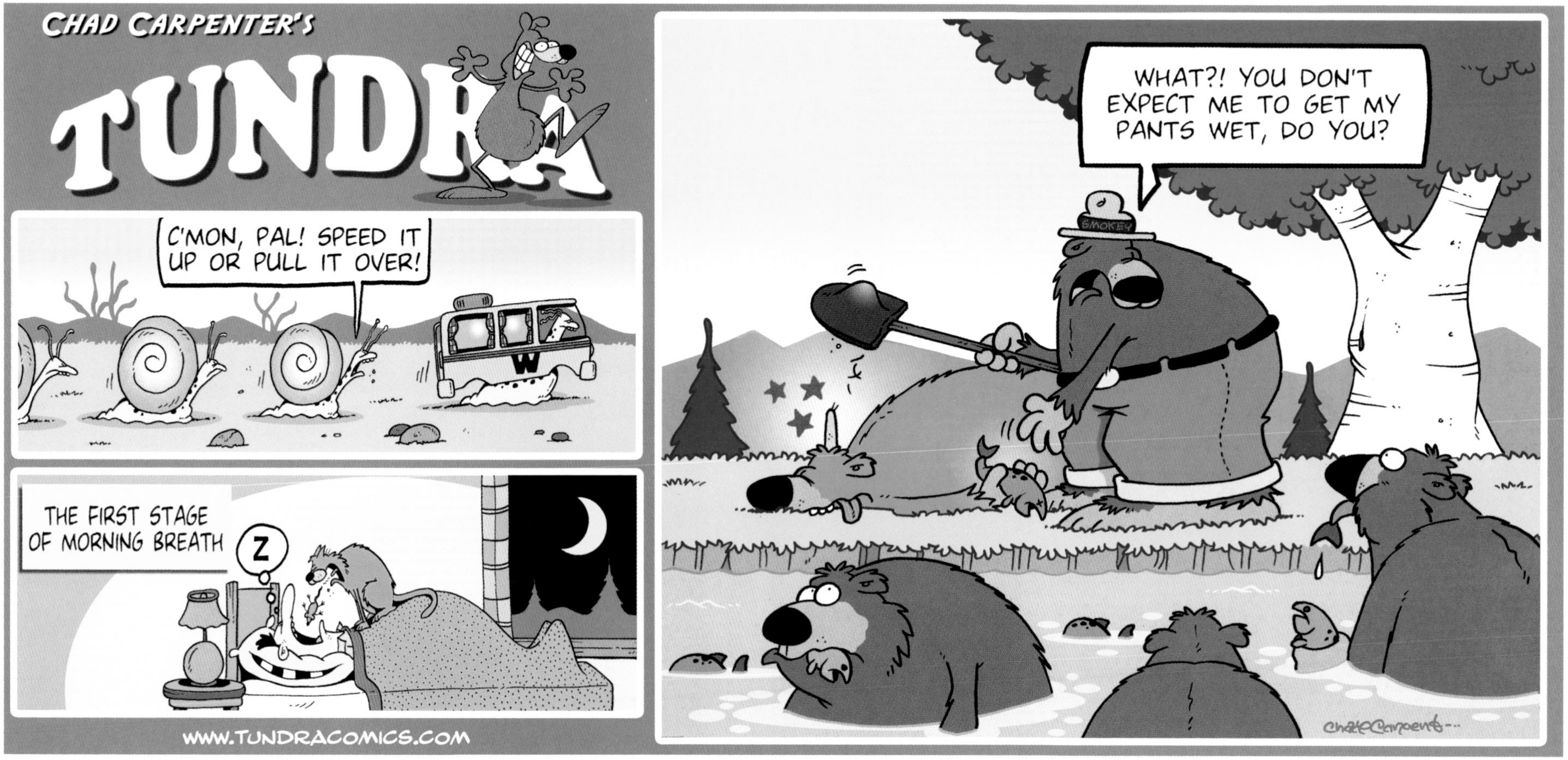
CHAD CARPENTER'S
TUNDRA
C'MON, PAL! SPEED IT UP OR PULL IT OVER!
W
THE FIRST STAGE OF MORNING BREATH
Z
WWW.TUNDRACOMICS.COM
WHAT?! YOU DON'T EXPECT ME TO GET MY PANTS WET, DO YOU?
SMOKEY

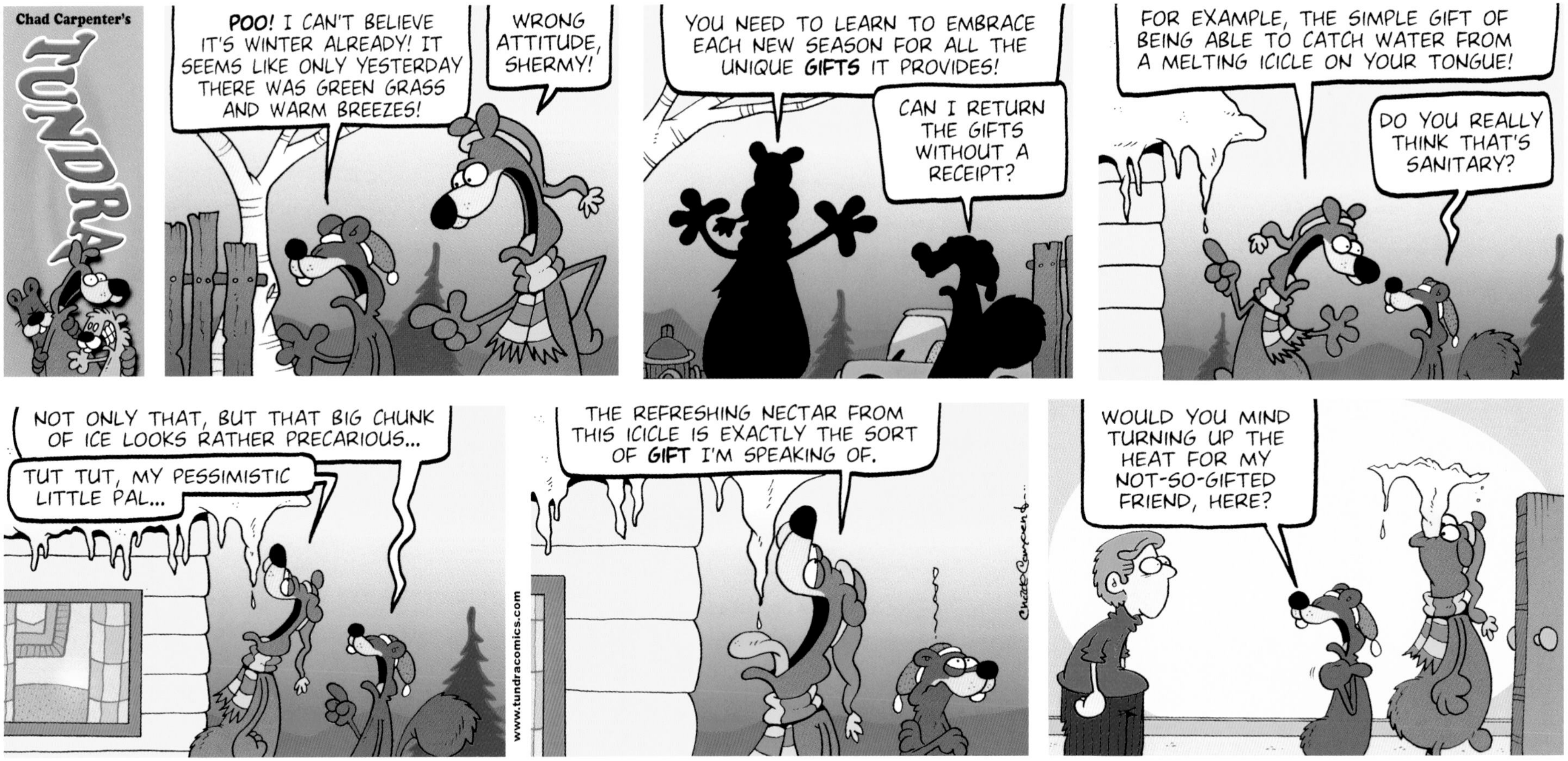
Chad Carpenter's
TUNDRA
POO! I CAN'T BELIEVE IT'S WINTER ALREADY! IT SEEMS LIKE ONLY YESTERDAY THERE WAS GREEN GRASS AND WARM BREEZES!
WRONG ATTITUDE, SHERMY!
YOU NEED TO LEARN TO EMBRACE EACH NEW SEASON FOR ALL THE UNIQUE GIFTS IT PROVIDES!
CAN I RETURN THE GIFTS WITHOUT A RECEIPT?
FOR EXAMPLE, THE SIMPLE GIFT OF BEING ABLE TO CATCH WATER FROM A MELTING ICICLE ON YOUR TONGUE!
DO YOU REALLY THINK THAT'S SANITARY?
NOT ONLY THAT, BUT THAT BIG CHUNK OF ICE LOOKS RATHER PRECARIOUS...
TUT TUT, MY PESSIMISTIC LITTLE PAL...
www.tundracomics.com
THE REFRESHING NECTAR FROM THIS ICICLE IS EXACTLY THE SORT OF GIFT I'M SPEAKING OF.
WOULD YOU MIND TURNING UP THE HEAT FOR MY NOT-SO-GIFTED FRIEND, HERE?

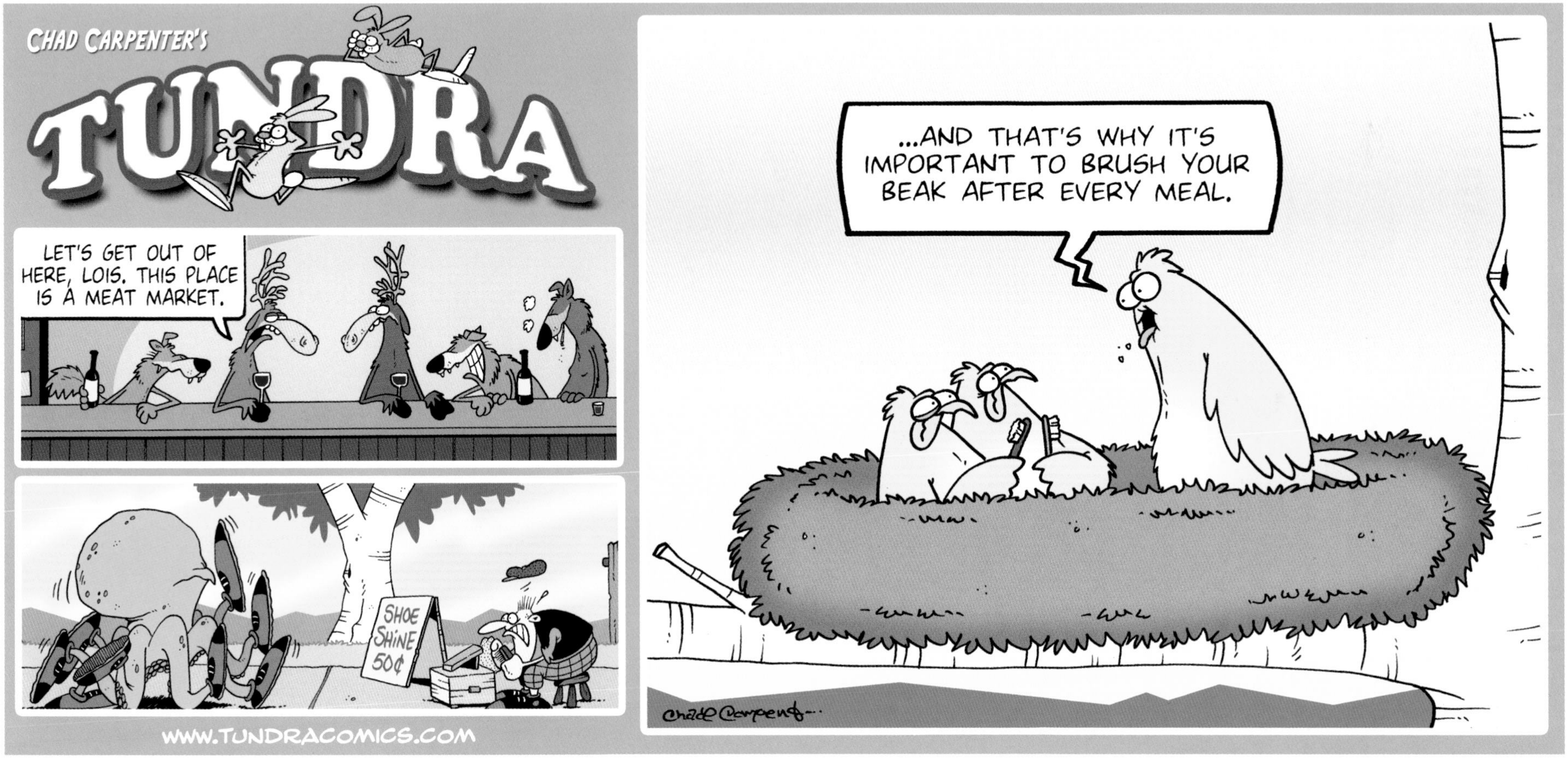
CHAD CARPENTER'S
TUNDRA
LET'S GET OUT OF HERE, LOIS. THIS PLACE IS A MEAT MARKET.
SHOE SHINE 50¢
WWW.TUNDRACOMICS.COM
...AND THAT'S WHY IT'S IMPORTANT TO BRUSH YOUR BEAK AFTER EVERY MEAL.

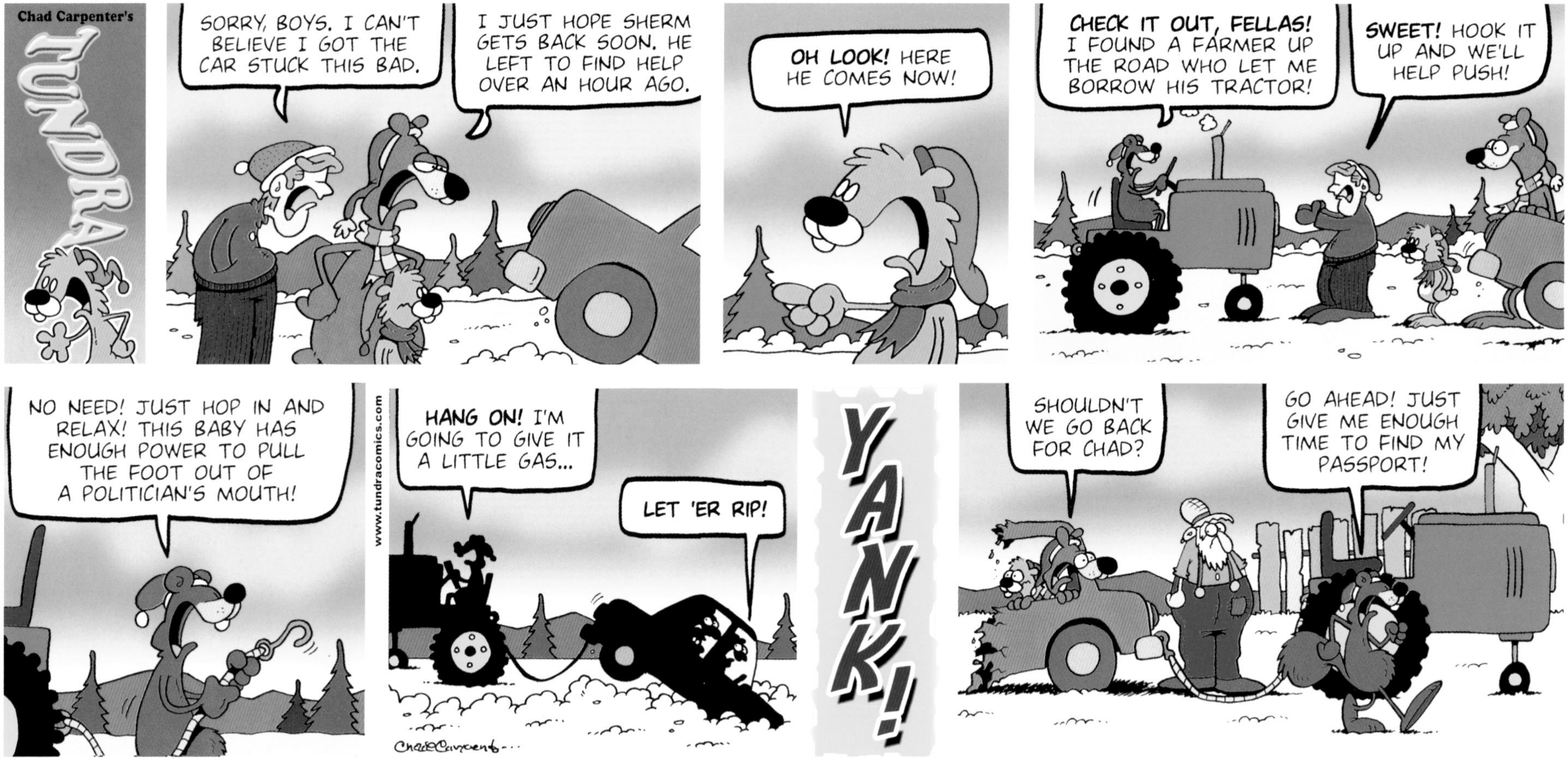
Chad Carpenter's
TUNDRA
SORRY, BOYS. I CAN'T BELIEVE I GOT THE CAR STUCK THIS BAD.
I JUST HOPE SHERM GETS BACK SOON. HE LEFT TO FIND HELP OVER AN HOUR AGO.
OH LOOK! HERE HE COMES NOW!
CHECK IT OUT, FELLAS! I FOUND A FARMER UP THE ROAD WHO LET ME BORROW HIS TRACTOR!
SWEET! HOOK IT UP AND WE'LL HELP PUSH!
NO NEED! JUST HOP IN AND RELAX! THIS BABY HAS ENOUGH POWER TO PULL THE FOOT OUT OF A POLITICIAN'S MOUTH!
www.tundracomics.com
HANG ON! I'M GOING TO GIVE IT A LITTLE GAS...
LET 'ER RIP!
YANK!
SHOULDN'T WE GO BACK FOR CHAD?
GO AHEAD! JUST GIVE ME ENOUGH TIME TO FIND MY PASSPORT!

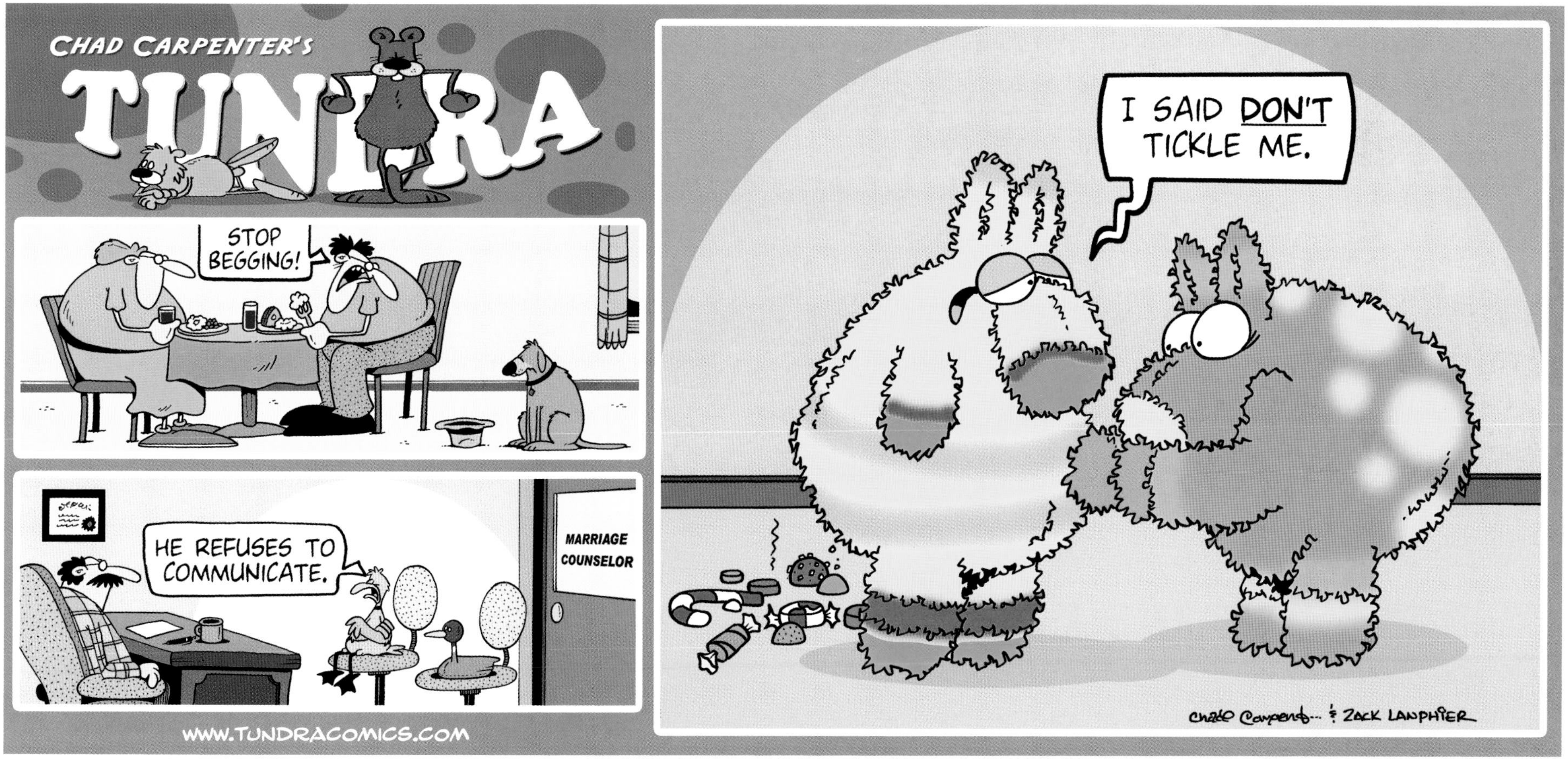
CHAD CARPENTER'S
TUNDRA
STOP BEGGING!
HE REFUSES TO COMMUNICATE.
MARRIAGE COUNSELOR
WWW.TUNDRACOMICS.COM
I SAID DON'T TICKLE ME.
ZACK LANPHIER

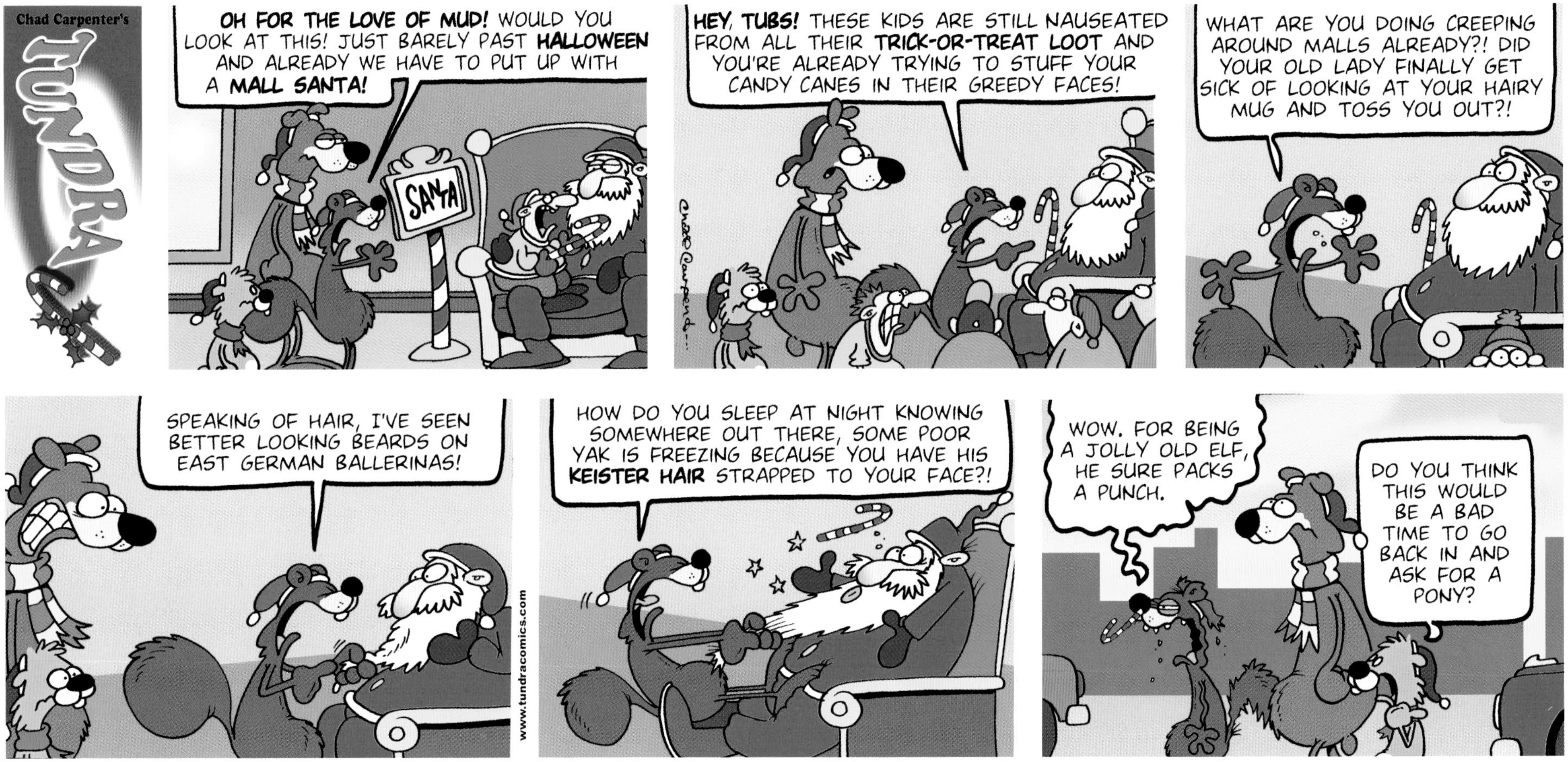
Chad Carpenter's
TUNDRA
OH FOR THE LOVE OF MUD! WOULD YOU LOOK AT THIS! JUST BARELY PAST HALLOWEEN AND ALREADY WE HAVE TO PUT UP WITH A MALL SANTA!
SANTA
HEY, TUBS! THESE KIDS ARE STILL NAUSEATED FROM ALL THEIR TRICK-OR-TREAT LOOT AND YOU'RE ALREADY TRYING TO STUFF YOUR CANDY CANES IN THEIR GREEDY FACES!
WHAT ARE YOU DOING CREEPING AROUND MALLS ALREADY?! DID YOUR OLD LADY FINALLY GET SICK OF LOOKING AT YOUR HAIRY MUG AND TOSS YOU OUT?!
SPEAKING OF HAIR, I'VE SEEN BETTER LOOKING BEARDS ON EAST GERMAN BALLERINAS!
www.tundracomics.com
HOW DO YOU SLEEP AT NIGHT KNOWING SOMEWHERE OUT THERE, SOME POOR YAK IS FREEZING BECAUSE YOU HAVE HIS KEISTER HAIR STRAPPED TO YOUR FACE?!
WOW. FOR BEING A JOLLY OLD ELF, HE SURE PACKS A PUNCH.
DO YOU THINK THIS WOULD BE A BAD TIME TO GO BACK IN AND ASK FOR A PONY?

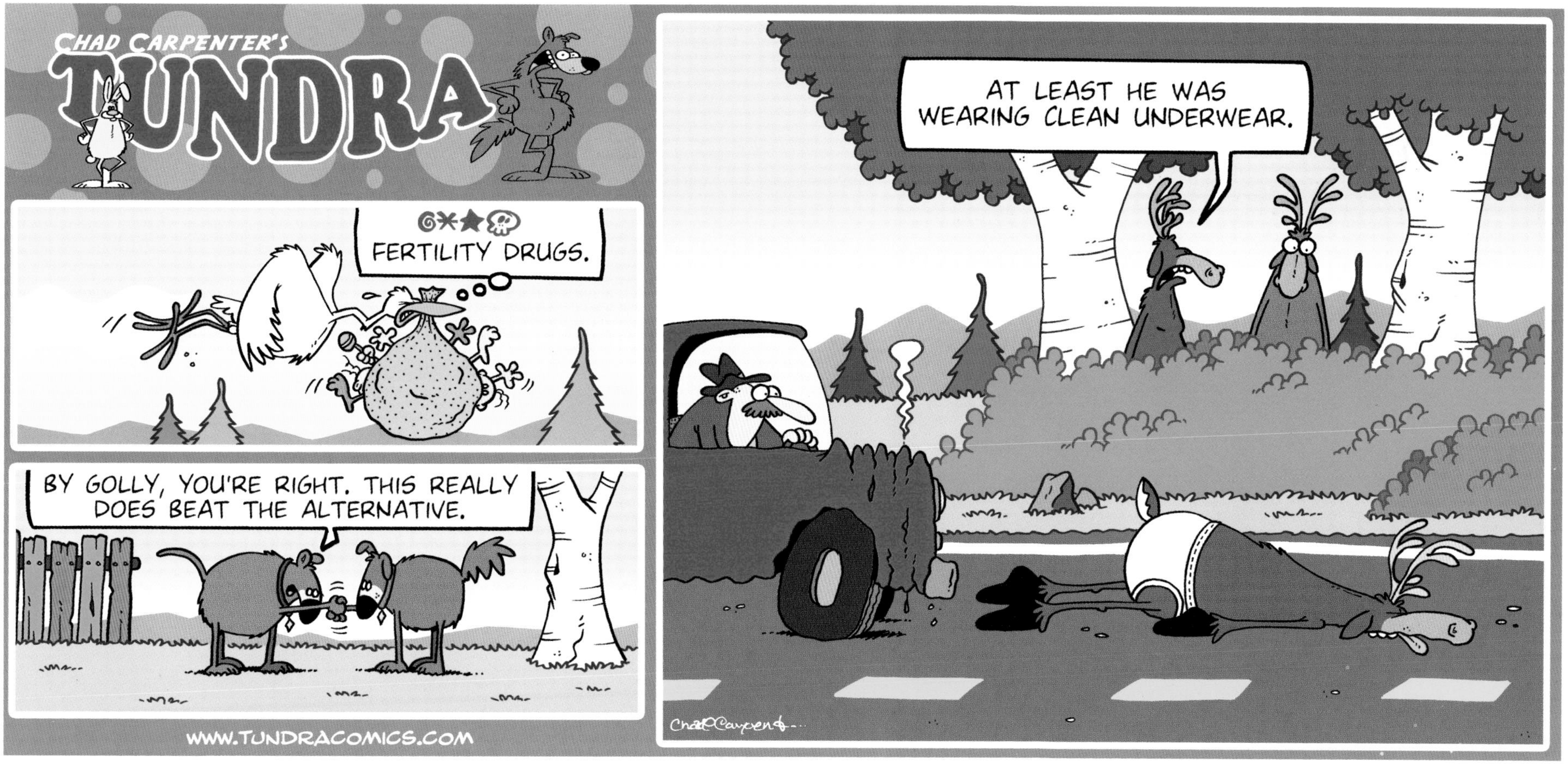
CHAD CARPENTER'S
TUNDRA
FERTILITY DRUGS.
BY GOLLY, YOU'RE RIGHT. THIS REALLY DOES BEAT THE ALTERNATIVE.
WWW.TUNDRACOMICS.COM
AT LEAST HE WAS WEARING CLEAN UNDERWEAR.

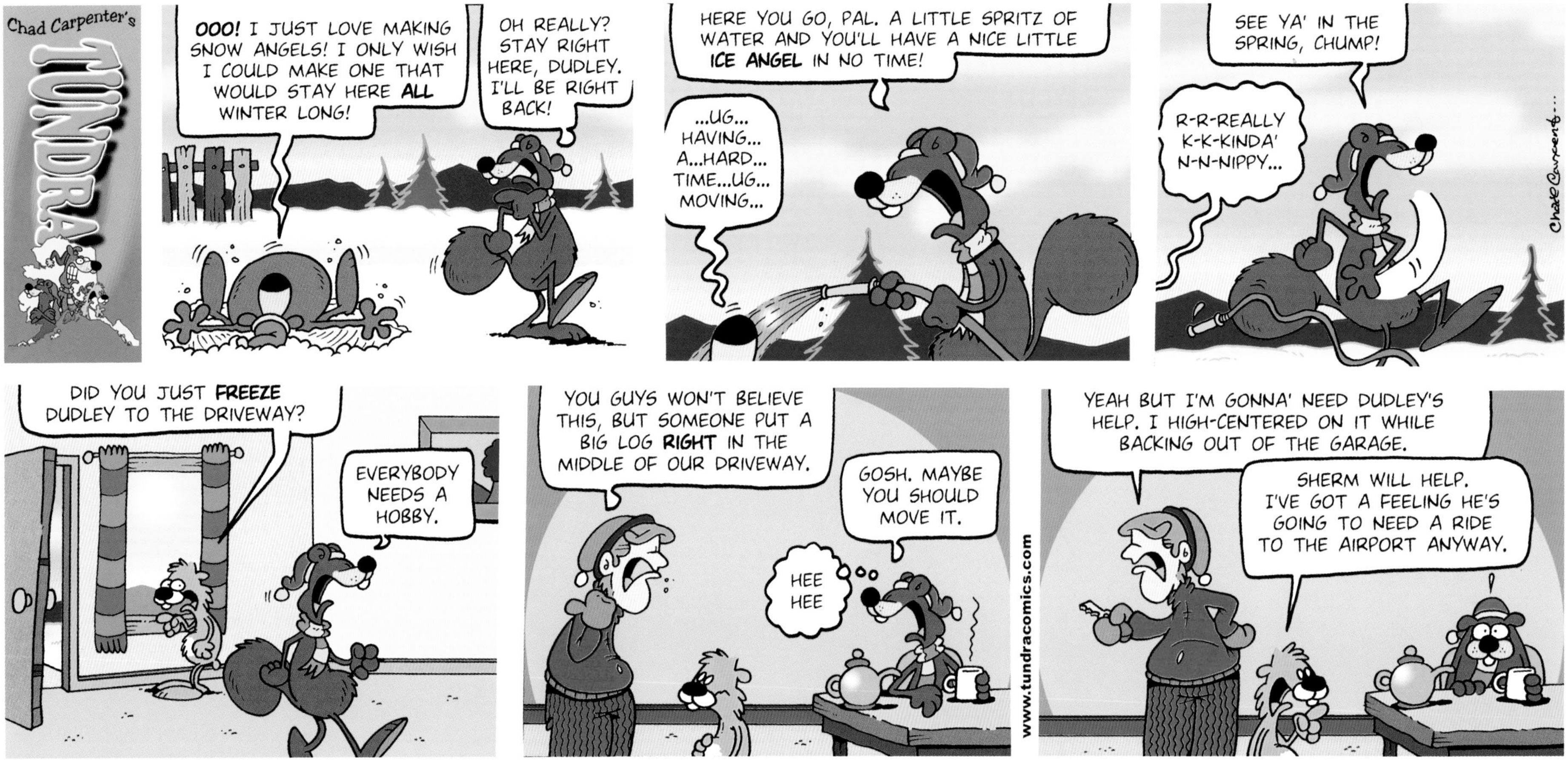
Chad Carpenter's
TUNDRA
OOO! I JUST LOVE MAKING SNOW ANGELS! I ONLY WISH I COULD MAKE ONE THAT WOULD STAY HERE ALL WINTER LONG!
OH REALLY? STAY RIGHT HERE, DUDLEY. I'LL BE RIGHT BACK!
HERE YOU GO, PAL. A LITTLE SPRITZ OF WATER AND YOU'LL HAVE A NICE LITTLE ICE ANGEL IN NO TIME!
...UG... HAVING... A...HARD... TIME...UG... MOVING...
SEE YA' IN THE SPRING, CHUMP!
R-R-REALLY K-K-KINDA' N-N-NIPPY...
Chad Carpenter
DID YOU JUST FREEZE DUDLEY TO THE DRIVEWAY?
EVERYBODY NEEDS A HOBBY.
YOU GUYS WON'T BELIEVE THIS, BUT SOMEONE PUT A BIG LOG RIGHT IN THE MIDDLE OF OUR DRIVEWAY.
GOSH. MAYBE YOU SHOULD MOVE IT.
HEE HEE
www.tundracomics.com
YEAH BUT I'M GONNA' NEED DUDLEY'S HELP. I HIGH-CENTERED ON IT WHILE BACKING OUT OF THE GARAGE.
SHERM WILL HELP. I'VE GOT A FEELING HE'S GOING TO NEED A RIDE TO THE AIRPORT ANYWAY.

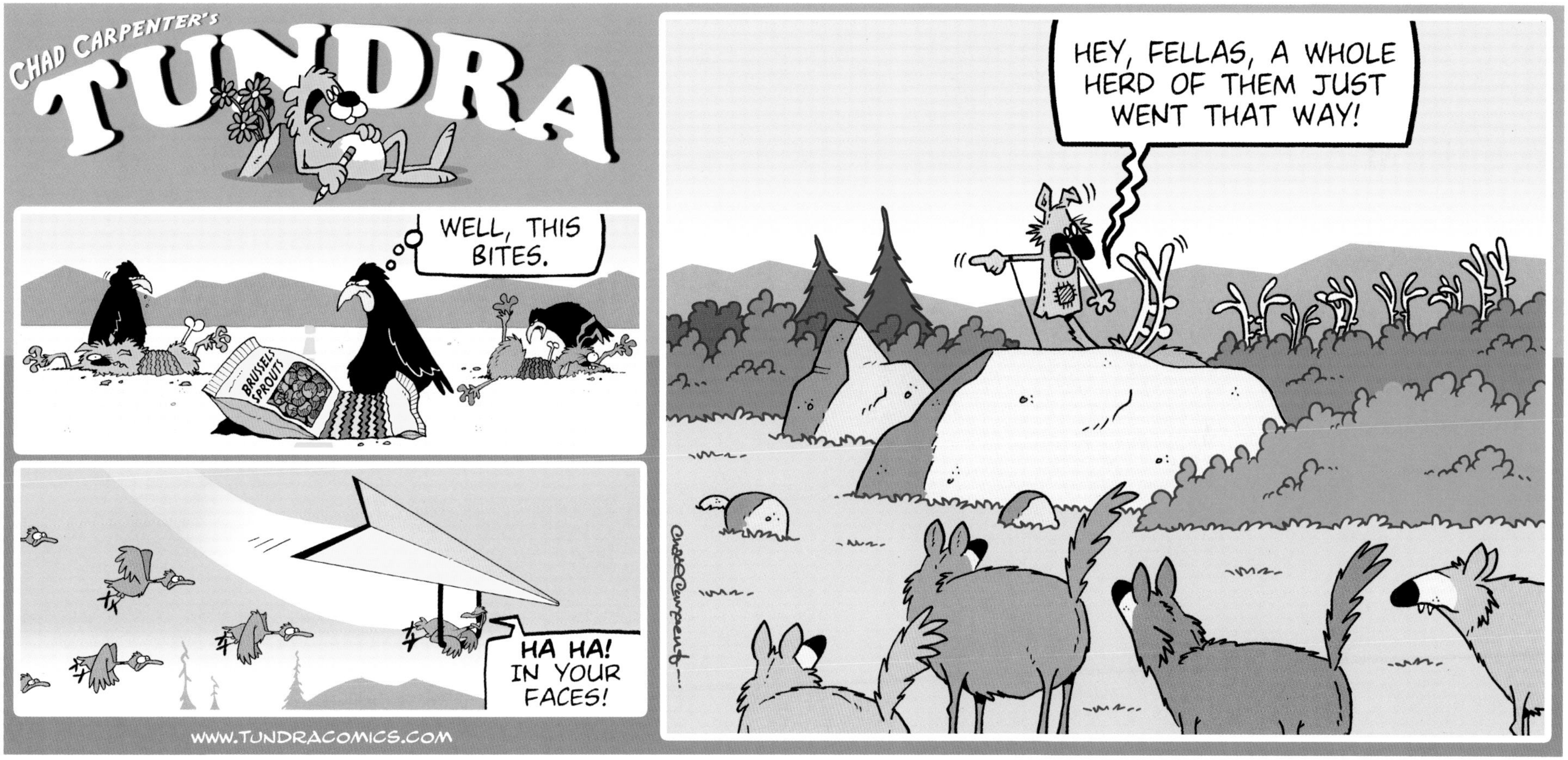
CHAD CARPENTER'S
TUNDRA
WELL, THIS BITES.
BRUSSELS SPROUTS
HA HA! IN YOUR FACES!
WWW.TUNDRACOMICS.COM
HEY, FELLAS, A WHOLE HERD OF THEM JUST WENT THAT WAY!

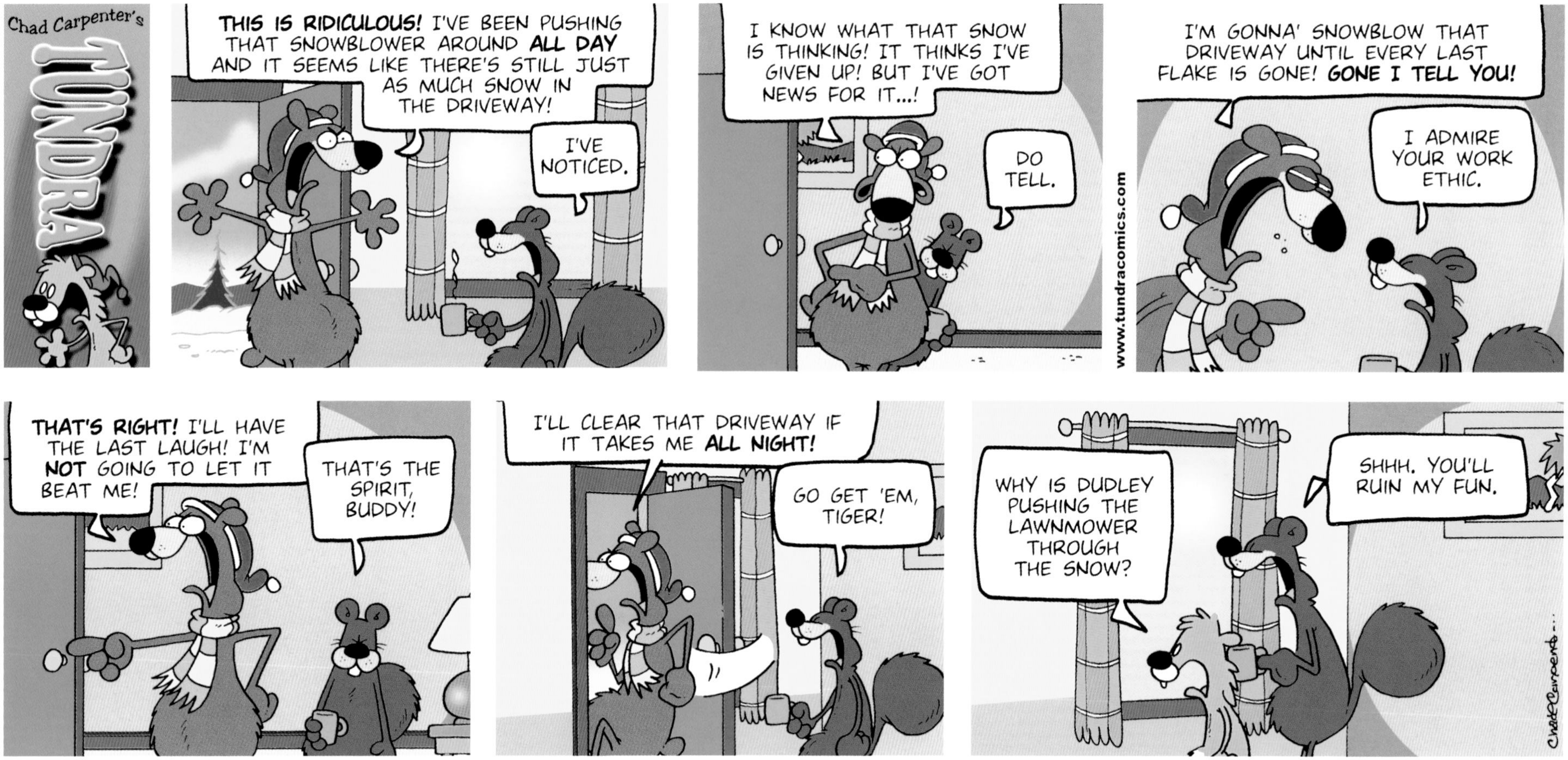
Chad Carpenter's
TUNDRA
THIS IS RIDICULOUS! I'VE BEEN PUSHING THAT SNOWBLOWER AROUND ALL DAY AND IT SEEMS LIKE THERE'S STILL JUST AS MUCH SNOW IN THE DRIVEWAY!
I'VE NOTICED.
I KNOW WHAT THAT SNOW IS THINKING! IT THINKS I'VE GIVEN UP! BUT I'VE GOT NEWS FOR IT...!
DO TELL.
www.tundracomics.com
I'M GONNA' SNOWBLOW THAT DRIVEWAY UNTIL EVERY LAST FLAKE IS GONE! GONE I TELL YOU!
I ADMIRE YOUR WORK ETHIC.
THAT'S RIGHT! I'LL HAVE THE LAST LAUGH! I'M NOT GOING TO LET IT BEAT ME!
THAT'S THE SPIRIT, BUDDY!
I'LL CLEAR THAT DRIVEWAY IF IT TAKES ME ALL NIGHT!
GO GET 'EM, TIGER!
WHY IS DUDLEY PUSHING THE LAWNMOWER THROUGH THE SNOW?
SHHH. YOU'LL RUIN MY FUN.
Chad Carpenter

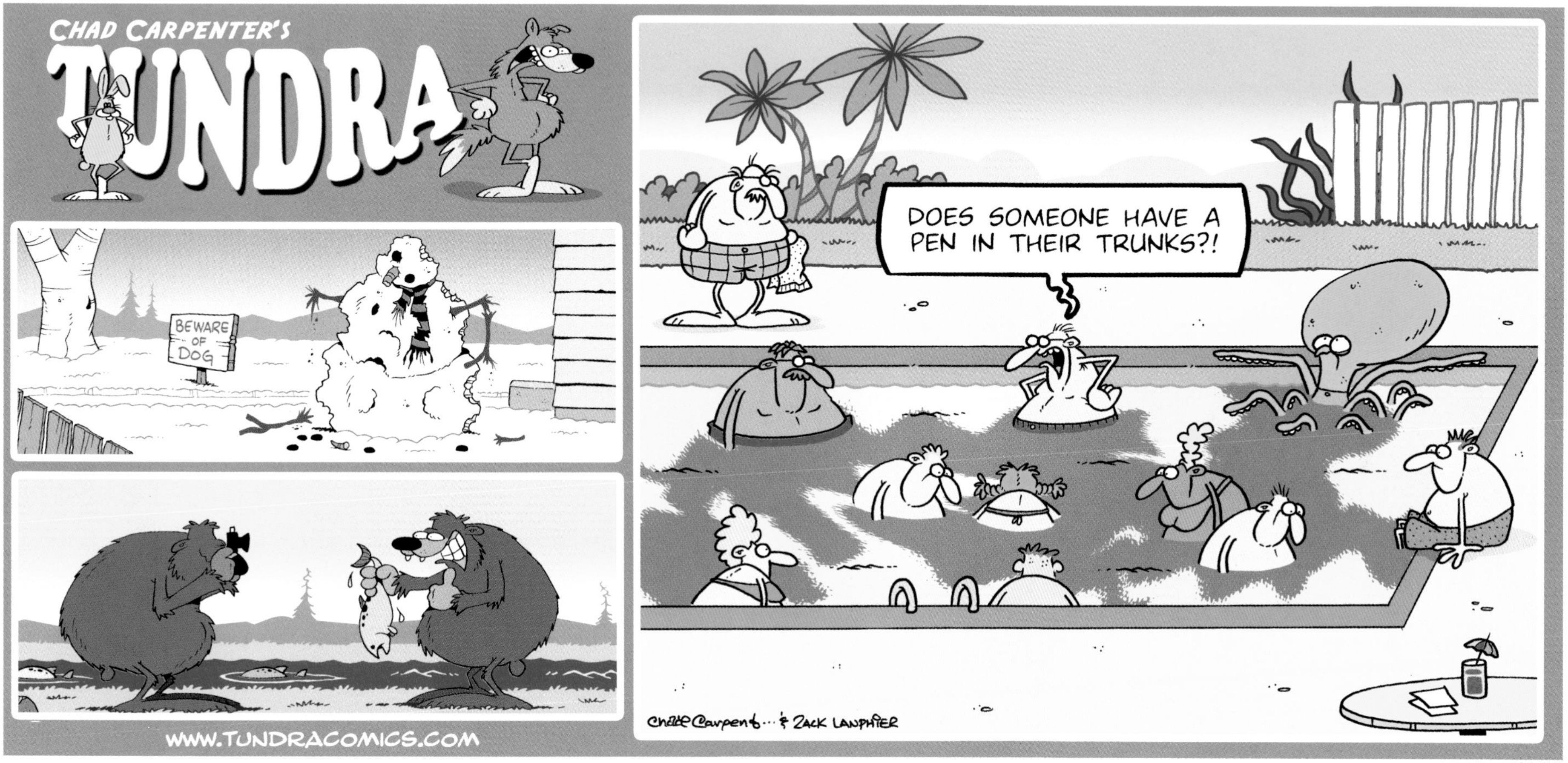
CHAD CARPENTER'S
TUNDRA
BEWARE OF DOG
DOES SOMEONE HAVE A PEN IN THEIR TRUNKS?!
ZACK LANPHIER
WWW.TUNDRACOMICS.COM

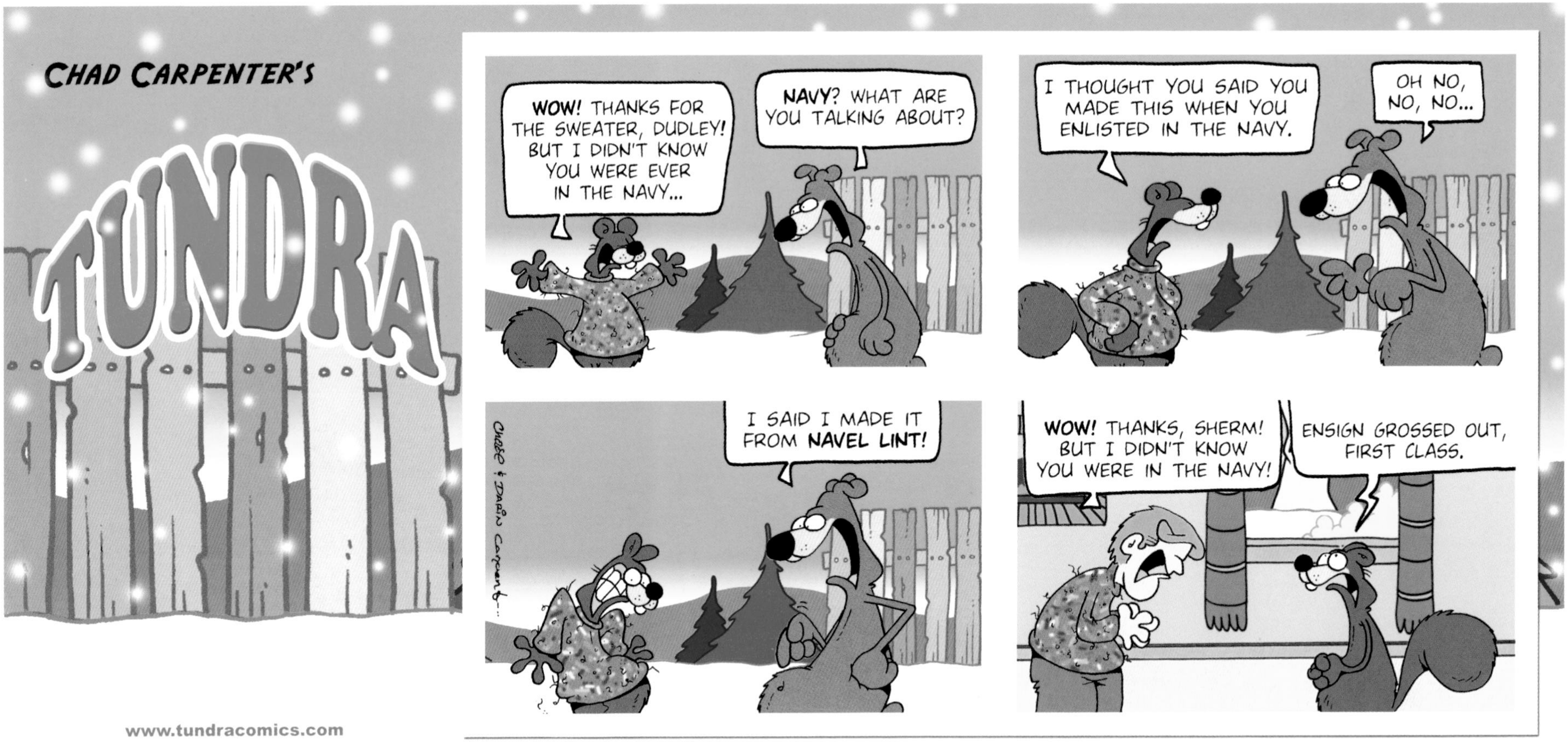
CHAD CARPENTER'S
TUNDRA
WOW! THANKS FOR THE SWEATER, DUDLEY! BUT I DIDN'T KNOW YOU WERE EVER IN THE NAVY...
NAVY? WHAT ARE YOU TALKING ABOUT?
I THOUGHT YOU SAID YOU MADE THIS WHEN YOU ENLISTED IN THE NAVY.
OH NO, NO, NO...
I SAID I MADE IT FROM NAVEL LINT!
WOW! THANKS, SHERM! BUT I DIDN'T KNOW YOU WERE IN THE NAVY!
ENSIGN GROSSED OUT, FIRST CLASS.
www.tundracomics.com

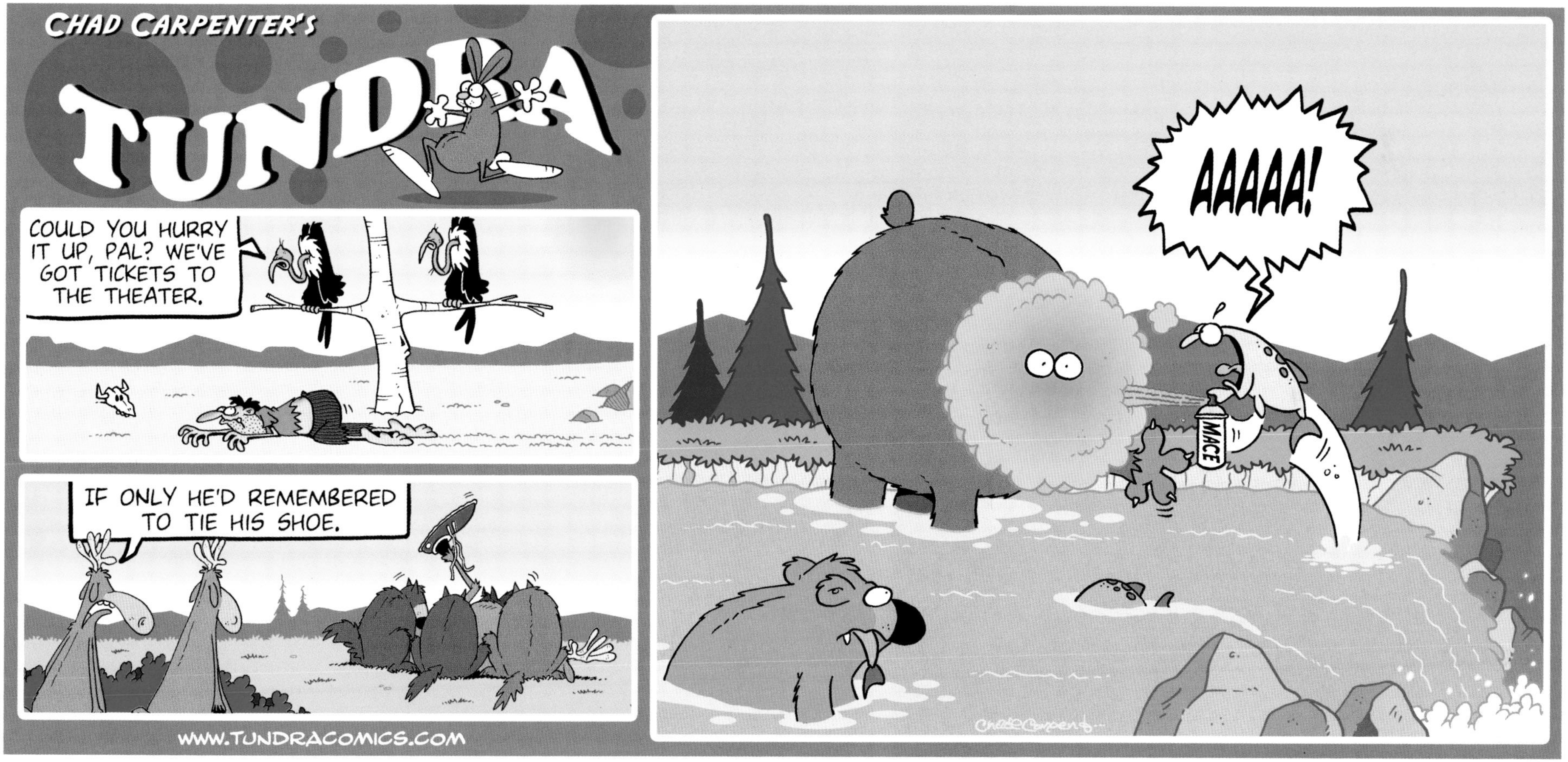
CHAD CARPENTER'S
TUNDRA
COULD YOU HURRY IT UP, PAL? WE'VE GOT TICKETS TO THE THEATER.
IF ONLY HE'D REMEMBERED TO TIE HIS SHOE.
WWW.TUNDRACOMICS.COM
AAAAA!
MACE

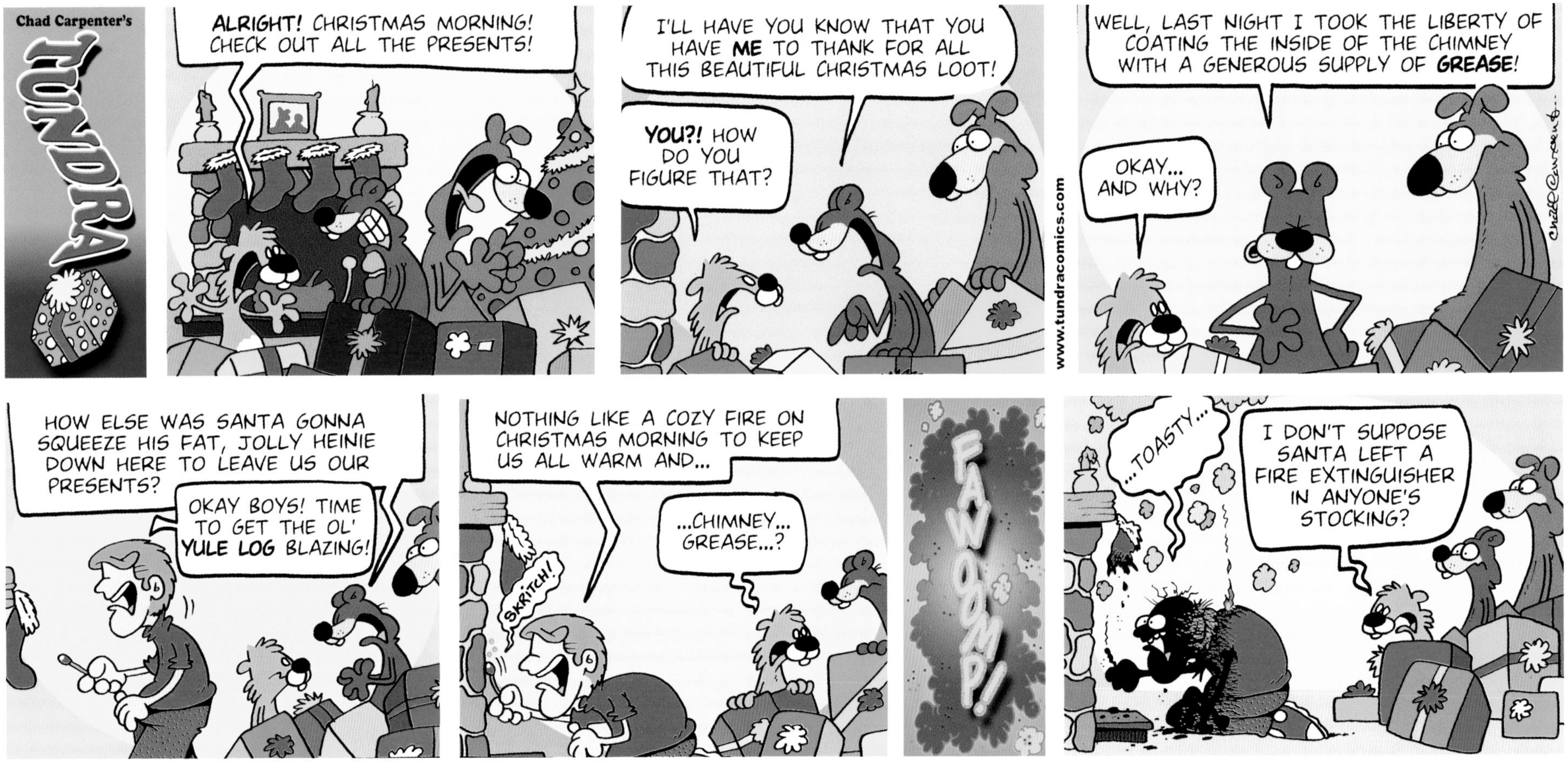
Chad Carpenter's
TUNDRA
ALRIGHT! CHRISTMAS MORNING! CHECK OUT ALL THE PRESENTS!
I'LL HAVE YOU KNOW THAT YOU HAVE ME TO THANK FOR ALL THIS BEAUTIFUL CHRISTMAS LOOT!
YOU?! HOW DO YOU FIGURE THAT?
www.tundracomics.com
WELL, LAST NIGHT I TOOK THE LIBERTY OF COATING THE INSIDE OF THE CHIMNEY WITH A GENEROUS SUPPLY OF GREASE!
OKAY... AND WHY?
HOW ELSE WAS SANTA GONNA SQUEEZE HIS FAT, JOLLY HEINIE DOWN HERE TO LEAVE US OUR PRESENTS?
OKAY BOYS! TIME TO GET THE OL' YULE LOG BLAZING!
NOTHING LIKE A COZY FIRE ON CHRISTMAS MORNING TO KEEP US ALL WARM AND...
SKRITCH!
...CHIMNEY... GREASE...?
FAWOOMP!
...TOASTY...
I DON'T SUPPOSE SANTA LEFT A FIRE EXTINGUISHER IN ANYONE'S STOCKING?

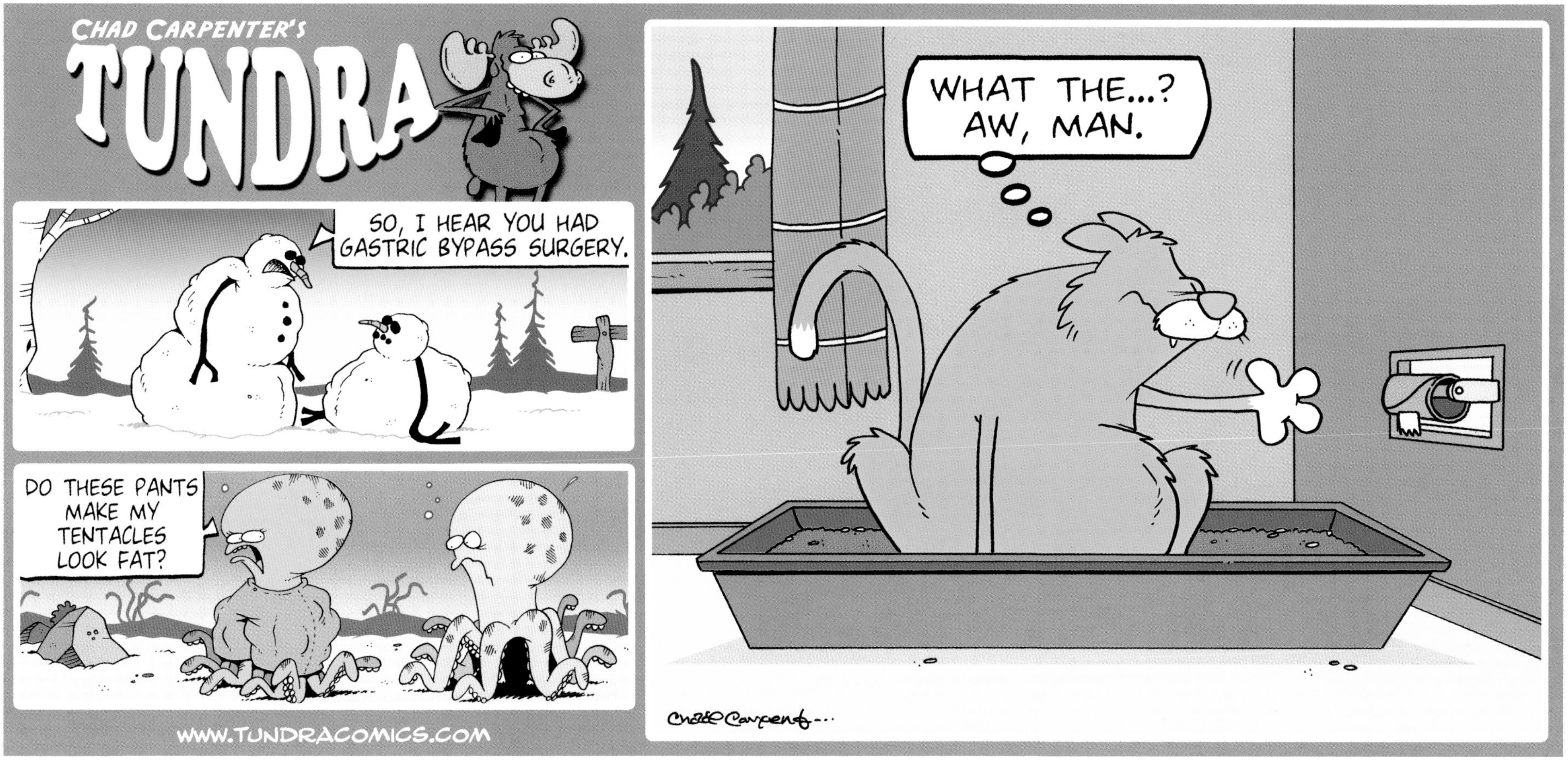
CHAD CARPENTER'S
TUNDRA
SO, I HEAR YOU HAD GASTRIC BYPASS SURGERY.
DO THESE PANTS MAKE MY TENTACLES LOOK FAT?
WWW.TUNDRACOMICS.COM
WHAT THE...? AW, MAN.

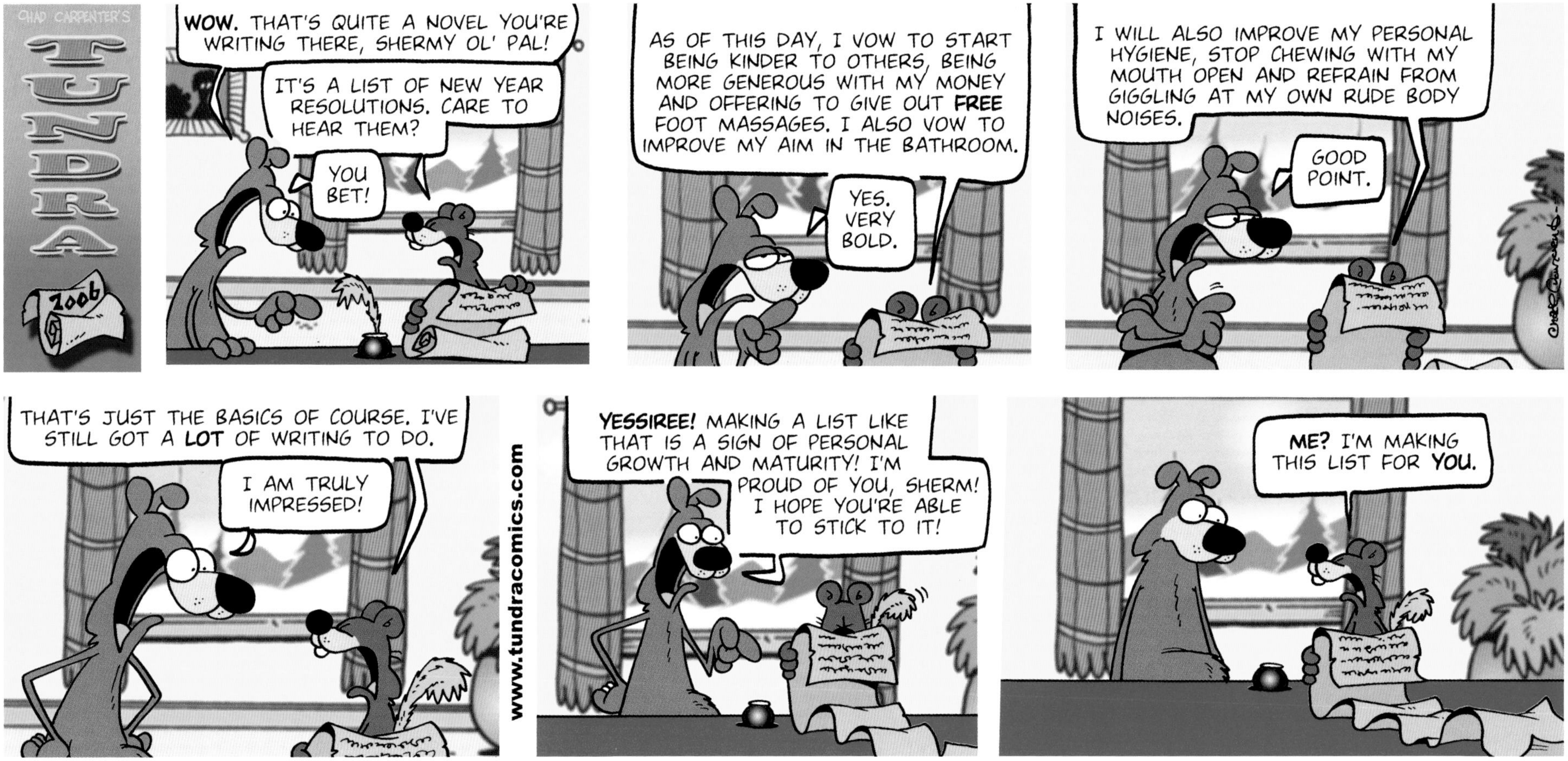
CHAD CARPENTER'S
TUNDRA
2006
WOW. THAT'S QUITE A NOVEL YOU'RE WRITING THERE, SHERMY OL' PAL!
IT'S A LIST OF NEW YEAR RESOLUTIONS. CARE TO HEAR THEM?
YOU BET!
AS OF THIS DAY, I VOW TO START BEING KINDER TO OTHERS, BEING MORE GENEROUS WITH MY MONEY AND OFFERING TO GIVE OUT FREE FOOT MASSAGES. I ALSO VOW TO IMPROVE MY AIM IN THE BATHROOM.
YES. VERY BOLD.
I WILL ALSO IMPROVE MY PERSONAL HYGIENE, STOP CHEWING WITH MY MOUTH OPEN AND REFRAIN FROM GIGGLING AT MY OWN RUDE BODY NOISES.
GOOD POINT.
THAT'S JUST THE BASICS OF COURSE. I'VE STILL GOT A LOT OF WRITING TO DO.
I AM TRULY IMPRESSED!
www.tundracomics.com
YESSIREE! MAKING A LIST LIKE THAT IS A SIGN OF PERSONAL GROWTH AND MATURITY! I'M PROUD OF YOU, SHERM! I HOPE YOU'RE ABLE TO STICK TO IT!
ME? I'M MAKING THIS LIST FOR YOU.

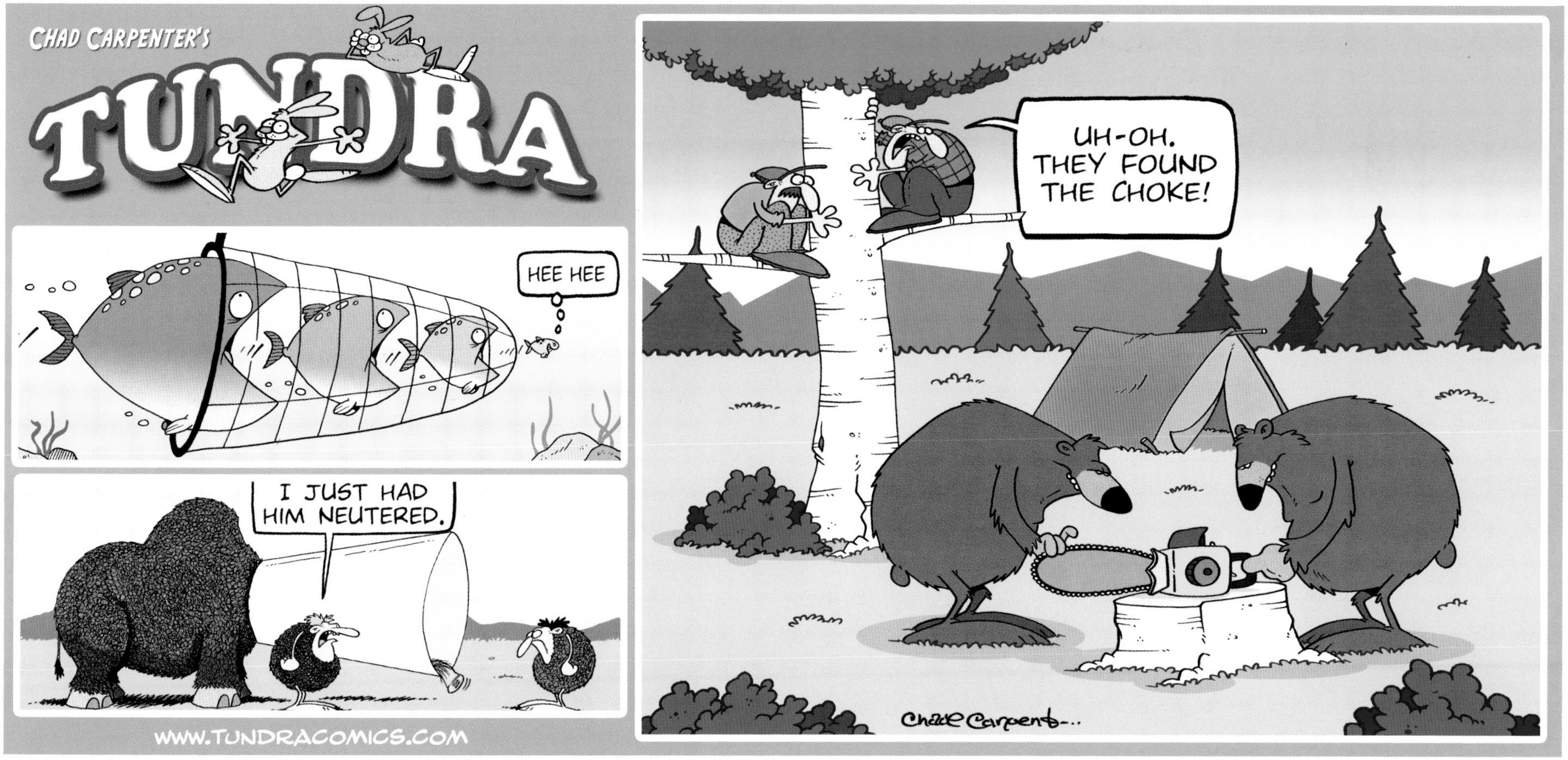
CHAD CARPENTER'S
TUNDRA
HEE HEE
I JUST HAD HIM NEUTERED.
WWW.TUNDRACOMICS.COM
UH-OH. THEY FOUND THE CHOKE!
Chad Carpenter

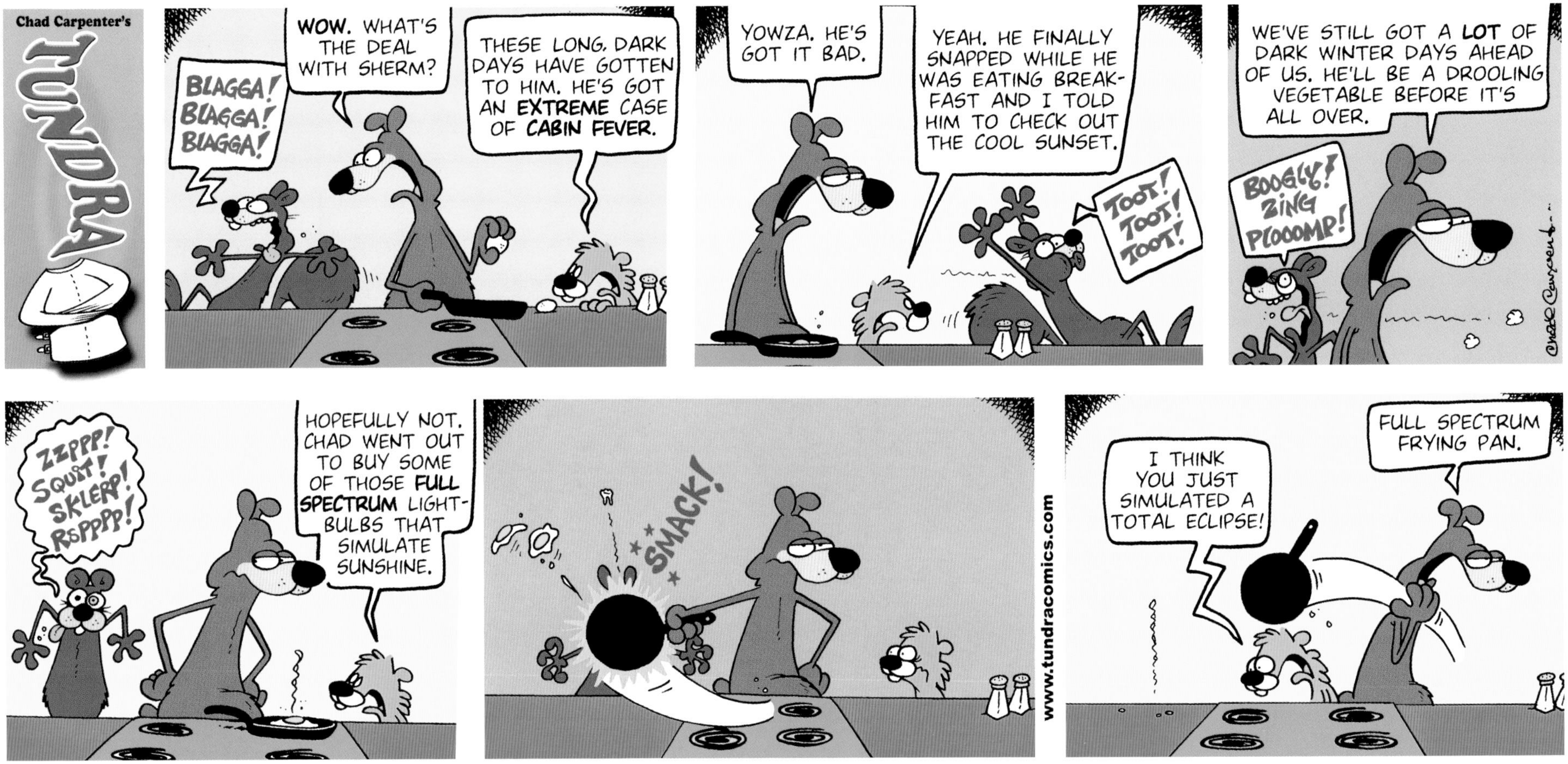
Chad Carpenter's
TUNDRA
WOW. WHAT'S THE DEAL WITH SHERM?
BLAGGA! BLAGGA! BLAGGA!
THESE LONG, DARK DAYS HAVE GOTTEN TO HIM. HE'S GOT AN EXTREME CASE OF CABIN FEVER.
YOWZA. HE'S GOT IT BAD.
YEAH. HE FINALLY SNAPPED WHILE HE WAS EATING BREAK-FAST AND I TOLD HIM TO CHECK OUT THE COOL SUNSET.
TOOT! TOOT! TOOT!
WE'VE STILL GOT A LOT OF DARK WINTER DAYS AHEAD OF US. HE'LL BE A DROOLING VEGETABLE BEFORE IT'S ALL OVER.
BOOGLY! ZING PLOOOMP!
ZZPPP! SQUIRT! SKLERP! RSPPPP!
HOPEFULLY NOT. CHAD WENT OUT TO BUY SOME OF THOSE FULL SPECTRUM LIGHT-BULBS THAT SIMULATE SUNSHINE.
SMACK!
www.tundracomics.com
I THINK YOU JUST SIMULATED A TOTAL ECLIPSE!
FULL SPECTRUM FRYING PAN.

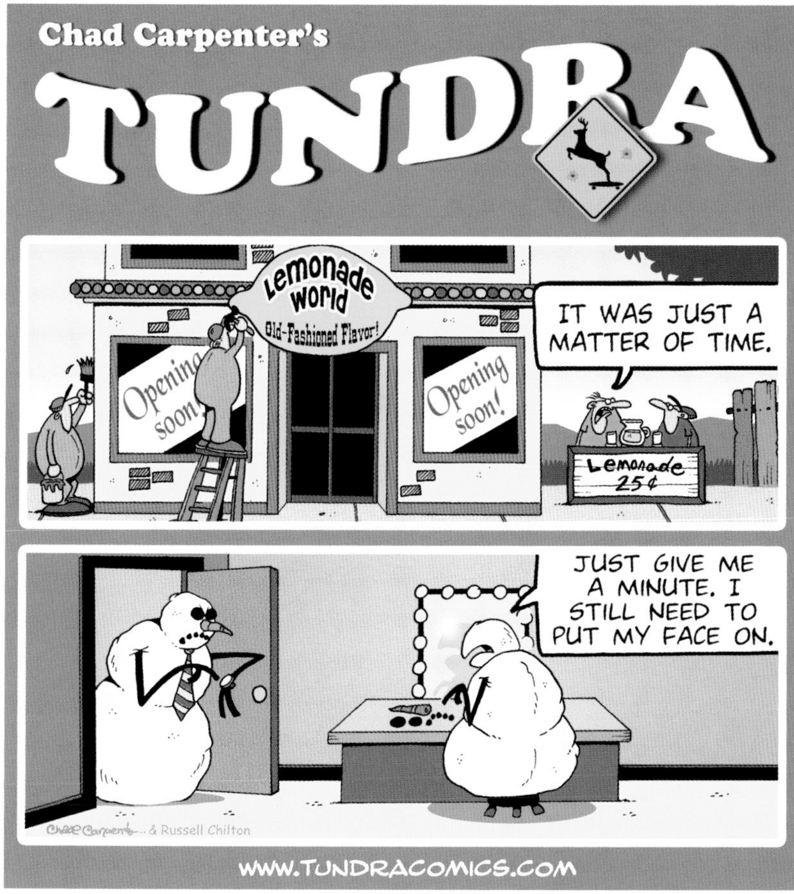
Chad Carpenter's
TUNDRA
Lemonade World
Old-Fashioned Flavor!
Opening soon!
Opening soon!
IT WAS JUST A MATTER OF TIME.
Lemonade 25¢
JUST GIVE ME A MINUTE. I STILL NEED TO PUT MY FACE ON.
& Russell Chilton
WWW.TUNDRACOMICS.COM

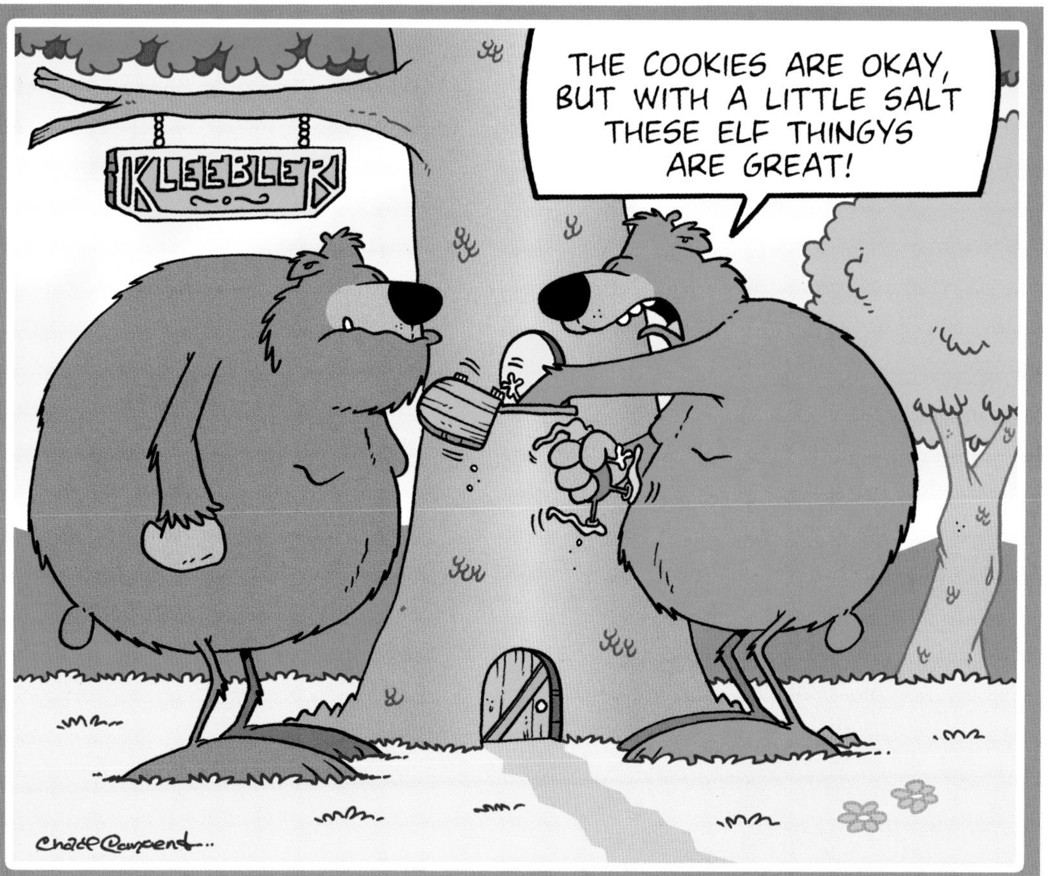
KLEEBLER
THE COOKIES ARE OKAY, BUT WITH A LITTLE SALT THESE ELF THINGYS ARE GREAT!

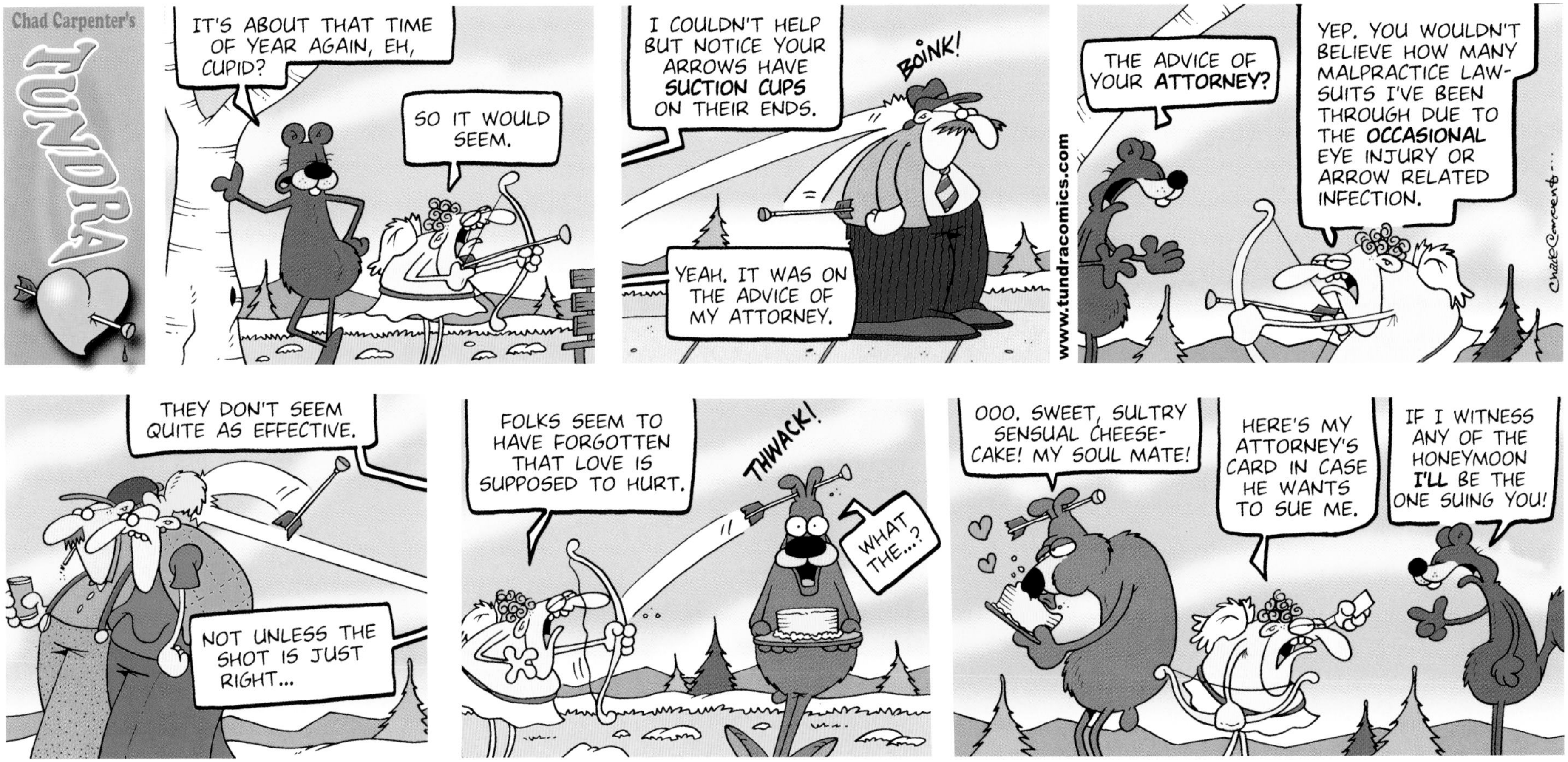
Chad Carpenter's
TUNDRA
IT'S ABOUT THAT TIME OF YEAR AGAIN, EH, CUPID?
SO IT WOULD SEEM.
I COULDN'T HELP BUT NOTICE YOUR ARROWS HAVE SUCTION CUPS ON THEIR ENDS.
BOINK!
YEAH. IT WAS ON THE ADVICE OF MY ATTORNEY.
www.tundracomics.com
THE ADVICE OF YOUR ATTORNEY?
YEP. YOU WOULDN'T BELIEVE HOW MANY MALPRACTICE LAW-SUITS I'VE BEEN THROUGH DUE TO THE OCCASIONAL EYE INJURY OR ARROW RELATED INFECTION.
THEY DON'T SEEM QUITE AS EFFECTIVE.
NOT UNLESS THE SHOT IS JUST RIGHT...
FOLKS SEEM TO HAVE FORGOTTEN THAT LOVE IS SUPPOSED TO HURT.
THWACK!
WHAT THE...?
OOO. SWEET, SULTRY SENSUAL CHEESE-CAKE! MY SOUL MATE!
HERE'S MY ATTORNEY'S CARD IN CASE HE WANTS TO SUE ME.
IF I WITNESS ANY OF THE HONEYMOON I'LL BE THE ONE SUING YOU!

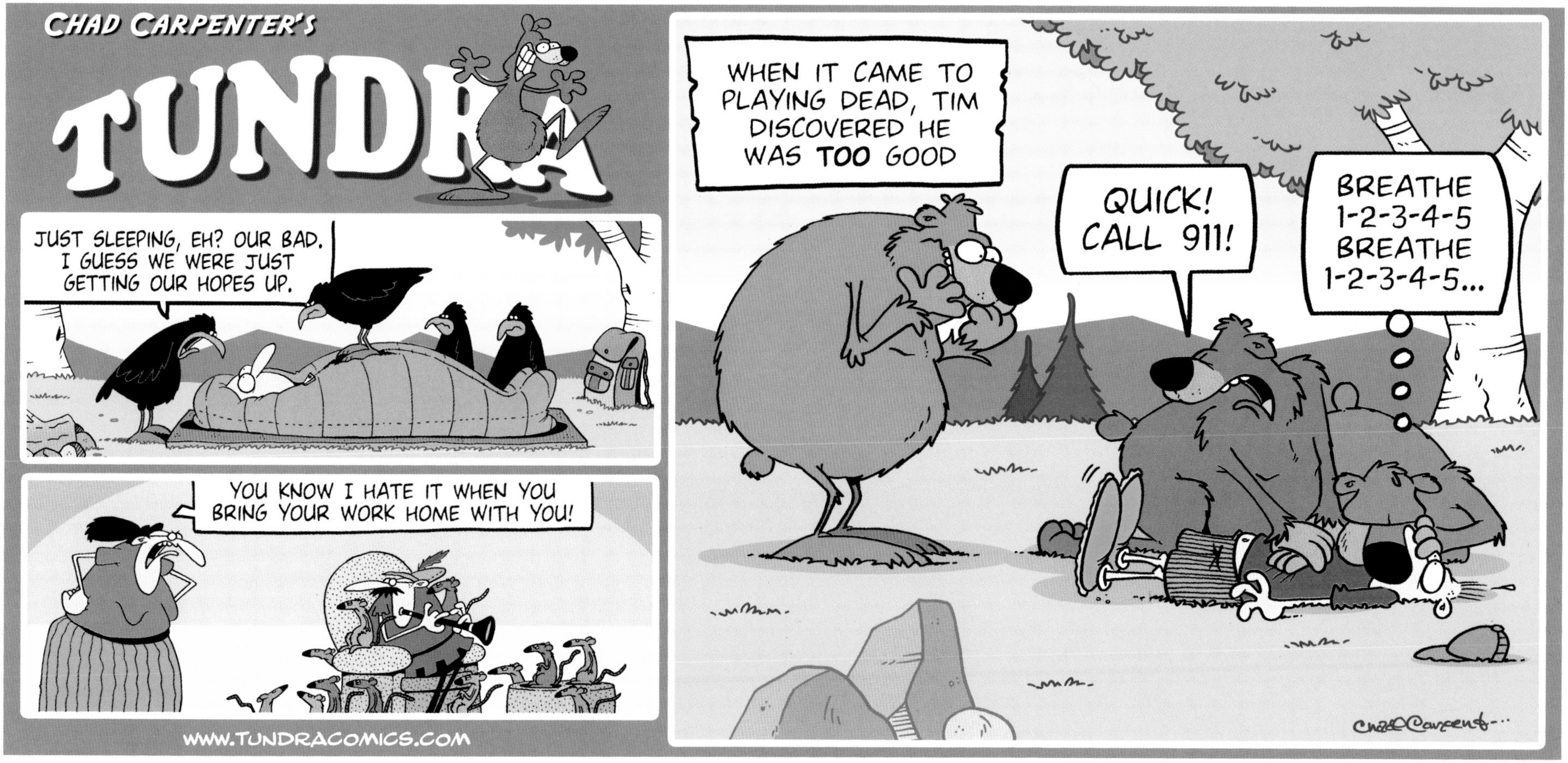
CHAD CARPENTER'S
TUNDRA
JUST SLEEPING, EH? OUR BAD. I GUESS WE WERE JUST GETTING OUR HOPES UP.
YOU KNOW I HATE IT WHEN YOU BRING YOUR WORK HOME WITH YOU!
WWW.TUNDRACOMICS.COM
WHEN IT CAME TO PLAYING DEAD, TIM DISCOVERED HE WAS **TOO** GOOD
QUICK! CALL 911!
BREATHE 1-2-3-4-5 BREATHE 1-2-3-4-5...

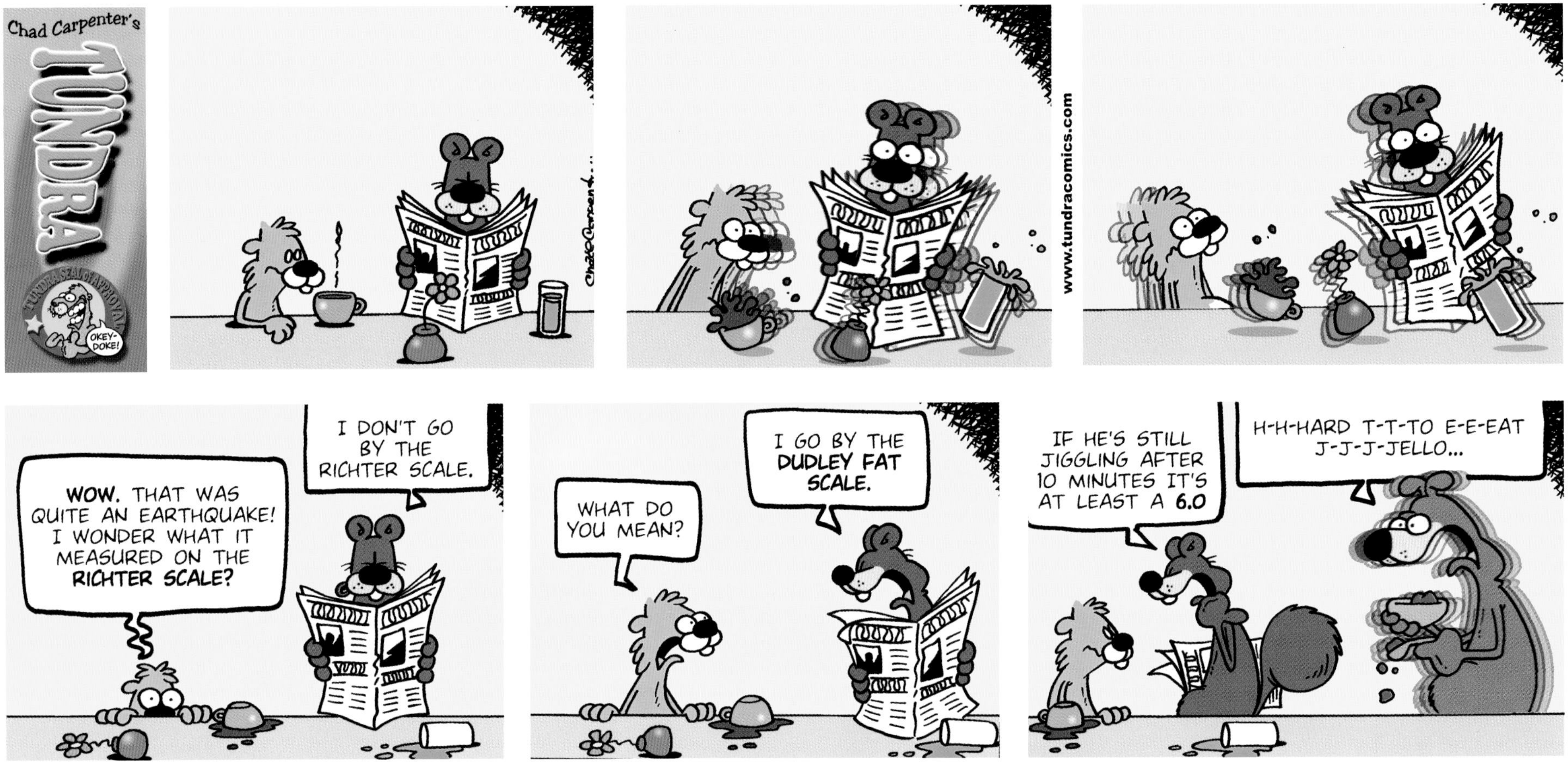
Chad Carpenter's
TUNDRA
TUNDRA SEAL of APPROVAL
OKEY-DOKE!
www.tundracomics.com
WOW. THAT WAS QUITE AN EARTHQUAKE! I WONDER WHAT IT MEASURED ON THE RICHTER SCALE?
I DON'T GO BY THE RICHTER SCALE.
WHAT DO YOU MEAN?
I GO BY THE DUDLEY FAT SCALE.
IF HE'S STILL JIGGLING AFTER 10 MINUTES IT'S AT LEAST A 6.0
H-H-HARD T-T-TO E-E-EAT J-J-J-JELLO...

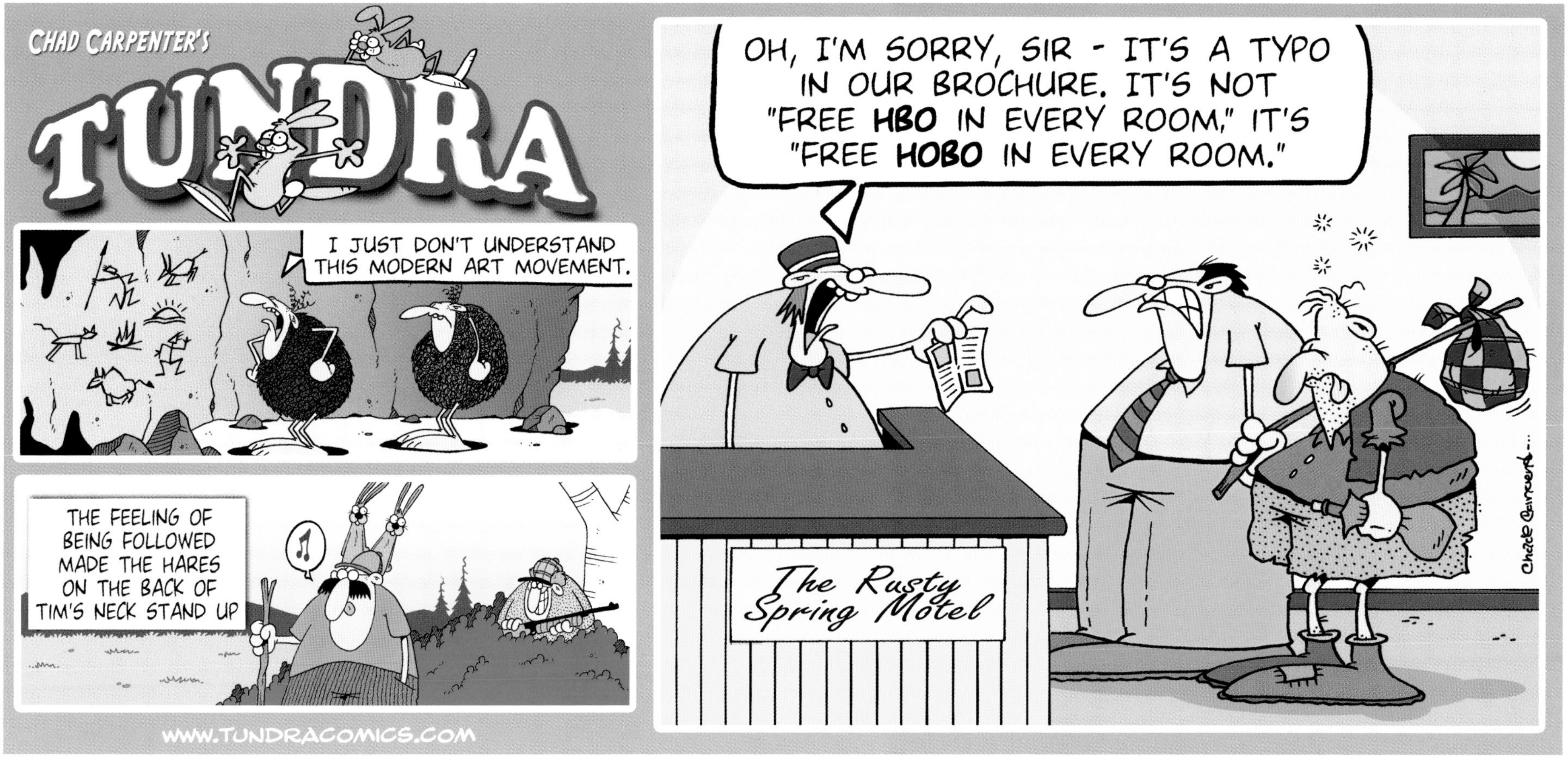
CHAD CARPENTER'S
TUNDRA
I JUST DON'T UNDERSTAND THIS MODERN ART MOVEMENT.
THE FEELING OF BEING FOLLOWED MADE THE HARES ON THE BACK OF TIM'S NECK STAND UP
WWW.TUNDRACOMICS.COM
OH, I'M SORRY, SIR - IT'S A TYPO IN OUR BROCHURE. IT'S NOT "FREE **HBO** IN EVERY ROOM," IT'S "FREE **HOBO** IN EVERY ROOM."
The Rusty Spring Motel

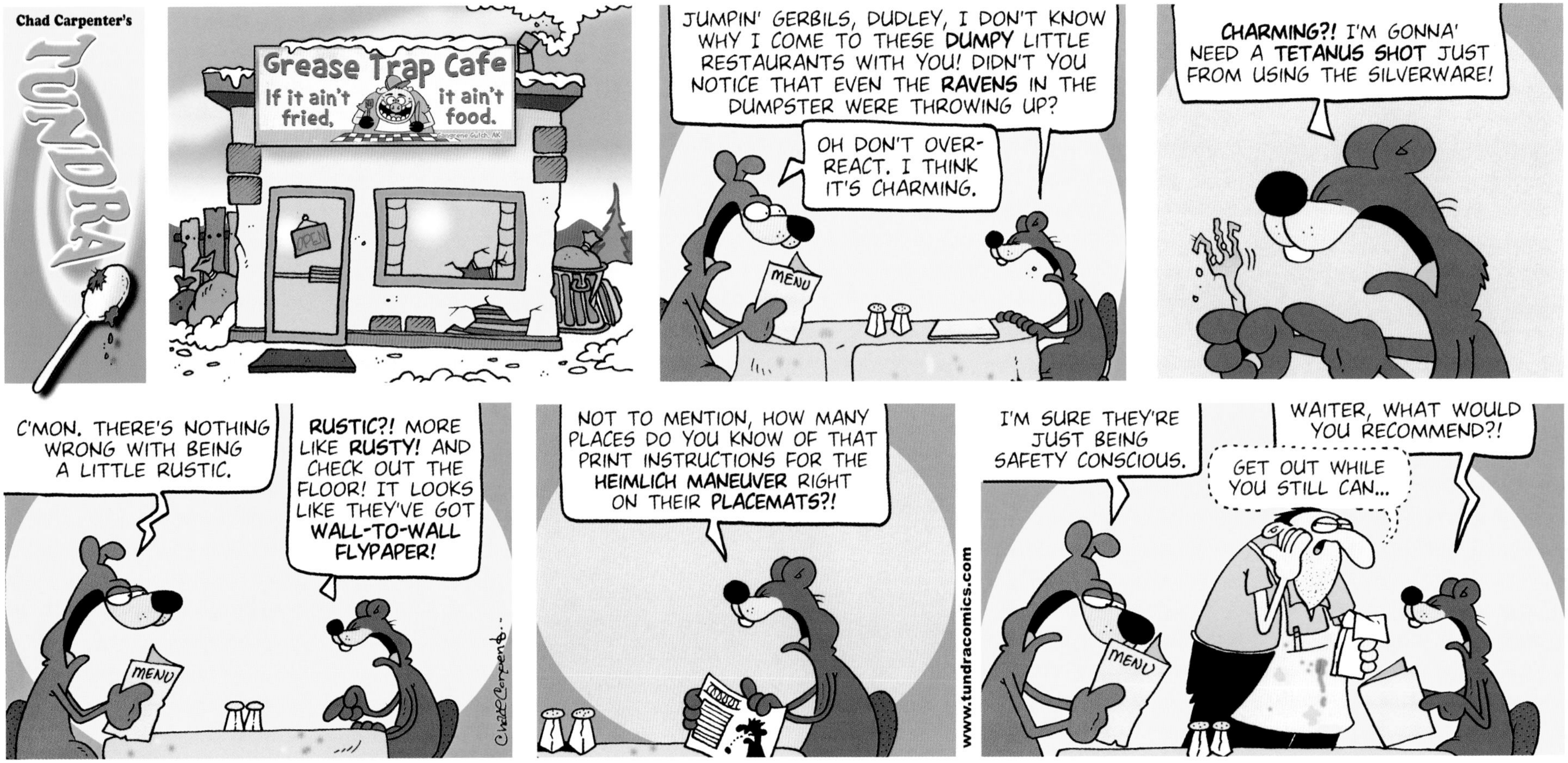
Chad Carpenter's
TUNDRA
Grease Trap Cafe
If it ain't fried, it ain't food.
Gangrene Gulch, AK
OPEN
JUMPIN' GERBILS, DUDLEY, I DON'T KNOW WHY I COME TO THESE DUMPY LITTLE RESTAURANTS WITH YOU! DIDN'T YOU NOTICE THAT EVEN THE RAVENS IN THE DUMPSTER WERE THROWING UP?
OH DON'T OVER-REACT. I THINK IT'S CHARMING.
MENU
CHARMING?! I'M GONNA' NEED A TETANUS SHOT JUST FROM USING THE SILVERWARE!
C'MON. THERE'S NOTHING WRONG WITH BEING A LITTLE RUSTIC.
RUSTIC?! MORE LIKE RUSTY! AND CHECK OUT THE FLOOR! IT LOOKS LIKE THEY'VE GOT WALL-TO-WALL FLYPAPER!
MENU
NOT TO MENTION, HOW MANY PLACES DO YOU KNOW OF THAT PRINT INSTRUCTIONS FOR THE HEIMLICH MANEUVER RIGHT ON THEIR PLACEMATS?!
www.tundracomics.com
I'M SURE THEY'RE JUST BEING SAFETY CONSCIOUS.
WAITER, WHAT WOULD YOU RECOMMEND?!
GET OUT WHILE YOU STILL CAN...
MENU

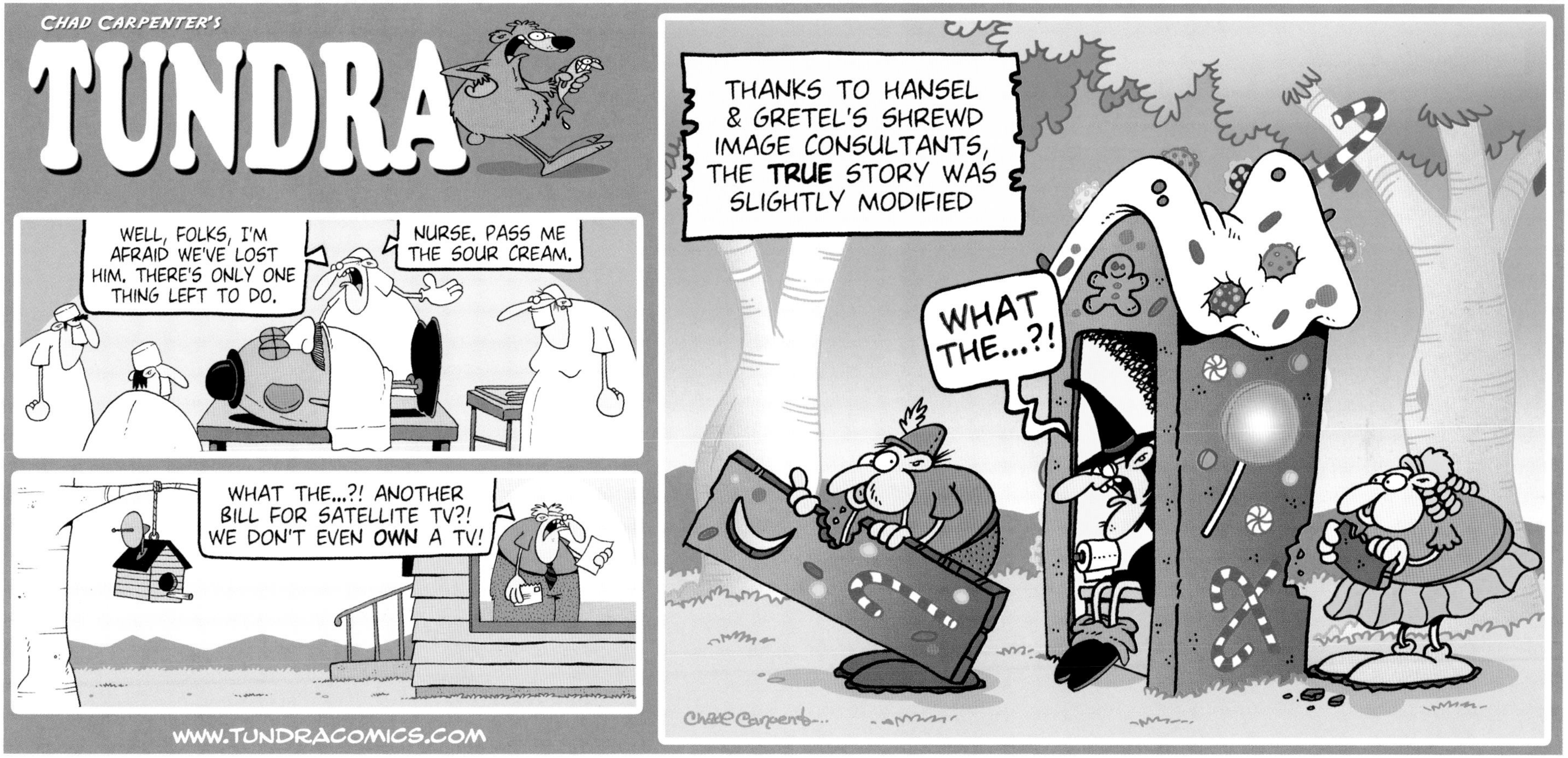

CHAD CARPENTER'S
TUNDRA
WELL, FOLKS, I'M AFRAID WE'VE LOST HIM. THERE'S ONLY ONE THING LEFT TO DO.
NURSE. PASS ME THE SOUR CREAM.
WHAT THE...?! ANOTHER BILL FOR SATELLITE TV?! WE DON'T EVEN OWN A TV!
WWW.TUNDRACOMICS.COM
THANKS TO HANSEL & GRETEL'S SHREWD IMAGE CONSULTANTS, THE TRUE STORY WAS SLIGHTLY MODIFIED
WHAT THE...?!

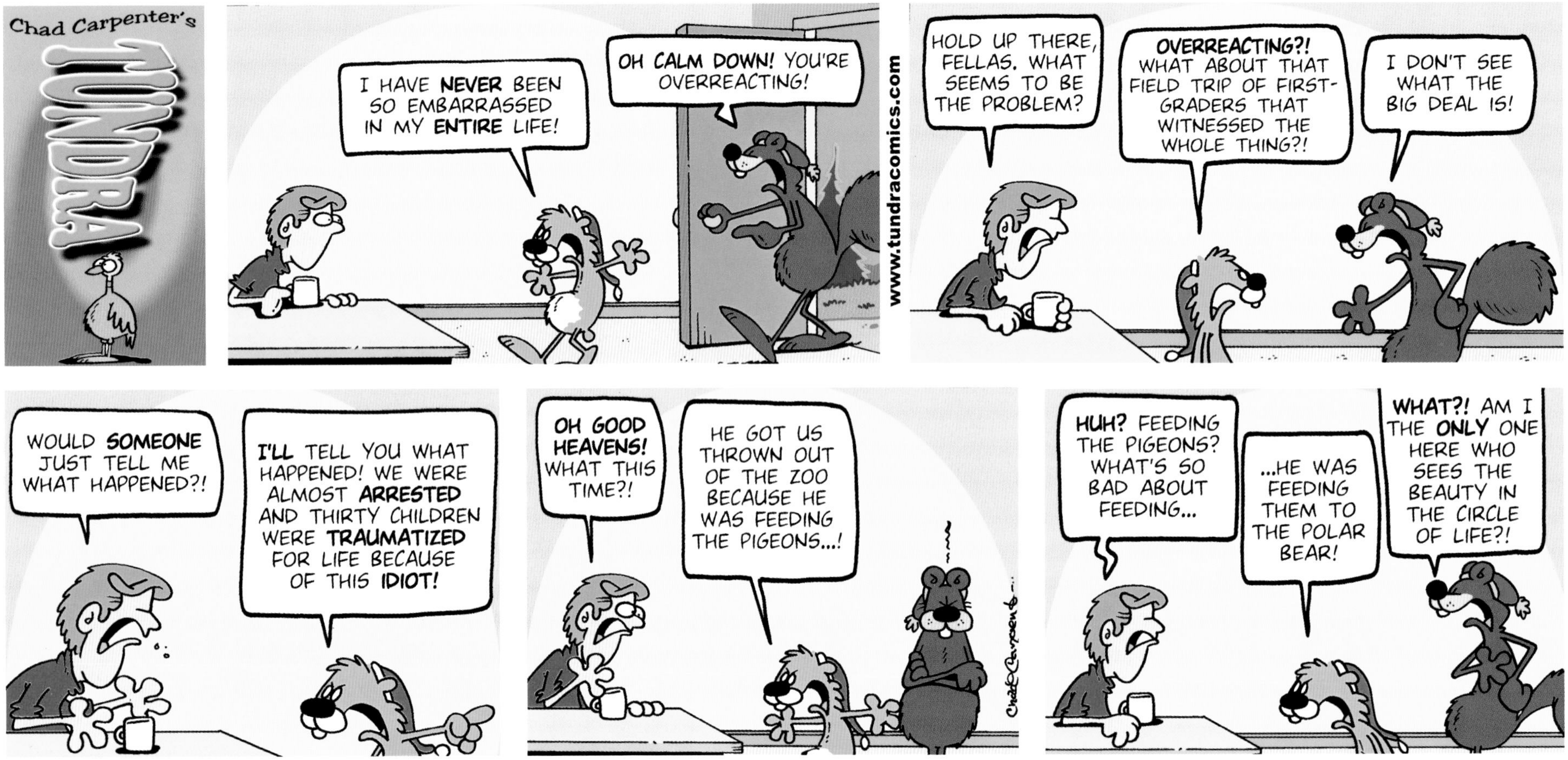
Chad Carpenter's
TUNDRA
I HAVE NEVER BEEN SO EMBARRASSED IN MY ENTIRE LIFE!
OH CALM DOWN! YOU'RE OVERREACTING!
www.tundracomics.com
HOLD UP THERE, FELLAS. WHAT SEEMS TO BE THE PROBLEM?
OVERREACTING?! WHAT ABOUT THAT FIELD TRIP OF FIRST-GRADERS THAT WITNESSED THE WHOLE THING?!
I DON'T SEE WHAT THE BIG DEAL IS!
WOULD SOMEONE JUST TELL ME WHAT HAPPENED?!
I'LL TELL YOU WHAT HAPPENED! WE WERE ALMOST ARRESTED AND THIRTY CHILDREN WERE TRAUMATIZED FOR LIFE BECAUSE OF THIS IDIOT!
OH GOOD HEAVENS! WHAT THIS TIME?!
HE GOT US THROWN OUT OF THE ZOO BECAUSE HE WAS FEEDING THE PIGEONS...!
HUH? FEEDING THE PIGEONS? WHAT'S SO BAD ABOUT FEEDING...
...HE WAS FEEDING THEM TO THE POLAR BEAR!
WHAT?! AM I THE ONLY ONE HERE WHO SEES THE BEAUTY IN THE CIRCLE OF LIFE?!

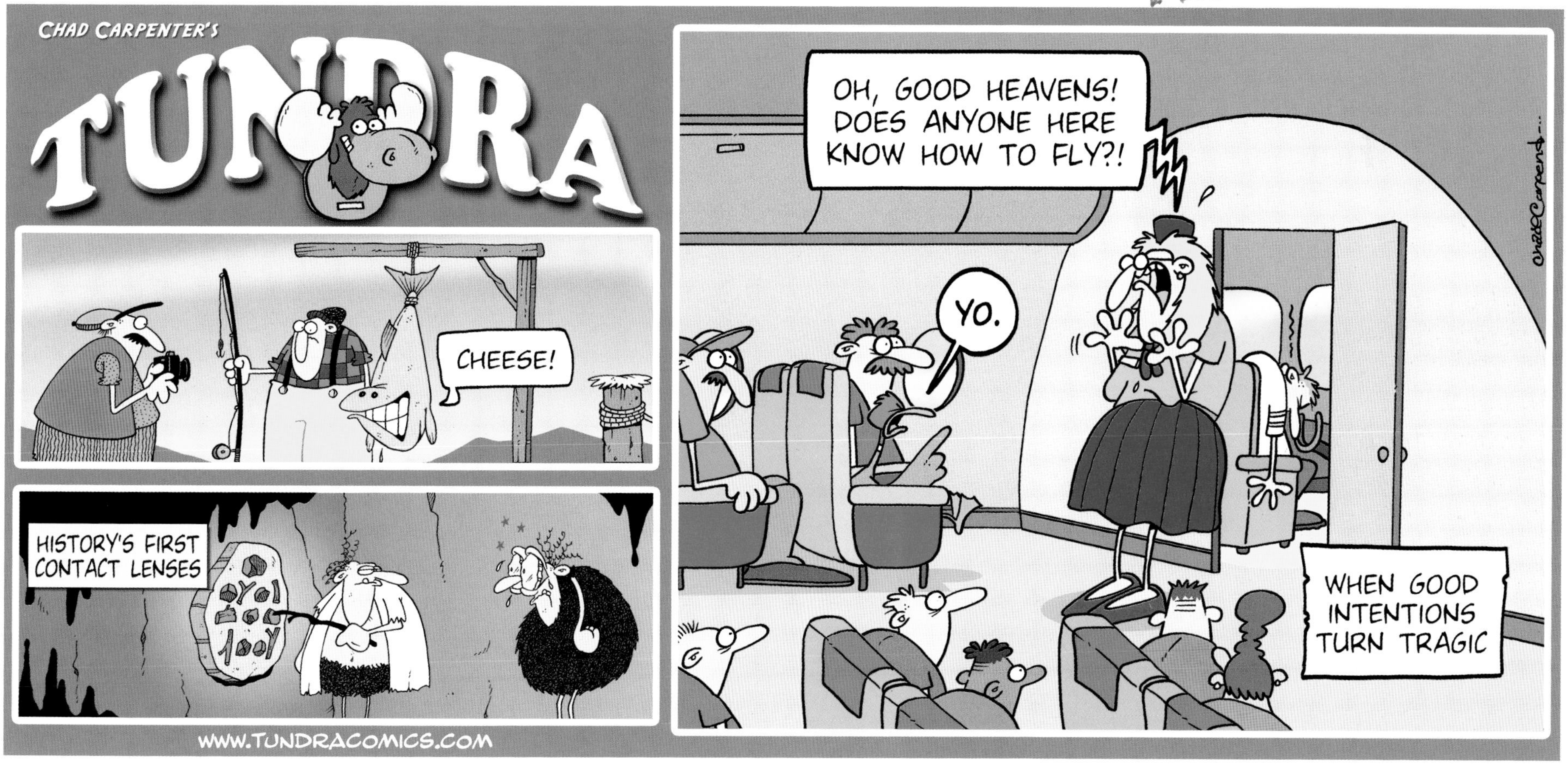
CHAD CARPENTER'S
TUNDRA
CHEESE!
HISTORY'S FIRST CONTACT LENSES
WWW.TUNDRACOMICS.COM
OH, GOOD HEAVENS! DOES ANYONE HERE KNOW HOW TO FLY?!
YO.
WHEN GOOD INTENTIONS TURN TRAGIC

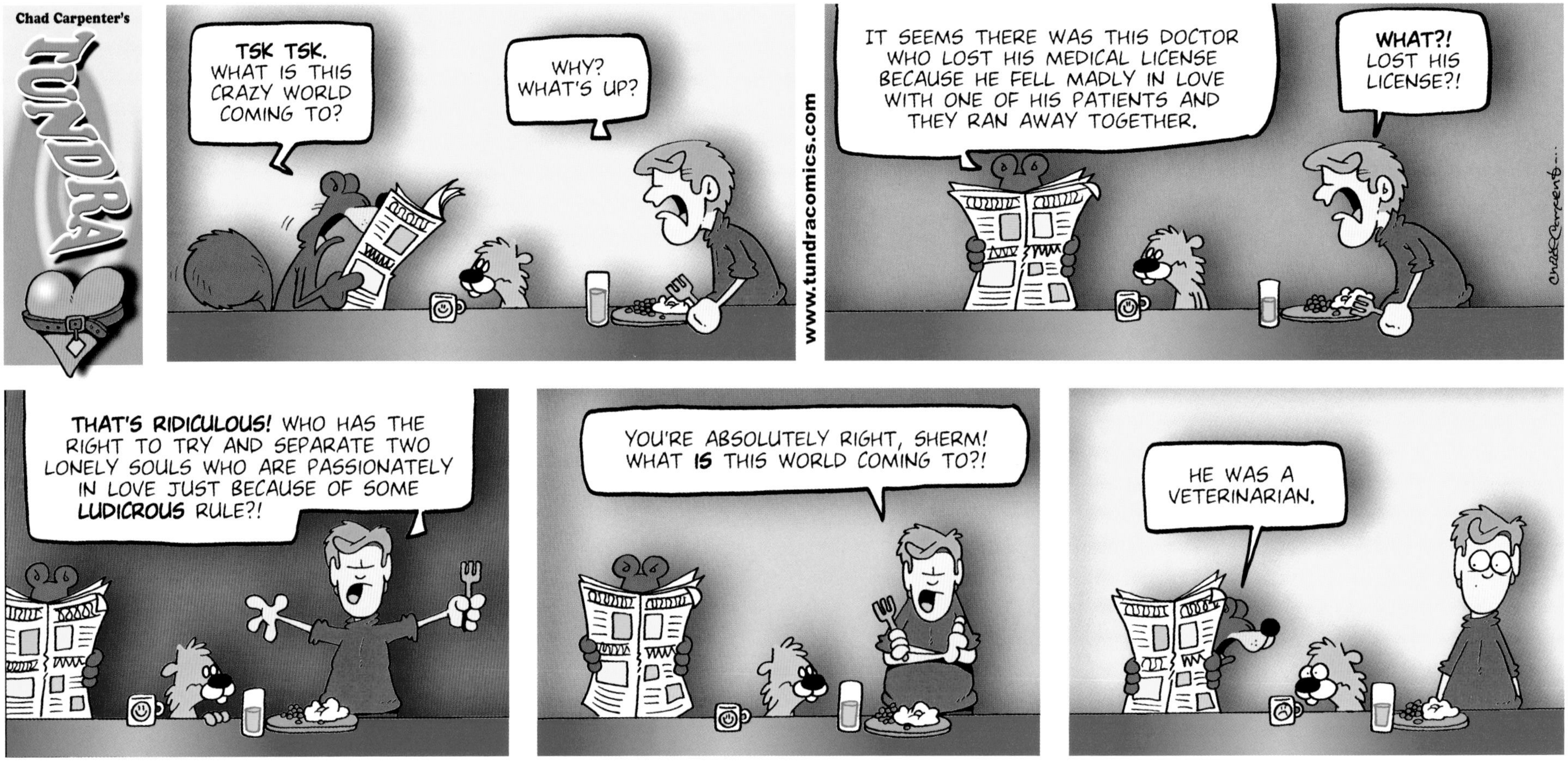
Chad Carpenter's
TUNDRA
TSK TSK. WHAT IS THIS CRAZY WORLD COMING TO?
WHY? WHAT'S UP?
www.tundracomics.com
IT SEEMS THERE WAS THIS DOCTOR WHO LOST HIS MEDICAL LICENSE BECAUSE HE FELL MADLY IN LOVE WITH ONE OF HIS PATIENTS AND THEY RAN AWAY TOGETHER.
WHAT?! LOST HIS LICENSE?!
THAT'S RIDICULOUS! WHO HAS THE RIGHT TO TRY AND SEPARATE TWO LONELY SOULS WHO ARE PASSIONATELY IN LOVE JUST BECAUSE OF SOME LUDICROUS RULE?!
YOU'RE ABSOLUTELY RIGHT, SHERM! WHAT IS THIS WORLD COMING TO?!
HE WAS A VETERINARIAN.

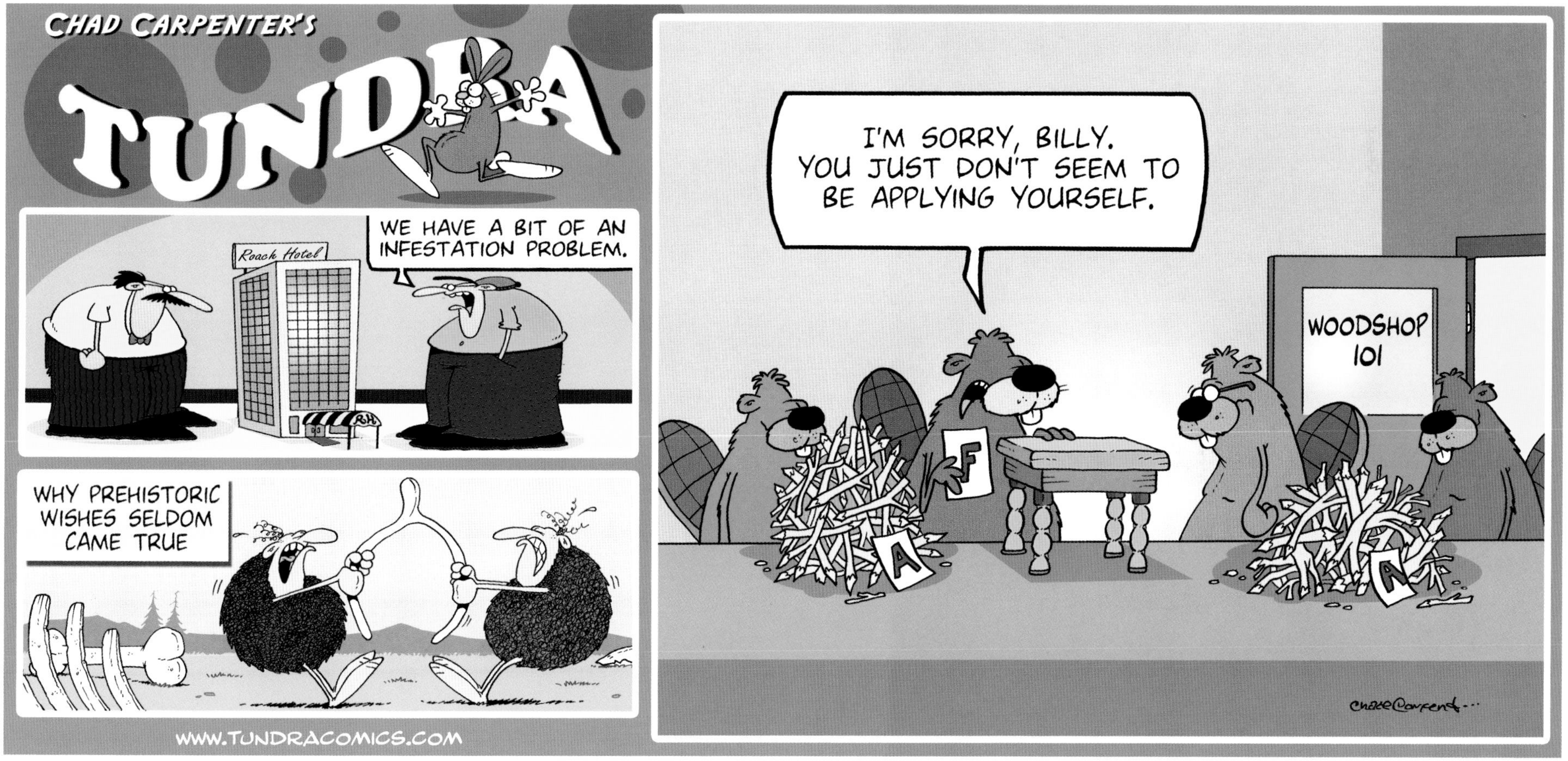
CHAD CARPENTER'S
TUNDRA
Roach Hotel
WE HAVE A BIT OF AN INFESTATION PROBLEM.
WHY PREHISTORIC WISHES SELDOM CAME TRUE
I'M SORRY, BILLY. YOU JUST DON'T SEEM TO BE APPLYING YOURSELF.
WOODSHOP 101
WWW.TUNDRACOMICS.COM

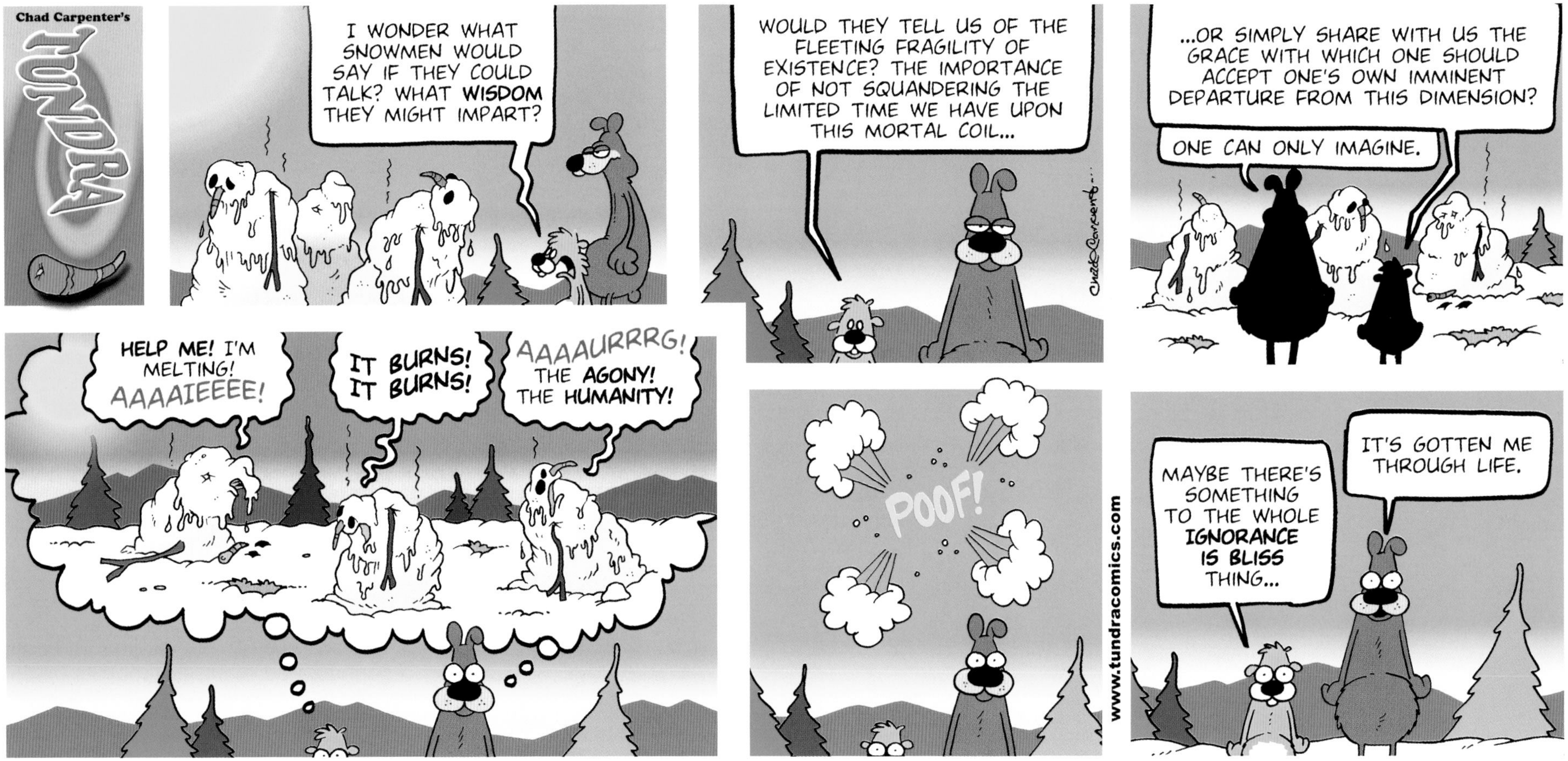
Chad Carpenter's
TUNDRA
I WONDER WHAT SNOWMEN WOULD SAY IF THEY COULD TALK? WHAT WISDOM THEY MIGHT IMPART?
WOULD THEY TELL US OF THE FLEETING FRAGILITY OF EXISTENCE? THE IMPORTANCE OF NOT SQUANDERING THE LIMITED TIME WE HAVE UPON THIS MORTAL COIL...
...OR SIMPLY SHARE WITH US THE GRACE WITH WHICH ONE SHOULD ACCEPT ONE'S OWN IMMINENT DEPARTURE FROM THIS DIMENSION?
ONE CAN ONLY IMAGINE.
HELP ME! I'M MELTING! AAAAIEEEE!
IT BURNS! IT BURNS!
AAAAURRRG! THE AGONY! THE HUMANITY!
POOF!
www.tundracomics.com
MAYBE THERE'S SOMETHING TO THE WHOLE IGNORANCE IS BLISS THING...
IT'S GOTTEN ME THROUGH LIFE.

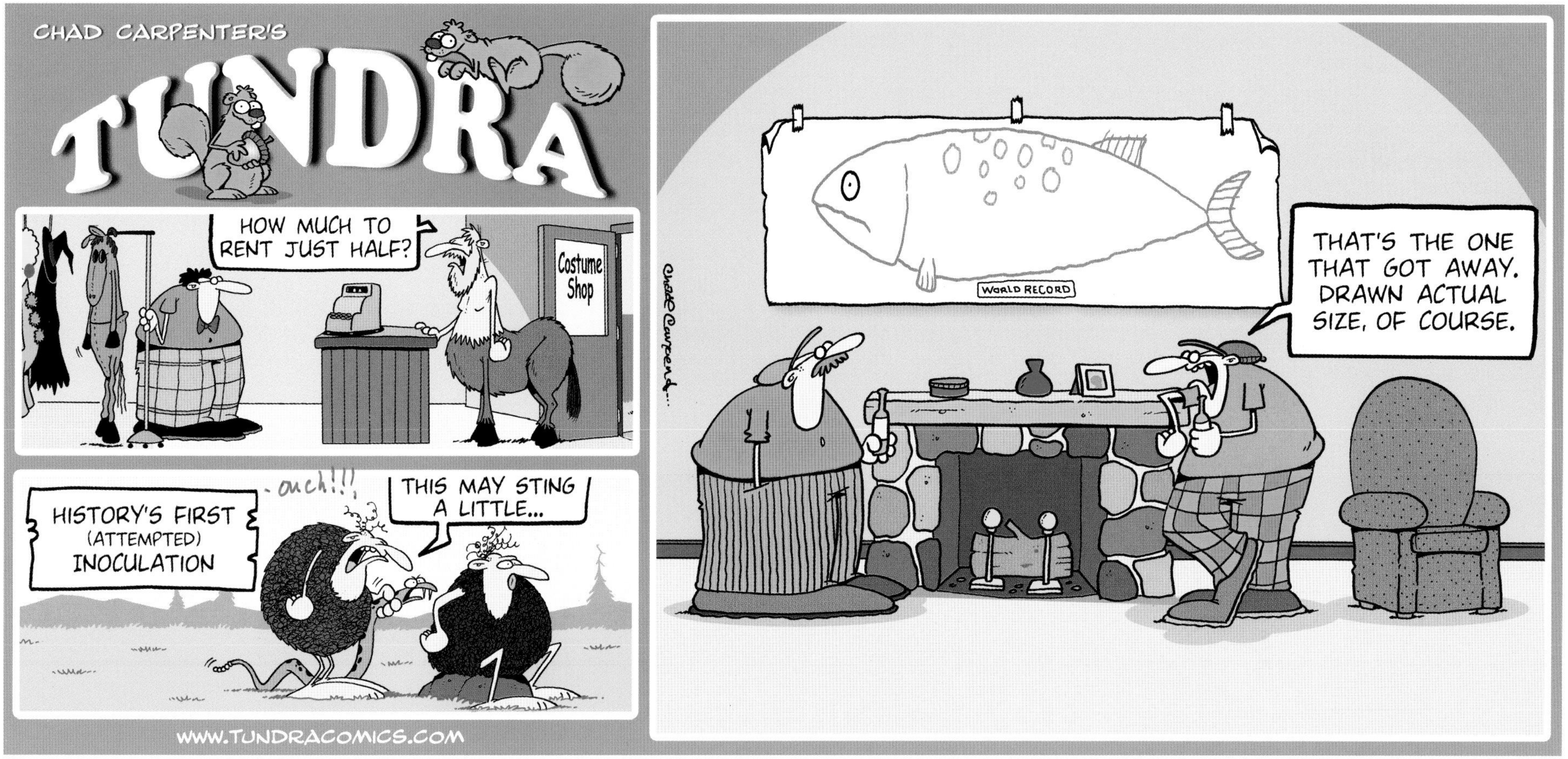
CHAD CARPENTER'S
TUNDRA
HOW MUCH TO RENT JUST HALF?
Costume Shop
HISTORY'S FIRST (ATTEMPTED) INOCULATION
ouch!!!
THIS MAY STING A LITTLE...
WWW.TUNDRACOMICS.COM
WORLD RECORD
THAT'S THE ONE THAT GOT AWAY. DRAWN ACTUAL SIZE, OF COURSE.

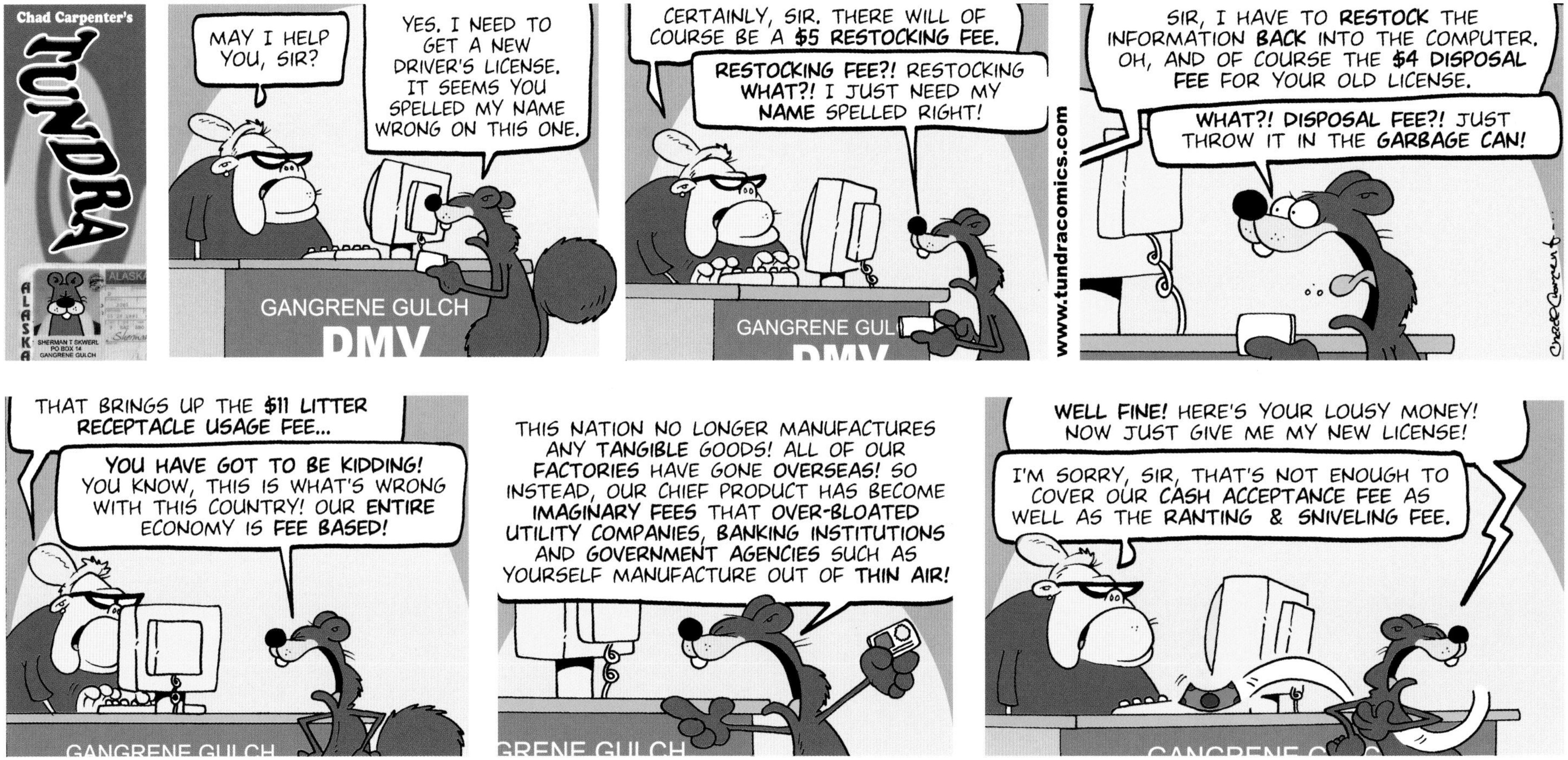
Chad Carpenter's
TUNDRA
ALASKA
SHERMAN T SKWERL
PO BOX 14
GANGRENE GULCH
MAY I HELP YOU, SIR?
YES. I NEED TO GET A NEW DRIVER'S LICENSE. IT SEEMS YOU SPELLED MY NAME WRONG ON THIS ONE.
GANGRENE GULCH
DMV
CERTAINLY, SIR. THERE WILL OF COURSE BE A $5 RESTOCKING FEE.
RESTOCKING FEE?! RESTOCKING WHAT?! I JUST NEED MY NAME SPELLED RIGHT!
www.tundracomics.com
SIR, I HAVE TO RESTOCK THE INFORMATION BACK INTO THE COMPUTER. OH, AND OF COURSE THE $4 DISPOSAL FEE FOR YOUR OLD LICENSE.
WHAT?! DISPOSAL FEE?! JUST THROW IT IN THE GARBAGE CAN!
THAT BRINGS UP THE $11 LITTER RECEPTACLE USAGE FEE...
YOU HAVE GOT TO BE KIDDING! YOU KNOW, THIS IS WHAT'S WRONG WITH THIS COUNTRY! OUR ENTIRE ECONOMY IS FEE BASED!
THIS NATION NO LONGER MANUFACTURES ANY TANGIBLE GOODS! ALL OF OUR FACTORIES HAVE GONE OVERSEAS! SO INSTEAD, OUR CHIEF PRODUCT HAS BECOME IMAGINARY FEES THAT OVER-BLOATED UTILITY COMPANIES, BANKING INSTITUTIONS AND GOVERNMENT AGENCIES SUCH AS YOURSELF MANUFACTURE OUT OF THIN AIR!
WELL FINE! HERE'S YOUR LOUSY MONEY! NOW JUST GIVE ME MY NEW LICENSE!
I'M SORRY, SIR, THAT'S NOT ENOUGH TO COVER OUR CASH ACCEPTANCE FEE AS WELL AS THE RANTING & SNIVELING FEE.

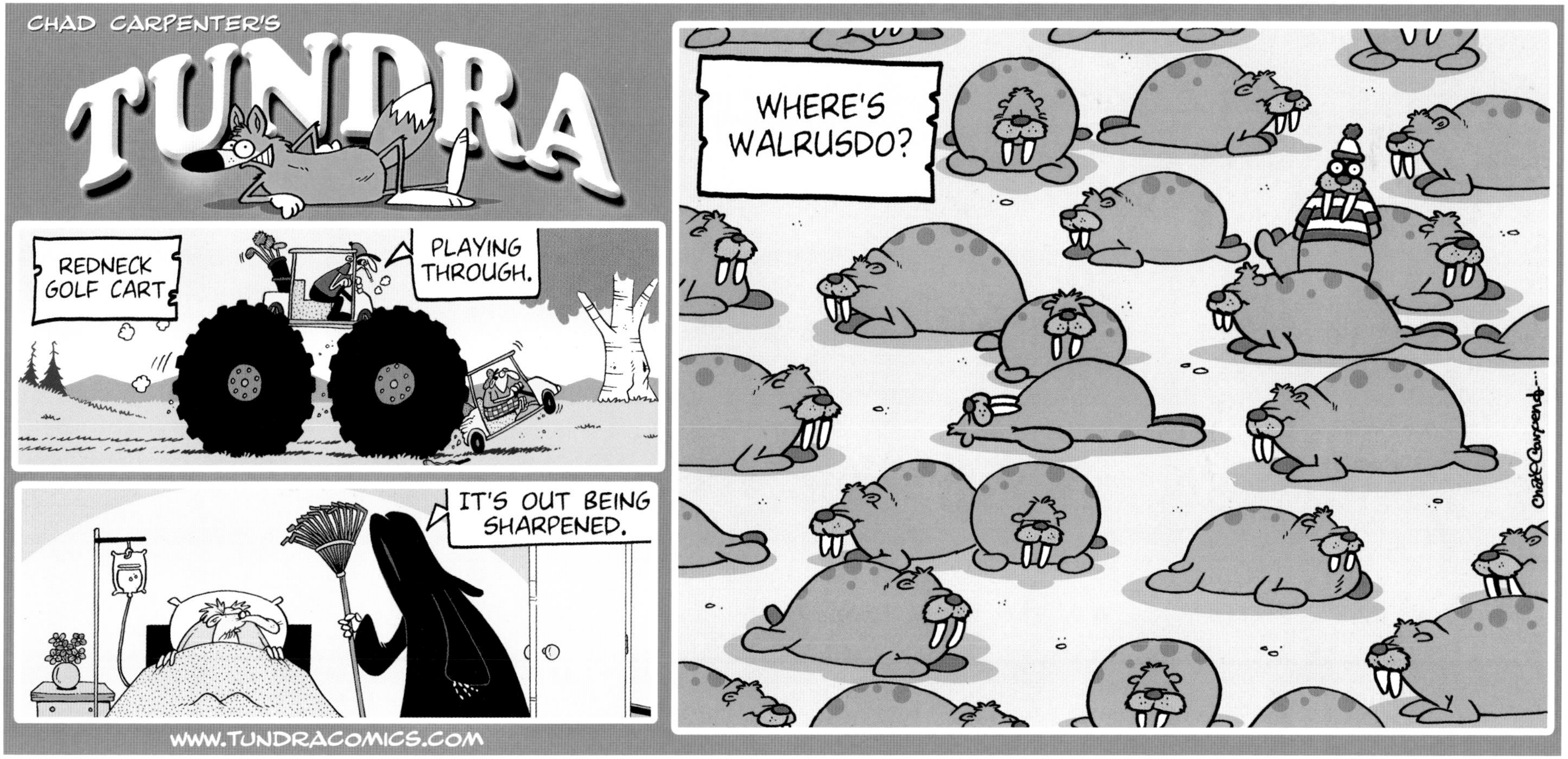
CHAD CARPENTER'S
TUNDRA
REDNECK GOLF CART
PLAYING THROUGH.
IT'S OUT BEING SHARPENED.
WWW.TUNDRACOMICS.COM
WHERE'S WALRUSDO?

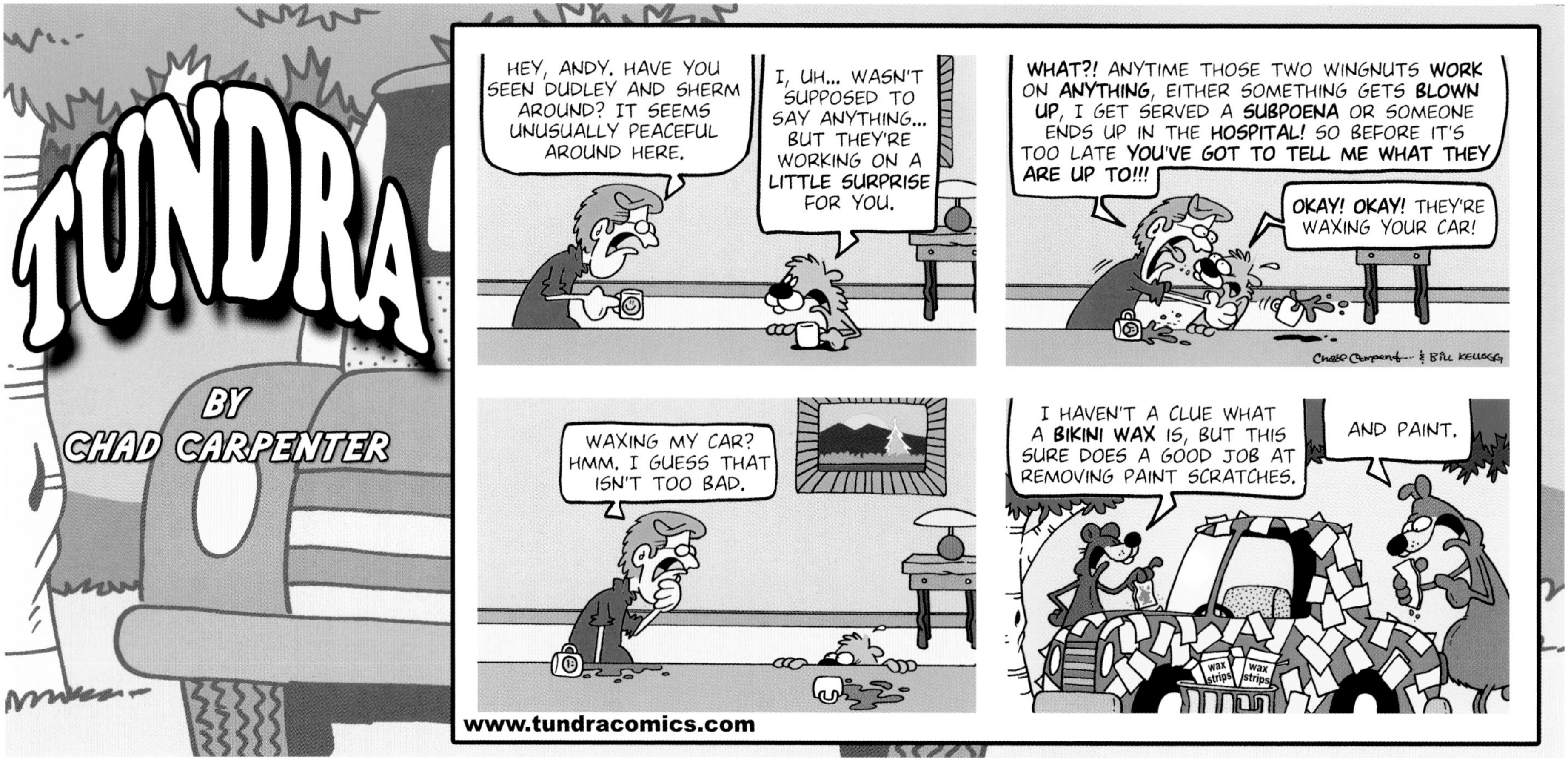
TUNDRA
BY CHAD CARPENTER
HEY, ANDY. HAVE YOU SEEN DUDLEY AND SHERM AROUND? IT SEEMS UNUSUALLY PEACEFUL AROUND HERE.
I, UH... WASN'T SUPPOSED TO SAY ANYTHING... BUT THEY'RE WORKING ON A LITTLE SURPRISE FOR YOU.
WHAT?! ANYTIME THOSE TWO WINGNUTS WORK ON ANYTHING, EITHER SOMETHING GETS BLOWN UP, I GET SERVED A SUBPOENA OR SOMEONE ENDS UP IN THE HOSPITAL! SO BEFORE IT'S TOO LATE YOU'VE GOT TO TELL ME WHAT THEY ARE UP TO!!!
OKAY! OKAY! THEY'RE WAXING YOUR CAR!
WAXING MY CAR? HMM. I GUESS THAT ISN'T TOO BAD.
I HAVEN'T A CLUE WHAT A BIKINI WAX IS, BUT THIS SURE DOES A GOOD JOB AT REMOVING PAINT SCRATCHES.
AND PAINT.
wax strips
wax strips
www.tundracomics.com

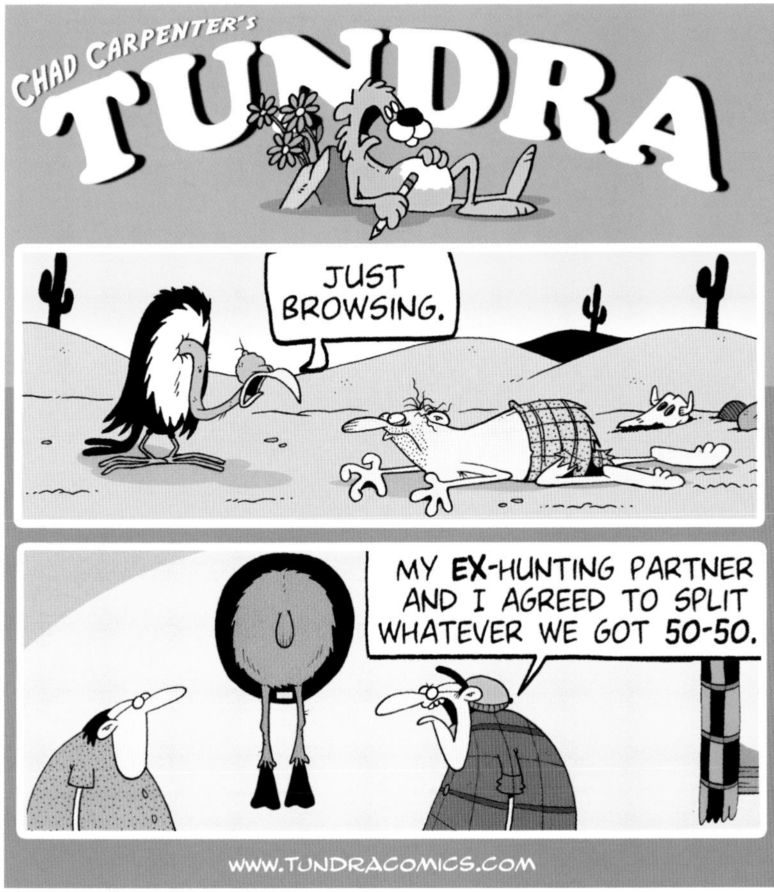
CHAD CARPENTER'S
TUNDRA
JUST BROWSING.
MY **EX**-HUNTING PARTNER AND I AGREED TO SPLIT WHATEVER WE GOT **50-50.**
WWW.TUNDRACOMICS.COM

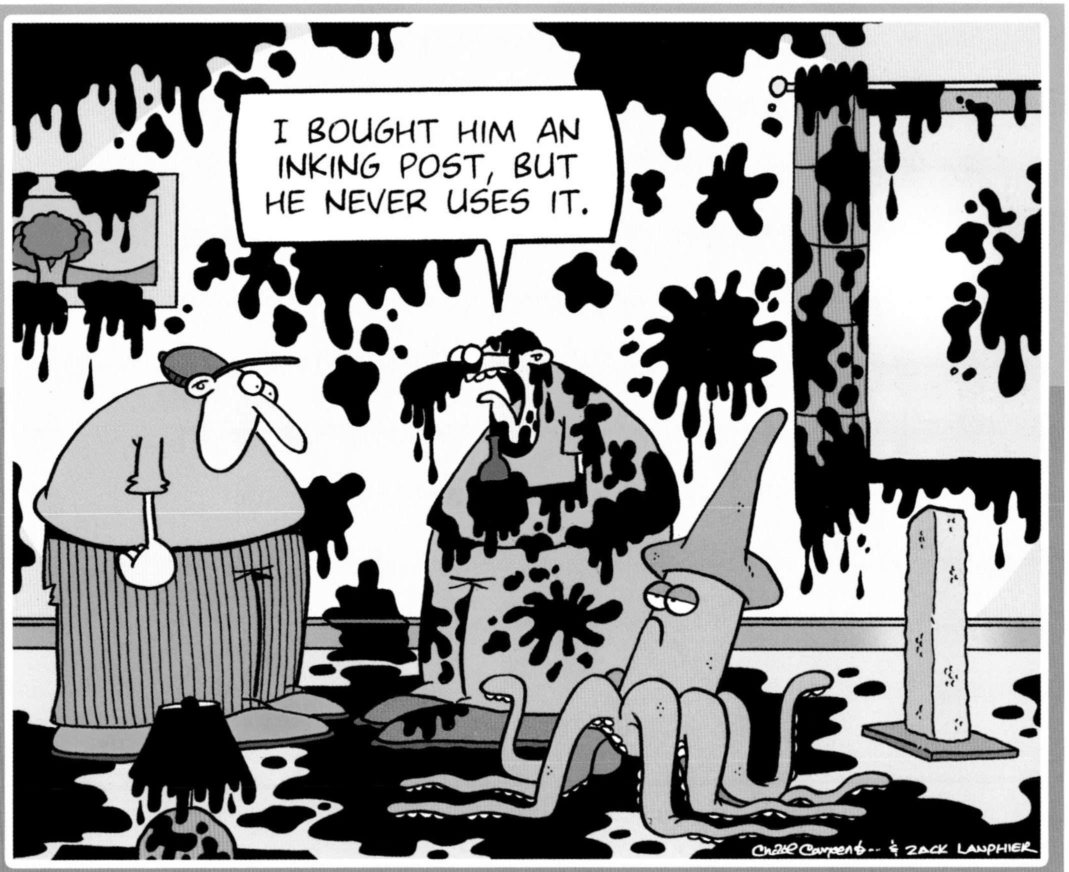
I BOUGHT HIM AN INKING POST, BUT HE NEVER USES IT.

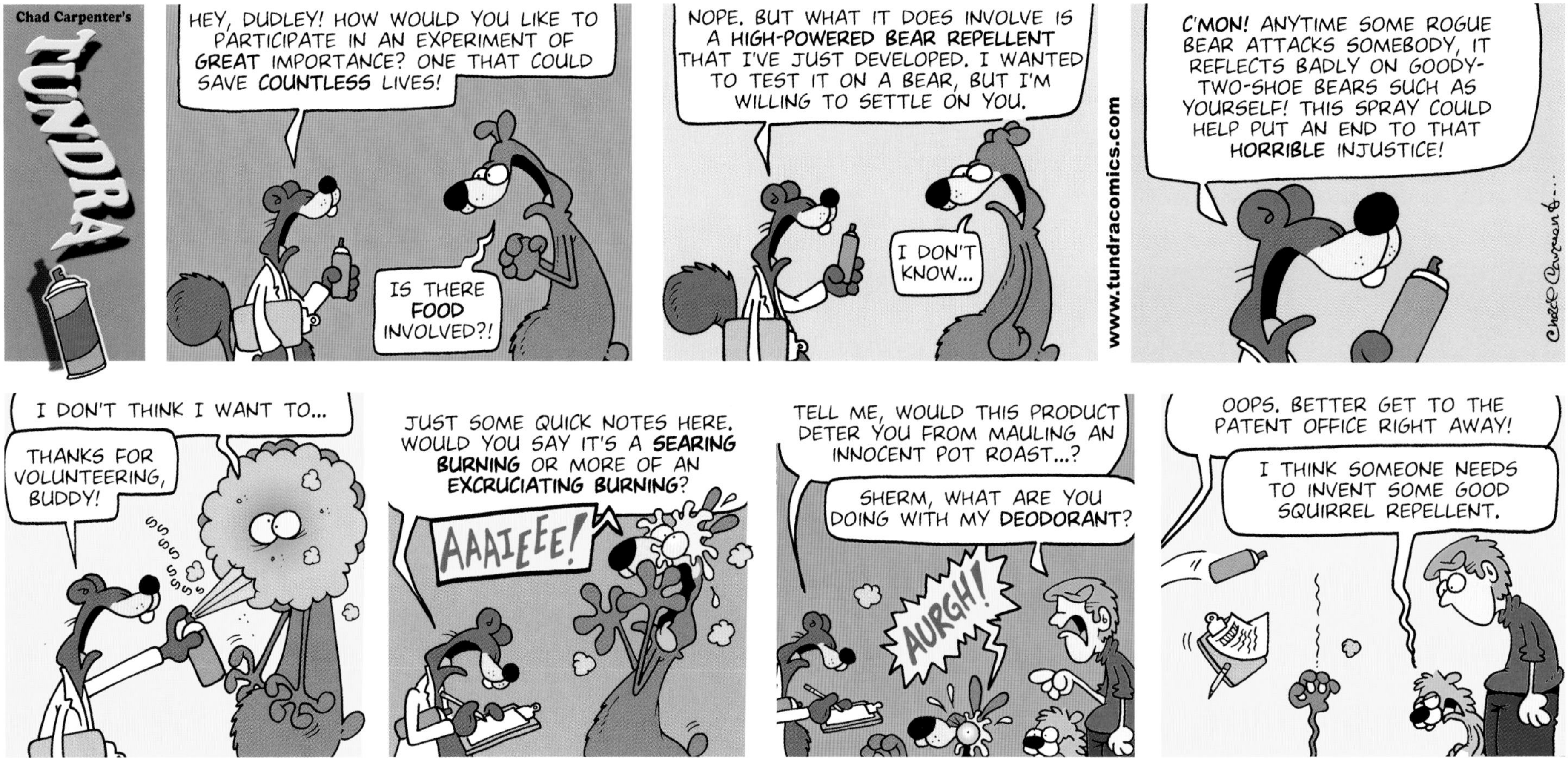
Chad Carpenter's
TUNDRA
HEY, DUDLEY! HOW WOULD YOU LIKE TO PARTICIPATE IN AN EXPERIMENT OF GREAT IMPORTANCE? ONE THAT COULD SAVE COUNTLESS LIVES!
IS THERE FOOD INVOLVED?!
NOPE. BUT WHAT IT DOES INVOLVE IS A HIGH-POWERED BEAR REPELLENT THAT I'VE JUST DEVELOPED. I WANTED TO TEST IT ON A BEAR, BUT I'M WILLING TO SETTLE ON YOU.
I DON'T KNOW...
www.tundracomics.com
C'MON! ANYTIME SOME ROGUE BEAR ATTACKS SOMEBODY, IT REFLECTS BADLY ON GOODY-TWO-SHOE BEARS SUCH AS YOURSELF! THIS SPRAY COULD HELP PUT AN END TO THAT HORRIBLE INJUSTICE!
I DON'T THINK I WANT TO...
THANKS FOR VOLUNTEERING, BUDDY!
SSSSSSSSS
JUST SOME QUICK NOTES HERE. WOULD YOU SAY IT'S A SEARING BURNING OR MORE OF AN EXCRUCIATING BURNING?
AAAIEEE!
TELL ME, WOULD THIS PRODUCT DETER YOU FROM MAULING AN INNOCENT POT ROAST...?
SHERM, WHAT ARE YOU DOING WITH MY DEODORANT?
AURGH!
OOPS. BETTER GET TO THE PATENT OFFICE RIGHT AWAY!
I THINK SOMEONE NEEDS TO INVENT SOME GOOD SQUIRREL REPELLENT.

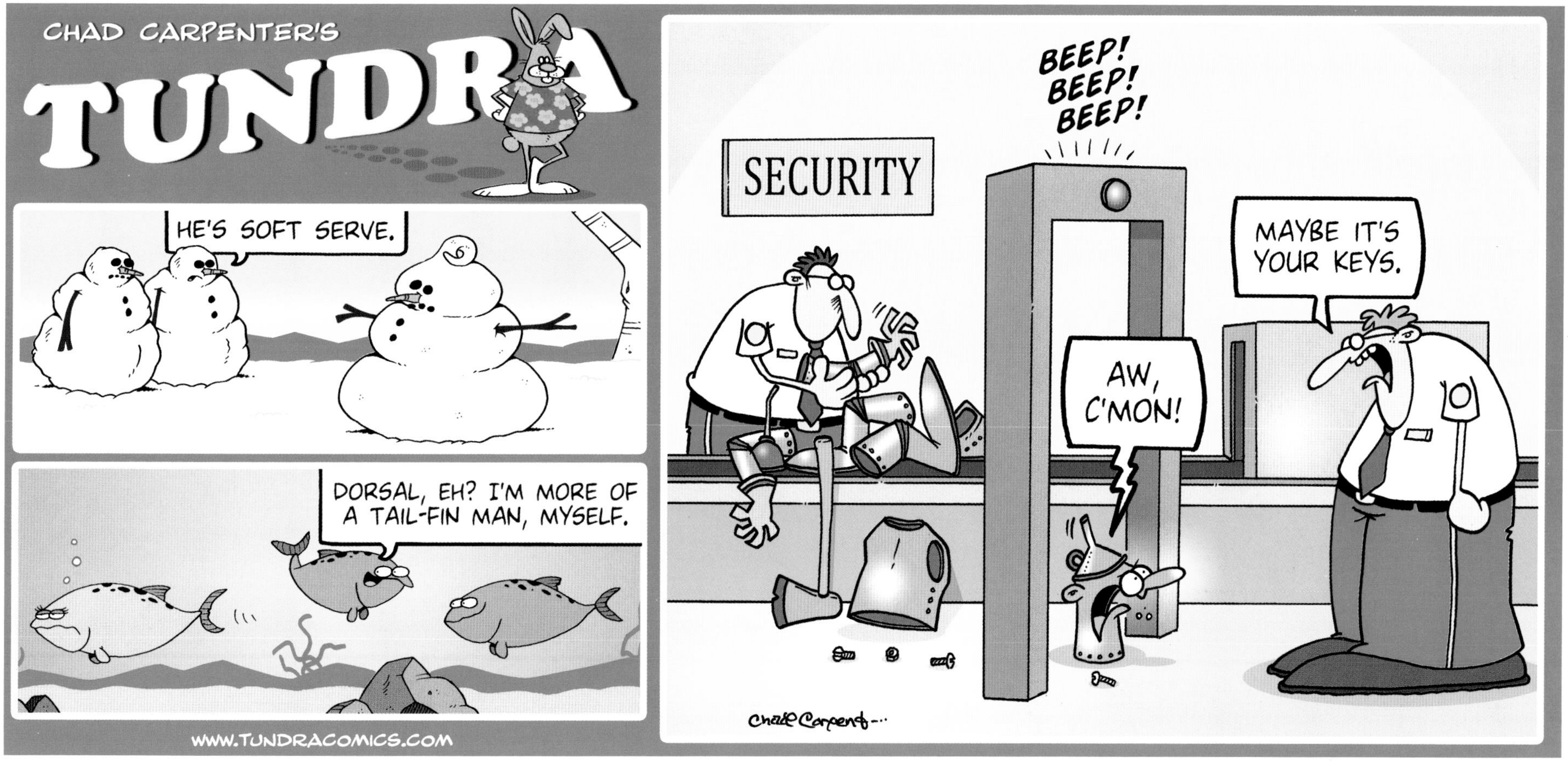
CHAD CARPENTER'S
TUNDRA
HE'S SOFT SERVE.
DORSAL, EH? I'M MORE OF A TAIL-FIN MAN, MYSELF.
WWW.TUNDRACOMICS.COM
BEEP! BEEP! BEEP!
SECURITY
MAYBE IT'S YOUR KEYS.
AW, C'MON!
Chad Carpenter

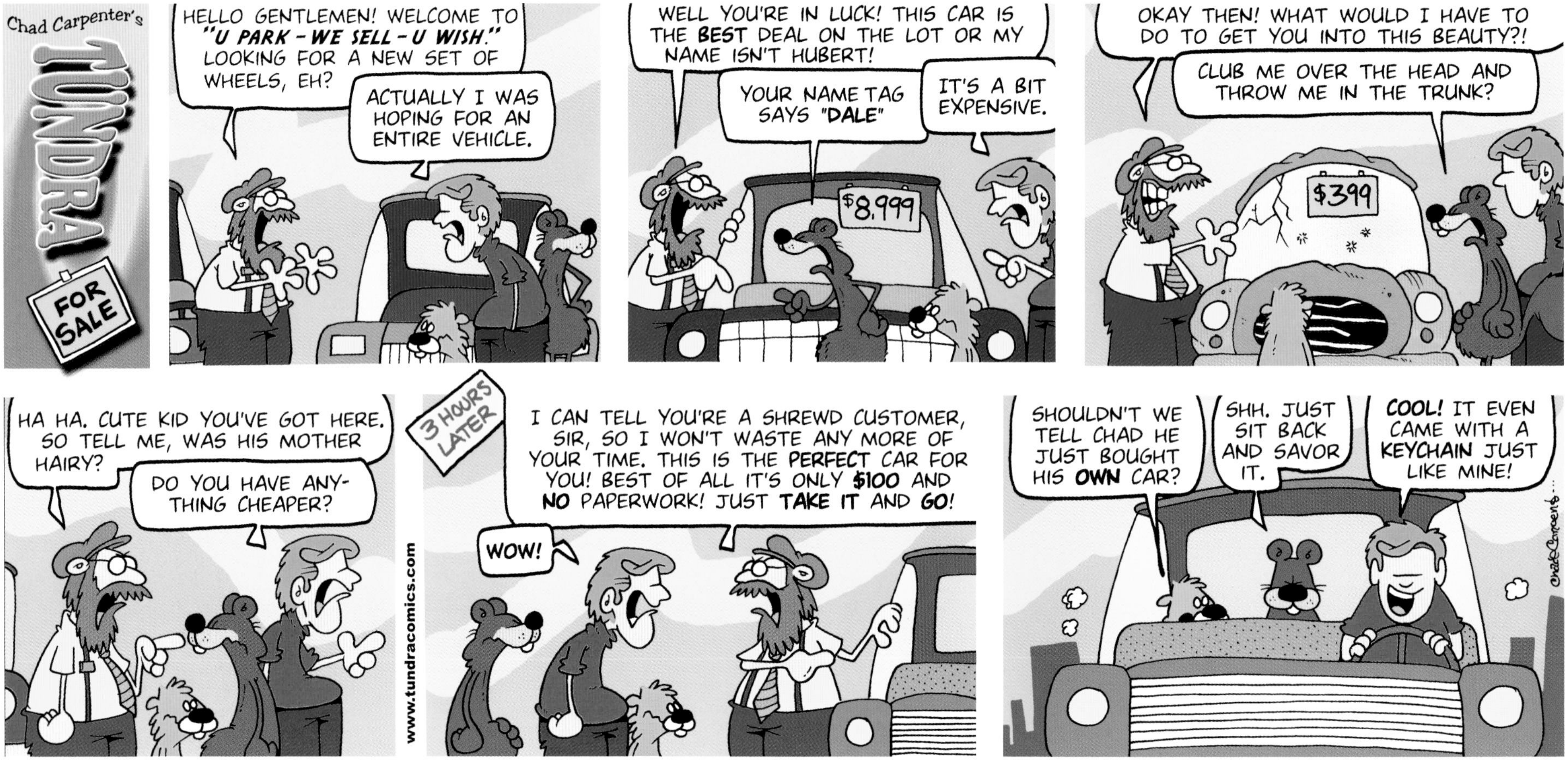
Chad Carpenter's
TUNDRA
FOR SALE
HELLO GENTLEMEN! WELCOME TO "U PARK - WE SELL - U WISH." LOOKING FOR A NEW SET OF WHEELS, EH?
ACTUALLY I WAS HOPING FOR AN ENTIRE VEHICLE.
WELL YOU'RE IN LUCK! THIS CAR IS THE BEST DEAL ON THE LOT OR MY NAME ISN'T HUBERT!
YOUR NAME TAG SAYS "DALE"
IT'S A BIT EXPENSIVE.
$8,999
OKAY THEN! WHAT WOULD I HAVE TO DO TO GET YOU INTO THIS BEAUTY?!
CLUB ME OVER THE HEAD AND THROW ME IN THE TRUNK?
$399
HA HA. CUTE KID YOU'VE GOT HERE. SO TELL ME, WAS HIS MOTHER HAIRY?
DO YOU HAVE ANY-THING CHEAPER?
www.tundracomics.com
3 HOURS LATER
I CAN TELL YOU'RE A SHREWD CUSTOMER, SIR, SO I WON'T WASTE ANY MORE OF YOUR TIME. THIS IS THE PERFECT CAR FOR YOU! BEST OF ALL IT'S ONLY $100 AND NO PAPERWORK! JUST TAKE IT AND GO!
WOW!
SHOULDN'T WE TELL CHAD HE JUST BOUGHT HIS OWN CAR?
SHH. JUST SIT BACK AND SAVOR IT.
COOL! IT EVEN CAME WITH A KEYCHAIN JUST LIKE MINE!

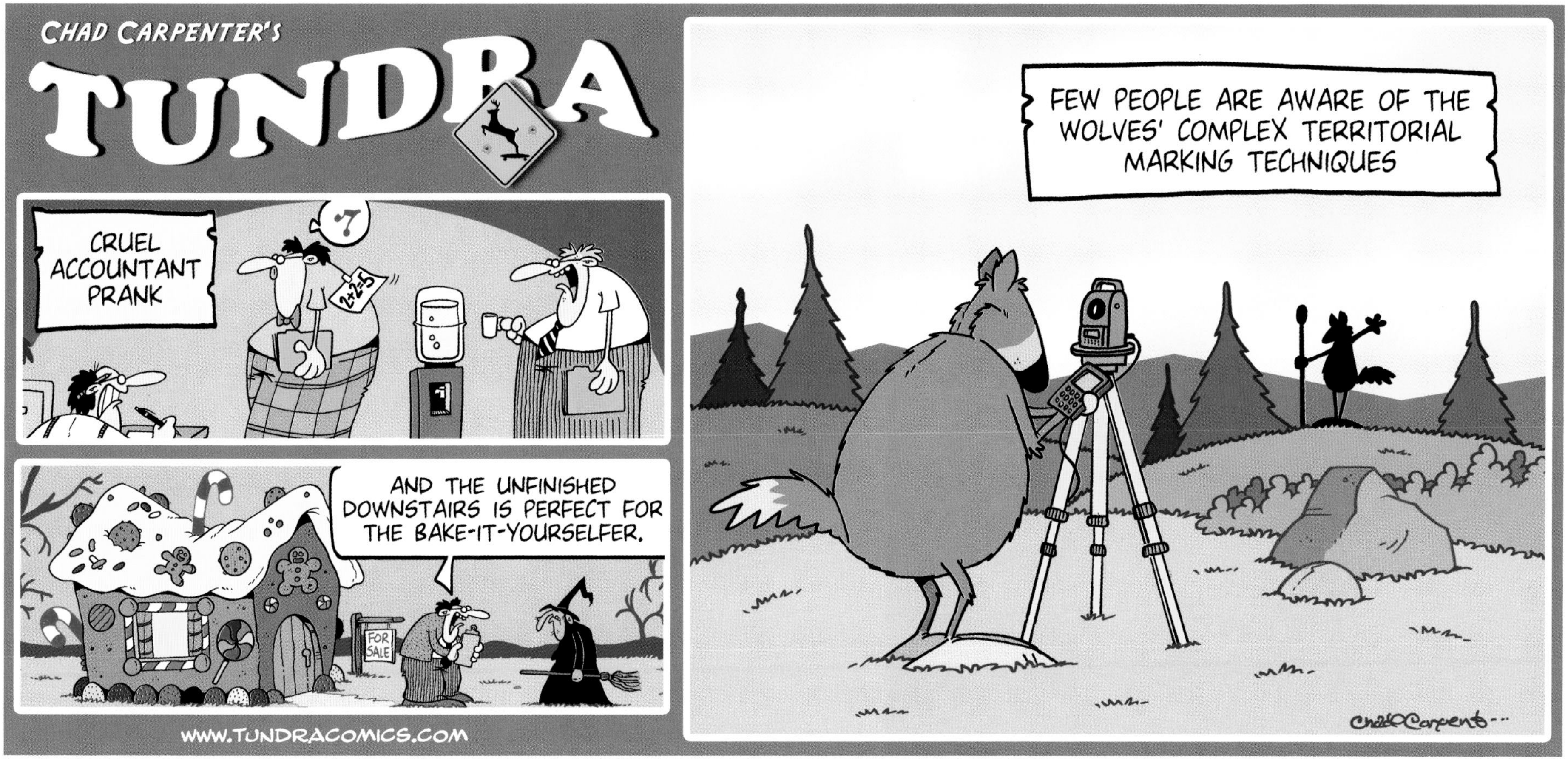
CHAD CARPENTER'S
TUNDRA
CRUEL ACCOUNTANT PRANK
2+2=5
AND THE UNFINISHED DOWNSTAIRS IS PERFECT FOR THE BAKE-IT-YOURSELFER.
FOR SALE
WWW.TUNDRACOMICS.COM
FEW PEOPLE ARE AWARE OF THE WOLVES' COMPLEX TERRITORIAL MARKING TECHNIQUES

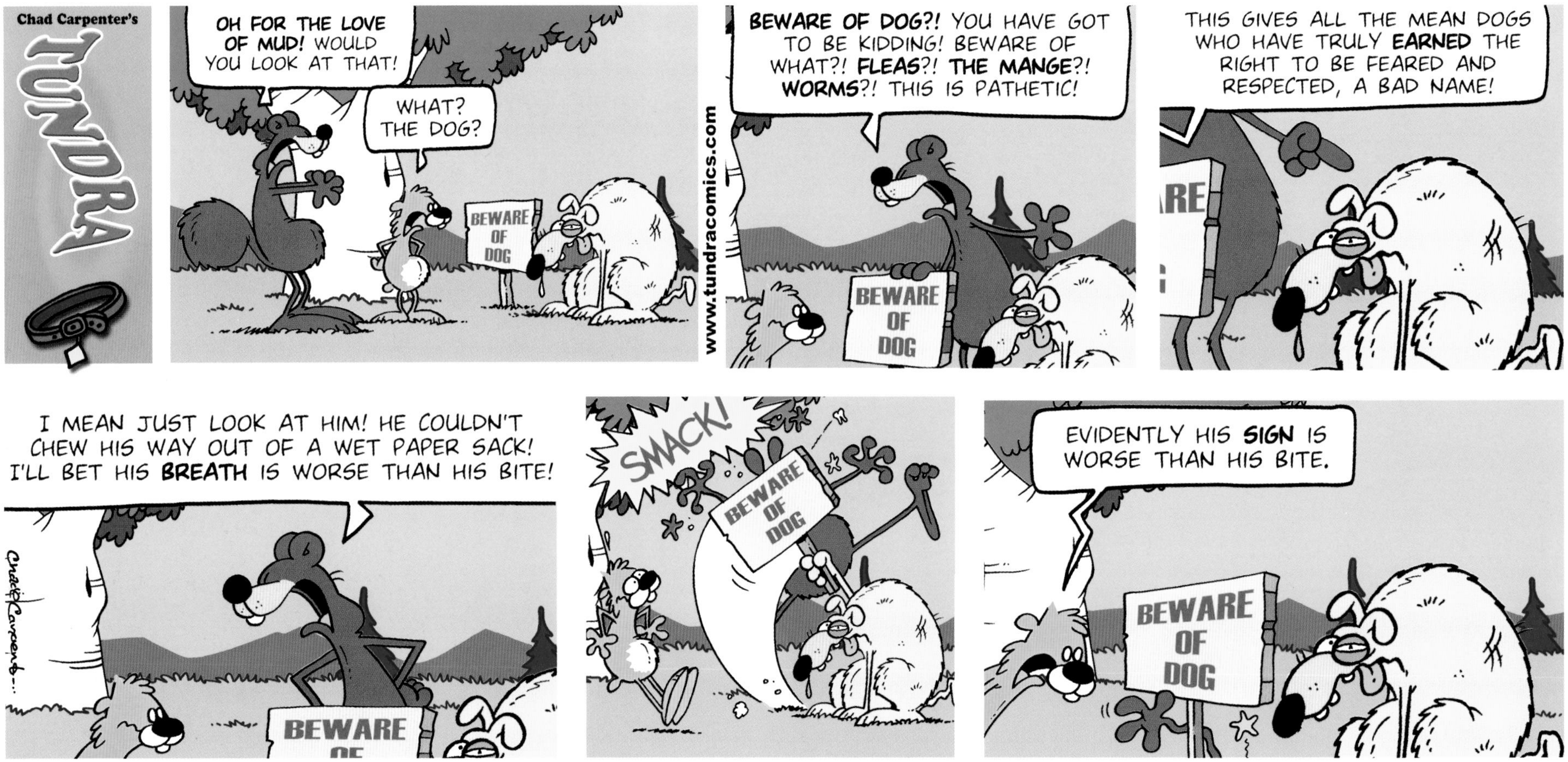
Chad Carpenter's
TUNDRA
OH FOR THE LOVE OF MUD! WOULD YOU LOOK AT THAT!
WHAT? THE DOG?
BEWARE OF DOG
www.tundracomics.com
BEWARE OF DOG?! YOU HAVE GOT TO BE KIDDING! BEWARE OF WHAT?! FLEAS?! THE MANGE?! WORMS?! THIS IS PATHETIC!
BEWARE OF DOG
THIS GIVES ALL THE MEAN DOGS WHO HAVE TRULY EARNED THE RIGHT TO BE FEARED AND RESPECTED, A BAD NAME!
I MEAN JUST LOOK AT HIM! HE COULDN'T CHEW HIS WAY OUT OF A WET PAPER SACK! I'LL BET HIS BREATH IS WORSE THAN HIS BITE!
BEWARE
SMACK!
BEWARE OF DOG
EVIDENTLY HIS SIGN IS WORSE THAN HIS BITE.
BEWARE OF DOG

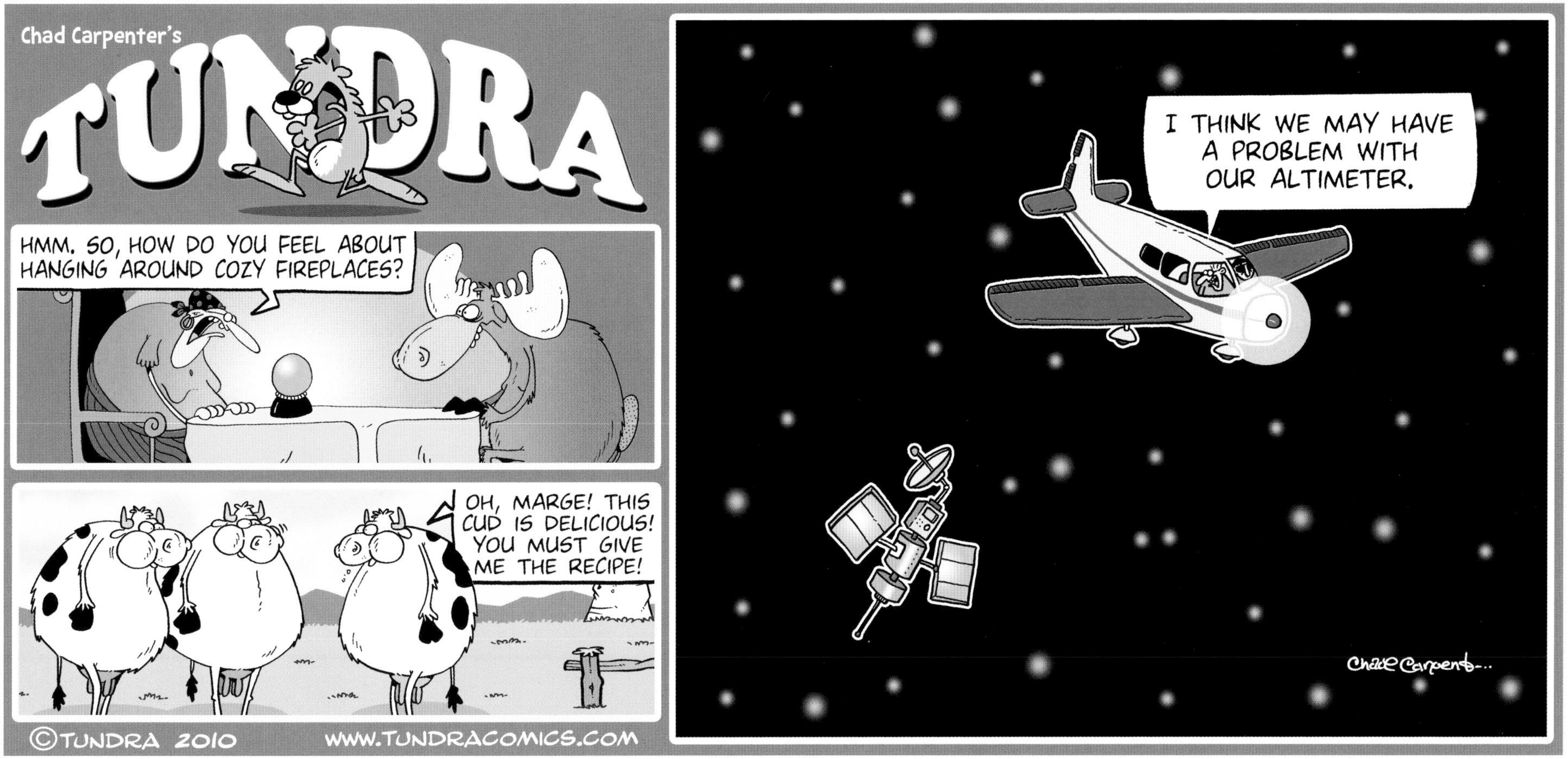
Chad Carpenter's
TUNDRA
HMM. SO, HOW DO YOU FEEL ABOUT HANGING AROUND COZY FIREPLACES?
OH, MARGE! THIS CUD IS DELICIOUS! YOU MUST GIVE ME THE RECIPE!
©TUNDRA 2010
WWW.TUNDRACOMICS.COM
I THINK WE MAY HAVE A PROBLEM WITH OUR ALTIMETER.

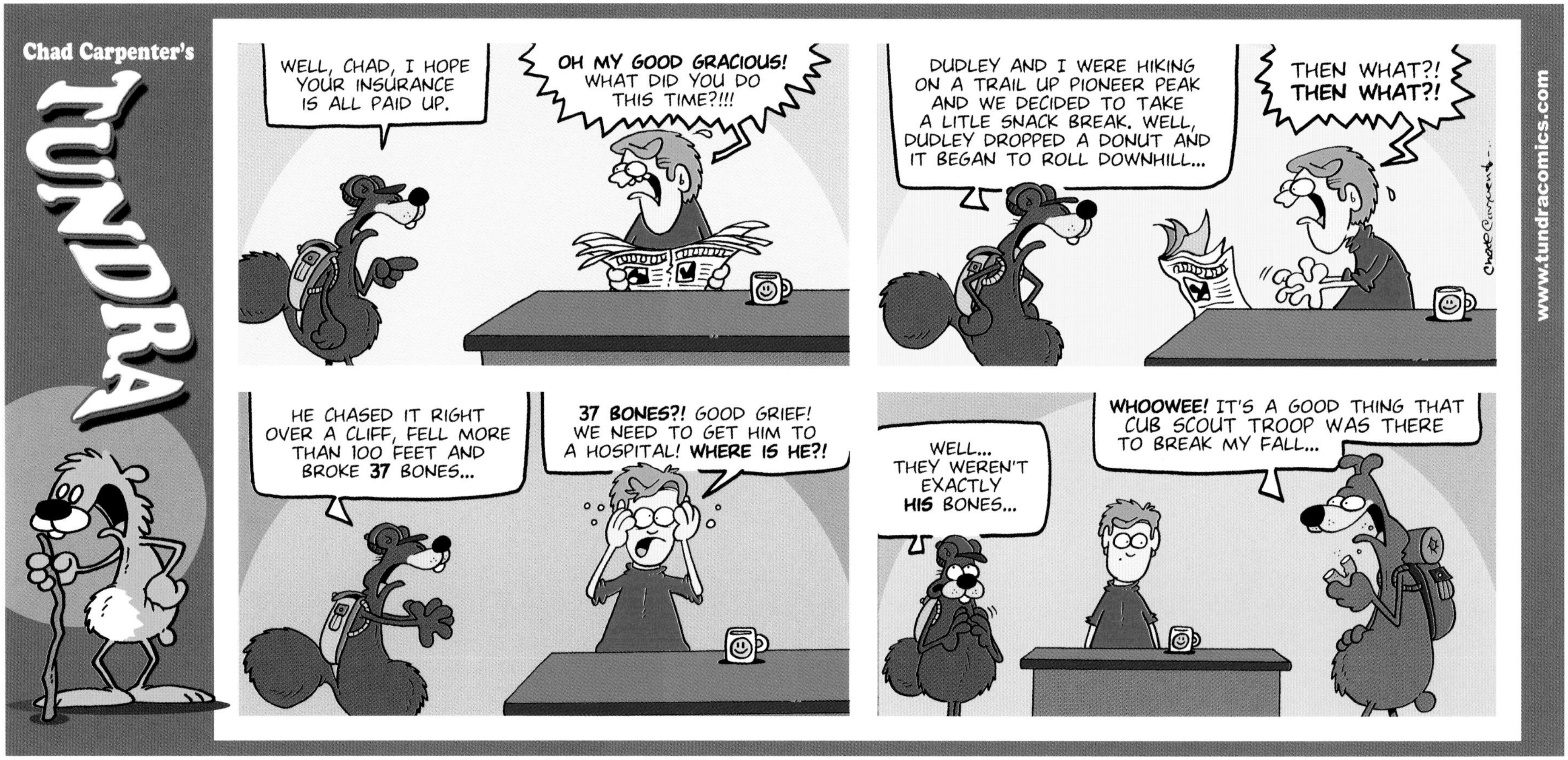
Chad Carpenter's
TUNDRA
WELL, CHAD, I HOPE YOUR INSURANCE IS ALL PAID UP.
OH MY GOOD GRACIOUS! WHAT DID YOU DO THIS TIME?!!!
DUDLEY AND I WERE HIKING ON A TRAIL UP PIONEER PEAK AND WE DECIDED TO TAKE A LITLE SNACK BREAK. WELL, DUDLEY DROPPED A DONUT AND IT BEGAN TO ROLL DOWNHILL...
THEN WHAT?! THEN WHAT?!
HE CHASED IT RIGHT OVER A CLIFF, FELL MORE THAN 100 FEET AND BROKE 37 BONES...
37 BONES?! GOOD GRIEF! WE NEED TO GET HIM TO A HOSPITAL! WHERE IS HE?!
WHOOWEE! IT'S A GOOD THING THAT CUB SCOUT TROOP WAS THERE TO BREAK MY FALL...
WELL... THEY WEREN'T EXACTLY HIS BONES...
www.tundracomics.com

No comment... ☺

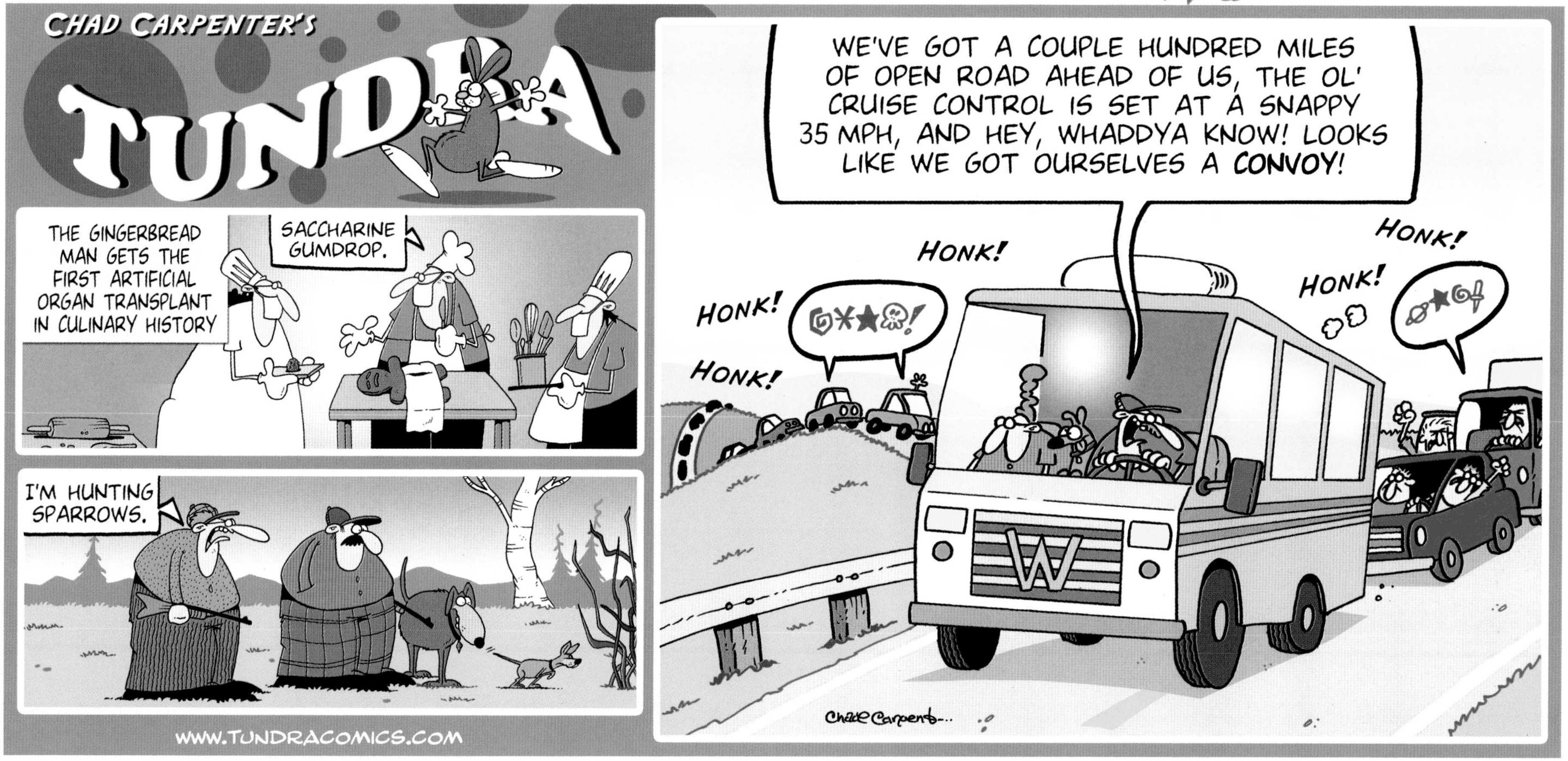
CHAD CARPENTER'S
TUNDRA
THE GINGERBREAD MAN GETS THE FIRST ARTIFICIAL ORGAN TRANSPLANT IN CULINARY HISTORY
SACCHARINE GUMDROP.
I'M HUNTING SPARROWS.
WWW.TUNDRACOMICS.COM
WE'VE GOT A COUPLE HUNDRED MILES OF OPEN ROAD AHEAD OF US, THE OL' CRUISE CONTROL IS SET AT A SNAPPY 35 MPH, AND HEY, WHADDYA KNOW! LOOKS LIKE WE GOT OURSELVES A CONVOY!
HONK!
HONK!
HONK!
HONK!
HONK!
W

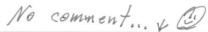

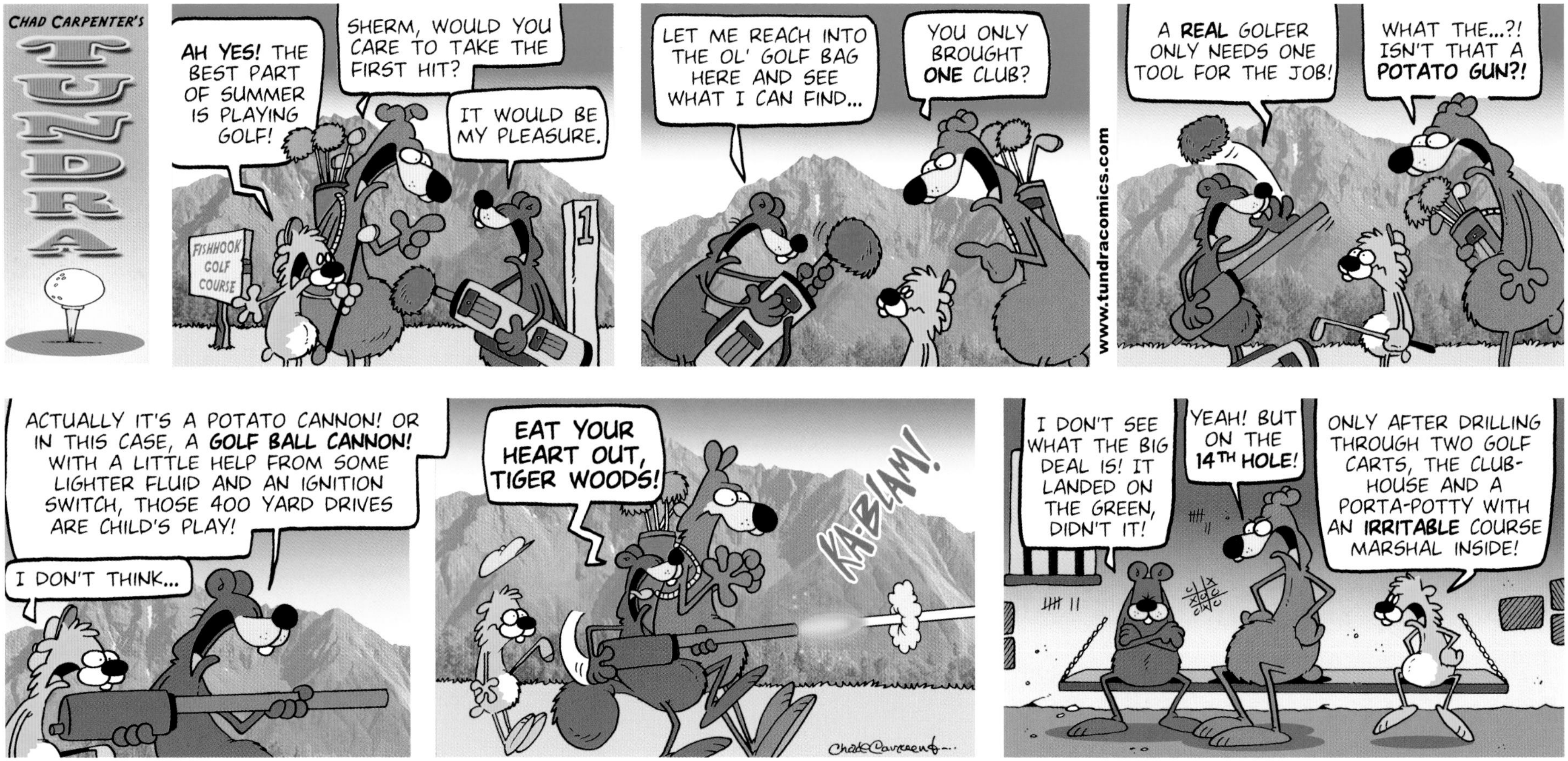
CHAD CARPENTER'S
TUNDRA
AH YES! THE BEST PART OF SUMMER IS PLAYING GOLF!
FISHHOOK GOLF COURSE
SHERM, WOULD YOU CARE TO TAKE THE FIRST HIT?
IT WOULD BE MY PLEASURE.
1
LET ME REACH INTO THE OL' GOLF BAG HERE AND SEE WHAT I CAN FIND...
YOU ONLY BROUGHT ONE CLUB?
www.tundracomics.com
A REAL GOLFER ONLY NEEDS ONE TOOL FOR THE JOB!
WHAT THE...?! ISN'T THAT A POTATO GUN?!
ACTUALLY IT'S A POTATO CANNON! OR IN THIS CASE, A GOLF BALL CANNON! WITH A LITTLE HELP FROM SOME LIGHTER FLUID AND AN IGNITION SWITCH, THOSE 400 YARD DRIVES ARE CHILD'S PLAY!
I DON'T THINK...
EAT YOUR HEART OUT, TIGER WOODS!
KA-BLAM!
I DON'T SEE WHAT THE BIG DEAL IS! IT LANDED ON THE GREEN, DIDN'T IT!
YEAH! BUT ON THE 14TH HOLE!
ONLY AFTER DRILLING THROUGH TWO GOLF CARTS, THE CLUB-HOUSE AND A PORTA-POTTY WITH AN IRRITABLE COURSE MARSHAL INSIDE!

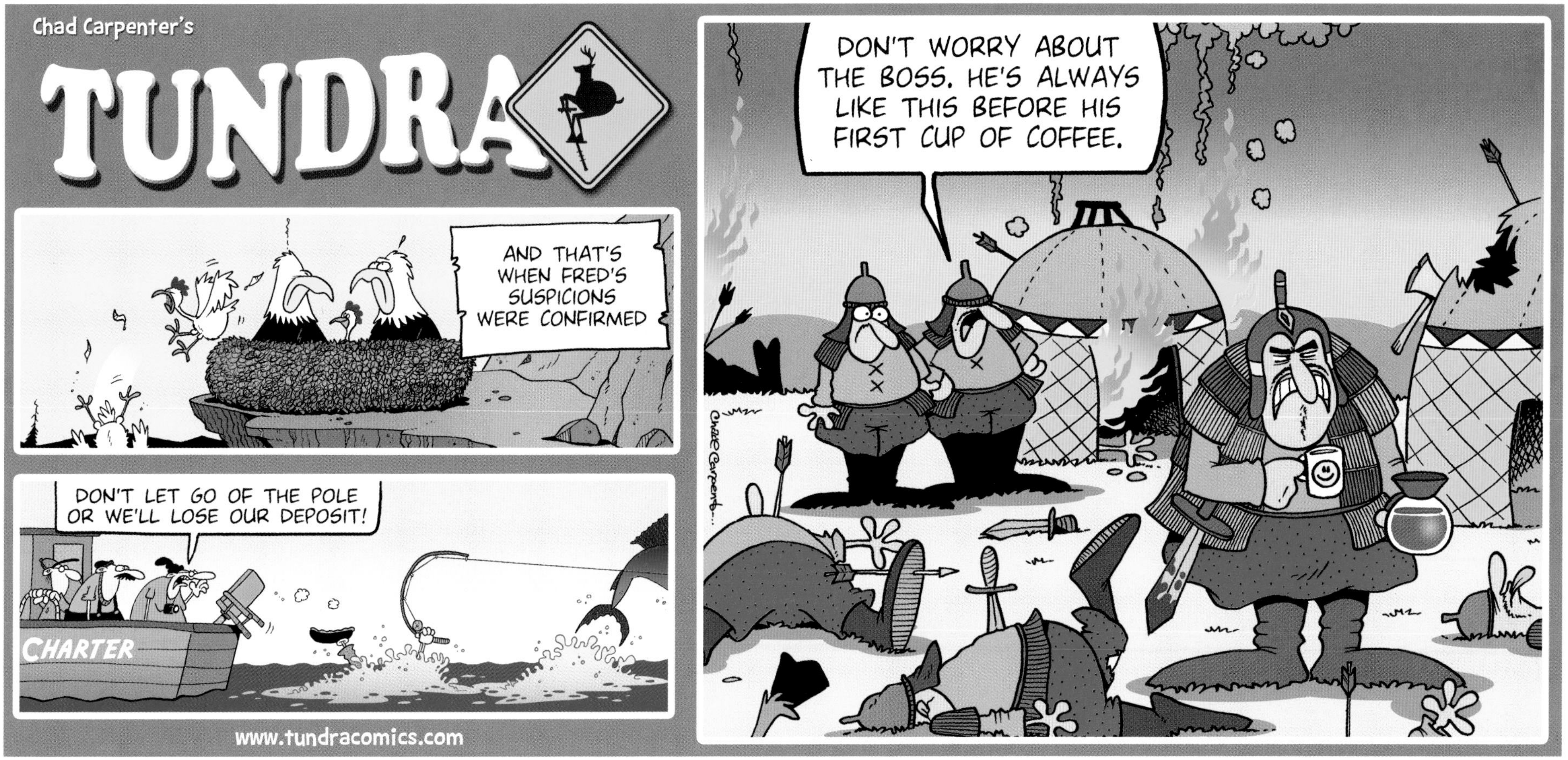
Chad Carpenter's
TUNDRA
AND THAT'S WHEN FRED'S SUSPICIONS WERE CONFIRMED
DON'T LET GO OF THE POLE OR WE'LL LOSE OUR DEPOSIT!
CHARTER
www.tundracomics.com
DON'T WORRY ABOUT THE BOSS. HE'S ALWAYS LIKE THIS BEFORE HIS FIRST CUP OF COFFEE.

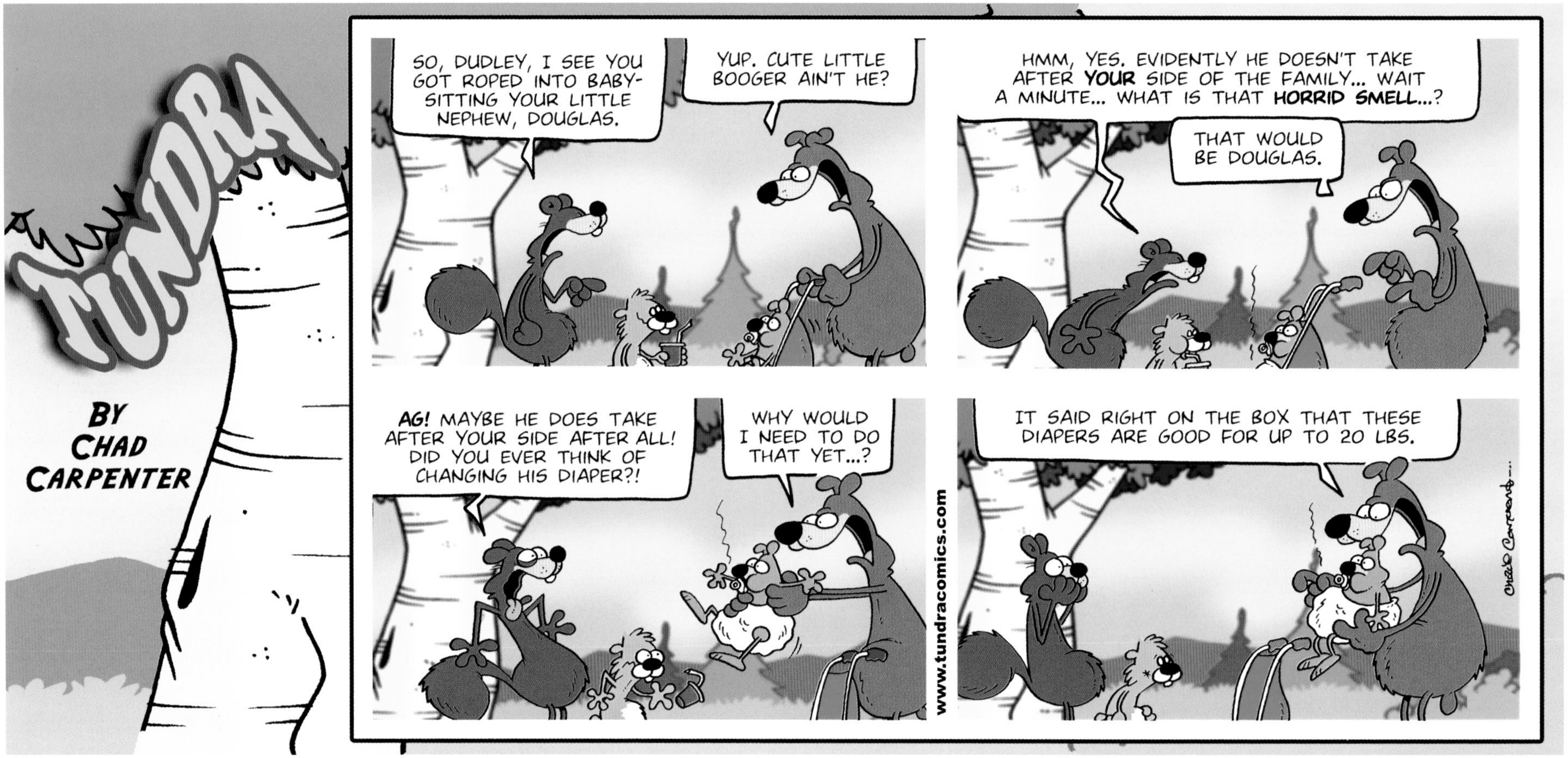
TUNDRA
BY CHAD CARPENTER
SO, DUDLEY, I SEE YOU GOT ROPED INTO BABY-SITTING YOUR LITTLE NEPHEW, DOUGLAS.
YUP. CUTE LITTLE BOOGER AIN'T HE?
HMM, YES. EVIDENTLY HE DOESN'T TAKE AFTER **YOUR** SIDE OF THE FAMILY... WAIT A MINUTE... WHAT IS THAT **HORRID SMELL**...?
THAT WOULD BE DOUGLAS.
AG! MAYBE HE DOES TAKE AFTER YOUR SIDE AFTER ALL! DID YOU EVER THINK OF CHANGING HIS DIAPER?!
WHY WOULD I NEED TO DO THAT YET...?
www.tundracomics.com
IT SAID RIGHT ON THE BOX THAT THESE DIAPERS ARE GOOD FOR UP TO 20 LBS.

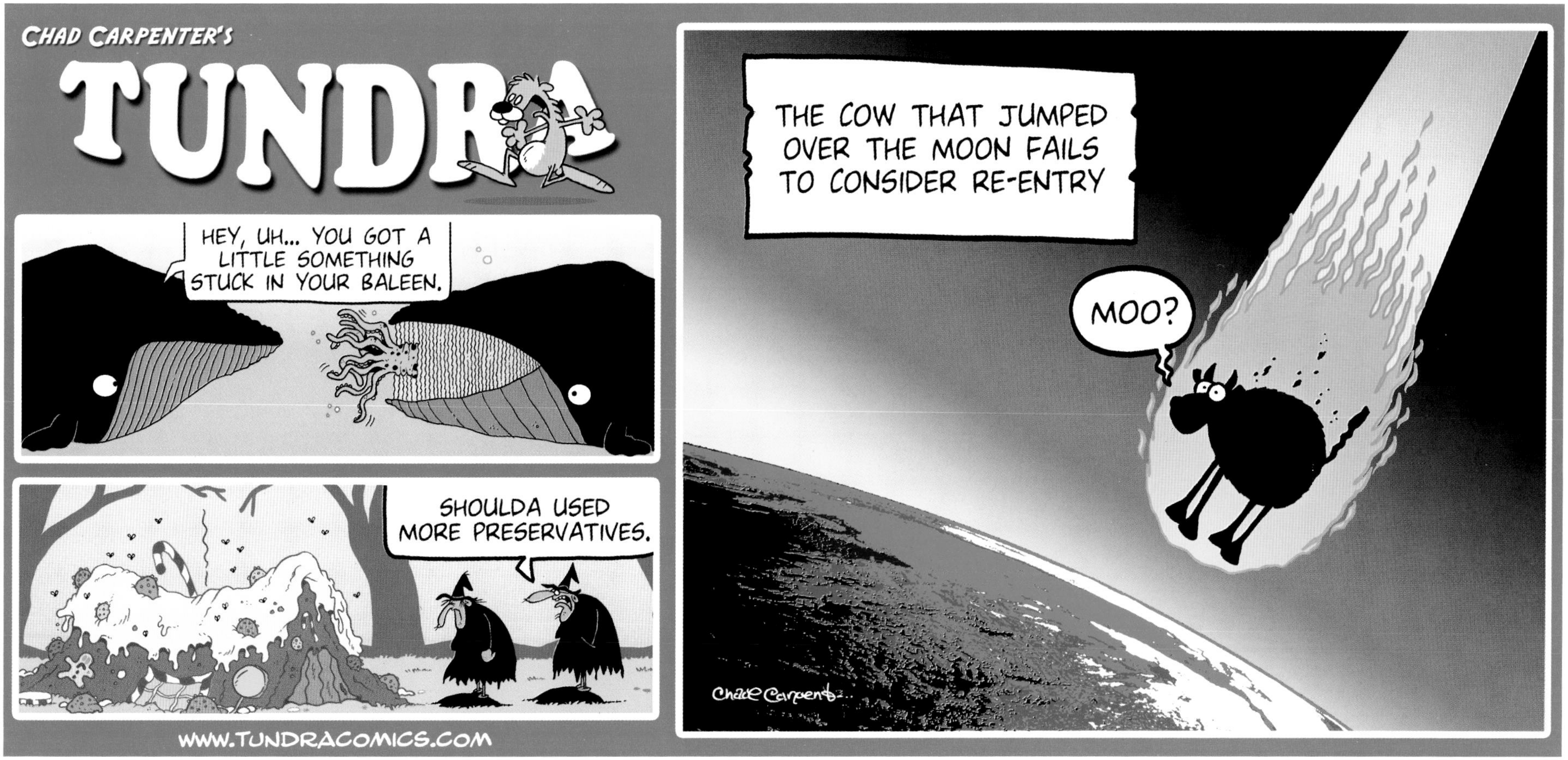
CHAD CARPENTER'S
TUNDRA
HEY, UH... YOU GOT A LITTLE SOMETHING STUCK IN YOUR BALEEN.
SHOULDA USED MORE PRESERVATIVES.
WWW.TUNDRACOMICS.COM
THE COW THAT JUMPED OVER THE MOON FAILS TO CONSIDER RE-ENTRY
MOO?

TUNDRA
BY CHAD CARPENTER
HERE'S YOUR KEYS, CHAD. THANKS FOR LETTING ME BORROW YOUR CAR.
WHAT?! I DIDN'T LET YOU BORROW MY CAR!
SURE YOU DID! YOU LEFT YOUR KEYS OUT WHERE I COULD SEE THEM. AS FAR AS I'M CONCERNED, THAT'S AN OPEN INVITATION!
THAT WOULD EXPLAIN YOUR POLICE RECORD.
OH, BY THE WAY. YOU MAY WANT TO HAVE YOUR CAR CHECKED OUT. I THINK IT HAS SOME ELECTRICAL PROBLEMS.
ELECTRICAL PROBLEMS?!
WHY IS IT THAT ANYTIME YOU TOUCH SOMETHING, IT ENDS UP BROKEN?!
BAD KARMA?
www.tundracomics.com
WELL, CONSIDERING THAT USUALLY WHEN YOU "BORROW" SOMETHING IT ENDS UP TOTALLY DESTROYED, I GUESS I SHOULD BE GRATEFUL IT'S ONLY AN ELECTRICAL PROBLEM.
HEY, CHAD. THERE'S A CAR THAT LOOKS JUST LIKE YOURS WRAPPED AROUND A POWER POLE DOWN THE ROAD.

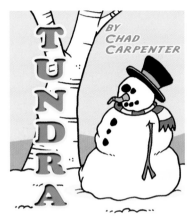

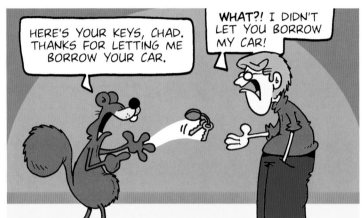

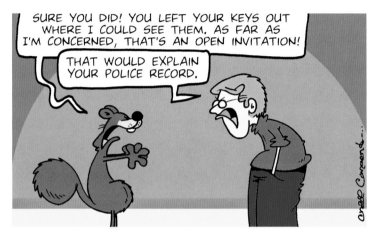

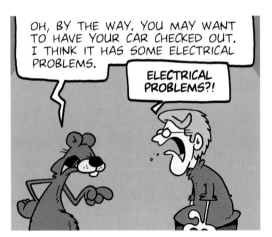

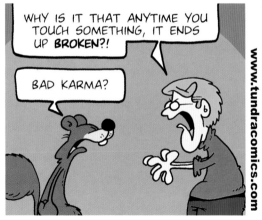

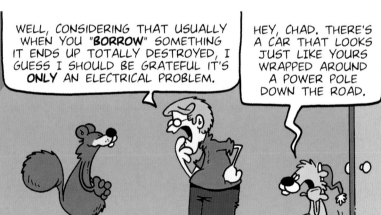

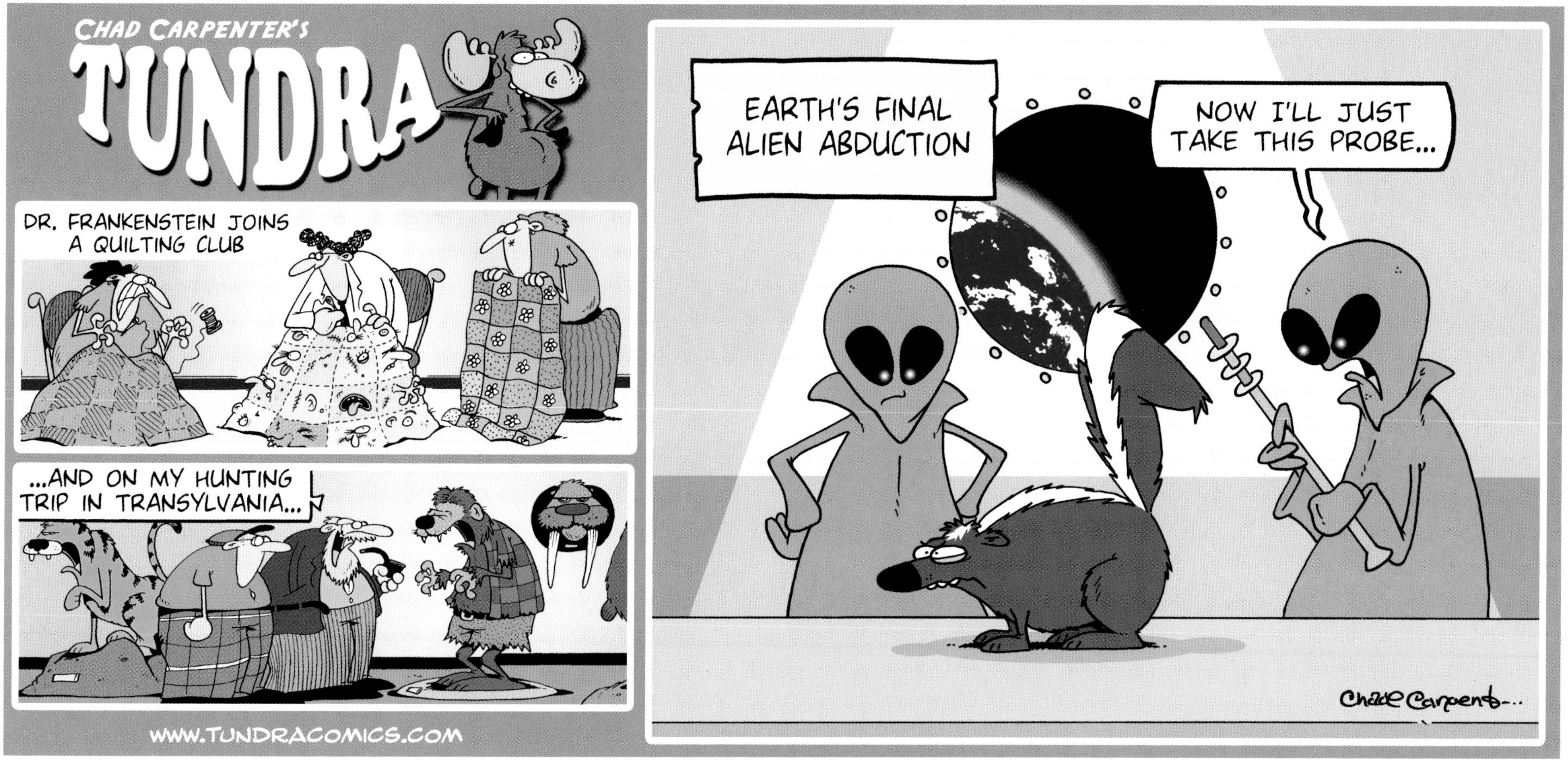
CHAD CARPENTER'S
TUNDRA
DR. FRANKENSTEIN JOINS A QUILTING CLUB
...AND ON MY HUNTING TRIP IN TRANSYLVANIA...
WWW.TUNDRACOMICS.COM
EARTH'S FINAL ALIEN ABDUCTION
NOW I'LL JUST TAKE THIS PROBE...
Chad Carpenter

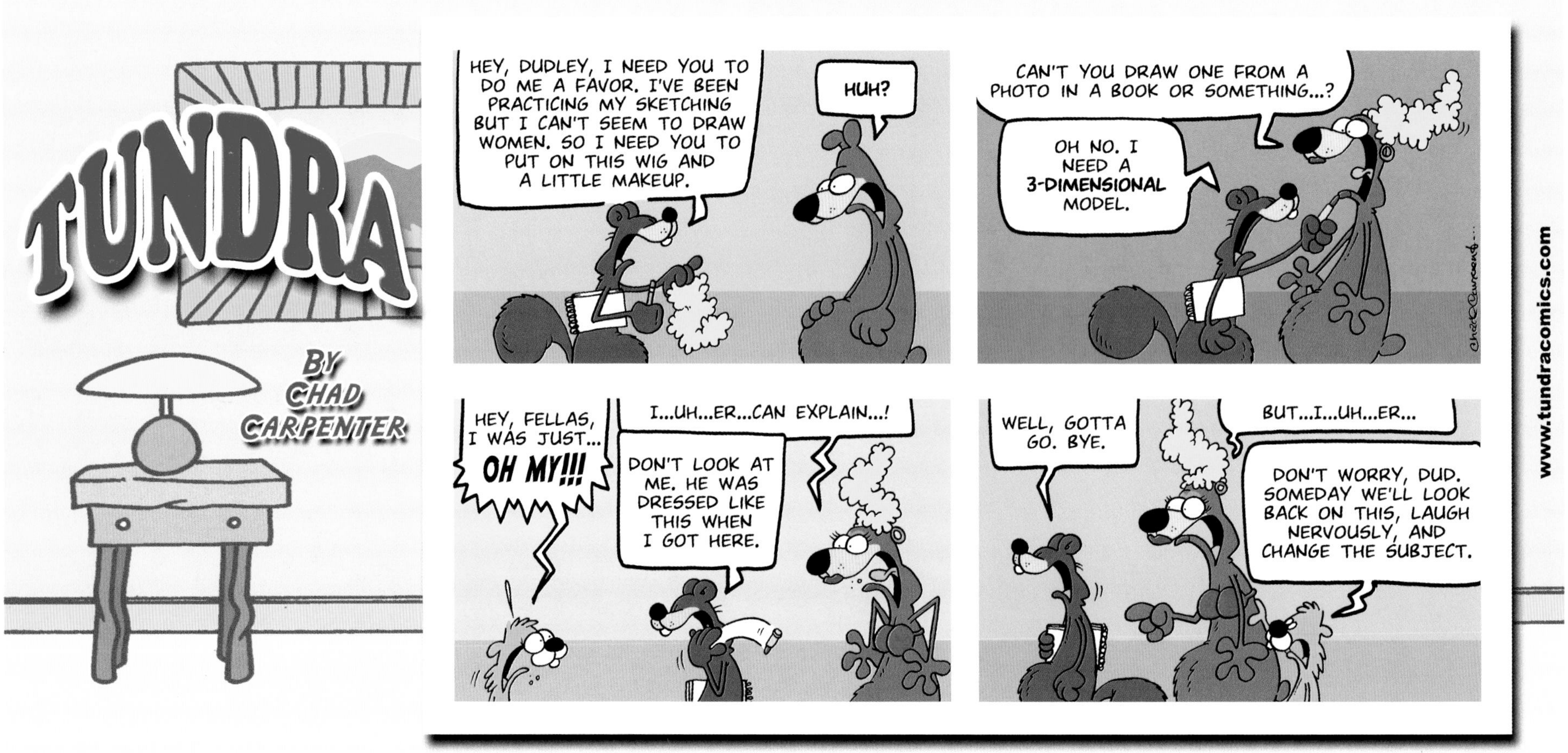
TUNDRA
BY CHAD CARPENTER
HEY, DUDLEY, I NEED YOU TO DO ME A FAVOR. I'VE BEEN PRACTICING MY SKETCHING BUT I CAN'T SEEM TO DRAW WOMEN. SO I NEED YOU TO PUT ON THIS WIG AND A LITTLE MAKEUP.
HUH?
CAN'T YOU DRAW ONE FROM A PHOTO IN A BOOK OR SOMETHING...?
OH NO. I NEED A **3-DIMENSIONAL** MODEL.
HEY, FELLAS, I WAS JUST... **OH MY!!!**
I...UH...ER...CAN EXPLAIN...!
DON'T LOOK AT ME. HE WAS DRESSED LIKE THIS WHEN I GOT HERE.
WELL, GOTTA GO. BYE.
BUT...I...UH...ER...
DON'T WORRY, DUD. SOMEDAY WE'LL LOOK BACK ON THIS, LAUGH NERVOUSLY, AND CHANGE THE SUBJECT.
www.tundracomics.com

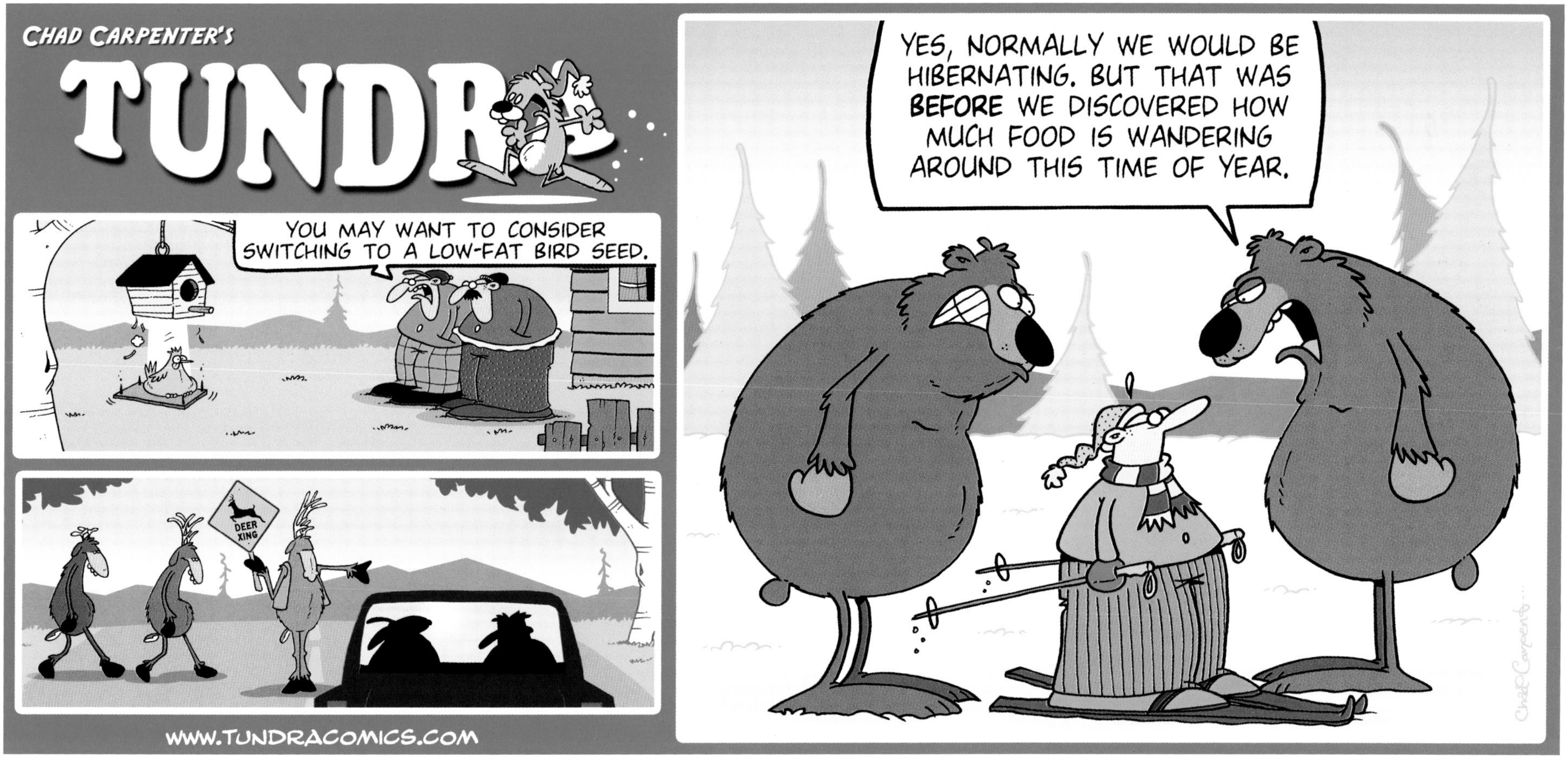
CHAD CARPENTER'S
TUNDRA
YOU MAY WANT TO CONSIDER SWITCHING TO A LOW-FAT BIRD SEED.
DEER XING
WWW.TUNDRACOMICS.COM
YES, NORMALLY WE WOULD BE HIBERNATING. BUT THAT WAS BEFORE WE DISCOVERED HOW MUCH FOOD IS WANDERING AROUND THIS TIME OF YEAR.

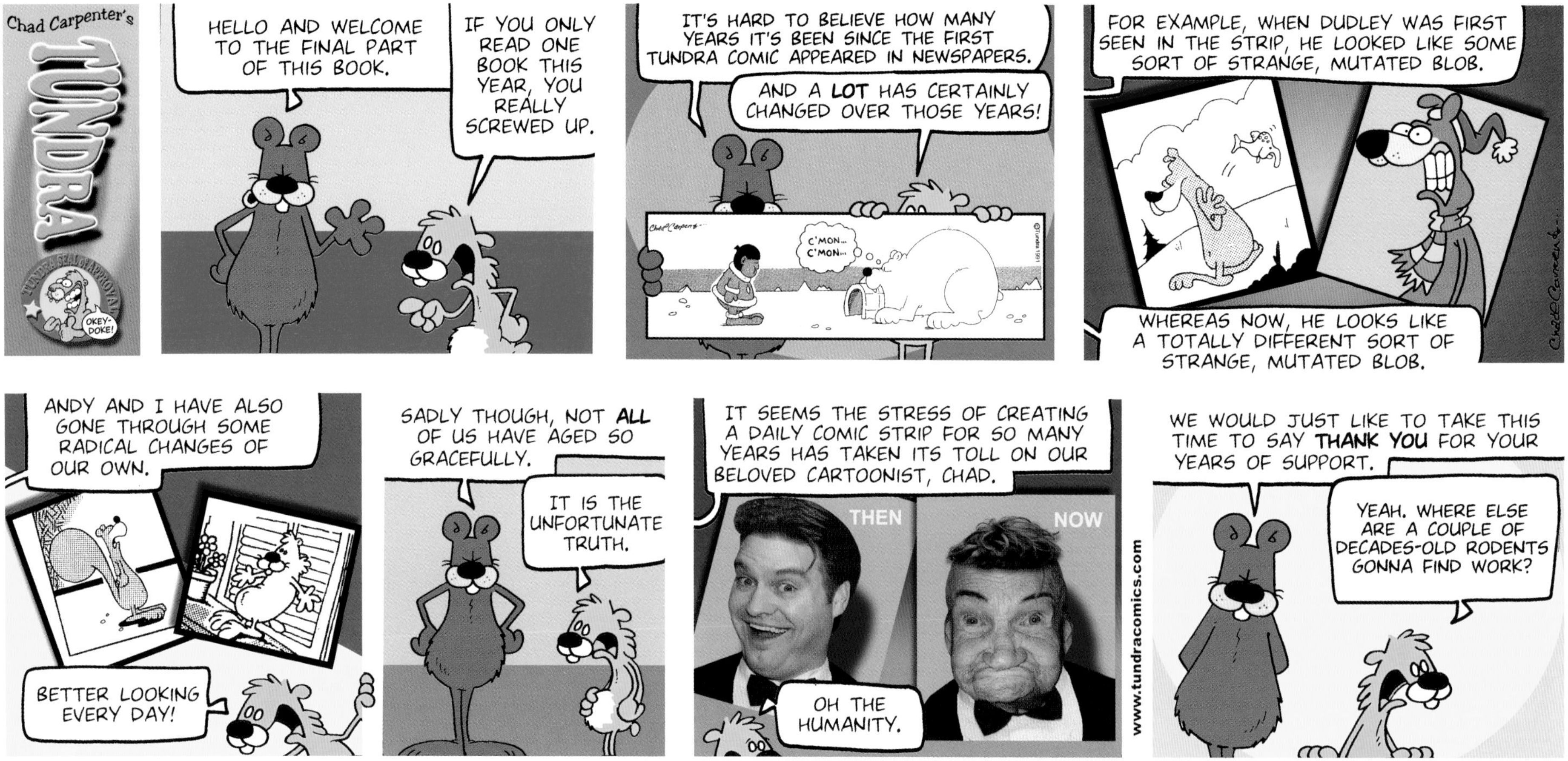
Chad Carpenter's
TUNDRA
TUNDRA SEAL of APPROVAL
OKEY-DOKE!
HELLO AND WELCOME TO THE FINAL PART OF THIS BOOK.
IF YOU ONLY READ ONE BOOK THIS YEAR, YOU REALLY SCREWED UP.
IT'S HARD TO BELIEVE HOW MANY YEARS IT'S BEEN SINCE THE FIRST TUNDRA COMIC APPEARED IN NEWSPAPERS.
AND A **LOT** HAS CERTAINLY CHANGED OVER THOSE YEARS!
C'MON... C'MON...
FOR EXAMPLE, WHEN DUDLEY WAS FIRST SEEN IN THE STRIP, HE LOOKED LIKE SOME SORT OF STRANGE, MUTATED BLOB.
WHEREAS NOW, HE LOOKS LIKE A TOTALLY DIFFERENT SORT OF STRANGE, MUTATED BLOB.
ANDY AND I HAVE ALSO GONE THROUGH SOME RADICAL CHANGES OF OUR OWN.
BETTER LOOKING EVERY DAY!
SADLY THOUGH, NOT **ALL** OF US HAVE AGED SO GRACEFULLY.
IT IS THE UNFORTUNATE TRUTH.
IT SEEMS THE STRESS OF CREATING A DAILY COMIC STRIP FOR SO MANY YEARS HAS TAKEN ITS TOLL ON OUR BELOVED CARTOONIST, CHAD.
THEN
NOW
OH THE HUMANITY.
www.tundracomics.com
WE WOULD JUST LIKE TO TAKE THIS TIME TO SAY **THANK YOU** FOR YOUR YEARS OF SUPPORT.
YEAH. WHERE ELSE ARE A COUPLE OF DECADES-OLD RODENTS GONNA FIND WORK?

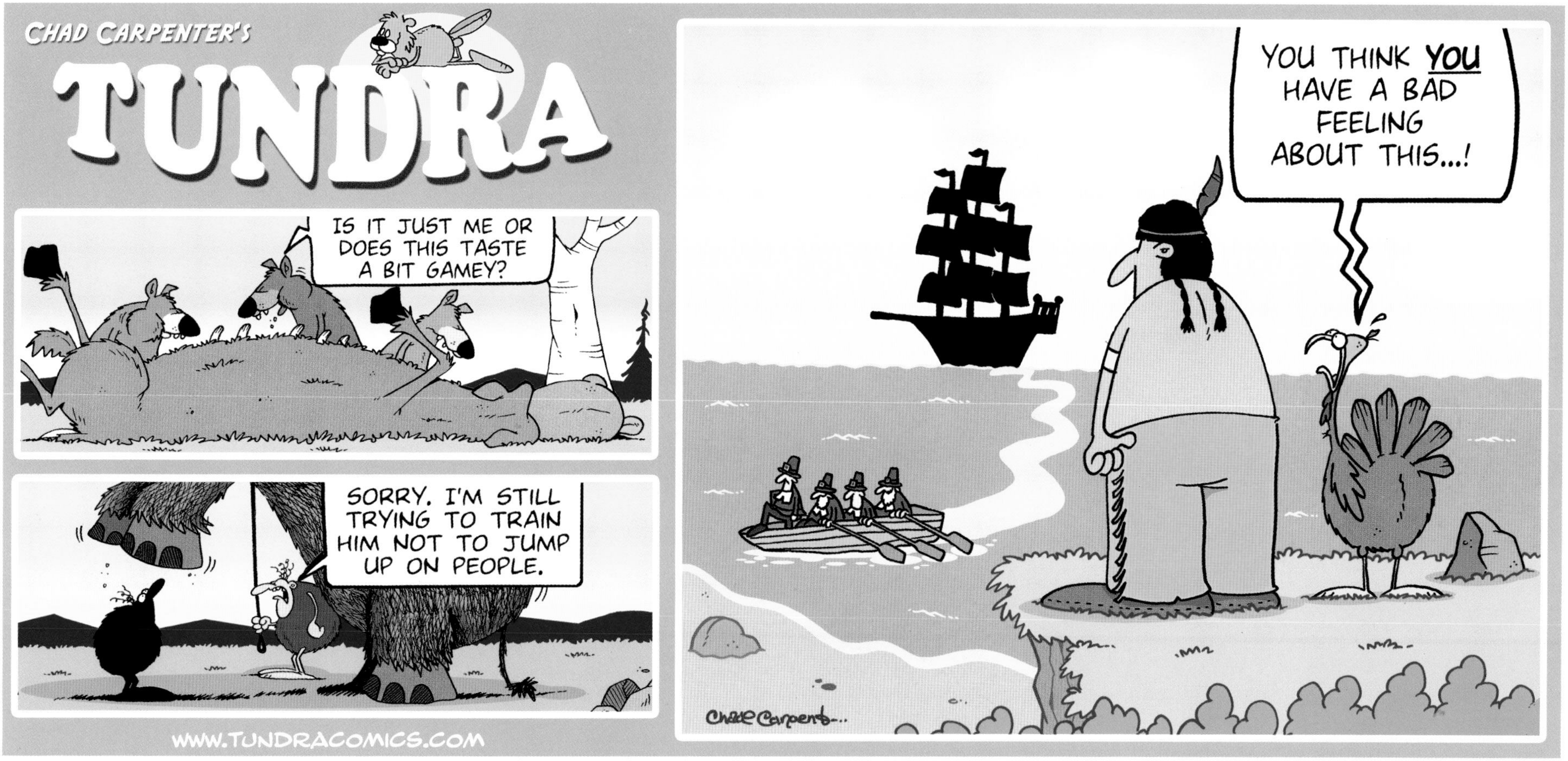
CHAD CARPENTER'S
TUNDRA
IS IT JUST ME OR DOES THIS TASTE A BIT GAMEY?
SORRY. I'M STILL TRYING TO TRAIN HIM NOT TO JUMP UP ON PEOPLE.
WWW.TUNDRACOMICS.COM
YOU THINK YOU HAVE A BAD FEELING ABOUT THIS...!
CHAD CARPENTER

For more **TUNDRA** silliness including books, calendars and lots of other stuff, please visit us at www.tundracomics.com